The

Ethnic

Food Lover's

Companion

THE
ETHNIC
FOOD LOVER'S
COMPANION

Eve Zibart

Menasha Ridge Press
Birmingham, Alabama

Menasha Ridge Press, Inc.
P.O. Box 43673
Birmingham, Alabama 35243

Distributed by The Globe Pequot Press

Cover design by Barbara Williams
Cover images provided by EyeWire, Inc.
Interior book design by Suzanne H. Holt
Decorative borders by Mary Holt, *TexStyles*

Library of Congress Cataloging-in-Publication Data:
Zibart, Eve.
The ethnic food lovers companion / Eve Zibart.
p. cm.
Includes index.
ISBN 0-89732-372-6 (alk. paper)
1. Cookery, International. 2. Food. I. Title.
TX725.A1 Z46 2001
641.59—dc21   2001030807

Manufactured in the United States of America

10 9 8 7 6 5 4 3 2 1

PREFACE

It is one of the most fascinating paradoxes of modern American life that we are obsessed with food, inundated with advertising, bombarded with advice, and offered thousands of varieties of consumables from all over the world—and yet we have forgotten the most vital truths about *eating*. Preparing food, serving it, and sitting down with friends or family is more than a physical necessity or social exercise; it's a ceremony, a re-exploration not just of our own short and visible history but of thousands of years of barter and translation and conquest and commerce and marriage and migration and famine. It encodes genealogies, tribal allegiances, taboos, languages, prescriptions, fears of pollution, and hopes of resurrection. Within a single menu item—lamb curry, for instance—is written whole romances: how the spices of Indonesia, the rice of China, the flatbreads of Mesopotamia, the compotes of Persia, and the meat of the conquering Mongols came to be lumped together under the casually mistranslated title bestowed by imperial Britain.

Centuries before refrigeration, before marked roads or sea routes, peoples and foods moved across continents: rice from China to India to the Middle East, Egypt to Greece to Portugal to South America to South Carolina to Africa. Corn from Peru to Spain to Morocco to Turkey to Italy; chilies from Mexico to Malaysia to Thailand; tempura from Portugal to India to Japan, sauerkraut from China to Rome to Germany. When we enter a restaurant, therefore—when we become a guest in another culture and participate in its traditions—we ought to appreciate the intricate piecing together of peoples that a nation represents.

Satisfaction is another thing we have forgotten with regard to food. A social meal should absorb us: capture our eyes with color, fascinate us with flavor and texture and aroma, feed our sense of wonder as well as the others. Nutrition, "diet," and convenience are all important considerations, but companionship, conversation (or the contemplation of a good book, even), and full sensual enjoyment of a meal are just as vital to our well-being.

This, then, is more than a restaurant guide, and less than an encyclopedia. It's an armchair traveler's companion to ethnic dining, a gazetteer to the overlapping cultures and waves of civilizations and discoveries that have framed our world. It's designed to make dining in an ethnic restaurant less intimidating, more illuminating, and more familiar, like a return to a favorite destination or even a childhood story remembered. To that end, it looks back to each cuisine's history, its natural limitations, its borrowed or impressed additions, its techniques and tools.

This guide also encourages you to re-examine some of the cultural assumptions our society makes about others. We'd like you to try dining in the traditional manner of each region, which is a way not only to show respect but also to lose a lot of prejudices. Eurocentric cultures have a tendency to look down on societies that eat with their fingers, although they themselves only gave up the habit—reluctantly—a handful of generations ago. We feel clumsy wielding chopsticks or rolling lettuce leaves or tortillas, a discomfort we confuse with a lack of sophistication. But eating with the hands slows you down, makes you concentrate on and enjoy your food more, so you actually eat less (tastes great, more fulfilling).

Eating by hand restores the human touch in metaphorical fashion as well: The proliferation of serving utensils, a particularly conspicuous form of consumption designed by the wealthy few, implicitly required the expansion of the servant class and a distancing of the kitchen labor from the privileged diner. This way you receive the food the way it is prepared.

Considering the history of a cuisine is another way to shake off some biases. If there is a great unsung hero of international cooking, it is the Persians, whose cuisine is not only maintained in so many countries today, from the Middle East to Afghanistan, but was also integral to the development of Mediterranean, Indian, and Indonesian foods as well. Yet Persian restaurants (many of which are owned by Iranians or Iraqis and suffer a sort of guilt by association with political events back home) are given short shrift by many critics.

The phrase "Middle East" itself recalls another assumption—that Europe was the center of the world. China was the Far East or the Orient, and Lebanon and Syria and so on were just halfway between here and there. (Britain, France, and the United States were "the West," if not quite the Blessed Isles.) Although we have managed to lose the "Oriental" habit, there isn't a real alternative to "Middle Eastern." However, we have eschewed the ethnocentric date markers "B.C." and "A.D." in favor of the more neutral alternatives B.C.E. (Before the Common Era) and C.E. (Common Era): After all, there are many cuisines in this book that are several thousand years older than the Julian calendar.

We have taken note, in a general way, of the various nutritional strengths and drawbacks of each cuisine. We have mentioned various religious taboos, too, but we pass no moral judgments on any diet, other than the classic "moderation in all things." However, you will probably notice that few other cultures overwhelm their plates with meat, which is not only a dietary issue but an economic one as well. Here in the United States, where meat is cheap and plentiful, we have a tendency to eat more than we need—more, arguably, than our share—just because we can. (In fact, one of the problematical accommodations cooks from other nations often make in restaurants here is to our inflated expectations of meat.) You may also find you like more kinds of seafood than you did when it only came frozen. Dining as others do may alter your tastes as well as your outlook.

One last thing to consider: cuisine as class distinction. When, in the unspoken etiquette of American society, does "immigrant food" become "ethnic cuisine"? What makes one country's food fashionable and another's merely fast? Is it a matter of political alliance, cultural chic, Hollywood romance, novelty? All these have some impact, of course: Jamaican and West African foods are gathering places for the emerging urban black entrepreneurial class; *Jewel in the Crown* and *A Passage to India* prompted a rush for Indian fashions; and the craze for hot chilies has made any number of otherwise unrelated cuisines, from Thai to Ethiopian to Tex-Mex, good investment bets.

But on a much more serious level, the answer is that we the consumers decide. We choose what styles evolve, not just by selecting a particular restaurant to dine in or talk about but also by the respect we afford a particular ethnic group. The quality and variety of a foreign cuisine doesn't reflect the sophistication of that culture—an assumption too many people make—but only the economic stability that immigrant community has achieved in our society.

The first members of an immigrant society are rarely prosperous. They are far more likely to be refugees from war or oppression, poverty, or political upheaval—and of that group, only a very few are apt to have any real cooking experience. (Many countries in the world do not even have a restaurant tradition, since it requires a successful middle class, those with some disposable income if not full-time servants, as customers.) Even those immigrants who do have some history as cooks will have limited access to the ingredients they are used to, and little money to spend on them anyway. Being able to afford to rent restaurant space, much less buy it, is usually years away.

So the first generation of immigrants traditionally recreates the simplest food they know—street food, in effect. Once they save up enough money or the community itself grows more stable, you begin to see mom-and-pop establishments serving family-style food; not for some time do you find "real" restaurants that offer more formal cuisine (with more expensive ingredients). Consequently, we should not assume that a particular ethnic group has only cheap food; rather, we should look at it in context. After all, you wouldn't want someone from another country to think the food at a truck stop was American haute cuisine.

These are difficult issues, and you can relax—there is less preaching in the text that follows. These are just impressions that took hold in the writing of this book, and you may hear echoes of them in your own mind as time goes on. But the main purpose of this book is for you to eat and to enjoy. We want you to have fun from here on. This is the first time we'll wish you "Bon appetit!" The next time, you'll be on your own.

—Eve Zibart

Contents

LIST OF ILLUSTRATIONS

ACKNOWLEDGMENTS

The quality of food writing and its scope have both increased so dramatically in recent years that it would humble any author of a guide as general as this. I'm grateful to the many chefs (and winemakers), historians, journalists, and friends for the pleasure they've brought me.

This book would literally not have made it to the printer without the tireless efforts of the folks from Menasha Ridge Press, especially Annie Long, who squinted over my tiny handwriting for hours on end (helluva job!); Holly Cross, who held my virtual hand and led the cheerleading section; Molly Merkle, who did her best not to panic as the deadlines passed (and the baby approached); Laura Poole, Georgia Goff, and Ann Cassar, the galley slaves; and Bob Sehlinger, who let me get it right this time.

And Dodger, who came home after hours of reading other people's copy and read mine instead of *The New Yorker*.

Menasha Ridge Press would like to thank the following people for last-minute reviews and suggestions: Prof. Milka Russeva, Ph.D., Center for Historical and Political Research, Sofia, Bulgaria; Diana Adjarska-Litzanova, Ph.D., Sofia University "St. Kliment Ohridski," Bulgaria; Prof. Cinzia Donatelli Noble, Brigham Young University; Prof. Franco Andreucci, University of Pisa, Italy; Thomas Cardoza, Ph.D, Eleanor Roosevelt College, University of California; Lisa Wolffe, Ph.D., Northwestern State University; Jeffrey L. Richey, Ph.D., The University of Findlay; Eric Shepherd, Program Officer, US/China Links; Mike M. Yamaguchi, Ph.D. candidate, University of California; Prof. James-Henry Holland, Hobart and William Smith Colleges; Katarzyna Cwiertka, Ph.D., Leiden University, The Netherlands; Russell Helms, Menasha Ridge Press; Edith T. Mirante; Prof. Robert Cribb, University of Queensland, Brisbane, Australia; Jeanne Jacob; Arne Kislenko, Ph.D., Ryerson University, Toronto, Canada; and Lydia N. Yu-Jose, Ph.D., Ateneo de Manila University, Philippines.

This book is for Terrell Vermont.

NORTH
PACIFIC
OCEAN

NORTH
ATLANTIC
OCEAN

SCANDIN

GERMAN
AUST

FRANCE/
BELGIUM

SPAIN/
PORTUGAL

NORTH
AFRICA

**PART II:
AFRICA**

WEST
AFRICA

THE
CARIBBEAN

CENTRAL
AMERICA

SOUTH
AMERICA

**PART VI:
THE AMERICAS**

SOUTH
PACIFIC
OCEAN

SOUTH
ATLANTIC
OCEAN

THE ETHNIC FOOD
LOVER'S COMPANION

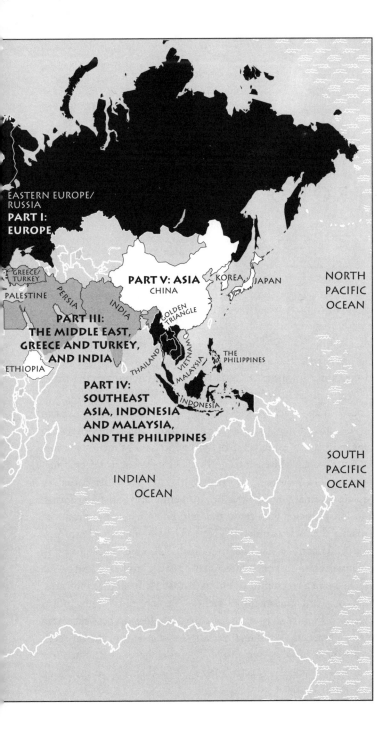

EASTERN EUROPE/
RUSSIA
**PART I:
EUROPE**

GREECE/
TURKEY

PALESTINE

PERSIA

INDIA

PART V: ASIA
CHINA

KOREA

JAPAN

GOLDEN
TRIANGLE

**PART III:
THE MIDDLE EAST,
GREECE AND TURKEY,
AND INDIA**

ETHIOPIA

THAILAND

VIETNAM

MALAYSIA

THE
PHILIPPINES

**PART IV:
SOUTHEAST
ASIA, INDONESIA
AND MALAYSIA,
AND THE PHILIPPINES**

INDONESIA

NORTH
PACIFIC
OCEAN

SOUTH
PACIFIC
OCEAN

INDIAN
OCEAN

INTRODUCTION

As the boom in culinary magazines and television cooking shows attests, Americans have never been more fascinated by food, or more adventurous in their dining habits. The great melting pot has suddenly become the world's most eclectic kettle as well.

Cuisines almost unheard of until recently, or confined to the larger urban centers such as New York and Miami, are working their way into the heartland; many, such as the Middle Eastern and Southeast Asian styles, have acquired new prominence as second- and third-generation Americans, now firmly established in this country, take time to rediscover their cultural roots. More familiar ethnic cuisines that had been cruelly homogenized in deference to American tastes (whether actual or assumed) are re-emerging in far more authentic and satisfying forms. The explosion of Pacific Rim trade and cultural exchange has produced pidgin cuisines that owe as much to "New World"—meaning both Australian and American—as to Asian traditions. The emergence of a black entrepreneurial class in the United States, the Caribbean, and West Africa has inspired a restaurant tradition that is new to all three cultures.

Hence our embarrassment of riches. No longer is dining out a choice between French and Italian, or carryout a toss-up between pizza and kung pao chicken. Nowadays, picking a restaurant for dinner more often recalls the method by which Dr. Doolittle chose his destinations: closing his eyes, letting the gazetteer fall open on the table, and stabbing downward with his finger.

And picking a restaurant is more and more frequently the answer to "What's for dinner?" The major shifts of the baby boom generation—the increase in two-career families, the decline of self-contained small towns, and the shift toward bedroom communities and rush-hour gridlock—have combined to strip the kitchen of its longtime role as the center of family life. At the same time, the disappearance of the domestic servant and the need to bring social partners together from across larger urban areas has made restaurant entertaining standard practice. Business meetings among residents of different countries are now commonplace; and since more and more Americans have friends and coworkers from other countries, they are even more likely to be invited to a restaurant that serves ethnic food.

That's the "riches" part: So many cuisines, so little time. We hope your having acquired this book means you're tempted to try them all. But we also understand that you may feel overwhelmed by the choices as well as perplexed by the novelties. What is Ethiopian food? How much of it is raw? How should you handle it? If you have vegetarian friends, kosher friends, squeamish friends, where should you go (or not)? How do you eat hard-shell crabs in spicy black bean sauce? What are the lettuce leaves for at the Vietnamese restaurant? How can you keep from dropping the fish into the soy sauce at the sushi bar? What's the difference between Hunan and Szechwan, Indian red curries and Thai green curries, samosas and sambusas, a Bellini and a blini? And how *do* you master chopsticks?

Read on. In this book you'll find a short history of just about any style of ethnic cooking you're apt to find in any restaurant in the United States, with a smattering of topographical information and social and political history (why a certain region produces spicier food, or emphasizes shellfish, or emulates a colonial power), key ingredients and staple menu items, and suggestions for ordering a complete meal. We'll tell you how certain dishes are eaten (if you don't like to eat with your fingers, you'll know which cuisines to avoid in advance) and, perhaps even more important, how they're not eaten—how not to offend your hosts unintentionally. We'll try to give you an idea of the relative expense of various cuisines, although of course that will vary depending on what city you're dining in and the formality of the particular restaurant.

And although this is not primarily a cookbook, we hope you'll find a few cuisines you particularly like, so we've included a few simple recipes you can reproduce or even preview at home. There are few better ways to get to know other people, or to appreciate their taste and the choices they make, than to go step by step through their recipe map. If the way to someone's heart is through the stomach, the way to their homes is through the kitchen. Each recipe feeds four to six people unless otherwise stated. And although any real explanation of a country's wine and spirits would require much more space and expertise, we have in a few cases tried to help you at least negotiate a dinner party order without embarrassment.

You could also consider the various chapters as preparation for traveling to other countries, since exploring restaurants is one of the best parts about taking vacations (and one of the inescapable elements of traveling on business). But note that this guide is primarily intended to help you negotiate ethnic restaurants in the United States, because while cooking techniques may be traditional and staple ingredients essential, one of the first things an immigrant cuisine must do is adapt to the available food supply. In the case of cuisines transplanted to the United States, this has been an advantage as often as a barrier, not merely because of the variety of foods available—and the increasing demand for more ethnic foods has certainly increased the quantity and quality of foods at chain as well as specialty groceries—but because in many countries, storage and refrigeration are extremely problematical. The vastly greater supply of meat and poultry in even the most pedestrian American pantry is an obvious difference, but the uniformly high quality of fruits and vegetables has also produced more vigorous interpretations of many traditional dishes from other countries.

Notice, too, that not every country in the world is discussed. That's because we're talking about restaurant dining, specifically; and although there are, for example, chains of "Australian steakhouses," and very fine restaurants all over Down Under, those establishments' ethnicity is generally limited to Aussie-ized item names and brands of beer. Similarly, though there are great restaurants in Vancouver and Quebec and so on—and plenty of Canadian chefs working in the United States—there are no "Canadian" restaurants here. There are plenty of "Irish pubs," but Irish stew (authentic or not) scarcely needs translating. South Africa may have a "cuisine," but it certainly hasn't been exported. Perhaps in a future edition we'll be lucky enough to need to explore those areas.

We also discuss some cuisines and provincial styles in combination, covering several Middle Eastern or Central American countries together, because the styles are so closely related and are frequently prepared interchangeably in the United States; as the regional styles become more prominent, they will be profiled more fully.

On the other hand, we do include some cuisines and provincial styles many people may already be familiar with, particularly if they live in larger cities. Even so, you may find tips, terms, and titles you hadn't known—and you might well discover that your neighborhood "Sichuan" restaurant isn't Sichuan at all but Taiwanese or even Korean. And that the "international" market down the street is just as all-American as the mega-grocery in the mall.

Reading this book is one way to begin to notice underlying similarities among apparently untranslatable cuisines and to feel more confident about trying new ones. Nearly every continent has stumbled upon such basics as the hot grill (the Tex-Mex fajita skillet, the European griddle, the Italian pizza stone, the Japanese teppanyaki, the Mongolian barbecue, the Chinese "sizzling platter"), the stuffed noodle (the wonton, the aushak, the ravioli, the piroshki), and the fried egg. Pasta, one of the staple foods even in cafeterias, is being rediscovered not only in finer Italian forms but in its "original" Asian varieties: Chinese, Japanese, and especially Vietnamese *pho* restaurants are tossing whole racks of noodles. Long, fat, flat, curly, stringy, springy, spicy—they're like rock musicals in menu form.

Even longtime batting champ Wade Boggs, who refused to eat anything but chicken every game night in more than a decade of baseball seasons, could order comfortably in almost any ethnic restaurant in the world. He could have it Southern fried, Cajun blackened, South American grilled, or Jamaican jerked; he could order African stew with peanuts, French coq au vin, Italian cacciatore, German Black Forest stew with cherries, Hungarian paprikash, spinach and feta–stuffed Greek chicken breast, chicken Kiev, Chinese kung pao chicken, Japanese teriyaki, Vietnamese hen stuffed with pork, Thai drumsticks fried inside out, and Korean tabletop barbecue without even needing a translator.

So come, explore, eat—*Mange! Kin khao! Bon appetit!* The world is waiting. The old saw has it that to understand another person, you need to walk a mile in their shoes. We think there's a better way to get to know another culture: Spend an hour at their table. It's a lot more fun.

No, we didn't forget those chopsticks. Here's the trick: Snuggle one down in the fold between your thumb and index finger, with one-third extending out the back side of your hand—the thicker end, or it may be the square end as opposed to the round part—and the longer section facing your palm. (Remember learning about levers in school? Let the chopsticks do the work, not your hand.) Curve your ring finger in and brace the chopstick against its first knuckle.

Now take the other stick and grasp it with your thumb and first two fingers just as you would a pen or pencil, and wiggle it. When you pick up food, you "write" up and down with the upper stick; the lower one just stays put—the base of your thumb becomes the fulcrum, to finish that comparison—and you pinch the food between the two sticks. Got it?

If not, don't worry. Just smile and ask for a fork. After all, this is the melting pot of the new millennium.

PART 1

EUROPE

FRANCE AND BELGIUM

BASIC CUISINE

DINNER FOR TWO:
Foie gras terrine, seafood vol-au-vent, truite meunière, tournedos rossini

DINNER FOR FOUR:
Onion tarte, frogs' legs, pâté, coquille St. Jacques, bouillabaisse, duck confit, leg of lamb, steak diane

STYLE:
Rich, refined, precise

KEY FLAVORS:
Cream, fine herbs, wine, wild mushrooms, garlic

EATING UTENSILS:
Forks and knives

DISTINCTIVE FOODS:
Foie gras, champagne, truffles, escargot, cheeses

UNIFORMITY OF MENUS:
Very good

NUTRITIONAL INDEX:
High fat, high cholesterol, high sodium

COST:
Moderate to expensive

"THANK YOU":
"Merci" (French); "Mercé" (Occitan); "Danku" (Flemish)

It's no mere coincidence—in fact, it's a masterstroke of cultural gamesmanship—that the phrase commonly used to describe fine cooking, "haute cuisine," is French. Most Americans have grown up taking for granted that French chefs and French restaurants were the finest; we've even been taking France's word for it, using the Michelin Guide ratings as the international standard.

There are a couple of twists to this legendary sophistication, however. First, very little of the French cuisine served in American restaurants qualifies as "haute." Just the opposite, in fact: Translated into English, the names of many dishes reveal their working-class origins, such as *bouillabaisse*, the "bubble and settle" soup made from the fisherman's leftovers, and shellfish *marinière*, cooked the way the barge workers did (with fish stock). Chicken *bonne femme* or *fermière* just means from the farmwife's recipe—good old home cooking—and fish *à la meunière* is the way the miller's wife makes it—i.e., coated with flour (and cooked in butter).

Second, many French favorites are French only in name: hors d'oeu-vres (foods "outside of the task") were lifted from the Russian *zakouski;* the spices and citrus sauces (for instance, the famous duck *à l'orange*) were introduced by the Arabs; the tomato and the sauces based on it came through Spain from the New World; and an astonishing number of recipes—pastas and noodles, meat flourings, pastries and creams—were introduced by Italian chefs at the French court. These adaptations led many white-linen restaurants in the United States to describe their menus as "Continental cuisine," embracing the whole of Europe.

Third, French cuisine as we know and admire it is more nearly mod-ern than classic; it began to take shape in about the seventeenth century but was mainly formulated in the eighteenth and nineteenth centuries. Compared to the other so-called great cuisines—those of China and India—*all* French food is nouvelle cuisine.

The truth is that when it comes to cooking, the French were never the most imaginative, the most adventuresome, or the most flexible: They were just the most obsessively perfectionistic. They knew what they liked (they bought so much Phoenician wine that by the seventh century B.C.E. there was a dedicated port at Marseilles) and they always believed that whatever anyone else could do, or brew, they could do better.

So they became the greatest technicians, and the greatest ambas-sadors, of Western culinary civilization. It was the French who made the craft of cooking into what Julia Child and company could honestly call an "art"; they made it sound like one of the anchors of Western civilization. ("Gourmandism is one of the chief links uniting society," the great epi-cure and food writer Brillat-Savarin pronounced.)

It was also the French who made the profession of cooking into a viable business. French culinary arbiters laid down elaborate and often intimidating rules for making sauces, serving banquets, and selecting wines. It was even a pair of French restaurateurs, the Troisgros brothers of Rouen, who in the 1970s decided that serving the portions in the kitchen and then "presenting" plates was more practical, and more profitable, than carving to order at the table. With their rules, their schools, their toques, and their wine tastings, the French succeeded in molding most ambitious restaurants in the United States, French or not, into their own image.

Which brings us to the fourth irony: Haute cuisine may be an endangered species.

Diners in the United States and Europe are becoming much more diet-conscious and wary of the cholesterol- and calorie-packed cream sauces; and they eat out far more often, meaning that they are less likely to want every restaurant meal to be extravagant and more likely to seek variety in flavor. The 1994 edition of the Michelin Guide eliminated nearly 50 previously ranked French restaurants and downgraded several more. The editors warned that "the cuisine of our country must adjust to a new behavior of its customers, use less sophisticated products and shoot for lighter additions without giving up the traditional quality."

French chefs are under pressure not only at home but, in a historical turnabout, from the United States, where classically trained but more eclectically minded chefs are exploring low-fat cuisine or applying French techniques to American and Asian ingredients.

So after 200 years of following every prescribed step of the recipes enunciated by Careme or Escoffier, French chefs have spent the past 25 years reinventing them. They are now finding ways to replace the rich cream sauces that were their signature and giving up the more elaborate Parisian fare in favor of the provincial specialties—especially those that, not coincidentally, are more closely related to the northern Italian dishes so popular in the United States. (This is not the first such shake-up: A cookbook published at the end of the fifteenth century includes 230 recipes, two-thirds of them then new. Vincent La Chapelle's three-volume treatise, published in 1733, was named *Cuisinier moderne*—and used the phrase "nouvelle cuisine." The French diet, and their attitude toward dining, lightened immeasurably after the Middle Ages and well before the cuisines of most other European countries.)

Because of this shifting state of affairs, and because so much of the mystery about a French restaurant is in the language, this chapter will focus more on preparations and provincial styles than on specific ingredients. And although Belgium is an independent nation, its cuisine is so closely associated with France's—and most of the Belgian-owned restaurants in the United States still describe themselves, for simplicity's sake, as French or German—that Belgian cuisine will be included in the section on provincial cuisine.

THE COUNTRIES

France is the leading agricultural nation in Europe—57% of its land is devoted to agriculture and viticulture—and so diverse in its climate, soil

Nutritionally speaking, exploring French cuisine is a little like Goldilocks tasting the Three Bears' dinners: Haute cuisine can be too big and rich; *cuisine minceur* can be too little and too light; and most people find nouvelle cuisine just about right. The differences are, as always, in the sauces: Classic cuisine uses the greatest number of cream- and butter-based sauces, usually poured over an already butter-sautéed fish or meat, and sometimes requires wrapping the whole thing in pastry doughs that are also heavily larded with butter.

Cuisine minceur, which borrowed from classic Japanese cuisine the idea of visual extravagance and severe simplicity of ingredients, is composed of many tiny courses of small portions and often ornate garnishes. Sauces and pastry may still be involved, but in tiny quantities. Nouvelle, which simply means "new," French cuisine (and also what is sometimes called "new Continental"

quality, and topography that different regions produce widely varying crops. Physically, France resembles a rather dumpy starfish with its most prominent "ray" sticking out to the west. It's bordered on the east by the Alps and the Rhine River, which runs beside Switzerland, Germany, Luxembourg, and Belgium. On the north France is washed by the English Channel and on the west by the Atlantic Ocean. The Pyrenees and Spain lie to the southwest, and the rest of the southern "corner" opens onto the Mediterranean.

Rivers cover the country like palm lines. The eastern crescent—Champagne, Burgundy, and the Rhône and Loire River valleys—encompasses the great wine-growing regions, along with the area around Bordeaux on the west coast. France produces all the food it needs, except for a few tropical crops, such as coffee. For more on regional agriculture, see the "Provincial Cuisines" section on pages 15–22.

Belgium, which has historically been tugged between France and the Netherlands, has an appropriately divided population: ethnic Dutch, who speak Flemish, and Walloons, who speak French. Their food follows the split patterns to some extent: abundant fresh seafood on the coast, bountiful German-style meats and sausages in the east, and in the middle, fields of grains— oats, rye, wheat, and barley—as well as beets, potatoes, and the famous endive (also known as chicory, *chicon*, or *witloof*). They also grow a large quantity of hops, with which they make some of the world's most potent beers. These beers are so potent, that they're often referred to as "the Burgundies of Belgium." However, both Flemish and Walloons share a passion for shellfish, particularly mussels and oysters, shrimp, eels, game, and ham.

THE HISTORY

Although there are ancient archeological artifacts in France, very little is actually known about the people who first inhabited the region, but by the time the Romans took over in the first century, it was already a crazy-quilt of "provinces."

France, which faces the Atlantic and Bay of Biscay along one side and the Mediterranean on the other, repeatedly absorbed invaders and refugees from both. The Gauls of Julius Caesar's famous "Veni, vidi, vici" campaign were actually Celtic; the Pyrenees were dotted with Basques; Brittany was populated by Britons driven out by the Anglo-Saxons; there were Greeks and Middle Easterners along the Mediterranean coast; and there were Germanic tribes in the east, including the Franks (actually Belgians), who gave their name to the region. Attila's Huns poked around in the fourth century, and the Saracens invaded in the ninth century, leaving behind pockets of Arab settlements along the Mediterranean and Spanish borders.

Not surprisingly, although the great majority of people speak French, there are still many other languages heard in France: The Basques speak Euskera, the Bretons have a Celtic dialect, the Alsatians speak a German dialect, the Corsicans speak Italian, the Provençal have a dialect called Occitan, and the residents of the districts near Belgium speak Flemish. And since the Franks ruled the Low Countries, western Germany, Austria, Switzerland, and northern Italy, there are family resemblances to all these countries in French regional recipes.

Just Right
Continued

cuisine) tries to provide rich flavors but in lower-fat dishes, frequently by poaching or steaming foods instead of sautéing them and by using reductions of stock, vegetable purees, or crême fraîche to thicken dishes instead of creams or roux.

If you're concerned about avoiding fat, you'll have to either memorize the basic sauces or learn to look perfectly comfortable asking for your hollandaise on the side; but there are a few dishes that you can just expect to break your cholesterol bank on. Anything *en croute* is wrapped in pastry; anything with *crême* most likely refers to heavy cream. Almost anything from Normandy will have cream in it, so titled or not. *Confit* is game, usually duck or goose or rabbit, cooked and stored in its own rendered fat; *blanquettes* are white stews thickened with cream and butter and eggs. Any dish described as *Milanaise* or *Velleroi* is coated and fried.

THE CUISINE

Early Frenchmen ate pretty much as their Roman and Greek predecessors had, depending heavily on fish, wild game, and fowl, boiled, roasted, or grilled and flavored with vinegar as often as oil. Winter meats had to be salted or dried, so spices and marinades were highly prized. The India-Constantinople trade supplied cumin, pepper, coriander, anise, galangal and ginger, mace, cinnamon, and caraway, to which the early French added green herbs such as dill, marjoram, and lovage. The Romans had mixed powdered thyme into soft cheese; the French experimented with fennel seeds. An early recipe for duck involved reducing the cooking liquid, already full of spices, and then adding wine, honey, vinegar, and more herbs and thickening the gravy with starch.

Fireplaces were huge, open affairs, with large spits and a few hooks to hang pots on. Although early records suggest that Frankish banquets were lavish, they were still largely matters of roasts or joints and small whole fowl; vegetables were almost always boiled and even stews were pretty much unknown until the twelfth and thirteenth centuries, when ovens appeared. Then smaller pans—including saucepans—became practicable, and a greater variety of dishes was possible.

By the Middle Ages, the French had gaped at the abundance and variety of Middle Eastern cuisine—it's estimated that fully half the French knights alive between 1100 and 1130 marched either to Spain or the Levant—and their banquets had become elaborate affairs, at least in terms of presentation. Feudal lords were served pheasants and whole calves and pigs, and peacocks with gilded bills, and swans that were baked and then re-feathered; but these meats were still basically either roasted or boiled—and they were still all being served at once, so they inevitably congealed and hardened. Rice was sometimes used as a thickener, as was bread; and the almonds introduced by the Arabs were now a staple. Eggs and cheese were used more widely, and cream sauces were now fairly common.

Not until the mid-sixteenth century, when Catherine de Medici, daughter of the Duke of Urbino, married Henry II and brought along her whole cooking staff, did the French look past their first joints, so to speak. Catherine imported butchers, pastry chefs, pasta makers—even forks, although she was signally unsuccessful in persuading people to use them. Both Catherine and her Tuscan cousin Marie, who married Henry IV in 1600 and brought along a new generation of Italian chefs, insisted that France take its place among the most sophisticated societies of the day.

(Catherine's role is being questioned these days, but there are many queens in culinary history, so we'll deal the full house.)

So food became fashionable, and France suddenly became the party capital of the world. The notorious "artistic temperament" took hold: One famous chef, Vatel, committed suicide in 1671 when the fish he had ordered for a banquet was not delivered on time. A seventeenth-century banquet menu for Louis XIV listed 168 entrees and accompaniments in the first five courses alone. Talleyrand, the great diplomat and gastronome, once remarked that "in England there are three sauces and 260 religions; in France there are three religions and 360 sauces." This is even more remarkable, when you consider they were still eating with three fingers and the point of a knife.

With this increased attention to cooking came a marked change in tastes. Recipes for vegetables increased in number, while those for starches decreased. Sheep and goats largely fell out of favor, replaced by veal and beef. Marine mammals (whales, dolphins, seals) disappeared from cookbooks, and though turkey was introduced from the Americas, many of the birds that had been hallmarks of medieval banquets, such as swans, herons and cranes, peafowl, storks, and cormorants, also vanished. Sauces became smoother, "bound" by roux or butter liaisons.

Most intriguingly, however, French chefs unilaterally lightenend their use of spices and seasonings, largely abandoning cumin, mace, ginger, and cardamom, and cutting back on salt and garlic so rigorously that the French who later traveled to other European courts routinely complained of the heavy salt.

After this point, however, the French obsession with exactitude took hold. Once established, recipes became immutable. No matter how far the French empire reached into Africa or Asia, it only rarely adopted any new culinary techniques or ingredients—even though the same regions had contributed to Mediterranean cuisines so long ago.

THE RISE OF WESTERN CULINARY CIVILIZATION

The relatively abrupt evolution of French cuisine also reflects much broader changes in the day-to-day life of nearly all medieval Europeans and deserves a moment's digression. Game and fish had always been relatively plentiful, and that was most of what early Europeans expected or desired. Consequently, farmers planted the same few crops for centuries, gradually leaching the nutrients out of the soil so that produce became progressively poorer, and the people who lived off them both poorer and weaker. (The Crusades thinned the men, and the plague culled out all but the strongest of both sexes.)

But in the fifteenth and sixteenth centuries, as the advantages of crop rotation were discovered, a wider range of foodstuffs, and more nutritious ones, became available. The larger supply of food meant less had to be preserved by salting or smoking, so that individual flavors became more apparent and people could afford to express preferences. As there was more food, there was more surplus—more to sell as well as subsist on—so the markets began to increase in size.

The improved quality of grain crops also improved the quality of the farm animals that were fed on them: As cattle became more productive, beef became as common as mutton. As horses became stronger, farmers began to use them for transport as well as labor, taking their products to more distant, larger markets.

Finally, Europeans began to have easier access to imported spices. Whole regions of France and Spain, particularly along the Mediterranean coast and Rhône River, that had been depopulated, gradually resettled. Shipments that had previously zigzagged from East to West—Indonesia to Baghdad to Byzantium to Venice, then over the Alps and up the Rhine—could now be steered more directly. Thus they also became more affordable—one of the major inspirations for the development of a fine cuisine.

Ironically, the Italians now found themselves effectively priced out of the imported spice market and had to learn to do with fewer ingredients; so just as French cuisine became richer, Italian cuisine became simpler. (Eventually, though for aesthetic rather than economic reasons, French cooking would, too.)

GETTING THROUGH THE MENU

Navigating a French menu isn't hard once you crack the code—the "à la" syndrome, so to speak. In fact, some dishes seem to lose more than their mystery when the veil of language is pierced: Everyone who's ever had the experience of being offered caviar and asking, "What's that?" will remember how unappetizing the answer "fish eggs" sounded. "Pâté" just means "patty"; "soufflé" means "puffed up." Worst of all, probably, "foie gras" means "fat liver," which is exactly what that silken delicacy is—the livers of geese force-fed into gross immobility.

Most dishes are named either for the sauce they are served with or for the major ingredient in the recipe; and when that ingredient is the prize product of a particular region, it is often called by the name of the province itself. Chicken *Dijonnaise*, for instance, means the poultry is served in a sauce honoring Dijon's most famous product, mustard. Calvados, the name of a province that produces fine apples and apple brandy, also refers to a dish containing either or both of those specialities. (There are also various recipes named for famous people or events, usually by the chef hoping to curry favor with a rich patron; you'll just have to memorize those.)

Of course, those sauces named for other countries, such as *indienne* or *grecque* (or *américaine*), don't reproduce other cuisines; they just represent the French image of Indian or Greek (or American) food.

The sauces may be applied to *boeuf* (beef), *veau* (veal), *venaison* (venison), *agneau* (lamb), *mouton* (mutton), *lapin* (rabbit), *porc* (pork) or *jambon* (ham), *volaille* or *poulet* (chicken), *caille* (quail), *canard* (duck), *oie* (goose), *poisson* (fish), *crevette* (shrimp), *ecrevisse* (crawfish), *homard* (lobster), or *huitres* (oysters), just to get you started.

The following is a glossary of some of the major "à la's" you are apt to see on a French menu and a practical, if not purist, pronunciation guide. Just remember that even the most classic of sauces is under revisionary scrutiny these days, and adventurous chefs may be experimenting with their own versions. The most important provincial and regional styles, in which a whole restaurant menu might be prepared, are described a little more fully in the next section.

Allemande (all mond): "German," but in reference to its pale color rather than its actual origin; *sauce allemande* is a basic white sauce, but the use of the word may imply horseradish or vinegar or sour cream in the recipe.

Alsacienne (all zah syen): Also Alsatian. From the Alsace region (see page 16).

Amandine (ah mon deen): Cooked with almonds.

Américaine (ah mare ee ken): Shellfish with tomatoes. A Parisian specialty, oddly; it's common to have lobster *américaine* in Paris.

Ancienne (ahn syen): "Ancient," or in the old style. Typically, ancienne recipes are cooked for a long time—braised or stewed—and sometimes served in pastry. They often use the more delicate sections (sweetbreads or kidneys) or rarities such as truffles and wild mushrooms as garnish.

Anglaise (ahn glehz): "English," implying rather plain fare, usually boiled or fried and without garnish.

Anna (ah nah): Specifically, a dish of sliced potatoes, seasoned with butter and layered in a casserole; but also any dish served with them.

Ardennaise (ahr den nez): Refers to the Ardennes mountains. Usually applied to fowl or game birds, but sometimes to meat, and characteristically flavored with juniper berries (or the juniper-based gin).

Au jus (oh zhu): With juice—that is, pan juices or stock.

Aurore (oh roar): A tomato-flavored sauce, hence pink-tinged and named for Aurora, the goddess of the dawn.

Ballottine (bal oh teen): Meat or poultry boned, stuffed, and rolled, then braised. A galantine is similar but usually served in aspic.

Basquaise (boss kez): Basque-style, after the indigenous peoples of the Pyrenees. Basquaise cuisine is similar to Provençal and Catalonian cuisine (see "The Iberian Peninsula: Spain, Portugal, Catalonia, and the Basque") but with a stronger Spanish (Mexican) influence. Typically it involves tomatoes, olive oil and olives, garlic, hot peppers, and perhaps air-dried ham or bacon. *Espagnole* is similar. *Bayonnaise* food is closely related but implies pork; *catalane* is also similar but more garlicky.

Bearnaise (bare nez): One of the primary sauces, a butter emulsion flavored with a reduction of wine, vinegar, shallots, and herbs, particularly tarragon. *Bearnaise* cuisine in general is somewhat similar to *basquaise*.

Béchamel (beh shah mel): One of the most basic white sauces, made of flour, butter, and milk.

Bercy (bare see): Generally means a dish finished with wine.

Blanc (blon): Literally, "white"—a dish with white sauce or just white by nature.

Bordelaise (bor deh lez): From Bordeaux, most often referring to a brown sauce flavored with red Bordeaux wine but sometimes meaning garnished with artichokes.

Bourgeoise (boorzh waz): Middle-class, i.e., *not* haute cuisine; generally refers to hearty but relatively simple, chunky-cut stews.

Bourguignonne (boor geen yon): Made with Burgundy wine; also refers to a provincial style (see page 19).

Bretonne (breh tuhn): From Brittany (see page 18); made with white beans.

Bruxelloise (bruk sell waz): From Brussels; Belgian food (see page 17). Similarly, *flamande* (flah mond) refers to Flemish cooking.

Champenoise (sham pen waz): Made with champagne. Similarly, *porto* means flavored with port wine, *madère* with Madeira, and *Xérès* with sherry.

Chasseur (shah sir) or *chasseuse* (shaw soose): "Hunter style," usually meats or game fowl with hearty sauces, but any dish with a brown tomato-and-mushroom sauce; livers are often used as flavoring. A *civet* is a related stew characteristically flavored with blood.

Dauphine (dough feen): Like Anna, refers either to a potato dish (a sort of croquette) or to a meat served with it. *Duchesse* is similar, too, but the potatoes are mashed and treated with cream and eggs.

Diable (dee a bluh): "Devil"; a dish with a hot and spicy sauce made either with cayenne or mustard.

Farci (far sea): Stuffed.

Florentine (flor ahn teen): Refers to the city of Florence; a dish (fish, chicken, omelet, etc.) served on a bed of spinach and topped with mornay sauce.

Gratin (grah tan): A dish topped with grated cheese or bread crumbs and butter and browned to a crust.

Grecque (greck): Greek, using a lot of olive oil, tomatoes, onions, and lemon juice.

Hollandaise (all ahn dez): Literally "Dutch," but refers particularly to what many people consider the queen of sauces, a lemon-flavored butter and egg emulsion.

Indienne (ann dee en): "Indian"; curry-flavored.

Jardinière (zhar dee knee air): From the garden; a dish garnished with turned, or trimmed to bite-size, vegetables.

Lyonnaise (lee ahn nez): From the province of Lyonnais or the city of Lyon (see page 20); but typically implies the use of vinegar.

Maitre d'hôtel (may truh dough tel): Refers to the restaurant host, of course, but in a recipe means a dish flavored with a seasoned butter.

Milanaise (mee lah nez): From the city of Milan; any dish coated in cheese and bread crumbs and then sautéed.

Mornay (more nay): One of the great sauces, a white cream sauce with cheese (frequently Parmigiano-Reggiano) and any dish served with it.

Mousseline (moose leen): Any puree lightened or stiffened with egg whites or whipped cream; also a hollandaise-like sauce.

Nage (naj): "Swimming"; shellfish served in its own poaching liquid.

Nantua (nawn tu ah): A city famous for crawfish, hence, a dish with crawfish.

Niçoise (niece was): From the city of Nice on the Riviera, a Mediterranean style with olive oil, tomatoes, garlic, and also potatoes (as in the famous *salade Niçoise*). *Parmentier* means that potatoes are involved.

Normande (nor mond): From the province settled by Norman (Norwegian) invaders, who went on to conquer England as well. Characterized by the use of apples, applejack, Calvados, or oysters (see page 21).

Papillotte (papy oat): Paper or parchment (or nowadays foil). A fish cooked en **papillotte** is seasoned, sealed in parchment, and baked in its own juices.

Parisienne (pair easy en): From Paris, and thus not provincial—a fairly light and generally "white" style.

Périgourdine (pair ih goor deen): From Périgord (see page 18), where truffles and foie gras are specialties, hence, dishes garnished or stuffed with them.

Poivre (pwov ruh): With pepper (peppercorns, not chilies).

Provençale (pro van sahl): From Provençe (see page 21); and one of the styles most influential in the current renaissance of French (and Mediterranean) food.

Savoyarde (sah voh yard): From Savoy (see page 22); two specific dishes: one an omelet filled with potatoes and Gruyère cheese, the other potatoes and Gruyère served in a crock.

Suprême (sue prem): A chicken recipe, specifically one involving the breast and wing.

Vigneronne (veen yair own): "From the vine grower," hence, a dish with grapes. *Véronique* is similar.

PROVINCIAL CUISINES
It used to be that even those French restaurants in the United States that advertised provincial rather than haute cuisine tended to mix and match their menus, preparing an Alsatian-style choucroute along with a Provençal bouillabaisse. Some of them, rather than specializing in a true regional cuisine, even used the term "provincial" to mean bourgeois or home-style food. However, many celebrated French chefs in the United States, having proved their proficiency at classical cuisine, are recreating more and more of their own regional specialties. (You may also see more restaurant reviews mentioning provincial styles.)

Again, technique and detail are the hallmarks of French cooking, and despite regional differences, once a recipe is established it can be reliably ordered anywhere—one benefit of those rote recipes. There are some broad distinctions to take note of, however: For instance, in the colder regions, the cooking fat is butter; in the temperate zones, duck and goose fat or lard; and in the south, olive oil. (Along the Rhône, they use all three.)

In the regions near Spain, corn was the primary starch, and in south-central France flour was generally made from chestnuts; wheat and rye flours were cheaper and used by "countryfolk" long after the wealthier classes, especially around Paris, demanded white flour. Now, of course, "French bread" is a universal commodity.

It is also true that there is much less dependence on cream sauces, and more on garlic, in the south, where the cuisine is clearly Mediterranean; and that the regions bordering Germany, particularly Alsace, show a strong German influence, involving cheeses, rich sausages, and pastries.

Here is a shorthand guide to some of the provincial styles you are apt to see more of in the next few years:

ALSACE AND LORRAINE This is one of the most fertile regions of France, with a broad variety of fruits, corn, hops, grains, and root vegetables. Not surprisingly, since the region borders Germany, the cuisine is strong on German-style *spaetzle* (dumplings) and sausages, particularly *boudin blanc*, blood puddings, and *civets* (blood-thickened game stews). The tough, long-legged hogs of the Ardennes forest are famous, as are the hams made from them. However, while across the border in Belgium the hams are pickled in brine, smoked, and then consumed quickly, the French hand-salt and air-dry them for six months before eating. The Ardennes is also home to a wide variety of game, especially stags and roe deer, wild duck, pheasant, rabbit, hare, and wild boar; in fact, the emblem of the region is a boar.

Alsatian foie gras is among the most highly prized, and Alsatian restaurants are apt to show it off gloriously, using it to top or even stuff game. The *choucroutes* of Strasbourg (hearty winter-warmer casseroles of white beans, goose or duck confit, sausages, smoked pork, sauerkraut, or, even more authentically, fermented turnips) are considered the apogee of the dish. This region is also the home of Munster cheese. Alsace is famous for its spring asparagus, which is consumed in vast quantities. The quiche Lorraine is a nonsweet tart of cream, eggs, and bacon, which sparked its own culinary revolution in the United States—did real men eat it or not? But no such question would have attended the version called *tourte à la Lorraine*, which has both veal and pork in it. Like Alsace, Lorraine produces good foie gras, boudin, and potted meats; it is also the original home of two famous desserts, *baba au rhum* and the *madeleines* that sent Proust to his pen. (Both were invented for poor King Stanislaus of Poland, who was robbed of his throne by Russia and placated with the Duchy of Lorraine; he apparently found the diet somewhat lacking.) Alsace is famous for its dry, spicy white wines, particularly Riesling (which can stand up to both fish and sauerkraut), Gewürztraminer (perfect with foie gras or cheese),

Pinot Blanc, and Muscat; it also produces sparkling wines like its neighbor Champagne, though bottle-fermented. Alsatian beer is well known, too, and this is also serious schnapps territory. Lorraine produces highly ranked reds, whites, and rosés; the best-known example here is Moselle.

ANJOU AND TOURAINE (LOIRE VALLEY) Bordered by the Loire River, Anjou is rich in freshwater fish, including pike, shad, salmon (now endangered), carp, eels, and bream; one of its specialties is *bouilleture*, a mixed fish stew with eels. The area around the port of Nantes is famous for spring vegetables, especially asparagus, leeks, carrots, mache, endives, and escarole. The so-called "champignon de Paris" mushrooms now come almost exclusively from the Loire Valley. There is still plenty of game around, especially wild birds, but no one makes more out of beef (or lambs or rams) than the residents of the Loire: Among organ meats prepared here are not just brains, kidneys, sweetbreads, and tripe, but ram's testicles, trotters, hearts, bull's cheeks, calf's heads, and the various chitterling sausages called *andouillettes*. (Frog legs are nothing after that.) Pralines and ganaches were first concocted here. The region is partial to fruits, particularly pears and prunes, which are often cooked with fish or game (a touch of the Arab influence). Anjou's soft cream cheeses and goat cheeses *(chèvres)* are extremely popular. Characteristic flavorings include sorrel and walnut oil. Anjou's dry white wines are very popular, notably the Sancerres and Pouilly-Fumés (both 100% Sauvignon Blanc) and the Chenin Blanc Vouvrays, which can also be made into late-harvest dessert wines.

THE BASQUE The Basque people are equally famous as sailors and as shepherds and farmers: they were the first to make an international trade of salted whale meat, starting about the eighth century C.E., and were almost certainly making regular trips to the great banks off New England and Newfoundland to harvest the essential cod before Columbus crossed the Atlantic. But their sheeps' milk cheeses, hams and salami, cider, lamb, and even their wines are highly prized. They are also noted for their free-range poultry—not just chickens and capons but also ducks, geese, turkeys, and even pigeons. The Basque country is still a major fishing area: In addition to cod, they harvest tuna, hake, lampreys, squid, sardines, anchovies, turbot, John Dory, and crabs. (For more on Basque cuisine, see "The Iberian Peninsula: Spain, Portugal, Catalonia, and the Basque.)

BELGIUM Belgian food has the same cheerfully hybrid style as the country as a whole: French techniques are applied to North Sea ingredients and served in German portions. However, unlike the French, the Belgians prefer to customize recipes to individual tastes. Sea bass may be topped with grilled foie gras; sea urchin is combined with oysters, artichokes, and asparagus; local baby shrimp or oysters are poached in Vouvray wine; and grilled fish and rabbit are typically dressed with coarse mustard. One-pot and casserole dishes are common: *Waterzooi* is a rich hot pot, usually of chicken but sometimes of rabbit or even eels or fish. *Carbonnades* are beef stews that use beer (these beer stews are often referred to by the French as "carbonnades à la flamande," meaning Flemish-style). The Flemish even "eat" their beer, cooking hops shoots in spring. Belgian endive is particularly popular wrapped with ham and covered with a cheese sauce. In cooler weather, the Belgians enjoy farmer's-style sausage platters or slow-cooked stews called *hutsepots*, which may be pork, beef, or game, usually with cream and sometimes varied by the use of dried fruits, such as prunes, and the dark, spicy beers of the region. There are several distinct soups: one of peas and beans, another a vegetable soup with pasta and milk, and one with crumbled gingerbread. And an odd reminder of Spanish rule remains: a fondness for escaveche. Here rooty, earthy vegetables are not just tolerated but are in fact preferred, most notably cabbages, leeks, turnips, carrots, and cauliflower. The smoked raw hams and pâtés of the Ardennes are famous, as is the game: wild boar, venison, and hare, especially. And everywhere are desserts, of course—hence the fame of Belgian chocolate.

BORDEAUX Although it produces particularly fine lamb, cheese, and foie gras, Bordeaux has been known since the fourth century as the wine-growing heart of France, source of the great Medocs (Margaux, Saint-Julien, and Pauillac), Graves, Sauternes, Saint-Emilions, and Pomerols. Even those who don't know Semillon from Saint-Estèphe know the names Lafite, Rothschild, Latour, and Margaux. But Bordeaux and its neighbors Gascony and Périgord have other reasons to boast: The region is rich in both freshwater and saltwater fish, and crayfish and eels are favorites. Périgord is famous for its truffles, Roquefort cheese, game fowl, and goose and duck confit and pâtés; Gascony is known for Armagnac and lamb, as well as foie gras and truffles. As in the other southern regions, Bordelaise cuisine emphasizes olive oil and garlic over cream, butter, and shallots.

BRITTANY The sharpest ray on France's profile juts out into the Atlantic Ocean close to Great Britain; in fact, the region is named for the Britons who escaped back to France after the Anglo-Saxons took over in the fifth century. Its Celtic-rooted cuisine shows a family relationship to

Welsh fare but with an even heavier emphasis on seafood: clams, oysters, cockles, scallops, mussels, trout, skate, mullet, bass, spiny lobsters, crabs, sardines, salmon, eels, sole, mackerel, pike, turbot, herring, and shad. Mackerel and herring have been major industries since the ninth century, here and in Boulogne to the north, which is still the primary fishing port in Europe. Crêpes were originally a Breton dish, but Crêpes Suzette were supposedly named for the dining companion of King Edward VII, then Prince of Wales. *Cotriade* is an eel soup or stew, and salt-meadow lamb served with beans is a Bretonne specialty; this meat is said to have a particular tang from the salt water that floods the meadows. Brittany is well stocked with duck and turkey, mutton and pork, and its cauliflowers, artichokes, strawberries, and apples are considered premium. It also produces the Guérande sea salt so popular among gourmets today.

BURGUNDY   Burgundy is to food as Bordeaux is to wine. Its poultry, including many smaller fowl such as squab, woodcock, and dove, is so good that even other Frenchmen admire it; the Charolais beef cattle is prime; the escargots are considered to be the finest; and the wines, including Chablis, Côte de Nuits, Pouilly-Fuissé, Mâcon-Villages, Meursault, Pommard, Chassagne-Montrachet, and Puligny-Montrachet—are big-bodied enough to go along. Not surprisingly, *marc*, a sort of brandy or eau-de-vie made from the skins and stems left over after the wine-making process, is widely made here. So was absinthe, until it was outlawed in 1915, and Pernod still is made. Wild mushrooms, currants (used for making Cassis), marc-washed Epoisses cheese and chèvres, Dijon ham, *coq au chambertin* (the original chicken braised in red wine), beef and rabbit *à la bourguignonne* (stewed in red wine), pike *quenelles* (poached "dumplings" made of fish mousse), smoked meats, and escargots, the legendary first course of snails in garlic butter, are quintessential Burgundian dishes. Many fine oils are produced here: sunflower, peanut, olive, and the gourmet favorites walnut, hazelnut, almond, pistachio, and pine nut. Cooking emphasizes not the four food groups but the four indulgences: wine, cream, lard, and pastry. No wonder they talk about "hearty Burgundies."

CORSICA   This Mediterranean island abounds in fish and seafood (and bouillabaisses), but oddly it is not as large a part of the diet as would seem likely. Mullet, sea bass, John Dory, dogfish, sardines, eels, squid, and octopus are among the most commom catches. Corsica also has an abundance of game, including blackbirds, which are considered a delicacy. It also produces a large variety of fruits and vegetables, most importantly almonds, figs, chestnuts (which for centuries served as flour and polenta starch), clementines, citrons, nectarines, wine grapes, and olives. Typical dishes include beef braised with juniper berries, and a sort of tripe deluxe called *tripa*, stuffed with spinach, beets, and herbs. Corsica has been Italian as well as French (and Byzantine, Arab, a Papal state, and briefly British), and many dishes and dialects recall the Italian connection: sun-dried goat or roast kid; *prisuttu* (prosciutto, Italian-style raw ham) and *panzetta* (pancetta) bacon; polenta, the corn-meal mush; and stuffed leg of lamb. Corsicans also make fine pastries, flavored with almonds, vanilla, aniseed, chestnuts, and pine nuts. Corsican sheeps' milk is made into Roquefort, among other cheeses, but an island specialty is *brocciu*, which is made not from the curds but from the whey.

GASCONY On the Atlantic coast just over the Pyrenees from Spain, Gascony is probably most revered for its Armagnac region, which produces the brandy that bears its name; but it also has fine oysters and truffles, goose, and duck (foie gras and confits). Ham here is often served "raw," meaning unsalted.

LANGUEDOC Named so after *langue d'oc*, language of the southerners (as opposed to *langue d'oil*, the Parisian dialect), this Mediterranean coastal region still shows strong Roman and Arab influences: Its most famous creations include *cassoulet*, the Roman-era mutton ragout with white beans; ragout of veal or duck with olives; blood stews of wild boar; and tripe with saffron and roast suckling pig; and to be cooked *à la languedocienne* means to be garnished with cèpes, eggplant, and tomatoes. (Further demonstrating its ties to old Mediterranean cooking, Languedoc dishes are often described as *à la catalane*, referring to the nearby coastal region of Spain.) Typical Languedoc menus highlight soups, particularly *pot-au-feu*, or hot pots; fish and shellfish stews (including a bouillabaisse entirely unlike the Marseilles version); and hearty vegetable soups made of garlic and cabbage. Egg dishes are unusually popular, especially omelets; and the many fine fowl as well as meats are made into sausages. Languedoc is also the source of Marsanne, Syrah, and Mourvedre wines and the home of Vermouth and Dubonnet.

LYON AND BEAUJOLAIS A major trading center since Roman days, Lyon revels in the produce from up and down the Rhône, as well as its own Beaujolais wines. The huge blue-collar workforce needed to run its markets and warehouses, who created a cuisine from the organ meats and offal, cheaper fish, and cheeses that more prosperous customers disdained, ultimately gave rise to the bistro fare so trendy today. Lyonnais tripe, chitterlings, and sausages are still famous. Lyonnais chocolate, Bresse fowl, quail, turkey, cockerel, pigeon, and rabbit are highly prized. The area is a major supplier of fish, particularly pike and carp. Along the Northern Rhône are some of the oldest vineyards in France, dating to perhaps the fourth century B.C.E. The great Côte Rôtie, Condrieu, Hermitage and Crozes-Hermitage, Cornas, and Saint-Joseph wines are all produced in the towns of Valence and Vienne. The famous Chartreuse liqueur is also from this region.

NORMANDY One of the most famous provincial cuisines, it richly deserves its reputation, so to speak—it's very proud of its butter and cream, which are obvious in almost all its dishes. Many Normandy dishes are even cooked in a special fat called *graisse normande*, which is clarified pork fat and suet with herbs and vegetables. *Tripe à la mode de Caen* is a very fine dish involving apples and cider, carrots, leeks, and such Middle Eastern spices as cinnamon, cloves, nutmeg, and cardamom. It is popularly said to date back to the time of William the Conqueror, whose favorite dish it's said to have been, but it's probably a sixteenth-century recipe. Another famous dish is *andouilles de Vire*, sausages made solely of pork intestines and stomach, marinated in salt and pepper, then smoked, then long-boiled. Normandy is also the home of many rich cheeses, including Camembert and the creamy Neufchâtel. Like neighboring Brittany, it has vast apple orchards (which produce both cider and Calvados, the great apple brandy), as well as meadows of salt-water grass that flavor its mutton and beef. The shellfish from the region are highly prized, especially the giant mussels, the prawns, and the small sweet lobsters called *demoiselles*, or "young girls."

PROVENÇE If any restaurant diner in the United States has escaped the Provençal craze, it's a surprise: The boom in lavender, monkfish, fennel, and, to a great extent, olives owes a debt to this "cuisine of the sun." Garlic certainly does, but while it is true that garlic (or *aioli*, a garlic mayonnaise) is a dominant ingredient of this quintessentially Mediterranean cuisine, it's also true that their garlic is much sweeter than what we are used to in the United States. However, there's no way of knowing what a particular chef is using. Other famous dishes include *pistou*, a typically Mediterranean dish of white beans, tomatoes, and vermicelli; bouillabaisse and similar *bourride*, a stew with white fish only and no saffron; *ratatouille*, the eggplant, tomato, and zucchini stew;

Cafe Society

In the United States, the words "bistro," "brasserie," "cafe," and "restaurant" are often used interchangeably, but originally they were all slightly different. A bistro was the homiest—a neighborhood tavern—hence it suggests a place where the food is hearty but unpretentious. A brasserie was a place where beer and cider were brewed and served, though now brasseries fall somewhere between bistros and restaurants, serving everyday rather than banquet food. Cafes also originally served only liquid refreshment, coffee and wine, but now tend to have what we call "light fare"—sandwiches, pâtés, cheese, and desserts.

tapenades, the savory spreads and tarts and breads with black olives and anchovies; grilled fish with fennel or swiss chard; and dried salt cod. The area is rich in greens and chicories, truffles, duck, lamb, garbanzos, artichokes, tomatoes, grilled peppers, and citrus condiments. The most important wines of the region include Châteauneuf-du-Pape, Gigondas, Côtes du Rhône, and the Tavel rosés.

SAVOY This northeasterly province, which adjoins Switzerland and Germany, is mountainous, but its slopes provide fine pasture and orchard space, and its dairy products, beehives, fruit and nut trees, and game are famous. Its cooking can be generously characterized as hearty: Its specialties include civet, a hare and pork stew with a rich blood, spice, and cream sauce; gratins in general, and gratin of cabbage in particular; and cabbages stuffed with potatoes, bacon, and lamb. Dishes featuring veal and lamb offal (sweetbreads, brains, and livers) are extremely popular. *Matafans* are cornmeal pancakes often served rolled around meat or poultry, something like an Alpine blini. The region has fine fish, which is often batter-fried or floured à la meunière. The influence of its neighbors can be seen in its fondues and especially its desserts, particularly *bonbons au miel des Alpes* (honied Alpine sweets), nougats, pastries, and chocolates.

HOW TO ORDER AND EAT LIKE A NATIVE

As described in the chapter on Russian cuisine, the manner in which dinners are now served—in courses, with all diners served simultaneously, and ideally at tables of no more than eight—was the Russian mode and replaced the French (and generally European) system of three mega-courses. The "correct" order of courses became: hors d'oeuvres, soup, fish, poultry, roast, salad, *entremets* (literally "in-betweens," often fruit or sorbet), cheese and, finally, dessert.

This system in turn prescribed the order of wines, from the lightest to the strongest, because in theory, drinking too dark a wine with the chicken would overpower the dish and spoil the flavor of the next wine. Traditionally, therefore, champagne was served with the hors d'oeuvres, lighter whites with the soups and fish, bigger-bodied whites (or lighter reds) with the poultry, full reds with the meats, the fortified wines such as port and brandy with cheese, and finally on to the great sweet wines, the Sauternes, with dessert. This light-to-dark color-coding was supposed to be fitting to the dishes, too, and for similar reasons—so that too strong a wine with the fish sauce didn't "kill" the chicken.

Obviously, this is more food (and alcohol) than most people want, even at formal banquets, so restaurants have made concessions. Many menus group the appetizers and soups together, and some group the meat and poultry entrées. The cheese course has almost disappeared (but any good French restaurant will have some cheese, even if it isn't on the menu, so ask).

In the United States, all but the finest French restaurants had given in to the American habit of having salad first, which was actually just a way of keeping the customer occupied while dinner was being cooked; but now that American diners have become intrigued by "authentic" dining, many restaurants have restored the old order. Some may ask which you prefer.

You may also see a special three- or four-course *prix fixe* menus: That means the meal has a fixed price, but you will probably have two or perhaps three dishes in each course to choose from. À *la carte* merely means you are ordering (and paying for) each course separately.

HOW TO ORDER AND SAMPLE WINE

The ritual—some people would say "ordeal"—of ordering and tasting fine wines at a restaurant should be fun, not frightening.

The supposed rules of ordering wines—only red with meat, only white with fish—are oversimplified and overrated. It's true that a sweet white will not ideally suit brown meats or game, and a very big red will overwhelm shellfish. However, many people prefer lighter reds with chicken or big whites with game fowl; "dessert wines" are ideal with foie gras, a dry Riesling or Gewürztraminer is good with smoked salmon or

The French take cheese as seriously as they do wines and sauces. There are 400 varieties made in France alone, and although in the United States they (or more often, American imitations) are available year-round, many fine French cheeses have "seasons." Some are even subspecialized: Certain Bries are eaten year-round, some only November till May. And like wines, certain cheeses may carry legal appellations—Roquefort, Camembert—only if they are produced in particular regions. In France, cheeses are served before the sweets, often with butter, though that is not always true in the United States; they are usually served with crackers, and sometimes dark bread and vegetables, rather than fruit. (With Munster, curiously, it is traditional to serve cumin.) If the cheese is uncut, it is traditional for the host to cut into it with the knife and then pass it around.

even curry. And champagne lovers believe that the "bubbly" can be drunk with almost anything.

Also, despite the accepted wisdom, many experts prefer red wines just slightly chilled, particularly with something other than red meat ("room temperature" in a medieval cellar, after all, was unlikely to have been anything near 72°); if you like yours that way, say so when you order it. Similarly, though Americans have a (deserved) reputation for liking both wine and beer over-chilled, serving white wine or champagne too cold will numb the flavor. If the restaurant has overcompensated, ask them to take the bottle out of the ice bucket for a few minutes.

Of course, selecting wines is at best a passion and at worst an obsession, so we suggest you buy a wine guide if you want to know which wines really do go best with certain dishes; or ask the waiter or the sommelier for suggestions. Don't be intimidated; it's their business to help you enjoy your meal.

When the bottle arrives, you (or whoever ordered the wine) will first be shown the label to make sure the correct wine has been brought out. Then the waiter will draw the cork and place it on the table beside your plate. Simply check to make sure it hasn't crumbled or dried out (it should be damp only about halfway up, or the seal is no longer tight); don't sniff it.

Then a sip will be poured into your glass; you may swirl it to release the "bouquet" (the aroma) before tasting it, but again, don't go overboard. If it's good, you may either ask the waiter to pour or, if the wine is a red, let it rest—"breathe," and mellow in the air—a few minutes before pouring it. A sour or moldy smell may be a passing problem; give the wine a moment to clear. The smell of wet cardboard, however, means the wine is "corked" and should be replaced. Some of this may be omitted if you've ordered an inexpensive or house wine; but in any case, if you are not happy with the wine, say so.

If you're entertaining at home, remember that the bouquet of a red wine is most accessible when served in a rounder goblet, while white wines are served in the more oval glasses. Champagne should be served in tall thin "tulips" or "flutes" rather than wide-bottomed, sherbet-style glasses so that the bubbles last longer.

COOKING AT HOME

It's probably not surprising that the French, who have made such a mystique of technique, should encourage people to think French recipes are difficult. Many certainly are; however, some of the recipes Americans typically shy away from, such as soufflés and hand-mixed hollandaise, are actually much easier and less temperamental than is rumored. The stew below is distinctively "provincial"—literally, as that's where Provence got its name—and incredibly simple. It's also perfect for entertaining, dirties only one dish from beginning to end, and can be made entirely in advance. Even the bouillabaisse is easy and so impressive.

PROVENÇAL BEEF STEW

This tastes best (and can be made much less fattening) when made two days in advance.

2 pounds stewing beef, cut in large chunks
2 leeks, thoroughly washed and sliced or coarsely chopped
2 cloves garlic, chopped
1 large carrot, peeled and sliced into coins
2 stalks celery (strings removed), sliced
1 1/2 tablespoons extra virgin olive oil
1 bottle hearty red wine
1 bunch fresh sage or thyme or both
(or 2 tablespoons dried of each), stalks tied together
1 sprig of fresh rosemary (or 1 tablespoon dried),
tied up with the thyme (optional)
2 whole bay leaves
salt and pepper to taste
1 2-inch strip of orange zest, minced

Combine all ingredients except orange zest in enameled casserole and refrigerate overnight. The next day, simmer gently 3–4 hours or until the meat is very tender. Cool, then return to the refrigerator overnight. The next day, remove all hardened oil and fat on the top and then reheat. Remove the bay leaves and the bunch of herbs, stir in the zest, and serve with noodles.

ENDIVE AND HAM GRATIN

8 medium Belgian endives, rinsed and trimmed
salt, pepper, and nutmeg to taste
2 1/4 cups milk
3 tablespoons unsalted butter
4 tablespoons flour
8 thin slices ham
1 cup grated Swiss or Emmenthal cheese
1/2 cup fine bread crumbs

Preheat oven to 350°F. Generously oil an enamel casserole with nonstick spray. Place the endives in the dish, season with salt, pepper, and nutmeg, and cover with 1 cup boiling water. Over high heat, bring the water back to a boil; cover, reduce heat to a bare simmer, and cook until tender (about 25 minutes). Remove endives with slotted spoon, reserving liquid, and drain.

Scald the milk. Meanwhile, melt butter in a heavy saucepan, stir in flour and cook just until it starts to take on color, then add hot milk and poaching liquid, whisking continually until smooth and thick. Simmer briefly, adjust seasonings to taste, and spoon a layer of sauce into the bottom of a baking dish large enough to hold all the endives side by side. Roll each endive in a slice of ham and place in the dish, cover with remaining sauce, top with cheese, and bake until top is crusty (15–20 minutes). Serves eight.

BOUILLABAISSE

3/4 cup olive oil
2 large onions, chopped
4 tomatoes, peeled, seeded, and chopped
2 strips orange zest, julienned

2 cloves peeled garlic, one minced and one split in half
1 teaspoon each taragon, fennel seed, and rosemary
1 tablespoon basil
4 tablespoons chopped fresh parsley
1 1/2 teaspoons saffron threads
3 cups fish stock, chicken stock,
or white wine or vermouth mixed with water
1 pound mixed light-fleshed fish such as John Dory,
sea bass, bream, snapper, halibut, monkfish, or cod
1 pound mixed shellfish such as scallops, calamari, or shrimp
1 dozen black mussels, scrubbed
1 pound small red potatoes
2 small spiny or rock lobsters, split (optional)
1 ounce Pernod, Ricard, or sambuca (optional)
8 slices crusty bread, rubbed with garlic halves and toasted
salt and pepper

Pour about half the olive oil into a deep-sided saucepan or enameled casserole; gently saute onions until translucent but not browned. Add tomatoes, zest, minced garlic, herbs, and saffron. Lay fish over vegetables, pour remaining oil over fish, and set aside to rest.

Meanwhile, bring stock to simmer, cook potatoes until almost done, and remove with slotted spoon; slice if desired or leave whole if small. Bring stock back to simmer if necessary. Return saucepan to high heat, add stock, and bring to boil; cover and simmer for 5 minutes. Add mussels, shellfish, and lobsters (if using); cover and simmer 5–7 minutes or until shells open and shellfish is done. Add potatoes and stir gently. Drizzle Pernod over stew and season to taste.

Place one slice garlic toast in each bowl, ladle out a mixture of seafood (giving each person a half-lobster), and dip the other toast into the side of the stew, or put the second toast on top of the fish and add a dollop of *rouille* (see notes).

Notes: To make the very best bouillabaisse, make homemade fish stock by simmering heads and bones from non-oily fish (your local fishmonger will be glad to save you some trimmings with a day's notice) and/or shrimp and lobster shells for 20 minutes in water to cover with a roughly chopped onion, celery stalk, and carrot. Bottled clam juice is not desirable except in emergencies, as it tends to be overly strong.

Rouille is a garlic paste traditionally served with bouillabaisse. To make it, soak 1/4 cup plain breadcrumbs in chicken stock or white wine; drain and squeeze out remaining liquid. Place two peeled cloves of garlic and two small chili peppers, trimmed and seeded, in a mortar; cream together to a paste and transfer to a small food processor or blender. Add a pinch of saffron (optional) and breadcrumbs; start processor and slowly pour in 2/3 cup olive oil to make emulsion.

ITALY

BASIC CUISINE

DINNER FOR TWO:
Stuffed artichoke, carpaccio, minestrone, bass with capers, osso bucco

DINNER FOR FOUR:
Mixed antipasti, risotto, grilled chicken, rabbit cacciatore, calamari fra diavolo

STYLE:
Hearty, aromatic, smoky

KEY FLAVORS:
Olive oil, garlic, anise, rosemary, tomato

EATING UTENSILS:
Forks and knives

DISTINCTIVE FOODS:
Pasta, risotto, bruscetta, prosciutto

UNIFORMITY OF MENUS:
Good

NUTRITIONAL INDEX:
Low sodium, medium fat

COST:
Inexpensive to expensive

"THANK YOU":
"Grazie"

It's entirely appropriate that so many people consider Italian food "Mamma's cooking": Even the French called it "the mother cuisine," and it goes back a long way.

In the first century C.E., when the Roman author Apicus was writing about cooking, he listed poaching, braising, basting, grilling, roasting, and steaming as common methods of cooking. Roman chefs were also serving egg- and roux-based sauces, cream sauces (including the one that was later dubbed "béchamel" in honor of a French marquis who adored it), fruits to offset fatty poultry (duck à l'orange), breads, and what sounds a lot like lasagne—and all this 1,500 years before tomatoes were even "discovered" by Europeans.

Not that they were short on exotic ingredients: For instance, Apicus also recorded a recipe that called for peas, leeks, coriander, oregano, ginger, nuts, wine, and honey, all of which were merely seasonings for a dish of bacon-and-sausage-stuffed thrush, topped with hard-boiled eggs.

The influence ancient and medieval Italian cuisine has had on what we casually term "classic" cooking techniques has been obscured primarily by the French writers' habit of appropriating recipes and giving them French names. Ragus, or stews, became the French *ragouts; millefoglie*, the "thousand-sheet" pastry, is now usually called *mille feuille*. At the same time, a lot of what seems old about Italian cooking—sun-dried tomatoes, rice, polenta—is relatively new and a testament to their curiosity. Until 150 years ago, eggplant was believed to drive people insane, and only the Sicilians championed it. Sun-dried tomatoes are Native American. *Carpaccio*, the pounded raw beef that is now a standard of virtually every Italian restaurant, was invented only a generation ago, at Harry's Bar in Venice. (This bar/restaurant was made famous by Ernest Hemingway, and the peach juice and Spumante cocktail known as the Bellini was also invented there.) Caesar salad is no older; it was invented in Acapulco by an Italian restaurateur named Caesar Cardini.

Italian cooking methods haven't changed much in the past two millenia; braising, poaching, steaming (*en papiotte*), grilling or griddling, and roasting remain the most common. There are still many villages that have one great wood-burning *forno*, or oven, in which temperatures routinely reach 1200–1500°F and in which casseroles left overnight in the "cooling" section cook for the next day. We have an increasing number of such ovens in the United States, too; Mamma would be proud.

THE COUNTRY

Italy, as children are always told, looks like a boot kicking into the Mediterranean—a very ornate cavalier's boot, with ruffles over the knees in the north and a powerful heel stretching toward Albania and Greece—and the islands of Sardinia and Sicily are like stones the toe is kicking. The frill at the top of the boot is actually the snaking line of the Alps, beyond which lie France, Switzerland, Austria, and Slovenia. Another mountain line, the Apennines, runs down the middle, like a seam, and on into Sicily. Down the east coast—the boot's calf—is the Adriatic Sea, and around the sole and shin lies the Mediterranean.

All but a handful of provinces in Italy touch the sea, and even in the north, no village is more than 150 miles from the ocean. And because the country remains staunchly Roman Catholic, the fish markets are teeming on Friday mornings and almost empty on Monday. (If you're a seafood fanatic, remember that even in the United States, Italian cooks are apt to concentrate on fish dishes on Friday.) The busiest port is Genoa, on the western continental shore near the Italian Riviera.

The mountains also shape Italian cuisine, however: Some parts of Piedmont have winters as cold or even colder than parts of Scandinavia. The plain at the foot of the Alps provides the primary pastureland, and so the major dairy supplier; naturally, many of Italy's cheeses and sweets come from this area. This is also the home of grains, such as rice and cornmeal, rather than wheat; so risotto and polenta go back further in culinary tradition than pasta. The fertile region to the east of the Apennines, Emilia-Romagna, provides fine durum wheat for pasta, as well as rice and maize; on the west is the great wine-growing region. Down the center of the peninsula and into Sicily, where the mountains are more amenable to olive groves than dairy cows, the use of olive oil increases.

Sardinia, over in the heart of the Mediterranean, is more than half pastureland and raises wheat, barley, grapes, and olives along with sheep and goats; it was the Romans' earliest bread factory and was seriously overcultivated for centuries. Sicily, hot but hilly, also supplies wheat, barley, and maize along with olives, almonds, wine grapes, sheep, and cattle.

THE HISTORY

Although there are plenty of archeological remnants, not very much is known about the earliest inhabitants of Italy. Egyptian records refer to Sardinia as early as the thirteenth century B.C.E., and the Greeks had established colonies along the southern coast by the fifth century B.C.E., but the first (of many) invaders into the central peninsula were the Etruscans, who probably moved over from Asia Minor in about the eighth century B.C.E. They were the first to turn wheat flour into a sort of mush, called *puls*, which became the basic hardtack of the Roman legions and probably left its name behind for polenta, the cornmeal mush that made its roundabout way from the Americas nearly 2,500 years later. They may also have been the first to manufacture salt for widespread consumption, although it was the more commercially inclined Romans who made it an international form of currency.

The Etruscans prospered for some 400 years before the Celts (Gauls) elbowed them further south; and soon after that, the Latins and Sabines between them produced that acquisitive and martial people, the Romans. The Roman nobles were heavy meat-eaters and drinkers—the Emperor Maximus reportedly consumed 40 pounds of meat and 40 bottles of wine a day—but the great mass of citizens and slaves of the empire continued to rely on grains, chicken, and a little fish.

Thanks to the innovations and subjugations of the Roman Empire, Italy remained at the center of the universe for a thousand years, until it fell to the various eastern "barbarians" and, like France, broke into a number of competitive states. Sicily fell to the Saracens in the tenth century; the Byzantines recaptured the southern provinces, only to lose them in the eleventh century to the Normans, who in turn gave way to Spain.

Over the next several centuries, France, Spain, Germany, and Austria carved off and juggled pieces of the once-great empire until, by the end of the fifteenth century, the country was loosely divided into three sections: the north, where the independent duchies of Genoa, Venice, and other little states were booming; the central regions, home of the great commercial city-states, such as Florence and the Papal States; and the south, where the Spanish feudal system was taking a cruel toll.

In the north and central plateau, the thirteenth, fourteenth, and fifteenth centuries were a golden age; the Renaissance artists and writers transformed European court culture forever and, thanks particularly to Venetian traders, transformed European cuisine as well. The Italians were unusually quick to appreciate and incorporate new foodstuffs from Asia and the Americas and to bring them together: A seventeenth-century Tuscan boar stew with Middle Eastern nutmeg and cured olives also includes chocolate, using the last ingredient in medieval meat stews much as the ancient Aztecs had. It was during the Italian Renaissance that most cooking techniques used today were perfected and taught to the French. (As Escoffier admitted, "If it had been an Italian who codified the world of cuisine, it would be thought of as Italian"—as if the Italians would ever think of "codifying" something so spontaneous as cooking.)

But if French chefs owe an irradicable debt to the Italians, they may have partially repaid it by preserving the techniques they had learned and returning them in the eighteenth and nineteenth centuries. And although Italy began the painful task of reunification in the late nineteenth century, its regional cuisines still show traces of the peoples who came and conquered before.

THE CUISINE

Having said all that, the very phrase "Italian cuisine" is itself an oxymoron. There is no single Italian cuisine; there was not even a single

Italy until the mid-nineteenth century, and the city-states of the Renaissance developed cultures and cooking techniques in various degrees of isolation.

Nevertheless, some broad-stroke descriptions may be helpful. In Italy, as in France, there is some regional distinction by cooking fats: In the northern areas, near France and Germany, the cooking medium is most often butter, and tomatoes are used more sparingly. Garlic is widely used in the north (although it may sound confusing, the north of Italy is closer to the south of France, so the cooking of the northwest Italian provinces, in particular, resembles that of Provence.) In the northeast, nearest Switzerland and Austria, fattier meats and sausages and cheeses and floured meats are more common. In Tuscany, the south, and in Sicily, the cooking fat is most often olive oil, as it is in Greece, southern Spain, and North Africa. And in Emilia-Romagna, the rich region that begins just beneath the "cuff" of the Italian boot and stretches across to the knee, cooks use all three fats—butter, oil, and lard.

There is also a preference in the north for egg noodles, which are softer, whereas in the south they are more apt to serve eggless pasta, which has more texture. For more on regional styles, see "Provincial Cuisines," page 48.

Italian cuisine is multicultural. Etruscans were making wheat into flour a thousand years before Marco Polo set out for the Far East, and they certainly understood something resembling pasta, whoever gets credit for coming up with the actual noodles. The Greeks introduced garlic, wine, and the essential (olive) oil. They also introduced the concept of fish

Oil and Vinegar

There is a good reason why "Mediterranean" cuisine is almost synonymous with olive oil; 98% of the olive groves in the world are found in Italy, Spain, and Greece. Although it is no longer only epicures who specify extra-virgin olive oil, you may be surprised to discover that "virgin" is not the next level down, but the lowest of four; "extra-virgin" is followed first by "superfine," then by "fine." (The crème de la crème is just that—skimmed off the top of the first pressing—and called *afiorato*.) The grades reflect the amount of oleic acid permitted; extra-virgin has 1% or less (.5% is considered correct), virgin 4%. Olive oils do not withstand high heat very well and should thus be used for flavoring, not frying.

Italy is also home to the greatest of vinegars, the sweet and redolent balsamic vinegar. The real stuff—the only vinegar that can be labeled aceto balsamic tradizionale—is made from the Trebbiano wine grape and is aged for about 40 years. The batch is periodically moved from one cask to another; the casks are each made of a different wood and impart the only seasoning allowed. All the while, the vinegar is getting thicker and sweeter. Some is 100 years old and as costly as vintage wine.

chowders—the beginning of a tradition that produced French bouillabaisse, Spanish zarzuela, and Italian *cioppino* (also called *cacciucco* or *brodetto*). Early on the Romans discovered that marinating meats tenderized and preserved as well as flavored them. Wine, vinegar, lemon, salt, bay leaves, garlic, and rosemary were the common ingredients. The Romans were early connoisseurs of seafood, and they farm-raised oysters, caviar sturgeon, and lamprey eels. Rome is also the home of an ancient and culinarily sophisticated Jewish community, whose recipes, particularly its artichokes, are justifiably famous.

But the Arabs and Byzantines are the unsung heros of the "mother cuisine"; they not only brought with them the Indonesian aromatics—mace, allspice, cinnamon, ginger, clove, anise, and the peppercorns that made Venice rich—but also showed the Italians how to distill the great vinegars now known as balsamic. They succeeded in persuading the Italians to grow their own rice—which the Romans had encountered in India but never felt much need to cultivate—thereby making possible the risotto. They even whispered the secret of ice cream, something they had learned from the Chinese. Their influence is readily visible in southern specialties, such as oranges with braised artichokes, fennel salad, and baked rabbit with preserved lemons.

It was also the Byzantines, incidentally, who taught the Europeans table manners: When Teodora, daughter of the emperor Constantine, married an eleventh-century Venetian aristocrat, she was revolted by the Venetians' habits of eating with their hands and passing communal goblets. She introduced napkins, table settings (some historians refer to solid gold plates and rock crystal cups), and the fork—for which innovations she was denounced as decadent by various cardinals. It took several centuries for the fork to catch on in Italy, and 500 years later, when the de Medicis carried it along to France, they weren't wildly successful, either.

The final major ingredients came via the Spanish, who carved off pieces of southern Italy at various times; they introduced the tomatoes, corn, hot peppers, zucchini, and chocolate they had found while searching for gold in the New World. (The word "salsa," used today almost exclusively for the tomato-pepper condiment in Central and South American cuisine, was picked up by the Spanish from the Italian word for sauce, which in turn had come from the Romans' lavish use of salt—*sal*.) However, to be fair, we owe that culinary favor at least in part to Cristoforo Colombo of Liguria.

Italy was ravaged by wars for centuries following the Renaissance, and meat has only become affordable, and hence a major part of the diet, since World War II. Italians typically eat their pastas with much less sauce than Americans, and a good Italian restaurant will not flood your dish. And Italian pizzas are much lighter; one can only think the real *capo di tutti i capi* would have paled at the sight of the kitchen-sink creations nicknamed "godfathers" in American pizza parlors.

In general, a Tuscan restaurant that specializes in grilled meats and seafood and uses the "good cholesterol" of olive oil is likely to have lower-fat fare than a northern Italian restaurant, particularly one that offers a lot of dredged and butter-sautéed dishes with prosciutto and fontina cheese. If you're worried about cholesterol, you may also want to remember that southern Italian cooking uses fewer eggs (particularly in the pastas), butter, or cream than northern styles. Even so, unless you pile on the Parmigiano (which is both high-fat and high-sodium), you can eat fairly well in any Italian kitchen—including a pizzeria. Just stick to the veggie versions.

> ### Tavern Fare
>
> Just as the French differentiate between bistros and brasseries, the Italians distinguish between trattorias, cantinas, and ristorantes. A trattoria is the most informal, a mom-and-pop place, often with an exposed kitchen, heavy plates, and jelly glasses for house wine. A cantina is more of a tavern. A restaurant that advertises *cucina stagionale* specializes in seasonal dishes, which is particularly authentic: In Italy, only fresh ingredients are ever used. *Cucina casalinga* or *casarecchia* is "home cooking," *cucina vecchia* is old-style cuisine, and *novella cucina* is the Italian equivalent of nouvelle cuisine—that is, lightened up (and probably hiked up price-wise as well).

THE MAIN INGREDIENTS

SEASONINGS Thanks to the Saracens, the "brown" spices of Indonesia—mace, nutmeg, cinnamon, coriander, anise, clove, and ginger—are as much a part of the Italian kitchen as the "green" herbs: tarragon, parsley, basil, fennel, oregano, sage, bay leaves, chives and leeks, thyme, chervil, rosemary, mint, juniper, and marjoram. Capers, a small green bud brined in vinegar (another Arab import), and pickled gherkins are also used to provide contrast, particularly to seafood (and particularly in Sicily). Anchovies are indispensable for meats, pastas, or green sauces traditionally served with boiled meats. (However, just as many Americans don't realize that sauerkraut is supposed to be rinsed of brine before cooking, ill-informed pizza- and Caesar salad–makers who have not learned to rinse the excess salt off anchovies have done their reputation a disservice.) Balsamic vinegar and green olives are popular in more pungent dishes; black and white peppercorns, truffles, and dried mushrooms are used in the earthier ones. Simplicity is a hallmark of main courses because freshness is so vital, but Italians are anything but shy about condiments and seasonings. *Salsa verde*, the green sauce considered essential with the mixed boiled meats called *bollito misto*, is a puree of parsley, capers, vinegar, anchovies, garlic, and olive oil. Horseradish sauce is used far more widely than in the United States.

VEGETABLES AND FRUITS Despite the fact that tomatoes did not reach Italy until early in the sixteenth century, and were viewed with suspicion in much of Europe, Italians (particularly those in the southern provinces) took to them immediately and have developed some of the juiciest varieties available today. Many Italian cooking experts say that the only canned tomatoes worth cooking with are the San Marzano tomatoes from Naples. (The route that tomatoes took into Italy is the source of some dispute, incidentally: As Naples was then a Spanish possession, that was long thought to be the first stop for the *pomodoro*, or "golden apple." However, some historians believe that the North African traders carried it from Spain into Italy, and that the word comes from "pomi di Mori" or Moorish apple. That might also explain the French name, *pomme d'amour*, "love apple.") Anise (fennel) is one of the most characteristic flavors in Italian cooking, as a spice and as a vegetable. Bulb fennel, celery, celeriac, the chicories (especially escarole and various types of radicchio) and endives, artichokes, thistles and cardoons, and Jerusalem artichokes are all popular.

Other large crops include cauliflower, broccoli and broccoli rape, brussels sprouts, eggplant, escarole, asparagus, chard, corn, sugar beets, spinach, turnip and mustard greens, zucchini, tomatoes, sweet and hot peppers, and beans, particularly peas, green beans, small black beans, white *fagioli*, limas, and cannellini beans. Wild mushrooms are legendary, particularly the porcini and portobellos, which are flooding American menus. Italians like these mushrooms both fresh and dried, especially in stuffings or sauces, where the more concentrated flavor of the dried funghi is preferred. And of course the redolent and earthy truffles, particularly the white ones from Piedmont, Tuscany, and the Marches, are a culinary icon.

A variety of citrus fruits, particularly oranges and lemons, are produced in the warmer regions, and so are tree fruits such as pears and peaches; the great grape regions are in Tuscany and Sicily.

RICE AND GRAINS There are only three types of rice considered suitable for making risotto, a creamy yet firm "braise" of rice, usually flavored with wild mushrooms or truffles, seafood, and Romano or Parmigiano cheese. Arborio rice is a short grain popular in the north and makes a stickier risotto. Vialone Nano retains more "body"; it is the rice of choice in Venice. Carnaroli was hybridized from Vialone and a Japanese variety in 1945: The rarest and most expensive of the three, it is increasingly popular among trend-savvy chefs in the United States. Cornmeal mush, or polenta, has been popular ever since the Arabs introduced it (trading with the Spanish, who found it in Mexico). Most polenta is a coarse yellow meal, although in the north it may be a finer white meal. Barley grains are often used in soups. Buckwheat, whole wheat, and rye flours are used not only for breads but also, particularly in the northern areas, in pastas.

DAIRY PRODUCTS Italians are among the foremost cheese producers (even the French bow to Parmigiano-Reggiano) and like both hard (Parmigiano and Romano) and soft varieties (mozzarella, ricotta, Fontina). These cheeses, incidentally, may be made from cow's milk, goat's milk, sheep's milk, or buffalo's milk, which is used to make the most expensive mozzarella. Gorgonzola is a fine blue cheese from Lombardy and Piedmont. Mascarpone is a sweet, very soft dessert cheese. "Ricotta" actually means "recooked," and therefore refers to a mild, slightly grainy, very soft cheese made from re-boiling whey. It was originally made from the popular ewe's milk Pecorino but nowadays is usually produced using cow's milk. In the United States, ricotta cheese has become popular to use in various pasta stuffings, both savory and sweet, as well as in many deserts.

FISH AND SEAFOOD   As we have noted, virtually every province has access to the Mediterranean as well as to numerous rivers, and the variety is mouth-watering: salmon and salmon trout, mackerel, tuna, carp, bluefish, swordfish, pompano, sardines, herring, anchovies, smelts, butterfish, cod, flounder, sole, pike, perch, red snapper, catfish, turbot, fresh- and saltwater eels, grouper, and tilefish, plus squid, lampreys, sea urchins, oysters, clams, mussels, lobsters, shrimp, sturgeon caviar, and scampi, the giant Adriatic prawns. In the United States, "scampi" is frequently seen on menus but rarely in the flesh; instead, shrimp or prawns are substituted. *Baccalà* is the Italian name for the Viking-dried cod now most often found in Portuguese and Brazilian food (*bacalao*). *Bottarga* is grey mullet roe that has been salted, pressed, and dried; a similar process is used on tuna roe. *Stoccafisso* (stockfish) is the name for the sun-dried cod that Norwegians call *stokkfisk*—the one that lasts 20 years.

No part of a fish goes untasted, incidentally: Sometimes pasta sauces are made of fish heads simmered in wine and tomatoes then passed through a food mill.

POULTRY AND GAME BIRDS   Chicken (which includes hens, young roosters, and capons) is almost daily fare, and turkey, duck, and goose are fairly common, but Italians also like the spunkier flavor of game birds—squab, partridge, quail, snipe, pheasant, guinea hen, and woodcock—that stand up well to being roasted, spit-grilled, or stewed.

MEATS   Although beef doesn't appear on Italian menus in the United States as much as veal and lamb (*agnelli*), Italian beef cattle are highly prized, particularly the Razza Chianina, a buffalo-like animal raised in Tuscany and Umbria, and the fattier, more tender Piemontese. Veal, or *vitellone*, can only be marketed as that if the calf is three or younger; at three-and-a-half, it becomes *manzo*. Liver and onions is a Venetian invention, not a school principal's, although it's more likely to be veal liver than calf's.

Pork and suckling pigs are popular as roasts and chops, but most often they are cured or salted: The word "prosciutto" usually refers to a raw, salted, and air-cured ham (although *prosciutto cotto* is cooked ham), and *pancetta* is a fine bacon from the belly that can be eaten "raw." *Mortadella* is a mild Bolognese salami, the original of what has become "bologna."

Capocollo is a long-cured, usually lightly smoked sausage from south and central Italy; the best-known, made in Umbria, is spiced with fennel and/or black pepper. An organ-meat sausage called *indugghia* (een-DEW-gia) is the ancestor of the French, and now more famously Cajun, andouille. *Bresaola* is air-dried beef. Pork and veal are ground into sausages or meatballs. The hams and sausages of the north are particularly good. Italians pay close attention to organ meats and offal, from jowls and pigs' feet to tripe and testicles; but only the "tamest" of these—brains, kidneys, livers, and sweetbreads—are apt to appear on American menus. Gamier meats are also popular, particularly wild boar and venison. Horse meat is still popular in some areas, especially the Veneto, but will not appear on a restaurant menu in the United States. Intriguingly, Italian cookbooks tend to group rabbit recipes under "poultry." (We *told* you it tasted like chicken.)

THE MAIN DISHES

Like French provincial cooking, Italian regional specialties may be made in any part of the country, but unlike the French, the Italians prefer to improvise a bit. They also insist on seasonal ingredients; you won't see asparagus risotto in the fall—not in Italy, at least. These are some of the more common dishes; for regional specialties, see "Provincial Cuisines," page 48.

ANTIPASTI These are appetizers, some of which are served hot (*caldi*) and some cold (*freddi*). *Bruschetta* are toasted bread crusts rubbed with garlic, olive oil, or butter; *crostini* are similar but are topped with garbanzo spreads, anchovies, tomatoes, or chicken livers. Mixed antipasti plates generally include olives, marinated mushrooms, hard-cooked eggs, roasted vegetables, particularly sweet peppers mated with anchovies, carpaccio (pounded-thin, raw beef drizzled with oil and dusted with black pepper and shavings of Parmesan cheese), prosciutto, or even salami. Grilled lamb is classic Tuscan fare. Other likely choices include fried or stuffed artichokes, clams or mussels, tomatoes stuffed with tuna or other seafood, fried sardines, poached fish, grilled or fried calamari, and garlic-sautéed scampi. *Fritto misto* just means a mixed fry and can include anything from sweetbreads and livers to mushrooms and cheese. See also "How to Order and Eat Like a Native," page 52.

SOUPS One of the most famous soups is *risi e bisi*—rice and peas in broth with parsley and cheese stirred in at the end: It's associated with the coming of spring and St. Mark's Day, April 25. *Pasta e fagioli* is beans, macaroni, tomatoes, and a little pork topped with grated cheese.

The vegetable soup Americans know as "minestrone" is a Genovese dish (though now made everywhere, with regional variations) and combines vegetables with string beans and cannellini, pancetta, prosciutto, tomatoes, and wine. Small stuffed pasta such as tortellini are frequently served *in brodo*, floating in broth. Seafood soups called brodetto or cacciucco (from a Turkish word for fish) are extremely fine. Lentil and bean soups, chicken soups with meatballs, potato purees, cabbage or sauerkraut soups, seafoods in broth, and green vegetable soups made from broccoli, escarole, or spinach are also common.

SALADS The mixed greens used in Italy (radicchio, escarole, arugula, romaine) tend to have body and a touch of bitterness that is tempered by simple dressings of olive oil and lemon juice or vinegar. Fresh mozzarella cheese paired with tomatoes is usually served only with oil (this is called *insalata caprese* or simply *caprese*). The Tuscans in particular are fond of *panzanella*, a bread, tomato, and olive oil salad that is a Mediterranean universal; this is sometimes called *caponata*, but in the United States, that word is usually short for *caponata di melanzane* (see the section on Sicilian regional cuisine, page 50).

VEGETABLES The Italians generally prefer their vegetables, like their seafood, fairly simple, partly because the vegetables are so fresh. Most often they are steamed or briefly boiled, then dressed with oil; blanched and then sautéed; prepared "agrodolce," or sweet-and-sour; or fried in a light simple batter, especially eggplant and zucchini and their flowers. Artichokes, carrots, and the bitter greens such as endive and escarole are often mellowed through braising or fricasseeing; cabbage and radicchio may be cooked this way, too, or fried, or wilted under hot dressings, as spinach is. In the northern regions, vegetables such as spinach and escarole are often steamed and creamed. Onions and cabbages are stuffed with pork or veal and sautéed. Carrots and green beans are usually lightly cooked in butter, though white beans and lentils are boiled and usually mixed with either bitter greens or a little meat. Eggplant used to be found only in the south, but nowadays *melanzane alla parmigiana* is available almost everywhere. Potatoes are less frequently "done" in Italy than in France, but they do show up pan-fried, or as croquettes, or mashed for gnocchi.

And now that the "Mediterranean diet" has become a buzzword for healthful eating, the Italians' reliance on beans, greens, and grains is no longer seen as a peasant's proclivity. In fact, while in the United States, the dishes involving white beans are usually limited to supporting roles in minestrone and bean, tuna, and red onion salad, Italian chefs consider them a primary ingredient, creating stews, soups, and entree salads around them (or, at their freshest, serving them up simply seasoned with a few tomatoes, prosciutto, and sage).

MEAT Meat in Italy was traditionally long-cooked, and much of it still is over there, although in the United States, steaks, chops, and roasts are more easily ordered rare. A classic Tuscan dish, *involtini*, features beefsteak strips pounded, layered with salami, raisins, pine nuts, orange zest, and cheese, then rolled up and sauced with a thick, sweet wine sauce; there is also a veal involtini, flavored with cinnamon and cloves and stuffed with sausage. *Bistecca alla Fiorentina* is a giant porterhouse steak that would make a Chicago cattleman proud—though sadly, the outbreak of "mad cow" disease has led the Italian government to ban the sale of beef on the bone. Beef kebabs, marinated in olive oil, lemon, red wine, and garlic, recall their Persian heritage, as does the immensely popular *osso buco*, veal shanks stewed with tomatoes (in some areas, white wine) until the meat falls off the bone, served over saffron rice.

Roast veal is a family favorite all over Italy; the breast is often stuffed or boned and rolled. Cold sliced veal with tuna sauce is a summer classic. *Stinco* is veal shank braised with anchovies. Veal cutlets or scaloppine, sliced and pounded top round, are commonly dredged in flour and sautéed, after which they may be flavored with lemon, marsala wine, anchovies, capers, grappa, asparagus, cheese, or cream, depending on the region: They are also stuffed and rolled. *Saltimbocca* is a sort of open-faced "sandwich" of veal and prosciutto, strongly flavored with fresh sage and so delicious it jumps—"saltare"—from the pan to the mouth, or "bocca."

Lamb is roasted, pan-roasted, fried, served upright in racks, and stewed, particularly with artichokes or fennel. Rabbit is simmered in white wine and rosemary or, especially in Tuscany, cooked in a ragu sauce for pappardelle. Organ meats are usually sautéed, fried, or braised, though sturdier livers may be grilled. Pork may be roasted, served as chops with German-style sweet-and-sour cabbage, or Sicilian-style with mint and oranges. But almost any other sort of dish—beef, veal, pasta, even seafood—may well include prosciutto or mortadella ham as a flavoring. Meatballs, although too often made of hamburger meat in the United States, are made with chuck, pork, veal, and various combinations depending on the region.

American waiters are usually instructed to offer you both ground Parmigiano and ground pepper for your food (and now that "fresh-ground" refers to cheese as well, watching young waiters juggling pepper grinders and cheese graters simultaneously can be pretty entertaining). However, many Italians consider cheese a flavoring for plainly dressed pastas or those with vegetable or seafood sauces; meat sauces, according to this school, do not take cheese.

Waiters also offer you large spoons, but these should only be used to serve from the platter, along with a serving fork. To eat pasta noodles, turn the tines of the fork downward and cage a few strands, then twirl the stem of the fork with your hand until the noodles wrap around the fork. Do not use the bowl of a spoon as a twirling aid or cut the noodles with a knife or with the side of your fork. If you can't manage long noodles, order the smaller, individual pastas, such as penne or agnolotti.

FISH AND SEAFOOD *Fra Diavolo* ("brother of the devil") is a peppery tomato-and-wine sauce often used with lobster, clams, squid, or mixed seafood; *marinara*, the milder version, is also commonly used with shellfish. (When restaurants list "clams with red or white sauce," marinara is the red sauce they mean.) Seafood stews are made with pesto or saffron, depending on the region; whole fish are most often either grilled simply with lemon and capers or garlic, glazed with wine, or dredged and fried; but particularly in the central plains, hollandaise sauce, or *salsa olandese*, is popular with steamed and poached fillets. The Byzantine flavor shows up when fish are sauced with ground almonds and grapes or raisins.

CHICKEN AND GAME BIRDS Poultry may be common, but it gets lavish treatment: grilled with rosemary; stewed with green or black olives, prosciutto, and chicken livers; stewed with peas and pancetta; even boned and left whole before being stuffed with beef and cheese and baked. Fillets are sauteed and stuffed with herbs or meats. "Cacciatore," or hunter's-style chicken, is stewed in wine, onions, and tomatoes. The gamier birds are tenderized either by hanging—the traditional treatment for pheasant—or by larding the breast, which is standard for pigeon and guinea hen. Duck and goose, on the other hand, are roasted to render the excess fat, then braised or stewed. In Tuscany and Umbria, duck is stuffed with its own liver, prosciutto, and herbs, and then grilled or roasted. Chicken *alla campagnola*, or country-style, has been skillet-fried with potatoes, sausages, and green peppers.

RICE AND GRAINS As mentioned, risotto is the most popular way to serve rice; it requires slow cooking and regular coaxing with broth. Among the most popular risottos are those flavored with wild mushrooms, eels, peas and pancetta, asparagus, and squid and scallops. Rice is also habitually paired with peas for risi e bisi. Sicilians roll rice into balls with various fillings (prosciutto and mozzarella, chicken livers, ground veal) and then fry them into what are called *arancini*, little oranges.

The phrase *riso nero*, black rice, usually means a dish flavored with squid ink, but if it's listed under the desserts, it means a chocolate-flavored rice pudding.

Polenta is a cornmeal mush that is cooked, left to cool, cut in slices, and then baked or fried; it can then be topped with almost any sort of meat, vegetable sauce, or poultry. Polenta slices are also used like fat pasta noodles in fancy "lasagne."

SWEETS Like everything else in Italian cooking, desserts echo the topography. Not surprisingly, it was the Venetians, with their Byzantine connections, who first grasped the extravagant potential of sugar, so Venetian desserts are particularly ornate, involving spun sugar, custards, and so forth. Chocolate ricotta cheesecakes, ricotta-stuffed cannoli, and *tiramisù* (espresso- and liquor-soaked ladyfingers or spongecake) origi-nated in the regions closest to Germany, where pastries and creams are common; in the Piedmont, where honeybees and nut trees are farmed, there are some almost Greek-style sweets. The ice cream, called *gelato*, and the sorbet-like *granita* are famous, and justly so. In Sicily, near North Africa, rice is flavored with orange and cinnamon, rolled in flour, fried, and finished with powdered sugar.

Nevertheless, such rich desserts are eaten far more rarely in Italy than in the United States, and at home Italians generally finish meals with fruit or cheese.

BEVERAGES Starbucks may be the buzzword, but Italy gets the thanks for the revolution in coffee-drinking and the flood of coffee bars in the United States. Among the Italian-style brews that have entered the vernacular are *espresso*, which is made from very finely ground beans pressed and forced with steaming water; *cappuccino*, which means "little hood" and refers to espresso topped with steamed and foaming milk; *latte*, which like the French "au lait" means a half-and-half blend of coffee and heated milk; and *macchiato*, or "stained" coffee, which is an espresso with just a little milk. Any of these can be ordered decaffeinated, with skim milk ("skinny"), in double doses, and so on, which makes for a lot of yuppie-drink jokes these days.

The Italians, you might note, have only plain espresso after dinner, because they do not think milk sits well on a full stomach. And while some put sugar in their espresso, none uses lemon peel; that is a reminder of a time when people were so poor that "coffee" had little flavor and the lemon had to mask it, much as in the southern United States during and after the Civil War, when chicory weed was used to stretch (or even replace) thin coffee.

Italian beers have also broken through the U.S. fashion barrier, and while the French Perrier and Evian waters may have been the first to habituate Americans to name-brand bottled waters, San Pelligrino and other Italian brands are making substantial inroads into the market.

WINES AND SPIRITS

Although Italian wines have until recently been considered a poor second to French vintages (like the cuisine, it has been slighted by the greater number of French and Francophile wine critics), the appearance in recent years of the so-called "super-Tuscans"—Sangiovese legally blended with small amounts of Merlot, Cabernet Sauvignon, Pinot Noir, Shiraz, and even Viognier and Chardonnay—has led to greater appreciation of Italian grapes. Nevertheless, while there are some very expensive Italian wines, the vast majority are still remarkable bargains. Italy actually has more acres devoted to grapevines than France, though Spain has the most, and exports more wine than either. Red wines outnumber whites two to one.

Wine is as old a drink here as anywhere: The ancient Greeks called the peninsula Enotria—Land of the Wines—and transformed casual domestic wine-making into a serious export industry. This early production may be one reason the Italian varietals seem to have such international bloodlines; many experts believe more than a thousand types of grapes have been grown here.

It was primarily from Italy that the rest of Europe learned viniculture, thanks to the Romans (Pliny noted that the vintage 121 B.C.E. was a particularly good one). The Antinori family of Tuscany, for instance, has been in the business since 1385; the Brolio family has been around since 1057 and is in its 32nd generation. But the "science" of winemaking (and marketing) were largely neglected until a few decades ago;

the collaboration of the almost equally ancient Frescobaldi family with the Mondavis of California in producing the super-premium Luce and Lucente wines—blends of Sangiovese, Cabernet, and Merlot—is just one of the more visible commercial successes.

The most important wine regions in Italy are Tuscany, which produces Chianti, Rosso di Montepulciano, Rossi di Montalcino, Vino Nobile di Montepulciano, and Brunello di Montalcino (all made from the Sangiovese grape but ranging respectively from light to tannic and imposing); neighboring Umbria, which produces Amarone and Orvieto; Veneto, home of the easy-going table red Valpolicella, its aged and more potent twin Amarone, and the dry white Soave; and Piedmont, home of the sparkling Spumantes, the chocolate-cherry Beaujolais-like Dolcettos, the similar but slightly more pugnacious Barberas, the powerful Barolos, and their more reticent siblings, the Barbarescos. Among sweet wines, the most famous are Sicily's Malvasias (Marsalas) and Tuscany's vin santo (which may be either Malvasia or Trebbiano). However, southern Italian provinces are beginning to produce big, rich, and affordable reds that may be the next craze, especially those made with the Primitivo grape, thought to be the ancestor of Zinfandel.

Other well-known Italian spirits include the aperitifs, digestifs, sweet liquers, and grappas, all of which are making a comeback in the age of the conspicuously elite consumer. Aperitifs, as the name suggests, are herb- or citrus-infused drinks intended to spark the appetite before a meal. Among the most common are the bitter-orange Campari (named for the Milanese Cafe Campari, where it was first brewed in 1860), vermouths, and a drier form of vin santo. Digestifs such as Punt y Mes ("a point and a half"), Averna, and Fernet Branca are even more bitter herbals that are believed to ease digestion; like concentrated root beers, they take getting used to. Among Italy's best-known liqueurs are the almond-citrus amarettos, the licorice sambucas, and the hazelnut Frangelicos.

Grappa is a strong (90 proof) *aquavit* that is a byproduct of the wine-making process (or used to be; nowadays some grapes are turned directly to its production). After the grapes were mashed, the skins, seeds, and small twigs were pressed and that rawer liquor allowed to ferment as a sort of laborer's drink. Over time, small wine producers began to experiment with higher-quality grappas, though few were exported; they were produced mainly for personal use. However, grappa has become very trendy in the United States and is now being produced in California and even Israel, as well as Italy. Grappas may be identified by the specific varietals used to make them (a far cry from the old recipes, which combined any and all grapes) or flavored with fruits or herbs; the modern versions are much smoother, though no less potent, than the originals.

PASTA

There are entire volumes on pasta, and there could be encyclopedias. Some of those volumes have whole chapters devoted to the question of whether the Italians invented pasta or whether Marco Polo brought it back from China. There is, in fact, a pasta museum—in Bologna, where the Italians believe pasta originated. We're not taking sides, just being grateful. As Sophia Loren once put it, "Everything you see I owe to spaghetti."

However, there are a few simple things to remember about pasta. The major distinction is between dried or "hard" eggless types and "soft" or "fresh" noodles with eggs. Neither is preferred in any way; it depends solely on the desired texture or the intended sauce, because the shape and weight are intended to complement the sauce. Thin or slippery sauces— tomato sauces, thinner cream sauces—are better matched to the textured shapes that will hold the sauce; and sturdy meat sauces go with thicker, flat noodles, such as linguine or fettuccine. Also, dried or hard pasta tends to have a slightly rougher surface and to swell more in cooking; it will hold on to oil-based or vegetable sauces better than fresh pasta.

Among the straight pastas are *capelli d'angelo*, or angel hair, the thinnest round noodles; spaghetti and *bucatini*, which is like a thick, hollow spaghetti; and the flat pastas—linguine, fettuccine ("*ribbon*"), the extra-wide pappardelle, and of course the broad lasagne sheet. Probably the most common in Italy itself is *tagliatelle*, a medium-width pasta.

Most pastas are named for their shapes. Among the spiral pastas are *fusilli* and *rotelle*. Tubular noodles can be smooth but cut with angled ends (*penne*, meaning "pen" and referring to a nib) or grooved (*rigatoni*). *Conchiglie* are little clam-shell shapes ("conchs"); *orecchiette* are "little ears"; *farfalle* are "bowties," pinched in the middle; *lombrichelle* are "worms," handmade and irregular (also called *stringozzi*, or "shoelaces"). *Maltagliati* means "badly cut" and is a sort of irregular triangular noodle good for soup. *Sedani* are curved and ridged like the celery they're named for. *Gramigna* is a curved Bolognese macaroni named for its crabgrass shape. *Semini* are seed-shaped (like the orzo of Greek kitchens), and *radiatore* are waffled—almost tripe-like, but rounded into little radiators.

There are a number of stuffed pastas, too: *Cappellacci* are round dumplings ("little hats") made by placing the meat or cheese filling onto one sheet of pasta, covering it with another, and then cutting out rounds; *ravioli* is similar but squarish; and *agnolotti* are sort of a "half-portion"— pasta first cut into disks, then filled, folded into half-moons, and pinched around the edges. *Tortellini* are "little rings," and *tortelloni* not-so-little rings. *Manicotti*, which is a square of pasta rolled around a filling of ricotta and prosciutto, literally means "hand-roll" and is named after a woman's muff. Add chicken, and it becomes *cannelloni*—"cannons."

Pasta, particularly linguine and fettuccine, is often made with vegetables to add flavor and color to the dish: Spinach, artichokes, tomatoes, beets, pesto, red pepper, garlic, and mushroom are the most familiar additions, but black pasta, colored with squid ink, can be very spectacular.

Strictly speaking, gnocchi is not pasta but dumplings, made of mashed potatoes rather than flour; it's more common in the north, near Germany.

As to pasta sauces, they are limited only by the imagination; some of the best known are mentioned in the descriptions of regional specialities.

PIZZA

We're not going to get into the question of who first invented pizza, either: We're just going to pass along that the Greeks settled in the south of Italy 2,500 years ago, and the Romans who followed them certainly ate something like white pizza. Tomatoes, of course, only arrived in the early sixteenth century. The first pizzeria on record opened in 1830, in Naples.

Italians make bread out of an astonishing array of flours: hard wheat, semolina, whole wheat, soy flour, barley, bran, cornmeal, walnut or almond flour, rice (which also shows up in some fritto mistos, rendering them something like transplanted tempura), and rye. The same dough can be used for bread, rolls, breadsticks, bruschetta, focaccia, calzone, or pizza. The only practical difference between pizza and focaccia is the thickness of the crust: Traditional pizza crust is thin, and something an inch or two thick (or, as it's called in the United States, deep-dish, Sicilian, or Chicago-style pizza) is more like focaccia. (True Sicilian stuffed pizza has two thin crusts, however.) Fold the dough in half over the fillings and seal it up and you have a *calzone*.

Unlike Americans, Italians consider the crust the pizza, and the topping just that—a light layer. The most famous types are *pizza margherita*, with tomatoes, basil, and mozzarella, which was prepared as a tribute to the Italian tri-colored flag when Queen Margherita visited Naples in the late nineteenth century; *napoletana*, a margherita with a dash of capers and anchovy; *frutti di mare*, margherita plus clams, mussels, squid, and/or shrimp; *ai quattro formaggi*, with four cheeses (chef's choice); *alla Romana* or white pizza; and *pizza al formaggio*, the traditional white pizza (except that sometimes pizza al formaggio turns out to be cheese bread).

Most bread is leavened, but *torta* or *piadina*, a flat griddle bread, is something like a cross between pita bread and a pizza crust. *Panettone* is a puffy sweet bread, studded with raisins, candied fruit, and citrus zest, traditionally served at Christmas; *colomba* is a similar loaf bread served at Easter.

PROVINCIAL CUISINES

As Italian food becomes more popular in the United States, chefs are less satisfied with calling their food "northern Italian" or "home-style." Increasingly, at least in the menus' small print and in restaurant reviews, you'll see Italian cuisine described with reference to the province, and these cuisines are some of the more distinctive styles. (Although the island of Sardinia is an Italian possession, its food is more closely related to that of Catalonia: see the chapter on "The Iberian Peninsula: Spain, Portugal, Catalonia, and the Basque.")

EMILIA-ROMAGNA Although the name may not be as familiar as Tuscany or Naples, Emilia-Romagna is Italy's major wheat-producing region, hence the ultimate source of pasta; home of prosciutto, the air-cured salted ham, and one of Italy's most famous cheeses, Parmigiano-Reggiano. Among the region's major cities are Parma, Ravenna, and Bologna, and to a great extent, a restaurant in the United States that advertises "northern Italian" cuisine is talking about Bolognese or Parmesan food. Pasta here generally includes eggs, and so is "soft": Among the finest varieties that originated here are capelli d'angelo, the very thin "angel hair" so popular in the United States, tortellini, tagliatelle, and lasagne. Spinach lasagne includes veal and beef and prosciutto; Romagna-style macaroni has sweetbreads, prosciutto, and truffles; and a Bolognese macaroni is topped with a pancetta, veal, chicken liver, and heavy cream ragout. Pastas with "four cheeses" were invented here. Earthy flavors— eel, kidneys, rabbit, salt cod—are common. The classic meat sauce, a poor imitation of which was many Americans' earliest experience with

Italian food, is actually made of a combination of ground meats: pork, veal, and beef, with pancetta, red wine, and milk as well as tomatoes. But that is only one of the region's claims to fame: Tortellini originated here, and there are scores of stuffings, ranging from cheese to chicken to veal to shrimp or fish to walnuts and cream. And the city of Modena is home to that great seasoning, aceto balsamico, balsamic vinegar.

GENOA Genoa is the centerpoint of Liguria, a long, skinny seafront region on the western coast of Italy; it adjoins France and bears some family resemblance to Provençal cuisine. The dishes there are apt to be baked and solid—lasagne, pastas with meat sauces, ravioli with walnuts, cauliflower with anchovies. A dish prepared *alla Genovese* is likely to have both basil and garlic as primary flavorings; soups and even rice are served with pesto—one of the region's most influential exports. In fact, nearby Portofino—a postcard-pretty resort of multicolored villas that has catered to the likes of the Duke and Duchess of Windsor and Bogart and Bacall—claims to be the home of pesto. Genoa is Italy's finest port, so seafood stews, seafood risottos, and seafood-sauced pastas are fine here. However, residents also enjoy fine game in season, characteristically with walnut or chestnut sauces. The region is rife with wild mushrooms as well. And Ligurians are famous for stuffing almost any vegetable before baking it: zucchini, eggplant, cabbage, artichokes, and tomatoes.

LOMBARDY AND THE PIEDMONT Both these regions are landlocked, so fish and seafood are markedly less important. The Piedmont region, in the northwest "frill" of the boot, adjoins France and Germany, so you are apt to find cheese fondue here and heartier farm dishes such as pork sweetbreads; offal stews; garlic and anchovy sauces; potato gnocchi; stuffed peppers; and veal chops stuffed with prosciutto and cheese, dredged, breaded, and cooked in butter. (The Val d'Aosta, a small province between the Piedmont, France, and Switzerland, is the source of the finest Fontina cheese, one reason for the popularity of fondue.) Polenta and risotto were historically more popular here than pasta. The Lombards use vegetables more freely than many other provincials, often stuffing pasta with pumpkin or spinach. *Osso buco*, pounded and breaded veal chops, and veal piccata are classic Milanese dishes; they also frequently stew tripe. Eggs and cheese are important here, and the rich mascarpone cheese, a sweet creamy cheese used primarily in desserts, is very common. Frying is more common here than in the south, and

Menus in Italian restaurants are fairly uniform, and so are spellings. Most menus are divided into hot and cold antipasti, pastas and risottos, pizzas (increasingly offered even in fancier restaurants), soups, seafood, meats, poultry, and desserts. Some may list salads separately; others may include them, American-style, under the appetizers.

among the characteristic dishes are fried sweetbreads and brains. You are also apt to find sauerkraut, sausages, juniper berries, bay leaves, and even strudels in this region.

NAPLES Naples is on the lower western coast, in an area known for hearty simplicity; *napoletano* is almost a synonym for "family-style." It is also closely tied to Catalan cuisine in its seasonings. Typical dishes include herb-stuffed squid and octopus; brains with capers and olives; spaghetti with clams, mussels, and/or plain tomato sauce (the origin of that classic menu item, "clams with red or white sauce"); pastas with tuna or anchovies; and a lighter version of *fettuccine carbonata*, a pancetta and mozzarella fusilli with tomatoes and dry white wine. Steak napoletano is an underrated dish of filet mignon broiled on a bed of chopped mushrooms, parsley, and prosciutto. Here, as in most of the south, grated cheese as a pasta topping is optional rather than habitual. Naples is also one of the centers of hard-sugar or "boiled" frosting and doughnuts.

ROME The Eternal City is actually in the region of Lazio, but that name is rarely used in the United States. Food in this region is typically rich, with lots of cheese, meat fats, eggs, organ meats, and oils. Pasta sauced only with olive oil, garlic, and a little hot chili pepper is a Roman standby. The fine sheep's milk cheeses Pecorino and ricotta are from this region. Salt and black pepper are applied liberally, a practice that goes back to the ancient Romans. The city of Amatrice has given its name to a pasta sauce, *Amatriciana*, a spicy tomato sauce traditionally served over bucatini. Make it even hotter and it's called *all'Arrabbiata*, "angry" sauce. *Carbonara* sauce with pancetta, cheese, and eggs is Roman through and through. Fettuccine *alla Romana* is sauced with chicken giblets, prosciutto, and tomatoes. *Saltimbocca* is also Roman. But the most famous Roman dish is probably the pasta dish known in the United States as *all'Alfredo*, named for the Roman restaurateur who made it famous.

SICILY This island, which was occupied by the Saracens, likes a strong dose of Middle Eastern flavorings, particularly pine nuts, raisins, fennel, and fresh sardines. Even pasta with sardines is traditionally flavored with saffron, fennel, and raisins. It was also the bastion of eggplant when, elsewhere, that vegetable was believed to be dangerous; and the home of *caponata*, which originally included tomatoes, celery, capers, olives, roe, and lobster but nowadays is usually something like a sweetish, olive-flavored ratatouille. Pastas are usually paired with a minimum of ingredients at a time: for example, onions in wine, anchovies, garlic, tomato and basil, eggplant and tomato, broccoli and pine nuts, fried bread crumbs and raisins, zucchini, tuna, dried cod. Steak Sicilian-style is sauced with black olives, chili peppers, garlic, and capers, as well as tomatoes. Sicily is also only about 80 miles from the coast of Tunisia, and Sicilians make a great seafood version of couscous.

TUSCANY In the past decade, Tuscany has become as hallowed a spot in the culinary hagiography as Paris used to be, with the cosmopolitan Florence at its heart and the Chianti vineyards in its backyard. Tuscan cooking is famous for its wood-burning stoves, used for roasting meats, fish, poultry, and even breads; for rabbit and wild duck cacciatore; for brown rather than tomato sauces on pasta (red-wine hare sauce, for example); and for massive open-faced sandwiches that may be the ancestors of American heros and subs. A traditional Christmas dish seems straight off the boat from Mexico: wild boar with sweet-and-sour chocolate sauce and dried fruits. Fish stews are substantial, bouillabaisse-style entrees here, not appetizers; whole fish are also grilled in crusts of either pastry or, sometimes, coarse salt. Rosemary is a classic Tuscan herb, particularly in grilled and roasted dishes, since it holds up well; rosemary, basil, tomatoes, tarragon, and olive oil are all most Tuscan chefs need. It is not true, incidentally, that *alla Fiorentina* means a dish has spinach in it; rather, it refers to the simplicity and freshness of the ingredients. Umbria adjoins Tuscany and has a similar cuisine—it is among the largest consumers of white beans, lentils, garbanzos, and fava beans—but is particularly noted for its risottos and Amarone wines.

VENETO Both Venice and Verona are in this province, so dishes described as Veronese or Venetian are apt to be rich and redolent of Persian spices. The classic local pasta is *bignoli* (bigoli), a round and somewhat thick noodle not rolled but pressed through a special sieve that looks something like a sausage grinder. Bignoli are served with anchovies and sardines, duck and chicken livers, and hearty sauces that match the heftier noodles. *Gnocchi* is also popular in this region and is expected to carry its weight under veal, livers, and even snails. The famous *pasta e* *fagioli*, noodle and cranberry bean soup, is typical. Sauce *puttanesca*, or "made in the whore's style" (not exactly *bonne femme!*), is generally said to have originated in the Venetian red-light district; it's a bawdy mix of anchovies, hot peppers, garlic, capers, and olives. Nevertheless, polenta is the preferred starch of the region. This has become a major center for the sparkling wine industry and is sometimes called "Little Champagne" (though not by the French). There is also a major lake district, which supplies lake shrimp, salmon, trout, perch, tench, and eels.

HOW TO ORDER AND EAT LIKE A NATIVE

Italians eat in courses and, perhaps in deference to the Dogess Teodora, on clean plates for each course. Traditionally, major courses are ordered one at a time, although in the United States, the full menu selection has become customary. It begins with the *antipasti*, or hors d'oeuvres, perhaps followed by *minestra*, or soup. Then comes the first course, called either *primi piatti* or just *i primi*, generally a pasta or rice dish, though in the south the soup may also be included here. This can be even more confusing because "minestra" is often applied to the primi course if it is served in a soup bowl, as risotto or pasta frequently are. Often "the first" is also the larger dish, and the *secondi piatti*, the meat course and any vegetable side dishes, are smaller. (The secondi is not considered a "main" course in Italy but rather one in a series; however, in the United States, the meat-heavy culture has unbalanced the diet.) This is the healthier way to go about it, since you fill up on the carbohydrate first—unless the first dish is fettuccine Alfredo and the second a grilled flounder.

With meat comes a salad and/or cooked vegetables as side dishes; then cheese or sweets—one or the other, rarely both; and, finally, fruit.

If the meal is particularly leisurely or fancy, there may be a sorbet or other palate-cleanser between the main courses. In some areas, too, *piatti di mezzo*—in-between dishes—come after the primi and are usually some variation on quiches or pies: meat or vegetable tortas, frittatas, soufflés, and so forth. A *sformato* is a molded egg-custard dish that can be filled with vegetables (artichokes, fennel, spinach, zucchini), game, or sweetbreads. In selecting dishes, one should avoid repetition of ingredients and having a spicy or rich *primi* course obscure a delicate *secondi*.

Two people can easily split a stuffed artichoke and a plate of cold meat, either carpaccio or prosciutto. Follow with minestrone or an escarole soup, if you like, then order one fish (sea bass with capers and lemon) or a meat (osso buco or veal piccata). Alternatively, skip the appetizers and share a simple pasta after the soup. Finish with fruit.

For four people, the restaurant may prepare a mixed antipasti platter; if not, order mussels or fritto misto, then, as your primi piatti, a risotto or vegetable ravioli dish to share. Split a grilled chicken, rabbit cacciatore, calamari fra diavolo, or other seafood dish.

Incidentally, although in Italy a "trattoria" is somewhat less formal or expensive than a "ristorante," the distinction is all but ignored in the United States; in fact, in recent years trattoria have been the trendier and pricier spots. An "osteria" was originally a wine shop-cum-bistro.

COOKING AT HOME

In the old days, entertaining Italian-style (as nearly every budget-conscious student and young married couple did) meant a red-and-white checked tablecloth, empty Chianti bottles as candlesticks, and over-sweet Americanized lasagne. Nowadays, it's much more fashionable to do it up Tuscan-style, dining al fresco if possible and using an assortment of brightly colored and painted ceramic dishes. And since this style is so chic, all sorts of franchise home-supply boutiques carry these dishes. Of course, you probably don't have a wood-burning oven, but you can always rub a fish with olive oil and rosemary and pop it on the grill.

If you have a few days' notice, infuse some extra-virgin olive oil with rosemary, basil, and a clove of garlic by dropping them all directly into the bottle; then serve the oil instead of butter for dipping the bread.

Making fresh pasta is not difficult and requires only cutting tools and maybe a drying rack. There are even fairly inexpensive machines that do it for you—add flour, egg, and water, and it churns out noodles. However, there is so much good dry pasta available now, both flavored and plain, that there is no reason to feel obligated to make your own. Just be careful not to overcook pasta; it should be *al dente*, which means "to the teeth"—that is, it should still have a little body but no raw flavor.

The seafood dish is Genovese; the white bean salad is typically Tuscan, as is the penne with Swiss chard. All are quite simple and quick.

SEAFOOD WITH POTATOES

1 pound potatoes
1/2 cup olive oil, divided
1 tablespoon garlic, minced, divided
1/4 cup parsley, chopped, divided
salt and pepper to taste
1 pound firm-fleshed fish (mackerel, anchovy, bluefish, cod),
baby octopus, calamari, or combination

Preheat oven to 450°F. Peel and thinly slice potatoes, rinse in cold water, and pat dry. Combine oil, garlic, parsley, and salt and pepper. Toss potatoes with half the oil and seasoning mixture, combining thoroughly, and place in a glass oven-proof dish or enameled casserole. Bake 15 minutes. Add fish (skin side down) or seafood, top with remaining seasoning mixture, and bake 15 minutes more, basting fish with juices once or twice and gently stirring potatoes if needed to make sure less cooked potatoes get a chance to brown. Serve in large bowls with fresh bread.

WHITE BEAN SALAD

1 pound dried white navy beans or cannellini
1 small onion, cut into chunks
1 carrot, cut into chunks
1 stalk celery with leaves, cut into large pieces
1 whole bay leaf
2 cloves garlic, crushed but left whole
1 sprig each of fresh rosemary, sage, and thyme
3–4 tablespoons extra-virgin olive oil, divided
salt and pepper to taste
wine or broth (optional)
2 tablespoons each of fresh thyme, sage, and rosemary leaves

Rinse and soak beans overnight. Drain, pour into large saucepan, and cover with fresh water; add onion, carrot, celery, bay leaf, garlic, herbs, and 1 tablespoon olive oil. Bring to simmer and cook 45 minutes, season lightly with salt and pepper, add more water or a splash of wine or broth if necessary, and cook until just tender, 15–20 minutes more. Drain, remove vegetables and herbs. Toss with fresh herbs, salt and pepper, and remaining oil to taste.

PASTA WITH CHARD

4–6 canned anchovy fillets in oil
1 pound Swiss chard (kale can be substituted)
1 pound firm, largish pasta such as penne or rigatoni
salt and pepper
3–4 cloves garlic, minced
1 tablespoon dried red chili peppers
2/3 cup extra-virgin olive oil
1/2 cup parsley, chopped
bread crumbs and grated cheese for garnish

Drain and lightly mash anchovies with a fork. Rinse the chard and chop, including stalks. Bring a large pot of salted water to a boil, add pasta and chard, and cook until the pasta is al dente. Meanwhile, sauté garlic, anchovies, and pepper flakes in oil until garlic is soft and golden but not brown. Drain pasta and chard, add parsley, and toss with hot garlic/ anchovy mixture. Top with bread crumbs and just a bit of cheese if desired.

The Iberian Peninsula:
Spain, Portugal, Catalonia, and the Basque

BASIC CUISINE

DINNER FOR TWO:
Gazpacho, tortilla, baked fish or shrimp, roast quail

DINNER FOR FOUR:
Sopa de pescado, miga, ceviche, roast pork, baked chicken, paella

GROUP DISH:
Tapas

STYLE:
"Mediterranean," earthy, aromatic

KEY FLAVORS:
Olive oil, tomatoes, shellfish, garlic

EATING UTENSILS:
Forks and knives

DISTINCTIVE FOODS:
Paella, tapas, gazpacho, salt cod

UNIFORMITY OF MENUS:
Good

NUTRITIONAL INDEX:
Medium fat, high protein, high sodium

COST:
Moderate to expensive

"THANK YOU":
"Gracias"

Iberia may never have produced a "great" cuisine, but it did forge revolutionary alliances. Whether conquered or conquering, the Spanish and Portuguese were always willing to come to the enemy's table.

Spain and Portugal fell to the Phoenicians, the Greeks, the Romans, and the Moors—and ate heartily on the offerings of all four—until they, too, became seagoing conquerors and began dining out on their colonies. The Portuguese all but monopolized the Indian and Asian trade routes, and Spain frog-jumped from the Americas into the Philippines. In 1494 the Iberian rivals even persuaded the pope to divide the "non-Christian world"—a sweeping assumption that covered Asia, Africa, India, and the Americas—by drawing a line that fell through the bulge of South America (which is why Brazilians speak Portuguese and most other South Americans speak Spanish).

Along the way, the Iberians became the great culinary go-betweens, first between Europe and

Asia, then between Europe and America. They absorbed Roman olives and Middle Eastern rice, hauled cattle into Mexico, appropriated Aztec tomatoes and Indonesian garlic, and monopolized olive oil in the New World and chocolate in the Old. They were given much and returned—or sold—even more. Like the alchemists of legend, they transformed the ingredients of disparate continents into "Mediterranean" gold; see also the chapters on Malaysia and Indonesia, North Africa, and Mexico and Central and South America.

THE HISTORY

Although the peninsula is named for the Iberians, who emigrated from Africa 7,000 years ago, they were not the original inhabitants of the region; the often-overlooked but extraordinarily resilient Basques, who still live in a sort of hybridized French-Spanish region around Bilbaõ and the Pyrenees, have probably been there since Paleolithic times: They are almost certainly the people who created the cave paintings at Altamira. They are the oldest distinct ethnic group in Europe, speak a language unrelated to any other, and disdained the Iberians and every other ethnic wave that has swept over the region; there is still a very strong and sometimes violent Basque separatist movement. Even Christianity took only a slow hold among the Basques, who were not converted for several hundred years after the rest of Europe. (Once converted, though, they showed their mettle by producing St. Francis Xavier and St. Ignatius of Loyola, among others.)

The Spanish and Portuguese, on the other hand, are closely related, became implacably Catholic, and were for much of their history an entangled if somewhat reluctant and highly impressionable region. Although they had already been conquered several times before the start of the Common Era—by the Phoenicians, the Greeks, the Carthaginians, and even the Celts, who left behind meat-stuffed pies and bagpipes—the Iberians became perhaps the most Romanized of all imperial subjects, vigorously taking to the innovations of language (Latin, the official language of the Roman Empire), agriculture (particularly olives, bread, garlic, and wine grapes), and politics (they produced two emperors, Hadrian and Trajan). The cuisine of the Catalonian region, the Mediterranean coastal region adjoining the south of France, remains almost anachronistically Roman.

The next invaders, the Visigoths, were Aryanists—and heavy meat eaters, the most obvious mark they left behind—but they allowed the Iberians to remain Catholic. Many of the coastal dwellers had Byzantine ties and were already experimenting with exotic spices; most cities had vigorous Jewish communities. When the Moors swept in from North Africa in 711 C.E., they not only imported dozens of vegetables and spices but showed the Iberians how to expand the arable territory beyond the river valleys through irrigation, thus permitting the cultivation of rice and groves of flowering almond and citrus trees and date palms. Their influence was industrial and aesthetic as well; the crafts and industries they fostered—Toledo steel, Cordoban leather, "Damascene" silver, Seville oranges, and Granadan silk—remain legendary.

However, it was the long battle to expel the Moors that inspired the Spanish and Portuguese to build empires of their own. In the United States, the Spanish conquistadors' victories in the Caribbean, Mexico, and South America are familiar stories, but the Portuguese were just as bold: Within a single 25-year span, from 1495 to 1520, Portuguese navigators rounded the Cape of Good Hope and established strongholds in India and Goa, Malaysia, Hormuz (on the Persian Gulf), the Caribbean, and Brazil. They began a highly profitable trade in spices and slaves—so profitable that in 1580, the covetous King Philip II of Spain added Portugal to a list of possessions that already included Sicily, Naples, Sardinia, the Netherlands, and virtually all of North and South America (he had valid claims to England and France, as well).

Philip was overly fond of rich German sauces and suffered from gout as a result, but he also revolutionized Spanish culture and cuisine in a completely serendipitous fashion: He moved the capital to Madrid, which was known as "the city of 300 taverns" and one of the first societies devoted to the art of dining out. In this milieu, amid the culinary revolution wrought by the tomatoes, peppers, squashes, potatoes, and beans brought back from the Americas, the Spanish practice of late dinners began. So much time was devoted to gossip and afternoon snacks that supper had to be put off until 10 p.m., and entertainments, as they came into vogue, were scheduled for midnight or later. It was also in Madrid that the tapas bar first appeared (see "Tapas," page 71).

The great irony of Spain's role in culinary history is that except for chocolate, which they managed to monopolize for a while, the Spanish vastly undervalued the agricultural riches of the New World. They were more concerned with the silver and gold the colonies provided, an influx of precious metals that not only took a horrific toll on the natives but that set off a chain of inflation so great it ultimately bankrupted the empire. And by handcuffing Portugal, the Spanish exposed the East Indies to Dutch predation and thus lost the great fortune of the Spice Islands as well.

THE COUNTRIES

Spain is divided from France by the Pyrenees, mountains running from the Mediterranean Sea to the Atlantic Ocean, and the whole country is striated east to west by mountain chains and rivers; Spain is the second-most mountainous country in Europe after Switzerland. The cooler north is a major cattle region, the eastern delta region near Valencia is prime rice-growing and citrus territory, the central plateau has limited arable land mostly turned over to wheat, and the dry south is covered in olive groves.

Though Spain is only about the size of Texas, its geography has always made unification difficult, and many of the peninsula's regions have distinct dialects and cultural traditions that represent topographical and historical segmentation rather than political boundaries. The Galicians, in the southern part of Spain, speak a Portuguese-influenced dialect, and Catalan is similar to Provençal French. Both Catalonia and the Basque have historically shared ambiguous borders with France, and Catalonia was legally French territory off and on from the seventeenth to the nineteenth century. Even the island of Sardinia, which has been a French possession and is now part of Italy, still bears the indelible imprint of Roman, specifically Catalonian, cuisine.

Portugal, to Spain's west, has no Mediterranean exposure, only about 500 miles of Atlantic Ocean shore. It has only a few good natural harbors, the best—and one of Europe's best—being Lisbon.

Portugal's summers are hot throughout the country; the humidity also produces much rainfall and fog, which makes the sailing prowess of the Portuguese even more impressive. Winters are fairly mild on the coasts and more severe inland. It has little fertile territory—another reason for its relentlessly outward-looking explorers—and most of that land is used to cultivate wheat, corn, rye, grapes, sugar beets, barley, olives, and citrus fruit. Most of the poorer land is used for grazing sheep. Fishing is still the primary industry, and sardines, anchovies, and cod are major exports as well as food sources.

Sardinia, incidentally, is more than half pastureland and was one of the Romans' major bread baskets, which also helps explain the unusual importance of bread in all the region's cuisines. It also produces such other Roman imports as olives, grapes, sheep, pork, and goats. Sardinia has an abundance of tuna, squid, mullet, eel, lobster, crabs, and, obviously, sardines (though they export most of them—maybe they're sick of the taste).

THE CUISINES

Spanish cuisine has been far more influential than has been recognized until fairly recently. The oldest known Catalonian cookbook dates to 1324 (parts of which were copied directly, with attribution, in later Italian cookbooks). Moorish-influenced Catalonian cuisine was so admired in France that one of the classic recipe styles, "à la catalane," refers to sautéed eggplant and rice pilaf. During the reign of Philip II, Spain was so dominant a world power that other European courts hired Spanish chefs. Dumas's 1873 *Grand dictionnaire de cuisine* spends nearly as many pages on Spanish cooking as on French. In fact, one of the most famous dishes in Escoffier, pheasant *à la Alcantara* with foie gras and truffles, was one of Napoleon's more lasting spoils: In 1807, his troops laid siege to the monastery of San Benito de Alcantara and brought back a copy of an ancient cookbook.

The relationship between Spanish and Portuguese cuisine has been debated for centuries, and despite the fact that there are Portuguese cookbooks almost as old as the Spanish, the food remains remarkably similar, especially as practiced in the United States. Among the distinctions worth noting are that the Portuguese are much fonder of corn meal and especially cornbread than the Spanish; use more chestnuts, including chestnut flour; cook with egg yolks rather than whole eggs, producing richer dishes; are fluent in puddings (a result of their long alliance with Great Britain); and care less for vanilla (which the Spanish charged dearly for).

It is not surprising that the two most visibly "ethnic" regions of Spain, the Basque and Catalonia (Catalunya), share many at least superficial traits. Though the Basque faces the Bay of Biscay and Catalonia the Mediterranean, along the strip called the Costa Brava, both are heavily dependent on seafood and, especially in Catalonia, on vegetables imported first by the Arabs and later from the American colonies. Seafood is so pervasive an element in these cuisines that even meat dishes are likely to have seafood ingredients.

However, in the past 25 or 30 years, Catalonian cuisine has undergone a renaissance both at home and in the United States, thanks to the followers of chefs Josep Mercader i Brugués, who ran the Hotel Ampurdán in Figueres, and especially of Ferran Adriá of the Michelin three-star restaurant El Bulli, on the Costa Brava north of Barcelona, who has been called by many critics the best chef in the world. (Catalonia is also at the center of Spain's booming wine industry; see "Spanish and Portuguese Wines," below.) This new, light, and intensely entertaining cooking, the liveliest segment of the *nueva cocina* movement, experiments with such modern—and diet-friendly—concepts as flourless pasta (made with agar-agar), concentrated fruit and vegetable purees, and "foams" (ingredients beaten to meringue-like emulsions); other novel dishes include white fish carpaccios and crisp-fried peelings of artichoke hearts, pistachio "tempura," and game bird drummettes with asparagus and blanched scallions.

Both chefs are known for deconstructing traditional recipe elements and reconfiguring them. For instance, the traditional tortilla combined slow-cooked onions, fried potatoes, and eggs; Mercader's version layers onion confit, egg yolk emulsions, and potato "foam" in a trifle dish. Instead of a traditional rabbit stew with wild mushrooms and potatoes, Adriá produces a strata of thin-sliced mushroom caps, rabbit loin, pork cracklings, and potatoes topped with a white sauce. Instead of roasting sweet peppers and eggplant and then dressing them with olive oil, Mercader turned them into a mousse; Adriá tops individually roasted vegetables—zucchini, endive, asparagus, tomatoes, eggplant, and truffles—with petal-thin slices of air-dried ham.

Not just food but the whole of Catalonian culture is evoked in Adriá's recipes; a dish of salmon fillets topped with brilliantly colored dice of peppers, onions, tomatoes, and zucchini, for instance, is named after mosaicist and sculptor Antoni Gaudí. His modern tapas include large shrimp or rock lobsters removed from their shells and given new shells of thinly sliced crêpes that stripe under heat so they look segmented; sea urchin flans served in their own shells; Oreo-colored sandwiches of sliced black truffles filled with pale truffle mousse; roasted baby octopus stuffed with raisins, pine nuts, and basil and topped with seared scallops and shaved Parmigiano. Jellies might be served hot, ice creams made from savories. Red mullet is served with codfish "tripe" (fish organs are an ancient delicacy), duck with seaweed.

Other Adriá-style dishes that have already appeared in gourmet food magazines in the United States include skate with yogurt and bonito with ginger and caramel. Typically these dishes are mere mouthfuls; a dinner at El Bulli may be as many as 20 courses long. If you are lucky enough to stumble into one of these nueva cocina establishments, prepare to settle in.

The Basque language, as mentioned above, is related to no other, but its dishes, and consequently the menus of Basque restaurants in the United States, are likely to bear strong resemblances either to French or Spanish—or Catalonian—menus, depending on the chefs' backgrounds.

Although not a regional cuisine, it should be noted that many Sephardic Jewish recipes, albeit adapted to kosher requirements, bear strong resemblances to the dishes listed below. The term *Sephardic* refers to those Jews of Spanish and Portuguese descent who were exiled by Ferdinand and Isabella in 1492—fortunately for many of their descendants, just as Columbus was sailing by orders of the same monarchs toward the New World—and also in the same year Their Most Catholic Majesties finally defeated the Moorish forces. Consequently, the recipes the Sephardic Jews carried with them into the Diaspora retained the heavy Persian and Roman influences seen below.

THE MAIN INGREDIENTS

SEASONINGS Particularly when it comes to seasonings, the Moors are more. Among the most characteristic flavorings are almonds, anise, cloves, coriander, garlic, pine nuts, peppercorns (white and green as well as black), bay leaves, chilies, cinnamon, chocolate, coffee, cilantro, cumin, sorrel, juniper berries, sesame seeds, rosemary, thyme, fennel, olives, wild oregano, paprika, and the sovereign powder saffron—made from the golden-red stamen of the saffron crocus, and the most expensive spice in the world. *Pimenton* or *pimiento del piquillio*, a "peaky" or pointed pepper particularly important to Catalonian cuisine, is a pungent paprika that can be either sweet or somewhat hot; though descended from the New World chilies, it is now a distinct and delicate-fleshed variety in its own right.

Up the Mediterranean coast toward Catalonia (and Provençe), the proportion of garlic increases; seasoning with fortified wines and vinegars are a natural in a region that so prides itself on wines and sherries. *Alioli* (or *allioli*), the Spanish version of the Provençal aïoli, is just what it says: garlic (all) and (i) olive oil (oli), and almost no meal goes without.

In fact, almost no dish mentioned in the chapter does not include garlic. Capers are also more prominent in the east.

Dipping sauces, or *mojos*, are particularly important with tapas; among the most common mixtures are sweet peppers and cilantro; dried red chilies and onions; almond and fish oil emulsions; green sauces of parsley, cilantro, and garlic; and mayonnaise flavored with nuts, herbs, or even salt cod flakes.

Because the combination of Old and New World flavors is extremely characteristic of Spanish food, many names still reflect this. *Ramillete albaicinero* is an herb bouquet, usually combining mint, parsley, oregano, savory, and bay, that is named for the last section of Granada that the Moors held. A dish marked "a la chilindron"—probably a conflation of "chili" and "Indian"—has a sauce that combines garlic, onion, tomato, sweet peppers, and ham. "Romesco" sauce combines ancho chilies and tomatoes with garlic, vinegar, ground nuts, and bread—a mini-compendium of Iberian history. "Veracruzano" refers to the Mexican port where the Spanish learned to cook fish with tomatoes and onions; but a form of *sofrito*, a paste of very slowly cooked onions and tomatoes, is an essential ingredient and is so ancient that it likely originated as simply onions and olive oil.

> ### Shell Game
>
> Coquille St. Jacques, curiously, though a French invention, was created because so many French Catholics were joining the Spanish in pilgrimages to the tomb of the miraculously restored body of the patron saint of Spain, the martyred disciple James—Jacques in French, and Iago, hence Santiago, in Spanish. One of the miracles associated with the saint's body, which according to legend was discovered just in time to help rout the Moors, had to do with restoring a drowned bridegroom, who reappeared covered with cockleshells. Hence the pilgrims wore cockleshell badges, and chefs served scallops in wine sauce on cockleshells.

SEAFOOD The great gift of Rome was olive oil; the great concept of the Moors was irrigation; the great prize of the Americas was vegetables. But in the beginning was the sea. Monkfish, cuttle fish, sole, hake, red and gray mullet, cod, sardines, skate, mackerel, sea bass, sea bream (orata), dogfish, sunfish, trout, swordfish, tuna, squid, octopus, crabs, spiny lobsters, spider crabs, scallops, clams, crayfish, barnacles, and eels are all harvested here. (One of Catalonian artist Salvador Dalí's most famous paintings shows the traditional harvesting of tuna, which were herded toward the shore, trapped, and then finished off with

In recent years, Iberian restaurants in the United States have lightened up a little on the olive oil that, combined with the cuisine's rich meats, often made dishes seem a bit greasy. However, the fat level is still fairly high; zarzuelas or roasted meats are lighter choices.

Portuguese dishes are generally similar to the Spanish versions, particularly in the United States, but may come as a shock to those who have lost the taste for heavy salt. Both the bacalhau and many pork dishes, even those cooked with potatoes or rice, remain extremely salty. Other seafoods and shellfish may be pickled with wine, if not brined, before cooking; and *mariscada*, Portuguese zarzuela or bouillabaisse, tends to be saltier than either the Spanish or French versions. But there are also paella-like dishes—sometimes called, with deceptive simplicity, "Portuguese rice"—in which the rice absorbs the seasonings.

spears.) The Mediterranean *espardeñas*, a type of sea slug usually referred to as a sea cucumber, has a scallop-like flavor that the new Catalonian cuisine has begun to make famous. *Paella*, Spain's most famous dish, is a showcase for shrimp, mussels, and clams (and there, but rarely here, freshwater snails as well); *zarzuela*, the soup version, is similarly embellished.

The sea fever the Spanish and Portuguese seemed to inherit genetically also accustomed them to foods that could be preserved and stored for months at a time: They learned to pickle, salt-cure, smoke, and dry meats and fish early on. *Bacalhao* or *bacalao*, dried and salted cod, is one of the most famous ingredients in Portuguese—and Spanish, and Italian, and Caribbean, and Scandinavian—cooking dating back at least a thousand years; though it may sound plain, the legend is that there are 365 recipes for it, one for every day—more than enough to keep a Portuguese Popeye happy. However, the name is somewhat misleading; the cod is always soaked at length, which not only removes much of the salt but also, between the drying and the rehydrating, softens the meat's texture.

STARCHES Bread is part of every meal in the Iberian peninsula; baked daily, it is grilled, dunked, and, if left over, fried in the little cubes called *migas*—after which it is used as a soup or salad ingredient, a stuffing, or even a sauce base. In the rural areas, it may be the only "meat" of the meal: Samuel Pepys, who visited Spain in 1683, wrote that "the greater part of Spain eat nothing but what they make of water, oil, salt, vinegar, garlic and bread, which last is the foundation of all." *Pace* Pepys, bread soups are even more common in Portugal. Around Catalonia, nearly every snack (or tapa) involves *pa ambo tomatique*, or grilled bread rubbed with tomatoes, salt, and olive oil, a sort of instant bruschetta. In some areas, a very plain, flat, pizza-like bread called *chapata* is used either with spreads for tapas or split into mini-sandwiches.

Wheat is also used to make a few forms of pasta, primarily the short, narrow noodles called *fiduea* and the flattened sheets used to make cannelloni; these are more likely to be found in Catalonia or other eastern regions because in the sixteenth and seventeenth centuries, when Spain controlled Naples and Sicily, the coastal ports enjoyed the closest contacts. In Portugal, pasta comes in a small, seed-like noodle similar to orzo; the Portuguese also depend more heavily on cornmeal than the Spanish do.

Rice, which is one of the most important products of the lagoons around Valencia, is most often served spiced or flavored in the fashion of the Moors who introduced it—that is, Persian-style—and is served with (not instead of) bread. As in Spain's former colonies in Mexico and Central America, rice comes red (with tomatoes), green (with parsley and cilantro), or black (with squid ink).

MEAT AND GAME From the mountainous north come the hearty goats, sheep, and hogs that made Spanish hams (*jamón*) and sausages famous. Ham is so highly prized that, as in Italy, different regions have perfected subtle flavorings; in one area of Andalusia, black pigs are raised only on acorns to produce a nutty-flavored meat. Spicy-garlicky *chorizo*, salamis, and blood sausage are consumed everywhere, but so are the more delicate pâtés, soft liver sausages, and pig's foot loaves. Organ meats and offal are very popular: brains and sweetbreads, particularly lamb, livers, kidney, and tripe and tongue.

The flavor of wild meat (and poultry) is still highly valued, particularly wild hare, wild boar, squirrel, and chamois, a kind of mountain goat. An alternative "meat," snails are as popular here as they are in France.

POULTRY AND GAME BIRDS Chicken is a staple, of course, but the turkey, another American transplant, has been greatly admired since its introduction and is a holiday staple just as it is in the United States. Darker wildfowl, especially geese, pheasant, quail, guinea hen, wood pigeon, wild and domesticated duck, partridge, and thrush, are extremely popular. (One bit of nonauthenticity in Spanish restaurants in this country is probably welcome: The Spanish traditionally like both their pork and their poultry extremely well aged. Pheasants were usually hung to the rotting point, and prime hogs still swing in butcher windows for years. Fortunately for the American palate, such practices are prohibited here.)

EGGS AND DAIRY Eggs are a significant element in the regional cuisines, not only as thickening agents but as ingredients and even main dishes; they are indispensable for the potato omelets called tortillas. Cheeses are extremely popular and produced from cow's, sheep's, and goat's milk, though few types are available in the United States except for the hard, Parmigiano-like Manchego (from La Mancha, the land of Don Quixote); the blue Cabrales, aged in mountain caves; the smoked sheep's milk cheese called Idiazábal or Roncal; the mild, soft Burgos, often used as a dessert; and the salty Tetilla, so named because the molds used to make it are breast-shaped, something like the Pompadour-inspired champagne glasses. However, the popularity of Roquefort, which is produced not far from the Spanish border, is worth noting.

VEGETABLES The primary vegetables of the Iberian pantry are reminders of the region's three great assimilations: Roman (olives, garlic, onions, asparagus), Moorish (eggplant, artichokes, garbanzos, lentils, broad and fava beans, cauliflower, and such greens as cabbage, chard, and kale), and American (white and sweet potatoes, onions, tomatoes, corn, avocados, hot and sweet peppers, many types of pumpkins, zucchini, black-eyed peas, and black, red, kidney, and lima beans). The peninsula does have some indigenous riches, however, particularly an extraordinary number of wild mushrooms, including chanterelles, morels, porcinis, and truffles. The Portuguese eat a green called *grelhado* that is a sort of nonflowering broccoli with fiddlehead-like tops.

FRUITS AND NUTS The Moors planted vast numbers of citrus fruits, most importantly lemons and oranges. The peninsula also produces pineapples, bananas, grapefruit, quinces (it was the Portuguese who taught the English to make marmalade), cherymoyas (also known as custard apples), date palms, figs, and pomegranates—fruits that, in Persian style, are often combined with poultry or even meat. The hazelnuts, almonds, walnuts, and pine nuts are not only ingredients and flavorings but, ground finely, are essential as thickeners, but peanuts are used primarily for oil.

THE MAIN DISHES

APPETIZERS AND SALADS Almost any of the smaller or lighter dishes that might be offered as a first course, or as a vegetable side dish, also appear as snacks or tapas (see below). The same is true for salads, although they generally consist of beans, potato salads (including salads with tuna or hard-boiled eggs), or some combination of tomatoes, sweet peppers, and onions; lettuce or other salad greens are not common. Other dishes include marinated asparagus, escarole salads, or sliced radishes and Middle Eastern mixtures of oranges, onions, and raisins. Fried bread salads mix leftover *migas* with tomatoes and olive oil. In Portugal especially, fresh-fried potato chips are almost synonymous with cocktail service.

SOUPS One of the most famous Spanish dishes is *gazpacho*, the raw vegetable soup that, depending on region and home recipe, may be coarse or chunky, sweet, tangy, or peppery. The simplest versions are just bread, tomatoes, olive oil, and seasonings; regional (and Americanized) recipes may include red onion, cucumber, bell peppers, and even a heretical avocado. There are white and green gazpachos, as well, flavored with cucumbers, cilantro, almonds, pine nuts, green melons, and white wine. Bread soups go back to early Roman times, and gazpacho and miga are both examples of Spain's role as intermediary: Both are derived from Middle Eastern dishes, and both were carried from Spain to Mexico.

Thick bean-and-greens soups, given the generic name *caldo verde*, usually combine white beans and kale or chard; even thicker versions involve ham hocks or pork chops, beans, greens, and potatoes. *Berza*, an Andalusian specialty, could be considered a Spanish cassoulet, combining ham hocks and necks, garbanzos, white beans, blood sausage and chorizo, pumpkin, chard, and the tangy brown spices of the clove family (some Spanish chefs claim that cassoulet is really French berza). Garlic soup by itself is extremely popular, too, as is the garlicky vegetable soup *pisto*. *Sopa de pescado* is a fish broth–based soup, often with rice or pasta added, served as a first course. Minorcans have a fondness for spiny lobster soup and for fish and potato chowders; octopus and potato soups, with or without fried bread, are also common.

Zarzuelas are both filling and fascinating, but, like paellas, made slightly differently in every region. Some are almost platters of mixed shellfish, such as crabs, clams, scallops, shrimp, and even lobster; but most have a fragrant broth and some tender vegetables; one school finishes the soup with swirls of sherry. Zarzuela is sometimes described on menus as a "Spanish bouillabaisse," with the same response as to the cassoulet.

CASSEROLES AND STEWS Because Spanish cuisine blends so many influences, it seems perfectly appropriate that its national dish combines European meats with Middle Eastern spices, American vegetables, and Asian rice. (Once the Spanish had perfected paella, they found it hard to live without; it is also a standard dish in Mexico, Cuba, and the Philippines.) Paella is a richly flavored but not heavy stew of shrimp and shellfish, chicken, sausage, ham, peas, artichoke hearts, sautéed onions, and tomatoes bedded down in a round, flattish pan of saffron-flavored rice. Any of these ingredients might be involved, depending on what region it's prepared in—there are meat versions, seafood versions, vegetarian versions, and even versions in which the rice is replaced by fideua, the small pasta noodles—but in the United States, the more-is-better super-combo style is the most popular. Paella is traditionally prepared for a group, but in the United States restaurants commonly offer paella for two.

However, paella is just the most elaborate of many rice dishes. *Arroz a banda* means "rice on its own," but even that is a sort of simple seafood paella, cooked with an elaborate fish broth, shellfish, and saffron. Other rice dishes or rice stews may be flavored with bacalao and garbanzos, pine nuts and raisins, sausages and pork chops, dried beans and turnips, rabbit, snails, greens and clams, meatballs, duck and garbanzos, or with squid ink and shrimp (called *arroz negres*, or black rice).

One of the most interesting characteristics of both Spanish and Portuguese dishes are their frequent combinations of meats and poultry or meats and shellfish, particularly pork and clams. One hearty hunter's stew combines rabbit, beans, snails, and chicken; another has rabbit, pork, and mussels or clams. *Cocido* is half soup, half stew, a hearty pot of assorted meats (chops, sausages, feet, ham hocks), poultry, chilies, white beans, onions, potatoes, kohlrabi, and lots of garlic, all cooked together and then strained from the broth; pasta or rice is added to the cooking liquid, it's served as soup first and the meats follow.

Matança is a Catalan stew of white beans topped with pork chops. Some clearly Arab-Spaniard amalgamations exist, such as beef and melon stew, beef or lamb with brown Persian spices, lamb thickened with ground almonds, and oxtail or lamb stew with juniper berries.

VEGETABLES Here again, the list of tapas might include any side dish or vegetable course, but among them are red or white beans with cabbage, wild mushroom fricassees, sautéed Swiss chard, green beans with ham, fava or white beans with mint, roasted peppers, eggplant or squash drizzled with olive oil, ratatouille with or without potatoes, eggplant or zucchini fritters, pimientos stuffed with bacalao, pork and/or squid, fried or roasted potatoes, twice-baked potatoes stuffed with mashed anchovies, baked onions stuffed with ground meat and topped with cheese, and, of course, tortillas, which in Spain are slow skillet-fried potato and onion omelets, not corn wrappers; and which may have minced ham, sausage, or seafood added. "Wrinkled" potatoes, incidentally, are small red potatoes that have been cooked in salt water then shaken in a dry, hot skillet so that their skins pucker.

SHELLFISH   *Ceviche* (or *seviche*) is raw fish and scallops "cooked" by a marinade of lime juice, onions, and chilies, a dish imported from the New World colonies. The famous fried seafood that is a staple of tapas bars includes squid, sardines, anchovies, shrimp, and fish chunks that have been lightly dusted with fine-ground flour and fried in the purest, freshest olive oil; unfortunately, few renditions in the United States match the originals.

More elaborate seafood dishes include clams and shrimp minced with ham, cheese, and a cream sauce and then covered with bread crumbs and fried; baby octopus roasted with potatoes; double-crusted eel pies; steamed mussels or clams; squid stuffed with ham and vegetables, grilled with sweet peppers and onions, or braised in its own ink; scallops and shrimp in white wine cream; shrimp sautéed with cognac and cream; and baby eels with chilies, a Basque favorite. Shrimp are served in a sauce of their own heads and baked lobster in a sauce using the heads and roe. "Clams with saffron rice" means the shellfish are the main ingredient; "rice with clams" literally puts the grain first. Arroz negres is usually rice with squid or cuttlefish and their ink, but fancier versions might also include monkfish, mussels, shrimp, and so on.

FISH   Although fish is occasionally seared on a griddle, it's more often baked or fried, though that may only be part of the story. It's baked in a green sauce of cilantro and parsley; baked whole with slow-fried potatoes, onions, tomatoes, and sherry; baked and covered in wine-flavored cream sauce; and, particularly on holidays, wrapped in puff pastry and baked. If it's fried, it might be marinated first. Even grilled at its simplest, it may come on a bed of coarse salt (or in a salt crust) with alioli, topped with diced ham and onions, or with a mashed anchovy sauce. Only occasionally will it be poached plainly in white wine or brandy, except in big cities where tourists may be more calorie-conscious.

Fish can be stuffed with ham and peppers or, vice versa, used as the stuffing for peppers or potatoes. Like shellfish, it's fried to a greaseless crisp rarely re-created in the United States—the original "tempura"—or mashed and turned into a terrine. *Escabeche* or vinegar-cured fish is so popular it migrated to the Caribbean. Swordfish is meaty enough to stand up to sweet-and-sour sauces with raisins, pine nuts, and sherry. Tuna is smothered in onions and oil and baked almost like a confit or tossed with tomatoes and capers.

The number of bacalao dishes, as mentioned, is in the hundreds, but among the most interesting (and those with the most obvious Moorish influences) are shredded salt cod with oranges and olives; cod topped with ratatouille; cod with spinach and pomegranates; and salt cod with apples and honey. Bacalao is also a common flavoring element in soups and stews

MEATS Meat courses also display a variety of influences from peasant heartiness (stuffed oxtails, braised pig's feet, pork roast stuffed with onions and leeks, roast pork ribs with cabbage) to Moroccan richness (lamb stewed in honey and nuts, meatballs with cinnamon and olives, and pork loin stuffed with spinach, prunes, and pine nuts or glazed with alioli and honey). Interestingly, especially in Catalonia, meats may be fried first and then simmered with vegetables; one recipe calls for boning and boiling a pork roast, then frying it, then stewing it with snails. In other places, pork or beef is grilled or fried (always sliced thin and always cooked well) and then served with spicy dips.

The Spanish often play off sweet-and-sour or spicy ingredients, such as sherry, olives, and crushed peppercorns, with oranges and sweet peppers. Roast suckling pig and roast lamb are favorites everywhere, as are lamb and kid chops, and roast legs with crackling skin. (In Sardinia, the suckling pig is traditionally split in half and roasted head-down beside the fire rather than whole and horizontal.) Casual eat-it-as-it-cooks barbecues, featuring skewers of chops, roasts, and whole quarters, are the original *churrasacrias* so common in South America and now popping up all over the United States. The classic treatment of calves' liver smothered in long-cooked onions is an old story here, as are veal shanks with apples.

POULTRY Chicken is baked with lemon and garlic, stuffed with sausage and vegetables, braised with peaches or with vegetables in a caramelized glaze; roasted and dressed with pomegranate, roasted pepper, or almond sauces; or braised in rice casseroles with saffron or cinnamon.

Quail are most frequently grilled or roasted and eaten whole; if they are baked, however, they may be stuffed with raisins and rice, ground pork and garlic, or, more elaborately, snails and pork. A tavern-style recipe obviously based on a New World dish calls for baking quail in lima beans. Roast duck with quince or prunes is a classic banquet dish, as is roast partridge with cabbage dumplings. Turkey is a Christmas tradition, stuffed with a rich mixtures of raisins, prunes, sausages, ham, and chestnuts. Pheasants are slow-braised in wine, though opinions differ on whether the wine should be red (with rosemary and other heartier herbs) or white (with a hint of vinegar or fruit).

Among the most frequent ways of cooking eggs are fried and served over tortillas or perhaps pork chops; fried and mixed with fried potatoes; softly scrambled with minced ham or chorizo or with spinach and shrimp; or, as tapas, hard-cooked and deviled.

DESSERTS Fruit is a common course, either as or before dessert, and frequently combined with cheese. Oranges, both the thicker-skinned varieties and the famous thin-skinned, bitter Seville oranges, are foremost among citrus fruits. Cherimoyas, dates, pomegranates, raisins, peaches, and bananas are also popular, often served with cream or a vanilla-flavored custard. *Membillo*, a sort of quince gelatin or aspic, is traditionally served with the salty, coarse Manchego cheese. More elaborate fruit dishes include peaches and dried apricots poached in red wine. There are vegetables desserts as well—fried bananas, sweet fried eggplants, and fried and sugared spaghetti squash.

However, the entire peninsula is passionate for sweets, the best-known of which are flan, a burned-sugar custard twin to the French crème caramel; similar but lighter condensed milk puddings; and rice puddings. Chocolate is often used as bittersweet, as it was when it was first introduced, but also in cakes and cake crumb–covered fruits. There are plenty of Middle Eastern–style indulgence, such as almond-powder marzipan, the sugar-powdered fried dough twists called *churros*, almond cookies, honey-baked pastries, dessert crêpes, butter cookies, and, the most basic, fried bread in honey.

TAPAS

Toward the end of the nineteenth century, when the light opera called zarzuela (just like the dish) was in its heyday, Madrilenos became fond of bars where they could come and go and eat small meals with drinks. These *tapas*—four- or five-bite dishes intended to while away hours of drink and conversation—are becoming the rage all over the United States.

There are scores of tapas possibilities, and a single restaurant, particularly in Madrid or Barcelona, may offer 40 or 50 choices, hot and cold. Even in the United States, a restaurant may lay out 25 or 30 tapas. The most familiar are chorizo sausages grilled or simmered in sherry or turned into the spreadable *sobrasada*, ham rolls, marinated mild or spicy olives, shrimp sautéed with garlic, grilled squid, grilled shellfish, fried smelts or squid, snails, sugared almonds, hard-boiled or deviled eggs, artichoke hearts marinated or stuffed with serrano ham, marinated quail eggs, meat- or vegetable-stuffed turnovers or empanadas, pickled green peppers, grilled leeks, pork and cabbage dumplings, fried green tomatoes, fried or mashed seasoned potatoes, marinated or grilled mushrooms, white bean or bean and sausage salads, bacalao and tuna salads, cheeses (either plain or in puffs or fritters), carpaccio (usually beef, but occasionally the trendier tuna), grilled quail, clams, anchovies, miniature paellas, potato and salt cod fritters, grilled eggplant or squash, pork ribs with cabbage, slices of roast suckling pig, sautéed *criadillas* (pig or beef testicles), spinach with chorizo, roasted and/or marinated peppers, baby octopus or squid stuffed with bread or pork mixtures, and, of course, tortillas. The tomato-rubbed grilled bread and similar bruschetta-like toasts are indispensable for spreading warm goat cheese, pureed bacalao, or sobrasada.

Not all these items are likely to be found in the United States, but on the other hand, American restaurateurs are racing to invent novel tapas (and "fusion tapas," and "new American tapas") designed to bring in trend-hungry crowds.

Tapas are traditionally served before lunch and again before, or what Americans would consider right through, the dinner hour, which in Spain is no earlier than about 10 p.m. Tapas are usually either served in a separate room, like a country bar or tavern, or displayed along the bar for customers to admire and point to; however, in the United States, many restaurants allow you to eat tapas in the dining room. The larger tapas bars may offer flamenco music or even dancing.

Incidentally, although the popularity of tapas in the United States has led many people to assume they are a Spanish invention, they are really adaptations of the *mezze* that Middle Easterners have been nibbling for centuries—in other words, another gift of the Moors. Just consider the pork kebabs, the quails in almond sauce, and the sugared nuts.

SPANISH AND PORTUGUESE WINES

Although often overlooked by wine snobs, Spain is the third-largest producer of wines in the world, behind France and Italy, and the Portuguese consume more wine per capita than any of them.

Spain and Portugal are best known as producers for fortified wines, and in fact they are the first names in such wines, so to speak: Both Madeira and port get their monikers from Portugal—Madeira from the island on which it is produced and "port" via Oporto, the country's second largest city—while "sherry" comes from Jerez (HER-ez,), a town in Andalusia originally named Seris by the Moors, the nice people who brought you distillation. Because both port and sherry are fortified with brandy spirits, it's not surprising that Spain is second only to the Cognac region in production of brandy as well.

Sherry was originally called "sack," whence the brand name Dry Sack; but eventually the city of origin became the shorthand for the style. Because Puerto de Santa Maria, where Columbus's boats were built, is very near Jerez, it is quite likely that sherry was the first wine to reach the Americas. (More romance: Although sherry is produced in Jerez, virtually all the grapes are grown in La Mancha.)

Sherry is the traditional beverage with tapas, and better restaurants can introduce you to the range of sherries from the dry finos and manzanillas, which make fine aperitifs (there are also good Spanish vermouths), to the nutty, mid-range palo cortadas, amontillados, and olorosos, to the sweet cream sherries. A tapas meal is actually a great opportunity to try several sherries, as different foods are best complemented by different styles: Chorizo, ham, cheese and kebabs might call for an amontillado, whereas the light aperitif sherries are better suited to grilled or fried fish.

Sherries are also categorized by age, "finest" meaning the sherry is three years old, "reserve" five, and "special reserve" ten years old. Sherries labeled "vintage" must by law be at least 15 years old. Madeiras are generally drunk when released, but by tradition, they are aged by being transported on ship all around the world, tossing and rolling.

The major difference between port and sherry is that the brandy is introduced into port during the fermentation process, which arrests the fermentation while the wine is still very sweet; in the production of sherry, the brandy is added after the fermentation is complete. Both are fairly high alcohol, port about 20% and sherry 18%. The most common types of port are the young, aggressive ruby ports; aged tawny ports, which develop a nutty, semi-dry quality and which come in 10-, 20-, 30-, and over-40-year-old varieties; white ports, which can be either dry or sweet; and vintage ports, which age to deep, musty, leathery, and nutty-spicy tones. (Unlike sherry, port is labeled "vintage" by year, not by age, and may last many decades.)

However, both Spain and Portugal produce other wines of note. Spain's northern region, near the border with France, produces most of the nonsherry wines, notably the *methode champenoise* sparkling wines called *cavas* and the red wines of the Rioja region. The Penedès region around Barcelona is the heart of the cava industry, producing 15 million cases per year; the dominant houses, Freixenet and Cordoníu, are both extremely popular in the United States and rivals for the position of world's largest producer of sparkling wine. Penedès is also home to the highly regarded table wines of Miguel Torres (trained in Burgundy and stylistically compared to Robert Mondavi) and the new super-Catalonian, so to speak, called L'Ermita. Many of Rioja's wineries were founded by winemakers from France who had to start new vineyards after the phylloxera epidemic of the late nineteenth century. Garnacha, one of the region's most important varietals, is the original Grenache.

Portugal actually produces more cork than wine, but it did develop the lightly sparkling, semi-sweet rosés, notably from the houses of Mateus and Lancers, that swept the international market in the 1970s and 1980s. More recently, a style of wine from the northwestern region of the country has attracted attention in the United States: "Vinho Verde" literally means "green wine," and refers to a light, crisp white generally drunk young, hence the word "green." Many have a tingle of effervescence to them, which also suggests youthfulness (and also supplies the sparkle for those rosés as well). There are red Vinho Verde wines as well, though that's sort of like saying "white Zinfandel"—you have to ask for it by name. Vinho Verde wines are a good match for seafood dishes or to the sometimes oil- and garlic-intensive dishes.

HOW TO ORDER
AND EAT LIKE A NATIVE

Dining in Spain is a full-time occupation, beginning with the two breakfasts (at about 7 and 11 a.m., respectively), tapas as a warm-up to lunch, which starts about 2:30 p.m., tea and cakes at 6, more tapas at 8, and dinner—the real stuff—starting about 10 p.m. or even later. Fortunately, dishes are generally more flavorful than rich, though they may seem oil-dense to American palates. The Portuguese are a little more restrained, dining at 8 or 9 p.m.; so Spanish or Portuguese restaurants in the United States tend to accommodate both styles.

Menus in the United States are divided up by courses, and some of the hors d'oeuvres may replicate tapas dishes or even be called tapas. A selection of them may also be listed as "entremeses variados," or mixed appetizers.

Two diners can easily share an order of gazpacho and a tortilla and entrees of either baked fish or shrimp and roast quail. A party of four might share two soups (sopa de pescado and miga) and ceviche, plus roast pork, baked chicken, and paella.

If you are planning to order paella, a dish that requires a fair amount of preparation, you may have to call the day before or specify paella when you make your reservations. Unfortunately, because it can be a lengthy process and Americans are notoriously impatient, partially precooked paellas are becoming more common in the United States; make sure to ask that it be made up fresh. A larger group should check out a tapas bar (where, depending on the kitchen, you may be able to sample paella as well).

Spanish and Portuguese restaurants are usually only moderately expensive, although there are more white-linen restaurants opening up these days. Tapas bars are like dim sum or sushi bars, because you pay by the plate, so you can spend a little or quite a lot.

COOKING AT HOME

The most important utensils in a Spanish or Portuguese kitchen are the flat, supple steel pans used for paella and the similar but smaller skillets used for toasting tortillas or frying (the wide rather than deep layer of oil allows for quick and even heating). Nonstick skillets and those of high-quality aluminum will do fine. Most dishes are cooked on top of the stove, in the skillets or soup pots, or grilled over open fires, with the exception of bread, which is made fresh constantly; however, some roasted entrees require baking dishes.

TORTILLA (POTATO OMELET)

4 tablespoons olive oil (or more), divided
1 large onion, sliced

1 sweet or mildly hot pepper, seeded and sliced
salt and pepper to taste
3 large potatoes, peeled, thinly sliced, and patted dry
6 large eggs
roasted red peppers (optional)

Heat 2 tablespoons oil in a nonstick skillet; add onion and pepper, season lightly with salt and pepper, and sauté slowly over low heat until very soft; remove with a slotted spoon to a plate. Add another tablespoon of oil and add potato slices in loose layers, seasoning lightly; sauté briefly, turning to coat, then return onions and peppers to skillet. Cover, and cook 15 minutes over medium-low heat, turning occasionally, until potatoes are lightly browned and tender. Set aside to cool slightly.

Meanwhile, lightly beat eggs with a pinch more salt and pepper; add potato mixture to egg mixture and let sit for 10 minutes. Wipe skillet clean; add remaining oil and heat. Pour egg mixture into skillet, spreading vegetables evenly, and cook about 5 minutes or until bottom is brown but eggs are still slightly soft in the middle; put a plate over the top of the skillet, invert the skillet to remove tortilla, and then slide the tortilla back into the skillet and cook just until the underside is brown and tortilla is firm but not dry. Slice into wedges and serve (with roasted red peppers if desired).

Note: Traditional recipes call for using much more olive oil, in effect smothering the onions and potatoes. (On the other hand, a crispier, lower-fat version can be produced by using just enough to keep the pan lubricated.) If you wish to add diced ham, sausage, bananas, or other flavorings, stir into egg mixture before adding potatoes.

PAELLA

4 tablespoons olive oil, divided
1/4 pound chorizo or other spicy sausage,
cut into 1/4-inch-thick slices
salt and pepper to taste
4 chicken breasts, legs, or thighs
1/2 pound small or medium shrimp, shelled
1/4 pound squid, cleaned and cut into rings
4 small rock lobster tails or langoustines

1 large onion, chopped

4 spring onions or scallions, white and light green parts, sliced

4 cloves garlic, minced

1 sweet red pepper, seeded and diced

1 small hot pepper, such as jalapeño, seeded and diced

1 1/2 cups short-grain rice

1 bay leaf

1/4 teaspoon saffron threads, crushed

2 medium very ripe tomatoes, grated (see note)

or 1 cup good-quality canned diced tomatoes

1/4 cup fresh parsley, chopped

3 1/2 cups defatted chicken broth,

or a combination of broth, clam juice, and dry white wine

4 ounces fresh small peas, cooked, or frozen and thawed

4 artichoke hearts, halved

1/4 pound ham, preferably Jubago or Parma,

or a combination of ham and lean pork

8 mussels, scrubbed and bearded

8 clams, scrubbed (optional)

In a paella pan or large skillet, heat 1 tablespoon oil; cook sausage until brown and remove with slotted spoon, leaving grease behind. Lightly season chicken with salt and pepper and brown; set aside. Add a little more oil if necessary and sauté shrimp, squid, and lobster; cook them just until opaque, and remove to plate. Sauté onions, garlic, and peppers until softened. Add 1 tablespoon oil and rice, stirring to coat rice grains; stir in bay leaf, saffron threads, tomato, and parsley and add broth. Cover pan tightly and cook about 10 minutes, stirring occasionally. Add peas and artichoke hearts; arrange chicken, ham, seafood, and shellfish around pan and cover tightly; cook until all liquid is absorbed, rice is tender (add more liquid if needed), and shellfish have opened—20–30 minutes depending on type of rice. Discard bay leaf and any shells that do not open, then serve.

Note: To grate tomatoes, halve them, squeeze halves gently to eject seeds, then rub against grater, holding over bowl, until skin is emptied; discard skins.

GERMANY AND AUSTRIA

German food is a lot more familiar than many Americans expect; in fact, you might not even recognize it as "ethnic" because so many family-style American meals, from diner blue-plate specials right down to the classic Fourth of July picnic, have German roots. Potato salad, deviled eggs, pickled beets, dill pickles, sugar cookies, meatloaf, mashed potatoes, pot roast, beef stew, chicken and dumplings, doughnuts, chocolate cakes and cookies are all typical German fare. A popular PBS series on Amish and Pennsylvania Dutch cuisine is called "Heartland Cooking." The whole meat-and-potatoes concept is primarily a German import, not to mention beer: Every year, 35 gallons per person of this quintessentially German brew is consumed in the United States. Hamburgers and frankfurters even get their names from German cities, and what could be more American than they?

A huge percentage of Western European strains within the American melting pot—not just Germans and Austrians but also Angles, Saxons, Franks, Burgundians, Lombards, Bavarians,

BASIC CUISINE

DINNER FOR TWO:
Vegetable soup, schlachtplatte, schnitzel, roast duck

DINNER FOR FOUR:
Schmeerkase, sausages, potato salad, duck, sauerbraten, pike in cream sauce, schnitzel

STYLE:
Sweet-sour, doughy, smoky, gamey

KEY FLAVORS:
Vinegar, bay, sour cream

EATING UTENSILS:
Forks and knives

DISTINCTIVE FOODS:
Sauerkraut, sausages, sauerbraten, game, beer

UNIFORMITY OF MENUS:
Good

NUTRITIONAL INDEX:
High fat, medium sodium, high cholesterol, high carbohydrate

COST:
Inexpensive to moderate

"THANK YOU":
"Danke (schön)"

Icelanders, and Teutons—all lead back to the Germanic tribes who stood Rome off and finally broke down her door.

Germans spawned the "greats" of various countries: Charlemagne and Otto I, emperors of the Holy Roman Empire; Frederick of Prussia, whose prescient appreciation of the potato prevented European famine in the eighteenth century; and Victoria, that sable symbol of British imperial propriety. And though German immigrants were not the first to settle the New World, their Reformation, which sowed similar Protestant and political upheavals across Europe, made its settlement inevitable.

In this century, and particularly since World War II, German food, which had a long and hearty frontier tradition in the United States, has become politically unpopular; more subtly, it has acquired an unsophisticated, out-of-step image as well, thanks to the increasing social prejudice against meaty, starchy "comfort foods." However, Germany's rich sauces, its delicate asparagus, fragrant hams, earthy, musty breads, and eye-watering mustards, and its almost legendary balance of assertive, gamey meats with green herbs and rich compotes make it one of the great cold-weather cuisines.

In the United States, German and Austrian restaurants, along with Swiss and even sometimes Alsatian ones, are indistinguishable. However, those particularly interested in Swiss and Alsatian foods should also see the sections on Italian and French regional cuisines, and the discussion of Eastern European foods, particularly Hungarian, may interest Austrian devotees.

THE COUNTRY

One of the reasons "German food" can be somewhat tricky to define is that Germany not only borders Poland, France, Belgium, the Netherlands, Switzerland, Denmark, and Austria; at various times it has also *been* Poland, France, Belgium, and so forth, or at least has controlled parts of them.

Germany is physically at the center of Europe, with equally close ties to the Slavic east, the Mediterranean south, and the Scandinavian north. A natural watershed, it slopes from the Alps across forestland and pastureland to the sandy lowlands of the Baltic, watered by rivers so powerful—the Danube, the Elbe, the Rhine—that for centuries they served as boundaries between ethnic rivals.

The mountainous south is turned over primarily to cattle and dairy farms, wheat and barley pastures, and vineyards: The wines of the Rhineland and the beers of Bavaria are all famous. The Black Forest is to the southwest, and its wild game, game birds, river trout, and tart fruits are among Europe's finest. The central plateau, a long narrowish belt between Dortmund and Dresden, is hilly and wooded; the famous spas are here, among orchards and herds of sheep. And the north coast is sandy and low, similar to its neighbors the Netherlands and Poland; grains are the most common crops here, particularly the potato. In 1756 Frederick the Great of Prussia commanded that the potato be planted all over his empire, and now it has become an integral part of the northern European and Scandinavian diet.

Germany has been divided innumerable times, by dynasty, by alliance, and by religion. The current boundaries of Germany, Poland, Austria, and the Czech Republic date only to this century. Ethnically, however, Germany and Austria are fairly homogeneous, with some Slavic, Turkish, and Italian minorities. During the centuries, Austria has had within its borders Celts and Romans, Slavs and Germans, Moravians and Magyars; due to all these ethnic influences its cuisine is richer, more aromatic, and more sweet-spicy than sweet-sour.

THE HISTORY

Not a lot is known about the indigenous tribes of the region. Although the Greeks mentioned meeting them trading in Norway in the fourth century B.C.E., there is little other record of them for several hundred years, when they began to expand their territories. They were halted on the west by the Celts and on the east by the Romans, who basically drew lines at the Danube and Rhine rivers. Tacitus, writing in the first century, described a taciturn people who lived on black bread, gruels (millet, oats, and barley), wild berries, game, and milk.

In the fourth and fifth centuries, the "Germanic tribes," who were closely related to the Slavs, began to break the Roman stranglehold, gradually making their way into England (as the Angles and Saxons), France and Belgium (Franks and Burgundians), and Lombardy and Germany (Goths and Visigoths). As the Roman Empire disintegrated, Europe came under invasion from the Norsemen, the Turkic Magyars, and the Slavs. Europe's borders shrank and shifted until 962, when Otto I assumed emperorship of the Holy Roman Empire, which at various times covered Germany, Austria, Moravia, Burgundy, the Netherlands, the Papal States, and Sicily.

Though the empire existed at least nominally into the early nineteenth century, its influence was diminished by a series of sundering blows—Martin Luther and the expanding waves of Reformation, the Thirty Years' War, and finally Napoleon, who, however briefly, reconfigured the whole of Europe.

The empire rose again to prominence in the late nineteenth century, thanks to Bismarck and alliances with Russia and Austria-Hungary; but its colonial ambitions in Africa and its ties to the Ottoman Turks gradually estranged it from the rest of Europe, and internal upheaval culminated in the outbreak of the First World War and, in a sense, the Second World War as well.

THE CUISINE

German food may remind one of that existential joke that goes, "If we had ham, we could have ham and eggs, if we had eggs." The Germans had a meat-and-potatoes kind of philosophy even before potatoes were discovered in South America and long before they made their meandering way to Europe.

Like its neighbors, pre-Renaissance Germany was somewhat hobbled by poor agricultural methods and the need to preserve food rather than present it. (See the chapter on France for a digression on the evolution of European cuisine.) Consequently, smoked, pickled, marinated, and salted foods are among the oldest techniques in this region: It's one reason the sausages of Germany are so famous. The prized Westphalian hams are dry-salted, then brined, and finally smoked in juniper berries.

Nevertheless, German cuisine is not nearly so straightforward as it is stereotypically portrayed. Its influences range from the Dutch and Danish, with whom it was closely allied beginning in the thirteenth century; to the

Cream of the Crops

Few cuisines are as rich in butter, cream, sour cream, eggs, and cheese as German food; it's meat-heavy and organ-rich, and when bacon grease, lard, and goose fat are figured in, it can be one of the fattiest diets known. Meats, fishes, noodles, even vegetables are habitually served under sauces. However, many of the game meats, particularly those with wine or vinegar marinades, are surprisingly lean; braised dishes, roasts, and even some of the lighter sausages grill out much of the fat. Soups are not only filling; they are usually nutritional bonanzas, combining legumes, grains, and vegetables. But the dumplings, the juicier sausages, the schnitzels, the cream sauces, and the fruit compotes pack a powerful weight. Many of the salted fish, smoked meats, and cheeses hide extra sodium and fat as well.

Italians, whose cookbooks were standard in the sixteenth and seventeenth centuries; to the Spanish, whose monopoly on the import of cocoa made them wealthy beyond imagination; to the French, who elevated cooking to "cuisine" in the nineteenth century.

Germany's own cookbook collection began in 1485; a century later, another published cookbook included 2,000 recipes. Using other European traders as middlemen, Germans acquired Peruvian potatoes (via English privateer Sir Francis Drake, who picked up provisions in Cartagena), Malaysian mustards (via the Poles, who got it from the Caucasians), and Persian almonds and saffron (via the Baltic markets). Going even farther back, it was the Chinese who taught the Romans how to make sauerkraut, and the Romans who taught the Germans—and the Tatars who reminded them how, more than a thousand years later.

Because of the shifting political influences, and the topographical differences as well, Germany's cuisine shows some regional tendencies, though they are not extreme. For example, flour doughs are more common in the south, and the starches—particularly *spätzle*, tiny egg and wheat-flour dumplings—are grain-based. Butter is commonly used for sautéing. In the middle and north, potato flour is the dumpling base, and bacon drippings are the cooking grease.

In the south, in Bavaria, fresh game and wildfowl are common and are often stewed with dried fruit; in Austria, which was often bound up with Hungary, goulash stews, with their paprika, are very popular. French and Italian dishes—pâté, trout meunière, frogs' legs, veal shanks, asparagus with hollandaise sauce—are also more common in the south.

In the central forestlands meats are smoked (raw Westphalia hams, short ribs), sauces are green with wild herbs (sorrel, chervil, borage, chives, tarragon, and dill), and stews and game are flavored with apples and pears and bread crumbs.

In the north—the ancient Prussia, near the Netherlands and Scandinavia, where warmer-weather food had to be stored for bad weather—dried fish, dried and pickled meats, dried fruits, pickled eggs and vegetables, smoked eels, and fatty pork sausages are mainstays. Cream and sour cream sauces are most common here, along with those other Norse staples, herring and salt cod.

THE MAIN INGREDIENTS

SEASONINGS Vinegar, sour cream, mustard, horseradish (Meerrettich), caraway, bay, juniper, black pepper, red wine, allspice, and honey are the most important seasonings in German cooking, but paprika, cinnamon, cloves, poppyseed, dill, almond, ginger, and fennel are also essential.

VEGETABLES AND FRUITS Green cabbage is king and potato its consort, but onions, carrots, turnips, asparagus, kale, spinach, white beans, red cabbage, sweet peppers, cauliflower, peas, and a wide variety of mushrooms are also important. Tomatoes, which were introduced belatedly, have less of a role here than in most of Europe; and although the Germans took to Middle Eastern–style stuffed cabbage and green peppers, eggplant is rarely served.

FISH AND SEAFOOD Herring, cod, mackerel, pike, salmon, trout, tench, and carp are plentiful, along with lobsters, oysters, prawns, and eels. Occasionally frogs' legs and mussels are harvested, too.

MEATS Traditionally, the German and Austrian cuisines are rich with game—venison, roebuck, mouflon (bighorn sheep), boar, bear, and hare—as well as the beef, veal, lamb, and pork more common today. They

---

Buds 'n' Spuds
Continued

liver cheese, but it contains no liver and may not have cheese. Bread might be white, wheat, whole wheat, cracked wheat, rye, caraway, pumpernickle, poppy seed, graham, black, egg, potato, sour, sweet, or sprouted. And beer might be dark, light, *bock* (dark and aged), pilsner (like most American beers), lager (left to age), *Weissbier* (weak wheat beer), *Malzbier* (low-alcohol malt brew), or *Marzenbier* (the Oktoberfest type). And that doesn't include the raspberry, cherry, double-bock, Maybock, and so forth.

Potatoes may be historically the newest addition to the menu, but their use has been thoroughly explored, too: They are boiled, mashed, baked, roasted, and turned into soufflés, salads, stews, soups, dumplings, pancakes, fried patties, and even bread doughs.

also prize offal and organ meats, from sweetbreads, kidneys, liver, tripe, tongue, and brains to trotters, snouts, knuckles, hocks, and so on. Anything that's left on slaughter day is usually turned into sausage on the spot.

Sausages are divided into three types, depending on the manner of their preparation, which in turn has much to do with whether the sausage is intended to be eaten right away. *Brühwurst* are finely chopped raw meat sausages that are parboiled and sometimes smoked as well; they include the familiar frankfurter or *Wiener*, a smoked mixture of lean pork and bacon fat; *Knockwurst*, made of pork and beef seasoned with garlic and cumin; the pistachio-studded *Bierschinken*; and the creamy white sausage or *Weisswurst* of Munich. So-called "raw" sausages (*Rohwurst*) are generally cured, air-dried, and smoked; pork and beef *Bratwurst* (grilling sausages) are the most familiar of this type in the United States. Fully cooked sausages, generally eaten fresh, include the liver sausages (*Leberwurst*) and blood sausages (*Blutwurst*).

In Austrian *heurigen* (taverns where only recently processed wine is served), sausages are sometimes pickled or marinated or turned into a spread for breads.

POULTRY   Goose and duck are the favorites, followed by game birds (partridge, pheasant, squab, woodcock, marsh hen, and quail) and chicken. Rabbit (as opposed to wild hare) is generally treated as chicken would be.

EGGS AND DAIRY   Butter, cream, sour cream, eggs, curds, cream cheese, and cheese are major ingredients, but cheese and eggs (most often shirred or boiled, and frequently pickled) are often eaten as main dishes as well. Among the best-known cheeses are Tilsit and the Bavarian cheeses Münster (an imitation of French Munster) and Limburger; Leiderkranz is actually an American invention. Germans both drink milk and buttermilk and use them in recipes. *Schmerkäse* is a sort of sour cottage cheese with dill that is spread on bread.

THE MAIN DISHES
APPETIZERS   Both hot and cold appetizers are popular, including the "continental" classics—foie gras, oysters, smoked salmon, caviar, sautéed mushrooms in split puff pastries, etc. Cold sausages and hams, cheeses and breads, pickled fish and eggs, and vegetable salads—particularly potato and coleslaws and pickled beets—are common; in the central lowlands, French-style mixed green salads are popular.

SOUPS The word to use about all but the clear soups is "hearty." The clear soups are not only French in style, they are often called consommés; they may include spätzle or even liver spätzle. Pureed soups—pea, cauliflower, bean, beet, lentil, turnip, or potato—may have garnishes of ham, bacon, sausage, or smoked fish. The cream soups are similar but are thickened with cream or sour cream and often egg yolks; there are also bisques with eel and crayfish and oxtail soup. Cabbage and bacon soup is particularly popular in the north. There is even a beer soup, which includes sugar and eggs. Both soups and stews may be thickened with bread crumbs.

DUMPLINGS Dumplings are particularly prized in the south, where they are made with bacon, liver, potatoes, or cheese. Softer dumplings are made from a noodle dough with eggs. The *knödel* (dumplings) of the south have several starches: flour, potatoes, and semolina. Dumplings, incidentally, need not be plain dough; they can be made with spinach or liver, stuffed with meat like ravioli, and flavored with anchovies or sauerkraut.

VEGETABLES Potatoes and sauerkraut are prepared in a number of ways, as mentioned above; these two are almost condiments. Potatoes mashed with apples is typical for the north and is called *Himmel und Erde*—Heaven and Earth. Red cabbage and apples (used in so many dressings and stuffings that they are almost more vegetable than fruit), spinach, green beans, asparagus, carrots, and peas are other vegetables served more or less plain. Cabbage and green peppers are stuffed, mushrooms and onions sautéed. Any of them may be creamed.

Our Daily Bread

Although nowadays the Germans tend to eat three meals a day, with a lighter lunch and heavier dinner, they traditionally ate five meals a day, with a second breakfast of coffee and pastry (called *Brotzeit*, or "bread time") and a late-afternoon meal of sausages and cheese. The midday meal was a hearty one, a practice passed on to millions of American laborers. The evening meal, called *Abendbrot*—literally, "evening bread"—bore a very strong resemblance to the Scandinavian smorgasbord: It was a meal of buttered breads and assorted cold cuts, cheeses, and condiments, which were assembled into open-faced sandwiches and eaten with knives and forks.

Even the big midday meal tended to be fairly plain, usually featuring an *Eintopf*—literally, a "one-pot" stew—which could be prepared and left to cook itself. Most of the dishes served in German restaurants are, in fact, just that: restaurant fare, derived from court and city cuisine rather than home cooking.

FRUITS Unlike diets that use most fruits raw, the Germans tend to either dry them and cook them into compotes to offset meat and poultry dishes (in which case they may have some vinegar) or simmer them in syrup for preserves or desserts. There are some almost habitual pairings: pork with apples, goose with cherries, duck with prunes.

MEATS Beef is used broadly: boiled, ground into meatloaf (*Hackbraten*), smoked and served cold, dried and then smoked, rolled around pickles and mustard, roasted with bacon, and braised (*Sauerbraten*) with vinegar, wine, or even buttermilk. *Braten* is simply roast of whatever kind. *Tafelspitz* is an Austrian dish of braised and horseradish-flavored roast beef. *Pfefferpotthast* is the original "pepperpot" or New England boiled dinner: short ribs or brisket given a little punch with bay leaves, capers, cloves, and black peppercorns.

Pork too is consumed entirely, with chops, the loin, and the hams the most popular cuts for smoking or grilling; it is also smoked or pickled and used to flavor primarily vegetable casseroles—kale, turnips, dried apricots, apples, and prunes and so on. Its affinity for mustard is well known, and chops are sometimes coated with mustard before being rolled in bread crumbs. Whole suckling pig (and boar piglet) are festival staples.

Veal is often turned into schnitzel and either breaded or sauced; the most elaborate version, *Holstein schnitzel,* named for the baron whose favorite it became, combines the cutlet, smoked salmon, caviar, a poached egg, and capers. (A simpler recipe—just a one-knight stand, so to speak—replaces the smoked salmon and caviar with sardines.) Weisswurst is a very light veal sausage with eggwhites. *Hasenpfeffer* is hare stewed with wine and peppercorns; venison is usually roasted or served as cutlets or fancy sausages, as is boar. Organ meats, particularly sweetbreads, are referred to in the French manner as ragouts and involve eggs and wine. A *Schlachtplatte* is a mixed plate of sausages and cold cuts, potatoes, and sauerkraut—the German ploughman's lunch.

POULTRY Goose is roasted and smoked; goose liver pâté is considered a luxury. Duck is marinated in beer or wine or stuffed with apples and prunes and perhaps sour bread crumbs; game birds are usually marinated before being roasted or grilled. Chicken is most often stuffed and baked or braised in wine French-style; both chickens and ducks are caponized (that is, castrated to increase body fat).

SEAFOOD Though less stereotypically "German," lobster dishes, including sauces poured over other fish such as salmon, are popular in the northern areas. Herring is fried, marinated, smoked, and turned into a sour cream salad with potatoes. Eel is smoked and made into sausage (it is also made into a stew). Fish are braised in wine and served with cream sausages and occasionally sweet-and-sour dressings; trout is served in several classic French styles, including steamed in foil or parchment and cooked in white wine and herbs.

DESSERTS Between the French and their layered pastry doughs and the Viennese and their ornate fillings, German and Austrian pastries became extremely elaborate. Under the French influence, honey, which had been the favorite sweetener, was replaced by sugar, which led to the creation of the meringue in Salzburg; under the Ottoman influence, the Austrians used jams as well as nuts in their sweets. *Strudel* is a yeast-dough pastry stuffed with ground apples; rice pudding, gingerbreads, raisin breads, almond cookies, and hazelnut cakes all show their Middle Eastern ancestry. An even more obvious example is marzipan, the ground almond-sugar-rosewater paste that is made into elaborate fruits, vegetables, and decorations and tinted to perfection. A town called Lübeck claims to be the home of the original marzipan; in any case, it has become the center of the marzipan industry.

Although the region offers hundreds of famous sweets, among the most common on U.S. menus are Black Forest cake (a layered chocolate cake with cherries) and Sacher Torte. Developed by Metternich's chef, Franz Sacher, it is a chocolate cake with a stiff chocolate shell that conceals apricot puree—and technically, the only "authentic" rendition is that served at the Sacher Hotel in Vienna. Another famous cake is Linzer Torte, which is made with red currant jam and almonds.

COFFEE While many of the cafes of Vienna have undoubtedly become tourist traps, there are over 500 of them, so you can probably find an authentic cup somewhere. But just as in its neighbor Italy, there are very specific terms for the many coffee drinks: A *melange* is a half-milk/half-coffee mix like cafe au lait with a bit of froth. *Kapuziner* is a small amount of coffee blended with a large amount of milk; it's like cappucino, and even shares a name, almost—"kapuziner" means monk and "cappucino" a monk's hood. *Einspanner* is sweetened strong black coffee with whipped cream. The word "goldener" for gold refers to milk in the glass; just a little milk turns it only brown or "brauner."

WINE AND BEER Even though the wine industry in Germany goes back at least to the Romans, and has the seemingly secure blessing

In the United States, a coffee-house is usually a folk music club or, more recently, an espresso bar. In Vienna, a coffeehouse is a far more important place: open almost around the clock, from 4 a.m. until the wee hours—and is something closer in both spirit and substance to a French cafe. These *Konditereien* are lavish bakeries offering pastries and cookies, plus omelets, cold cut sandwiches, and the classic small pan-fried steak. *Heurigen* are a bit like pubs—wine-makers' taverns, specializing in the owner's product (if the barrels are full, a piece of grapevine is often tacked over the door) and country fare such as grilled chickens and simple buffets. A *Beisel* is more like a bistro, with a more formal wine list and heartier food: meats, sausages, suckling pigs, and sauerkraut. And a *Ratskeller* is literally a cellar, traditionally a wine vault, that serves more elaborate food.

of having been the province of various religious orders during the Middle Ages, Germany is still the most beer-centric culture in the world. Germany produces only 2–3% of the world's wines, and mostly from very small vineyards—an estimated 100,000 winemakers own fewer than 2.7 acres—so it exports only a small amount of fine wine. So if you only know a tiny bit about German wines, know this:

The two great wine-producing regions are those around the Mosel (or Moselle) and Rhein (Rhine) Rivers. The most important varietal is Riesling, which accounts for 85% of the wines produced (Germany produces some red wines, but not notable ones). Riesling is a remarkably versatile grape that can make fruity or floral but also crisp wines with refreshing acidity, ranging from honey to melon to apple blossom to butter. Those from the Moselle region (in tall-necked green bottles) tend to have a more apple-like crispness and an elegant but lighter structure; those from the Rhine (in brown bottles) are bigger-bodied and more floral, with apricot or pear-like notes. (Wines in black porcelain or fake enamel bottles can be safely disregarded.) German wines typically have somewhat lower alcohol levels than French wines, 8–10% as compared to 11–13%.

The major words in labeling are *Tafelwein*, or table wine (don't—they're rarely exported anyway), and *Qualitätswein*, or "quality wine" (do). *Kabinett* wines are made from the first-harvested grapes, and so are the most delicate; they are usually dry or semi-dry. *Spätlese* are produced from grapes left a week or so past harvest, and so are usually semi-dry to semi-sweet (although some are dry) and full-bodied. *Auslese* wines are made from grapes left even longer and are heavier and sweeter. *Sekt* indicates a sparkling wine.

The dessert wines are also of note, especially *Trocken* and *Eiswein*, the original "ice wine," which is made from grapes left on the vine until frozen; these are very concentrated, sweet, high-acid, and more expensive.

The revival of microbrewing in the United States, as well as the increased interest in quality imports, has made the labeling of German beers of interest as well. A few of the more popular styles available are *Märzen*, a high-malt, sweet, and fairly high-alcohol beer traditionally brewed for Oktoberfest; *Bock*, a high-alcohol (8–10%) and assertively malty brew; *Weissbier*, a tangy, lighter-bodied brew made with 50% malted wheat and often flavored with raspberry or other fruit; *Dunkelwiesen*, a Bavarian-style dark wheat beer with a roasting or caramel tone; and *Maibock*, a pale bock brewed in spring. *Pils* (or pilsner) is a blond lager with a hoppy flavor, the ancestor of most American-style beers; *Dunkel*, in contrast, is a dark Munich-style brew with dominant malt and a creamy finish; and *Dortmunder* might be said to be in the middle, high hop content, golden tone, and moderate body. There are also occasionally smoked beers, triple bocks (so malty they were intended as a substitute for bread to fasting monks), and fruity, all malt *Alt* beers.

And just for the record: Oktoberfest is actually mostly in September, a 16-day spread that ends the first Sunday in October.

HOW TO ORDER
AND EAT LIKE A NATIVE

There are only a few tricks to eating as the Germans do. The first is that open-faced sandwiches are eaten with a fork and knife, as they are in Scandinavia; the second is that smoked eel is eaten with the fingers. In fact, it's eaten by itself, accompanied only by plain bread; and at the end of the meal, the waiter traditionally pours not water but schnapps over your hands to remove the odor. Otherwise, eat as you would at home.

German food is not only rich in texture; it's rich in flavor as well and ought to be dealt out slowly on both accounts. Two people might order a vegetable soup and a mixed platter of sausages with bread to start, then a schnitzel dish and duck or goose. If it's spring, large platters of plain asparagus may be offered. Four people should try schmerkäse, mixed hot sausages, hot potato salad, roast duck, sauerbraten or hasenpfeffer, fish in cream sauce, and schnitzel.

Remember, dessert will be waiting.

COOKING AT HOME

Your mother cooked this stuff. If she didn't, your school cafeteria cook did. You probably have everything you need to cook anything in this chapter.

SAUERBRATEN

1 cup dry red wine
1/2 cup red wine vinegar
1 cup beef broth, stock, or water
1 onion, sliced
6 black peppercorns, crushed
8 juniper berries, crushed, or 1/4 cup gin
2 bay leaves
1 3-pound beef rump roast or top round
2 tablespoons oil
1 carrot, finely chopped
1 stalk celery, finely chopped
1 leek, finely chopped
2 tablespoons flour
2 tablespoons powdered ginger (optional)

In a nonreactive saucepan, combine wine, vinegar, broth, onion, peppercorns, juniper berries or gin, and bay leaves and bring to boil; let cool. Meanwhile, place roast in an enameled casserole or Dutch oven just large enough to hold it, and pour the wine marinade over it; cover and refrigerate, turning occasionally, for at least 48 hours, preferably several days.

On the day of cooking, remove meat from marinade and pat dry; strain and reserve marinade. In a deep casserole, heat oil and brown roast on all sides, adding more oil if necessary. Remove meat to a platter; add chopped vegetables to oil and cook until soft; sprinkle with flour and ginger until colored and smooth. Pour in marinade and bring to boil; return meat to casserole. Cover, lower heat, and simmer until tender, about 2 hours. Remove meat to platter; strain the liquid, skim off as much fat as possible, and boil down slightly to thicken. Slice meat and pour sauce over it. Serve with potatoes, potato pancakes, and red cabbage.

POTATO PANCAKES

3 pounds potatoes, peeled and grated
3 eggs, beaten
2 small onions, grated
1 1/2 teaspoons salt
1 teaspoon pepper
4 tablespoons flour
oil for frying

Press potatoes between paper towels or dishtowels to remove moisture; turn into bowl. Combine potatoes with eggs, onions, seasonings, and flour. Pour oil about 1 inch deep in skillet and heat; drop in spoonfuls of potato batter; brown, turn, and drain on paper towels.

ROAST DUCK WITH APPLE STUFFING

1 5-pound duck
salt and pepper to taste
1/2 pound veal, ground
1/2 pound sirloin or round, ground
1/2 pound lean pork, ground
2 tablespoons raisins
1 egg, beaten
3/4 cup dry bread crumbs
1/2 teaspoon dried sage
pinch nutmeg
pinch allspice
2 tart cooking apples, peeled, seeded, and diced

Preheat oven to 450°. Rinse duck inside and out and pat dry. Season cavity with salt and pepper; with meat fork, prick skin all over.

In a large bowl, combine all remaining ingredients except apples with a little more salt and pepper; then add apples and stuff duck, leaving space for expansion. Skewer or sew cavity shut and truss bird. Place breast up on rack in shallow pan and roast 15 minutes or until lightly browned, then remove from oven; reduce heat to 350°, pour off accumulated fat, and return to oven for 1 hour or until juices from thigh joint run clear (start testing after 45 minutes). Remove and let rest before serving.

SCANDINAVIA

BASIC CUISINE

DINNER FOR TWO:
Herring, smoked lamb,
fish chowder, reindeer
stew, poached salmon

DINNER FOR FOUR:
Herring, prosciutto, veg-
etable stew, stuffed pork
roast, salmon, veal rolls

GROUP DISH:
Smorgasbord

STYLE:
Tart, sour, salty, creamy,
"fishy"

KEY FLAVORS:
Caraway, dill, juniper,
sour cream

EATING UTENSILS:
Forks and knives

DISTINCTIVE DISHES:
Pickled herring, gravlax,
lutefisk

UNIFORMITY OF MENUS:
Good

NUTRITIONAL INDEX:
High sodium, high fat,
high cholesterol

COST:
Moderate

"THANK YOU":
"Tack" (Swedish)
"Takk" (Norwegian)

Mention Scandinavian food, and most people think "smorgasbord"—and while it may be oversimplifying things to suggest that all Norden food is one big buffet, that word is a fair reminder of the cuisine's homey abundance and straightforward simplicity.

Scandinavian cuisine may not offer great variety or elaboration; but it seems to come almost directly from the Earth itself, with its traditions nearly intact. The salmon and herring, goose and wildfowl, reindeer and mutton, root vegetables, mushrooms, and berries that characterize Scandinavian cuisine are the constant gift of its long coastlines, snow-melt rivers, thick timber plateaus, lakes, and marshes. The food does not come easily, but its fats and proteins offer strength; and it is best enjoyed in company—another hedge against the long winters.

Perhaps because food doesn't come easily here, good (and tireless) cooks are highly prized. In Denmark, the farmwoman in charge of the kitchen is addressed as *madmor*—"food mother." The very best *kjøttkaker*, or meat patties, are always said to be "mors kjøttkaker"—Mom's meatloaf. And that food involves hard work makes even more admirable the Norwegian farmwives' tradition of hanging baskets filled with fresh flatbread, butter, sausage, and a clean cloth under the storehouse eaves for any hungry person who happens by.

THE HISTORY

Denmark's "dual citizenship"—culturally associated with Scandinavia and geophysically joined to northern Europe—has made it a natural crossroads between the regions. In fact, in prehistoric times, a broad land bridge existed across what is now the strait between Copenhagen and the southern tip of Sweden. The Danes had probably settled there by 2000 B.C.E., but they left few records before the ninth century, when the Vikings launched the first great raids on northern Europe. In their heyday, the Danish and Norwegian Vikings—or "Norsemen," which was eventually corrupted to "Norman" (hence the "Norman Conquest" of England)—ranged as far as Spain, France, the Low Countries, Germany, and Great Britain. Their influence waxed and waned, but never collapsed, for several hundred years. (Denmark's periodic "enlightenments" produced at least one fine irony: Danish nobles, who had once forced a king on the English, eventually hobbled their own king by forcing him to sign a declaration closely copied from the Magna Carta.)

Finland, which shares a long border and strong ethnic connections with Russia to the east, has also been a sort of bridge and not infrequently an actual battleground between Sweden and Russia. It was probably first inhabited about 7000 B.C.E. by nomads who followed the retreating ice north in search of game and fish; in the early centuries of the Common Era, their descendants, the Samis (also known as Lapps or Laplanders), were gradually forced to the extreme north by the Finns. Sami cuisine and culture is still as thoroughly centered on the reindeer as the American Prairie tribes' were on the bison.

Sweden, the more hospitable country, was inhabited first; traces of settlement go back nearly 12,000 years and evidence of trade with Europe around 4,000 years. Not close to their Scandinavian neighbors—the "Vikings" with whom they are often confused—the Swedes actually spent most of their early history battling Norway and Denmark and expanding east across Russia. Throughout the Middle Ages, Sweden was a potent military and political presence in Europe, but it emerged after the Napoleonic Wars as an early and visionary liberal society. One of Napoleon's idealistic and eventually estranged generals even became the King of Sweden. Swedish culture is the most eclectic culture in the region, and Sweden was the only country to establish a serious court cuisine. Veal Oscar, in fact, is named for King Oscar II, who preferred his veal cutlets topped with asparagus, bearnaise sauce, and lobster meat.

THE COUNTRIES

Scandinavia looks something like a drooping lily with three long, irregular petals—Norway on the west, Sweden in the center, and Finland on the east, bordering Russia, which actually forms a fourth petal—and, to the south, several dropped "seeds" that comprise Denmark. Although the northernmost part of the Scandinavian peninsula is subarctic tundra (a third of Norway lies above the Arctic Circle), the central regions are humid, fertile, and rich in both wildlife and fresh- and saltwater fish.

Because of its somewhat warmer climate—the edge of the Gulf Stream keeps it between about 30° and 60°F—Denmark is much more widely cultivated than its neighbors; three-quarters of its land is devoted to pasture and agriculture. Not only is Denmark richer in grains than most of its Norden neighbors (which may be one reason they drink more beer than the others), the Danes are also much more reliant on pork as a source of protein. This is not coincidental: In the latter half of the nineteenth century, the Danish government actively encouraged its farmers to shift their emphasis from grain production (they tended to "buy American," as we say) to dairy and pork, and as a result, Denmark became the most prosperous small-farming economy in Europe. Even today, although it has greatly expanded its industrial base as well, pigs, cattle, and poultry remain as important as cereals and root vegetables.

Heavily forested and, like Norway, with a third of its territory lying above the Arctic Circle, Finland is dotted with some 55,000 lakes and vast marshlands. Only about 9% of the land is arable, and the primary commodities are grains (hay, oats, barley, wheat, and rye), sugar beets, potatoes, poultry, cattle, hogs, reindeer, and sheep.

Norway, a 1,100-mile-long and often narrow strip of coast, is 60% mountain and has even more lakes than Finland—nearly three times as many, in fact. It remains a heavily fishing-dependent society; only about 3% of its land is devoted to farming. The mountain pastures are given over to cattle, some goats and sheep, and reindeer in the north. The northern region of Norway, like that of Finland, is dominated by Finns and Lapps or Samis.

Sweden's climate ranges widely from the mountainous northern region, which comprises nearly two-thirds of the country, to the densely populated south. Like its neighbors, Sweden is more than half forest. Only 8% of its land is arable, and most of that land is devoted to sugar beets, potatoes, grains, and fodder for the poultry, hogs, and cattle.

THE CUISINE

The Vikings knew early on how limited the food supply was—it was one of the primary reasons behind their aggressive quest for new territories—and they also knew how to make the most of it. Their methods of preserving foods, salting, smoking, and drying, are still in use today; in particular, their reliance on dried cod during long sea voyages inspired many Portuguese dishes and allowed the Europeans to make their own long treks to distant nations. The Finns even cure lamb in their saunas!

Although few so-called Scandinavian restaurants in the United States are particularly authentic, and most tend to mix Danish pastries with Norwegian lamb, there are substantial differences in each country's cuisine, primarily having to do with topography. Denmark, the farthest south (and a near neighbor to Germany), is a green and dairy-rich nation whose food is thick with creams, cheeses, and butter. Danes prefer sweet cream, the others primarily sour cream. Norway, long and exposed, has a spare, sturdy style strong on preserved meats and cereals. Sweden, down the center, is the wealthiest and most eclectic, with elements of French, German, Polish, and Russian styles; and Finland, the most heavily forested, delights in earthy flavors—wild game, lake fish, wild mushrooms, and black sour breads. (Whether or not it has any basis in fact, an old saying has it that "The Danes live to eat, the Norwegians eat to live, and the Swedes eat to drink.")

One of the great ironies of Scandinavian history is that despite the apparent ubiquitousness of salt, there isn't enough hard sun, and the Baltic isn't sufficiently saline, for the Scandinavians to rely on the evaporation method of producing salt for preserving foods. So German and Low Country merchants managed to take over the salt trade, particularly in connection with herring, and made immense profits.

THE MAIN INGREDIENTS

SEASONINGS Dark green, "fruity" spices are prominent, including green and black pepper, juniper berries, dill, pine needles, allspice, anise, dried citrus peel, caraway seeds, bay leaves, and coarse salt. Vinegar, lemon, honey, and sugar are the other main flavorings. The Danish prepare a very distinct condiment called *fiskesennep*, "fish mustard," of coarse-ground brown and yellow mustard seeds, molasses, vinegar, and salt. They also like a very mild sort of curry powder.

FISH AND SEAFOOD This is so much the major class of food in the region that many restaurants list the lunch special as *dagensratt*—"fish of the day." Cod, salmon, haddock, Arctic char, trout, pike, and mackerel are eaten with dedication, but the greatest regional fish is herring, the alpha and often the omega of Scandinavian meals. In some areas, herring comprises three-quarters of all the fish consumed. Roes of all sorts are a particular favorite of the Finns, who consume not only the true (sturgeon) caviar but salmon, whitefish, trout, cod, and lumpfish eggs. The so-called "Norway lobster," also known as the Dublin Bay prawn, is a pale pink or orangy rose langoustine. Shrimp is also popular, particularly the small, delicately flavored baby shrimp; and the warmer regions offer eels, oysters, mussels, langoustines, crayfish, and *muikku*, a tiny type of salmon with a delicate roe.

POULTRY AND GAME BIRDS Chicken is widely raised, though more for eggs, it seems, than fricassees. Game and "free-range" birds, with their more assertive flavor, are more popular: snow grouse, goose, pheasant, duck, woodcock, and the dark-breasted ptarmigan.

DAIRY PRODUCTS Cheeses may be the most obvious, and may be made from sheep's, goat's, or cow's milk; but cream, sour cream, butter, and an extraordinary number of soured or fermented dairy foods (curds, buttermilk, and particularly one called *skyr*, which is something like yogurt) are also popular. Nothing goes to waste: In some regions, fermented whey is recycled to make cheese. Once the Danish set out to learn cheese-making from the Germans and the Swiss, they got it almost exact: There are Danish duplicates of Gouda, Roquefort and Gorgonzola (the so-called "Danish blues"), Emmenthal, Port Salut, and Edam.

MEATS In the northernmost regions in particular, reindeer is a whole grocery store, providing tongue, sausage, meatballs, marrow, saddle, cutlets, milk and cheese, liver, stew, steaks, sandwiches, and pâté.

(Actually, to the Sami, it's a whole general store, providing skins for boots and clothing, horns for utensils and souvenirs, and transportation and portage as well.)

Pork is more popular farther south, particularly smoked and salted; and while reindeer is quite lean, pork provides much of the fat of non-Sami diets. (One of the features of Valhalla, the Viking heaven, was that it served a perfectly roasted wild boar that could be consumed every night but reappeared whole the next morning.) Beef is most common in Denmark—partly because the reputation of Danish ham is so high that much of it is exported. Goat, lamb, and mutton are common, but the Scandinavians, particularly the Finns and Norwegians, also prize game meats: elk, reindeer, roe deer, red deer, venison, bear, hare, even whale and horse (although the last two are unlikely to appear on any menu in the United States). Here, too, everything is used: tongue, tripe, jowls, and even calf's and sheep's heads— the "mock turtle" of the soup. Not surprisingly, any and all meats, wild or domestic, are dried, salted, smoked, brined, ground up for sausage, or given any combination of the above treatments.

VEGETABLES AND GRAINS Since winters are long and sunlight short, roots and winter vegetables that can be cold-stored (or pickled) are the most important: potatoes, onions, celery root (celeriac), parsnips, carrots, leeks, kale, cabbage, rutabaga (so popular it's known elsewhere in Europe as the "Swede"), and some greens. Wild mushrooms are especially plentiful in Finland, where some 50 varieties are eaten (including some shunned elsewhere as poisonous).

Pick and Choose

It is possible, though difficult, to avoid a lot of salt and fat when eating at a Scandinavian restaurant. First of all, you're expected to butter the bread at the smorgasbord, and if you don't, the toppings will drip on you. Second, many of the dishes (on either the smorgasbord or the regular menu) have cream sauces or mayonnaise; many pastry-wrapped dishes do, too. Even a lot of meat stews have heavy or sour cream mixed in. Your best bets are roasts, ham, dry-cured lamb or mutton, wild game, poached fish, and shrimp. Fermented dairy products, such as buttermilk and yogurt, tend to separate out the fat and are thus better than whole cream or butter. Vinegar is better than salt, so pickled fish is better than salt; smoking is better than either. But all things considered, sodium is a passing problem, while fat hangs around a long time, so choose salty dishes over creamy ones.

Barley and rye are raised in the south, wheat and oats farther north. The Norwegians traditionally made flatbread from potato flour; leavened breads were only introduced about a century ago.

FRUITS AND NUTS   From the forests come a variety of berries, sweet and tart, including lingonberries (cranberries), strawberries, cloud-berries (golden raspberries), blueberries, honeyberries, and rowanberries; they are used not only as fruit but as seasoning elements, especially to offset rich game. Nuts are also harvested but are primarily served in desserts.

THE MAIN DISHES

SOUPS   Scandinavian meals contain both hearty stews and chow-ders and more delicate vegetable bisques. The lighter ones are generally Danish cream of shrimp soups or light mushroom-barley soups, but the more traditional include fish chowders; beer and bread soups; thick pea soups; the Viking-era "black soup" (*svart soppa*), made with pig and goose blood (but nowadays tamed with wine, port, cinnamon, and gin-ger); hot pots of mixed veal, pork, and beef; and "slaughter soup," which uses all the offal. The sometimes-Russian Finns make borscht.

FISH AND SHELLFISH   Herring, cod, halibut, sturgeon, and salmon are served nearly every way possible: boiled, baked, smoked, pickled, poached, dried, grilled, salt-cured, "moussed," or boiled in soup. On special occasions, fish is baked *en croute*—wrapped in pastry—or roasted whole.

But it's the variety and pungency of the preserved fish that really shows off the "Scandinavian" resourcefulness (and some would say, courage). Plain dried cod is *stokkfisk* (which lasts up to 20 years), and salted dried cod is *klippfisk*. The salt- and sugar-cured salmon called *gravlax* was originally buried and allowed to ferment—literally, "grave" salmon. *Rakefisk* (or surfisk) is a fermented trout buried the way gravlax used to be. (In Iceland they even bury sharks and let them ferment, which is really clever, as it breaks down the cyanic acid that otherwise makes the meat toxic.) *Lutefisk* is a very common dried and lye-cured codfish that is soaked, boiled, and then turned into soup or a jelly-like spread for flat-bread. There is even a fermented and potentially explosive herring called *surstroemming* that only a madmor could love. (For more on herring, see "The Smorgasbord," page 100.)

POULTRY AND GAME BIRDS   Pickled goose (called "burst goose") is boiled with vegetables or served hot with a chilled horseradish cream; fresh goose is stuffed with apples and prunes. One of the preferred sauces for game birds, and game meat as well, is a combination of goat cheese and cream.

VEGETABLES Most vegetables, as we noted above, are rooty and tough; they are most often used in soups or stews, braised or boiled, or chopped and then creamed; this method is used for spinach, cauliflower, cabbage, carrots, and so on. Just as popular, however, are sweet soups made from fresh fruits. Potatoes are eaten relatively plainly—baked, skillet-fried, julienned for fritters, or mashed into dumplings—but they are eaten a lot. Swedes and Norwegians venerate the potato as much as the Irish do, and for an ironically related reason; it saved them from famine in 1771. Some Swedes eat as many as four or five potatoes a day.

MEAT Danish hams and bacon are famous but expensive, because so many are exported, and thus are eaten sparingly; thin-sliced mutton and smoked lamb are often substituted. Pork loin is frequently stuffed with prunes and apples and accompanied by red cabbage, particularly in the regions near Germany; it is also sometimes ground and stuffed in or even around cabbages. Pork is often combined with veal, especially when it's ground; it may be turned into meatballs or a sort of meatloaf or into fried croquettes.

Lamb is stewed, roasted, dried, salt-cured (both legs and whole chops), and sometimes smoked—or, in the case of the Norwegian *fenalar*, dried, salted, *and* smoked. The Swedes have a dish called *lökdolmar* that is surely related to the Middle Eastern dolmas (lamb-stuffed grape leaves), only since grape leaves are not available, the Swedes use blanched, softened, and separated onion layers. Beef is roasted, pot-roasted with anchovies, stewed with beer ("seaman's stew"), or hash-browned and chopped with diced beets and onions into a sort of hamburger with internal relish. Mutton-cabbage stew is popular in Norway. A really macho dish is the Finnish *vorshmack*, a mixture of ground mutton, beef, salt herring, garlic, and onions.

BEVERAGES Meals are accompanied by beer and distilled liquor, specifically the fiery caraway-flavored clear grain alcohol called, with forgivable enthusiasm, *aquavit*—the "water of life." Also popular are berry-flavored teas that are nearly juices. Finns prefer vodka and make and export many first-rate brands.

BREADS All shapes, types, and flavors are made in the region, from the huge flatbread to the sweet *pulla*, a yeast bread or roll usually served with coffee (which perhaps explains the use of the word "Danish" to mean a sweet roll) to crisp (hardtack) to rye to the "black" bread used for the smorgasbord. *Limpa* is a sweet Finnish rye popular at Christmas; at Easter they make an even richer loaf of wheat and rye flours, cream, butter, eggs, raisins, almonds, and cardamom—all baked in a milk can.

DOUGHS AND PANCAKES Scandinavians make plenty of sweet and nonsweet doughs, particularly waffles and pancakes (usually served as desserts, not breakfast) and crêpes. The Danish are fond of crisp-edged crêpes filled with baby shrimp in dill and cream. There are dumplings stuffed with pork and dipped in butter, and there is also some pasta. The Finns make Russian blini, a rye-dough version of *kulebiyaka* (coulibiac), and a version of pirogi. Pastries are occasionally made to be stuffed, like the sour cream dough stuffed with meatloaf called *lihamurekepiiras*; if you see it on the menu, just point.

DESSERTS Denmark, partly because of its proximity to Germany, is particularly rich in pastries, huge cream-and-cake tartes, whipped cream–berry mousses, and fruit-flavored liqueurs. The *romfromage* is a soft whipped-cream meringe suffused with dark rum. Berries are also popular in crêpes; and the Finns, who are particularly fond of ice cream, sometimes make dessert blintzes. In the north, however, plain fruit and cheese are more frequently the finale.

THE SMORGASBORD

A smorgasbord meal is a series of courses always beginning with her-ring—lots of herring—and eaten over dark multigrain "black" or rye bread (white bread for shrimp and very light dishes). The bread is sliced thin and placed on round flat disk to the left of the dinner plate, called in Danish *smørrebræt*, literally "buttering board." (If you think that's funny, try the Finnish term, *voileipäpöytä*.) The bread is always buttered, which serves as a sort of seal for the toppings. After the bread is buttered, it is moved to the large plate, where it becomes the base of the open-faced sandwiches (*smørrebrød*) that make up the smorgasbord (the whole "bread-and-butter table"). Everything that is not bread or butter, inci-dentally, is *paalæg*—"laid on."

Herring is the whole first course, but there may be a dozen dishes of it, pickled, salted, peppered, sugared, smoked, fried, marinated, and poached in aspic. The pickled herring (which is slightly sweet, as opposed to the marinated herring, which is vinegary) generally appears first with onion and then perhaps with dill sour cream, curry sauce, mustard sauce (fiskesennep), sweet-and-sour sauce, Madeira, and so on; first you taste the herring, then you toast with the aquavit.

After the herring comes the second course, and a clean plate; now you get the other fish (smoked salmon, gravlax, eel, poached salmon with mayonnaise, and lobster or crab salad), hard-cooked eggs, apples, and some sort of salad or pickle to offset it. The third plate consists of meats and salads: roast beef, ham, salami, liver pâté, sausage, pasta salad, hard cheese, pickled tongue. Then come the hot dishes: meatballs, herring croquettes, egg and bacon tartes, omelets, potatoes. Finally, the cheese board arrives (and then dessert, although that may be delayed while you still recover).

All these courses are prepared, served, and eaten with the familiar utensils, *exclusively*—that is, even things you might expect to pick up with your fingers, such as the tiny sandwiches, are cut up in the European manner (fork, tines down, in the left hand, knife in the right) and eaten off the fork. This may take some getting used to, especially for curry-sauced, hard-boiled eggs, but that's how they do it. (It's actually a good idea, since most of the sauces are creamy and the thin bread crumbles easily.)

Incidentally, about those Swedish meatballs: As an appetizer or part of the smorgasbord, meatballs are served without gravy. As a main course, over rice or pasta, they are served with sauce.

HOW TO ORDER
AND EAT LIKE A NATIVE

As the old saying goes, the Danes live to eat, and traditionally they eat a half-dozen meals a day. Here, however, Scandinavian restaurants have adopted the American hours and the common menu organization. Nomenclature and menus are fairly standard, and you should have no difficulty ordering.

Meals generally begin with multiple appetizers—pickled or salted fish, open-faced cucumber and onion sandwiches, some cheese—followed by soup (most often a dill-flavored fish or shrimp and potato chowder) and then the main courses of fish and meat.

A good meal for two might include some pickled fish or a plate of fine smoked or dried meats, followed by potato and fish chowder or creamed vegetable soup and, if possible, a main course of either reindeer or venison along with poached salmon; pastry-wrapped fish or lamb would be a good alternative. Ask for cheese (sliced Finnish *lappi* or the Swiss-like *vasterbotten*), fruit salad, or berry pie for dessert. A party of four would add a stuffed pork roast or goose, stuffed veal rolls, and perhaps a couple more Danish pastries—unless of course you go to an all-you-can-eat smorgasbord place. Then you're on your own. Just remember: Herring always comes first, and cheese is always last.

Be sure to ask for special imported beers or aquavit.

COOKING AT HOME

It is probably easier to make lowfat Norden food at home than in a restaurant. Now that more and more specialty markets import game, reindeer is not hard to find and is certainly the most flamboyant dish to offer guests. (Elk, venison, or even buffalo are perfectly acceptable substitutes.) Start by laying out pickled herring and rye or cracked wheat bread, some cheese, and strong drink—aquavit and beer, for example. The pork roast can be accompanied by red cabbage and apples. Serve the reindeer stew over mashed potatoes with a side dish of parsnips and carrots, (and pass lingonberries or cranberry relish).

STUFFED PORK ROAST

8 pitted prunes, soaked in hot water or apple cider
1 tart apple, peeled, cored, and cubed
1 teaspoon lemon juice
3 1/2–4 pounds boned center-cut loin of pork
salt and pepper to taste
2 teaspoons thyme
1 tablespoon butter (more if needed)
1 tablespoon oil (more if needed)
3/4 cup white wine or vermouth
1/2 cup heavy cream (or substitute half-and-half or sour cream)
1 tablespoon currant jelly

Preheat oven to 350°F. Drain prunes and pat dry; sprinkle apple with lemon juice and add to prunes. With a sharp knife, cut a slit down the length of the loin to make a pocket reaching almost end to end; season with salt, pepper, and thyme, stuff with fruit mixture, and sew up the pocket with kitchen thread. (If you prefer to buy the roast already rolled, cut a tunnel all the way through with a skewer, widen it with a wooden spoon handle or knife sharpener, and force the fruit down either end of the tunnel, alternating prunes and apples.)

In a casserole just big enough to hold the loin, over medium heat, melt 1 tablespoon butter and 1 tablespoon oil; brown the roast on all sides, adding more oil if needed. When it's brown all around, pour off fat and add wine. Whisk in cream, bring to simmer, and cover; then move it into the oven and bake until tender (75–90 minutes). Remove to platter and let rest. Meanwhile, on top of the stove, skim the fat from the cooking liquid and bring to a boil; reduce to about a cup, add jelly, and simmer until dissolved and smooth. Slice roast and pass with sauce.

SAMI REINDEER STEW

3 tablespoons butter
3 pounds boneless reindeer meat, shoulder or roast, frozen
2 cups coarsely chopped onions
1 cup sliced mushrooms
1 cup sour cream (optional)
2 tablespoons crushed juniper berries or gin (optional)
salt and white pepper to taste

Melt the butter in an iron pot. Slice the frozen meat into slivers and add to pot; cover and simmer until all the water from the frozen meat has evaporated and the oil is clear. Add a little water and onions and continue simmering until tender (about 30 minutes). Add mushrooms, sour cream, and juniper berries or gin if desired, simmer 5–10 minutes more, then serve.

CELERY ROOT FRITTERS

1 large celery root, peeled and coarsely grated
1 onion, coarsely grated
1 sweet bell pepper, cut into matchsticks
2 teaspoons chopped hot pepper or 1/2 teaspoon hot pepper sauce
1/2 cup frozen corn, thawed and drained
4 eggs, lightly beaten
3 tablespoons flour

1/2 teaspoon baking soda

3 tablespoons fresh dill

4 tablespoons butter or margarine, divided

3–4 tablespoons oil, divided

salt and pepper to taste

optional garnishes: sour cream, crème fraîche, caviar, sliced red onion

Wrap grated celery root in a dishtowel and squeeze moisture out; turn into a bowl, repeat with grated onion, and add to bowl. Add peppers, corn, eggs, flour, baking soda, and seasonings and toss until well mixed.

In a skillet, melt half the butter and half the oil and heat to medium. Drop spoonfuls of vegetable batter into hot oil and flatten slightly; fry about 2 minutes on each side, drain on paper towels, and continue, adding butter and oil as needed, until the batter is used up. Garnish as desired.

RUSSIA, POLAND, AND EASTERN EUROPE

From the culinary standpoint, as from many others, the Cold War was a terrible waste. Russian food, once one of Europe's most admired cuisines, is known to most Americans only at its extremes—opulent Kremlin caviar fare on the one hand and the borscht and boiled potatoes of quota lines and black markets on the other. And too many of the Russian restaurants in the United States seem to cling to their own form of continental nostalgia, focusing more on "name" dishes (chicken Kiev, beef Stroganov, steak tartare, charlotte russe, veal Orlov) than authentic ones. Polish cuisine, once similarly admired, has been similarly slighted, reduced to ball-park sausages and beer gardens.

But with the fall of the communism and the economic reconstruction of Eastern Europe, we can hope for a revival of not merely classic Russian and Polish dishes but Hungarian, Romanian, Czech, Bulgarian, or Ukrainian ones as well. These are substantial cuisines, meaty, rooty, smoky—part comfort food, part extravagance.

Over a vivid, passionate crazy-quilt of Greek, Byzantine, Asiatic, Scandinavian, Turkish, and Germanic influences was installed a layer of eighteenth-century European custom and economy; and despite decades of reckless and ruthless agricultural "redevelopment," many parts of the former Soviet sphere remain fertile and potentially prosperous.

THE COUNTRIES

Even in the post-Soviet era, Russia (or the Russian Federation, which comprises 21 autonomous republics) remains physically the largest country in the world, covering some 6,670,000 square miles, stretching 5,000 miles from the Baltic Sea to the Pacific, and crossed by geographical belts that run virtually the entire climactic range.

The Ural Mountains are generally used to divide the northwest, "European" region of Russia, including Moscow and St. Petersburg, from the Asiatic subcontinent, which bred ruthless and incredibly adaptable tribes—the Scythians, the Mongols, the Manchus, the Huns, and others. In the northern tundra, fur-trapping, fishing, reindeer herding, and sealing remain major occupations. The central steppes are among the great grain pastures of the world, producing wheat, oats, and rye (and supporting the dairy herds that graze on them) as well as sunflower seeds and sugar beets. Siberia is 40 percent forest, and many of the game foods that became famous in Russian cooking originated there.

The southern belt of Russia is subtropical, and the produce and cuisine resemble that of Georgia, Turkey, and Russia's other Middle Eastern neighbors: citrus fruits, some wine grapes, tobacco, tea, poultry, pigs, and cattle. (It was to Georgia, intriguingly, that Jason led his Argonauts; along with the Golden Fleece, they discovered the pleasures of pheasant.) Ukraine, which adjoins Romania and Poland, was the breadbasket of the old empire; it produced 25 percent of the staples consumed in the old Soviet Union, primarily wheat but also corn, rice, barley, potatoes, beets, and vegetables.

The Danube River creates fertile plains down through the central plateau of Hungary, through the northern plains of Bulgaria, and into Romania. Much of the region has cold winters and hot summers, with only short intermediate seasons; farmers here primarily produce grains (wheat, barley, rye and corn) but also grow potatoes, beets, and grapes (wine-making is widespread) and raise pigs, sheep, and some cattle.

The population of the East European countries is a nonhomogenized blend of ethnic Slavs, Turko-Tatars, Mongols, Greeks, and descendants of Finnish and Germanic tribes; more than 60 ethnic groups are represented.

The greatest bond among the East Europeans is their speech—more than 300 million people speak a Slavic language. However, the cultural rift emerges even here: The Bulgarians, Russians, Ukrainians, Byelorussians, Serbs, and Macedonians use the Cyrillic alphabet, while the western Slavs—Poles, Czechs, Slovaks, Croats, and Slovenes—write in the Roman alphabet, reflecting their Roman Catholic background. The two non-Slavic languages in the region are Romanian, which, like French, Spanish, Italian, and Latin, is a Romance language; and Magyar, or Hungarian, a language that is part of the Finnish-Ugric family.

THE HISTORY

About 3,000 years ago, the Scythians left Asia and worked their way west. A series of Asiatic armies—Huns, Avars, Magyars, and other Turco-Altaic tribes—pushed into Germany and the Balkans, bringing Chinese noodles, red meat, soured dough, and the indispensable *kasha* (a buckwheat grain) into the fruit-heavy Prussian and Byzantine diet. Meanwhile, the Norsemen, who lent their name to the region— Varangians, sometimes called "Rus" or "Rhos"—instilled the practices of salting and smoking fish.

By the ninth century, Kiev, on the trade route between Scandinavia and Constantinople, became a major commercial center and spice market; this is one reason why cardamom, cinnamon, and ginger were known in the north. Potatoes and oils were imported through Poland from Scandinavia and Italy.

But just after the turn of the thirteenth century, Genghis Khan stormed through Persia, Russia, Eastern Europe, and the Balkans; within decades the Mongols had left their culinary marks all across Russia, particularly the use of yogurt, sweet fermented alcoholic drinks, boiled meats, and a variety of bread and pasta products from the steppes. To the south, the Byzantine Empire, Bulgaria, Serbia, and central Hungary fell to the Ottoman Turks, who preferred spitted meats and pilafs to fruit-sweetened stews.

At the beginning of the eighteenth century, when Peter the Great became determined to bring Russia into full commerce with the rest of the European world, Russia was suddenly launched on an almost unprecedented culinary binge.

Peter imported European-trained chefs, a practice that became routine among Russian aristocracy. (Alexander I's personal chef was the celebrated French gastronome Careme, the father of "grande cuisine," who had already worked for Talleyrand and turned the future King George IV down to cook for Baron Rothschild.) Over the next decades, the influx of Dutch, French, and German dishes; the introduction of vegetables such as potatoes, asparagus, and lettuce; and the techniques of making sauces, mincing meats, and blending pastry transformed the Russian cuisine forever.

Devouring the Black Sea territories of the faltering Ottoman Empire, Russia also grabbed up fields of bell peppers, tomatoes, and eggplant. So successful was the synthesis that under Catherine the Great, Russia was the chief power and social presence of continental Europe, and Russian-style banquets—particularly the ornate appetizer courses called *zakouski*—were all the rage.

Poland had an early advantage in the culinary competition. Like France, it had the benefit of a food-savvy Italian queen—Bona Sforza of Milan, who in the fifteenth century married the Polish heir Sigismund and brought along pasta and ice cream with her dowry. But in the eighteenth and nineteenth centuries, Poland was annexed right off the map, gradually devoured by Russia on the east and Austria and Prussia to the west. As a result of these enforced alliances, Polish cuisine adopted German-style smoked meats and pastries and learned to produce desserts that rivaled those of the Viennese.

Hungary, too, owes Italy a culinary debt and a queen: Beatrice of Naples, who married King Matthias I during the country's late-fifteenth-century height. (It's a good thing that Italy had so many duchys, so many princesses, and so many royal cooks to spare.) The advent of pasta and the whisking of meat juices into cream sauces dates from her arrival. The next great influx of ingredients arrived with the Turks, who conquered central Hungary in the sixteenth century; they introduced not only pilafs, flatbreads, eggplant, and phyllo dough (which opened the way to the great tortes and strudels of Budapest), but also the tomatoes, paprika chilies, and corn they traded the Spanish and Portuguese for. And last came the

Habsburgs, who matched the pastry dough of the Middle East with the sweetened cream, chocolate, and spun sugar of Vienna.

Romania, Yugoslavia, and Bulgaria retain much stronger ties to their Turkish and Middle Eastern neighbors—moussaka, kebab, bourek, baklava, ayran, and other Turkish favorites are rather common—and even incorporate a few Mediterranean flourishes.

Though Russia is dominated by Christians, who fast but are permitted all foods at other times, in the south and central regions there are many Muslims, whose dietary taboos, primarily pork, are consistent. There are also still strong traces of Jewish kosher-inspired cuisine in the Eastern European areas.

THE CUISINES

To a great extent, the evolution of the region's cuisines parallels those protracted and uneasy meetings of East and West—Europe vs. Asia, Roman vs. Byzantine, Turkic vs. Germanic. Here the medieval European fascination with sauce and display meets the crude vitality (and protein) of those meat-and-bread-wolfing Tatars who conquered the known world.

There are two great paradoxes in traditional Russian cuisine: The first is the almost unequaled abundance of wild game and fowl, conflicting with the huge number of fast days—250 of them—mandated by the Russian Orthodox Church, which banned not only meat but also milk or eggs. Fortunately, the region's seas and rivers produce great numbers of fish, particularly sturgeon (source of the almost mystically prized caviar), salmon, sable, mackerel, shad, whitefish, carp, pike—including Hungary's famous fogas—and trout, along with crawfish, eels, frogs, and oysters.

The other paradox is the cheerful eclecticism of its starches—the Middle Eastern grains, the European potato, and the quintessentially Oriental dumplings, noodles, and kasha.

In medieval times, Russian foods—not just large cuts of meats, such as legs or roasts, but vegetables, poultry, and fish as well—were cooked whole, not chopped or sliced. And since the Russian wood-burning "stove" was usually only an oven built into the wall of one room and extended as a bed platform and heater into the next, there was no direct-heat cooking, either; meals were braised or boiled or baked. Hence the preference for stuffed and poached or boiled noodles and dumplings over the long, fast-boiled noodles adopted elsewhere. Fish could be smoked in separate smokehouses, or they were even more commonly salted and brined—again, caviar.

Not until Peter the Great's forcible Europeanization of Russia did stove-top cooking become known (or even possible). Then the grinding and chopping of meats became almost a national pastime. And the methods of making egg-dough pastry that Russians learned from their European tutors transformed their braised and baked meat dishes into the glorious variety of *pirogi, kulebiaki,* and *pirozhki* that became signature dishes. Most Russian/Polish sauces are French transplants, particularly the white béchamels, salad dressings, and cheese sauces; sour cream and yogurt are used primarily as toppings, not as ingredients.

Among other regional distinctions: The Turkish strain, and the fondness for grilling meats, remains more important in the southern regions. While Hungarians cook sour cream into a recipe, Polish cooks generally stir sour cream into a dish after it has been removed from the heat and just before serving.

THE MAIN INGREDIENTS

SEASONINGS The most important herbs and spices in the northern regions are parsley, dill, horseradish, bay leaves, cloves, pepper, and mustard. Onions and mushrooms are used widely for flavor, but garlic is used very sparingly, particularly in Poland (maybe Dracula should have relocated). In Georgia, which served as a stopping-off point for caravans trading between Venice and Baghdad, such eastern herbs as basil, cardamom, bayberry, coriander, marigold, cinnamon, allspice, and ginger are popular; even peanuts, which came in from Indonesia, crop up sometimes.

Paprika, Hungary's most famous spice, is a cayenne brought to Central Europe via the Byzantine trade. (Just as corn was mistakenly called "the Turkish grain," the cayenne was sometimes referred to as "Turkish pepper.") Around the seventeenth century, some of the heat was bred out, and a deep color and fuller flavor bred in: True Hungarian paprika is far more aromatic and pungent than the adulterated powder that used to pass for it in the United States. It's interesting to note, however, that the Hungarians were already rubbing raw meat with black pepper, both to preserve and flavor it, even before cayenne was introduced. The poppy seed is a Turkish innovation too, quite common in Eastern European cooking.

EGGS AND DAIRY PRODUCTS

Yogurt, sour cream, *smetana* (which is a sort of half-sour cream, lighter than American sour cream), and cottage cheese are among the staples in the East European cuisines. Eggs are used most frequently as an ingredient in doughs and pastries; when they are cooked separately, even as a layer in *kulebiaka*, they are usually hard-cooked. In Bulgaria, cheese is brined just as it is in Greece to make feta.

GRAINS AND BREADS

The usual juxtaposition of fairly rich soil and a relatively harsh climate early on made Poland, the Baltic States, and Western Russia heavily dependent on cereal crops, including rye, barley, wheat, and millet, but the most important grain has always been buckwheat. The nutty kasha groats, which serve as stuffing, side dish, and entree, remain Russia's characteristic grain; it's used as rice is used elsewhere, as a sort of risotto and in stuffings. True rice comes in a distant second and is usually called for in recipes derived from Turkish or sometimes French dishes. Cornmeal is common in Romania, where it is served as a mush or polenta called *mamaliga*.

Hard-Hearted Fare

One of the regional distinctions involves the cooking fats. In Georgia, for example, housewives use a clarified butter called *erbo* that seems to bridge the gap between India's ghee to Morocco's smee. (So, incidentally, does the Hungarian practice of sautéing the paprika into the onions before the meat is added.) Around the Baltic, butter and cream are extremely common. Traditional Czech recipes called for bacon grease; in Hungary, with its strong Turkish influence, olive oil dominates. Hungarians, displaying the Viennese influence, are fond of richer flavors in general: They specialize in gamey wild boar and venison and the fattier pork; they prefer to cook with lard or goose fat rather than oil; and they thicken virtually all stews with either a flour-lard roux or sour cream—or both.

The breads of Eastern Europe, particularly the dark rye, caraway-flavored loaves, and wheat breads, are used not just as sandwiches or side dishes but in soups and sauces; the French refer to a topping of fried bread crumbs as "à la Polonaise." Russian and Bulgarian breads are generally leavened, while the Hungarians are addicted to a deep-fried and garlic-topped flatbread called *langos* that is purely Mongolian. And a popular Polish snack is *zapiekanka*, which is very like the "French bread" pizzas with mushrooms and cheese.

VEGETABLES AND FRUITS Produce that can be preserved for year-round consumption, either in cold storage or by pickling, are the most common. Beets (essential for borscht), cabbage, cucumbers, eggplant, mushrooms, potatoes and tomatoes (which were both introduced in the late sixteenth century), onions, peas, lentils, kohlrabi, turnips, brussels sprouts, savoy cabbage, and cauliflower are plentiful; the more westerly regions also grow spinach, sorrel, and vegetable marrow (what we call zucchini). Wild mushrooms are so essential to the Polish diet that they, rather than fish, were the usual meat substitute on Catholic fast days. In the south, Turkish eggplant, squashes, pomegranates, dates, and figs are plentiful. Preserved lemons, pickled watermelon rind, and pear and plum preserves remain popular. Sour cherries, raspberries, and gooseberries in particular are used for desserts and for a variety of strong, sweet liqueurs.

FISH AND SEAFOOD The prized sturgeon (source of caviar), salmon, pike, carp, and herring are far and away the most important fish in Eastern European fare. The original "gefilte" ("stuffed") fish was a whole pike or carp that was cooked, the meat and bones removed, and then the meat stuffed back into the skin.

GAME BIRDS AND OTHER POULTRY Wildfowl are particularly popular in classic Russian and Eastern European cuisine, among them pheasant, partridge, duck, quail, grouse, goose, turkey, chicken, guinea fowl, and even (for really elaborate banquets) crane, swans, and peacocks.

MEATS Thanks to the breadth and variety of topography, meat dishes cover the spectrum, from game (including rabbit and hare, reindeer, elk, venison, and bear) to the lighter meats, such as veal and suckling pig, and the heavier ones, such as beef, smoked pork, and mutton. Organ meats are relatively popular, particularly in Hungary, where brains and kidneys are not only used in stews but also ground and stuffed inside dumplings; and in Poland, where tripe and fried goose livers are specialties.

THE MAIN DISHES

SOUPS The most famous recipes from the region are borscht, the hot or cold beet soup (called *borszcz* in Polish); and the Hungarian *Szegedi halaszbe*, a fish chowder named for the city that reputedly perfected it. Bread soups, such as the rye meal mash often served at breakfast or lunch in Poland, are common. Other common soups include *kharcho*, the Armenian meat and vegetable stew related to Hungary's heavier *harcho* (see below); Polish barley and split-pea soup; bouillons with or without dumplings; and cream soups of potato, cauliflower, sorrel, and dried beans or peas. Cold fruit soups are also popular, particularly in Hungary and Poland. A chicken and vermicelli soup with chicken liver dumplings is another Polish favorite.

DUMPLINGS, PIES, AND OTHER DOUGHY DELIGHTS The doughs—pies, pastries, crêpes, and especially the dumplings and ravioli—of Russian and Eastern European cooking are ubiquitous; they can also be hard to differentiate. Some are divided by size: *Pirog* refers to a large pie, big enough to cut, while *pirozhki* (*pierogi* in Polish) are little pies, usually half-moon shaped, that can be held in the hand. *Pyshki* are also small but square and deep-fried. Some are classified by dough type and some by stuffing. Yugoslavian *bourek* (i.e., the Turkish *borek*) and Bulgarian *banitza* are pastry-dough pies stuffed with cheese or sometimes meat. *Kreplach* are Jewish egg-dough dumplings stuffed with meat, chicken, or cheese; the word is probably derived from "crêpe." Some dumplings are nicknamed by shape: *Rastegai*, the nickname for canoe-shaped pastries pinched together at the ends but with the stuffing exposed in the middle, means "unbuttoned." Some are boiled, some are fried, and some might be served either way.

There are other dough substitutes as well. Polish and Lithuanian chefs are famous for their *latkes* (potato pancakes) and *knishes* (potato turnovers), as well as the potato pudding, made with noodles in Germany, called *kugel*. The Hungarian *tarhonya* is a granulated pastry, something like

Oh, Garçon!

One of the surprises of classic Russian cuisine is that the presumably "French" table etiquette dictating service and presentation is not French at all but Russian; in fact, this etiquette replaced the French style in the late eighteenth century. "Service a la française" was a medieval hangover in which harried teams of servants laid out dozens of dishes in three major stages; first the soups, hors d'oeuvres, and fish; then the meats, roasts, large and small fowl, savory pies, and vegetables; and, finally, the sweets. Admittedly, the arrival of castle guests was somewhat less prompt or predictable in those days, but a great many dishes spent too much time congealing, melting, or souring. The "service a la russe," which the French admitted was an improvement in quality and control, assigned a waiter to a table of 10 or 12 seated guests, whom he served one dish at a time—soup, fish, meat, salad—offering the food from the left and removing plates from the right.

Name That Noodle

When it comes to dumplings and such, near-identical names can breed confusion. Russian *pelmeni* are small, noodle-dough ravioli stuffed with potatoes, cheese, ground beef, cabbage, or mushrooms; they can be served either boiled in soup or fried with sour cream (Siberians prefer to use a mustard or vinegar dressing). The Russian *pirogi* are large, rectangular, brioche-style pastry doughs stuffed with meat, fish, or kasha and mushrooms. The Polish *pierogi* aren't *pirogi*, however—they are what Russians call *pelmeni*. So are the Ukranian *vareniki*, although they are more likely to be cheese-stuffed noodles, like Afghani aushak—but *valeniki* are cheese-stuffed *blini* (buckwheat pancakes or crêpes) rolled up and deep-fried. *Kulebiaka* (or coulebiac in the French style) is another large pie, a double-crust layering of salmon, rice, and either hard-boiled eggs or filet of salmon or sturgeon. Polish *kulebiac* may be fish, but it may also be cabbage. *Kurnik* is another piroghi, this time with a chicken and hard-boiled egg stuffing. The Russian *pirozhki* and the Hungarian *piroshki* are, fortunately, the same—a pastry-dough turnover filled with ground meat or perhaps shredded cabbage and rice and deep-fried.

the Greek orzo, made by forcing noodle dough through a sieve; it is then cooked like rice. The dumpling doughs themselves can become stuffings or, rolled in bread crumbs and deep-fried, croquettes (or *kromeskis*), although croquettes more often contain a nugget of chicken, fish, ham, or pâté. Almost anything stuffed can be fried in this culture: Polish *golomaki* are stuffed cabbage rolls that are breaded and fried. The utmost in cholesterol indulgence might be *bourreki*, dumplings of thickened béchamel sauce mixed with cheese, rolled into balls, encased in noodle dough, rolled in eggwash and breadcrumbs, and then fried.

MEATS Old French and Russian court dishes still intermingle: A Russian menu is as apt to include chateaubriand, venison, rabbit, or Stroganov. Hungarians still like to roast on spits, using whole joints or fowl and carving them rather than cutting them up for the skewer. Hungarians also have one specialty with a characteristically Persian flavoring—the mutton stew called *harcho*, which is flavored with pickled plums.

Kebabs, called *raznijici*, are popular in Romania; the ground-meat type is called *lule* (*cebapčici* in Yugoslavia). Romanians also like mixed grills called *mititei*, which combine cigar-shaped lule with smoked beef and bacon. *Shashliks* are thinly pounded, marinated, then skewered and grilled; relatives of the donner kebabs, they are often served with purely Persian pilafs.

Polish cuisine displays its German-Austrian history in its sausages, particularly the garlicky kielbasa (or *kolbasz*), and its smoked meats. Similarly, Transylvania's old ties to Hungary show up most vividly in a layered casserole of rice, sauerkraut, smoked sausage, pork, bacon, hard-boiled eggs, sour cream, and onions fried with paprika.

STEWS Perhaps the most famous Hungarian family of dishes is what in the United States is interchangeably called paprikash or goulash. Correctly speaking, goulash (or *gulyas* or *gylyas* or *goulasch*) is a soup: The word "gulyas" means "cowboy," and it was originally a sort of bunkhouse special. It generally has the paprika added via the lard-flour roux as thickening and may include potatoes or noodles (or both). Paprikash contains no starches, just fried onions, meat (pork, veal, beef, or chicken), paprika, and herbs, plus sour cream—pretty much the opposite of the way generations of American cookbooks have it. *Pörköit* is paprikash without sour cream. *Tokany* is a variation on paprikash with thinly sliced meat (and perhaps more than one type of meat). *Szekel gylyas* is a pork and sauerkraut version.

The Polish national dish is *bogos* or "hunter's stew," a glorified leftover of mixed meats or sausages, sauerkraut, mushrooms, apples, and tomatoes; "Warsaw-style" stew ups the ante with red wine and potatoes. And the kosher prohibitions against cooking on the Jewish Sabbath are traditionally satisfied by preparing one-pot stews the day before and allowing them to sit until sundown; they are generally combinations of meat, barley, potatoes, and beans.

POULTRY AND FOWL Chicken can be given a paprikash sauce, too, but it is more frequently served as *koltetki*, ground and seasoned then breaded and fried; or *tabaka*, whole marinated game hens pressed and grilled. Polish-style roast chicken has a rich mushroom, herb, breadcrumb, and onion dressing stuffed under the skin as well as into the cavity. Wild-

> ## What's in a Name?
>
> So: Beef Stroganov is a dish of beef, cut in strips, sautéed, and then sauced with a mixture of mustard (preferably Dijon), sour cream, and tomato paste. Chicken Kiev is breast meat with pockets cut in to hold extra butter and parsley, all rolled in fine bread crumbs and sautéed in more butter. Steak tartare is probably just that—knife-minced raw beef on bread, perfect for the Tartar warrior on the run. The so-called veal Orlov isn't really Russian at all but French; named in admiration of the five brothers who put Catherine the Great on the throne, it's roast veal served with truffles and asparagus. Careme did invent charlotte russe, a ladyfingers and Bavarian creme dessert, but he was in Paris at the time. And the Polish mushroom–sour cream dish called *po Nelsonsku* is named for Lord Nelson, the hero of Trafalgar, but no one knows why.

fowl may be dressed with berries, preserved citrus, or even Persian-style walnut sauce. Various "continental" duck dishes, usually with sour-fruit sauces, are very common; roast goose is, too, though less likely to appear on menus in the United States.

BEVERAGES Even the popular drinks reveal the region's multiplicity of influences: tea from China via Siberia and Central Asia; *kefir*, a fermented milk of Mongol ancestry; coffee from Peter's European wanderings; and wine and grapes from the Middle East and France. Vodka, of course, is the Russian national drink, distilled from potatoes, wheat, and occasionally rye. (The Russian fondness for strong drink is nothing new: A sixteenth-century book describes the frequent banquets as involving Greek and Italian wines, both cold and hot; beer and the sweet beer-like *kvass;* brandy; and a variety of fruit liqueurs.) Polish vodkas, too, are superior, and increasingly popular in the United States, though the Poles traditionally drink beer with meals. Hungary produces many fine wines, the best-known being white Tokay, and an apricot spirit called *barack*. Bulgarian and Romanian red table wines are increasingly popular as inexpensive table wines here.

ZAKOUSKI

The zakouski are the smorgasbord of Russia and Poland (where the word is *zakąski*) and for centuries were served to announce a host's prosperity as well as his generosity. They were also polite excuses for extending the cocktail hour. The zakouski course became the rage in the rest of Europe as well, and they may represent the beginning of the great caviar craze.

Like a smorgasbord, the zakouski were more than hors d'oeuvres, although they were sometimes preliminary to a full dinner; the table itself comprised a banquet, and there were unspoken (and sometimes spoken) rules of etiquette that dictated its laying out and provisioning. Among typical zakouski were cold meats, ranging from cold cuts to cold roast fowl to steak tartare; chicken, pigs' feet, fish, eggs, ham, and even asparagus and brains in aspic; jellied pork and veal and pâtés and liver terrines; pickled beets, mushrooms, or gherkins; boiled salmon with mayonnaise, horseradish, or "Greek" (tomato-vegetable) sauce; hard-cooked eggs; sautéed mushrooms; and greens, kidneys, tripe dumplings, herrings (what Chekhov called "the finest zakouska of all"), sardines, anchovies, meatballs, and multiple kinds of caviar and breads, laid out with dozens of garnishes, mustard, horseradish, and chopped onion.

Blini are a descendent of zakouski, and one that is particularly popular in the United States. Buckwheat crêpes are brushed with melted butter and topped with caviar or sour cream—but not both in combination, an American corruption—and then rolled and served with more melted butter; other fillings include hard-cooked eggs, smoked salmon, salted herring, or other fish.

HOW TO ORDER AND EAT LIKE A NATIVE

Traditionally, Russians ate four meals a day: breakfast at about 8 a.m., consisting of buns, open-faced sandwiches, and cold cuts; a substantial lunch of fish, meat or vegetable casseroles, crêpes and perhaps dumplings, at 1 p.m.; the multicourse dinner (and primary social meal) at 6 p.m., which would involve at least three or four courses, beginning with the zakouski, even without company; and, at 9 p.m., an almost immediate last supper of pirozhki and desserts. Here most restaurants limit themselves to a half-dozen zakouski, and you may be able to order a preassembled platter with several types.

Caviar at a restaurant is apt to be fairly expensive, but if you order blini you'll get a good sampling automatically and a more filling dish for the money. Blini, as mentioned, are dressed with melted butter and either sour cream or caviar, but not both. In the old days, plain blini (or bliny) might be rolled up, dipped in butter, and popped straight into the mouth (although that was considered macho or unpolished); but nowadays they are rolled up (preferably with two spoons, in the French fashion) and eaten with knife and fork. An order of blini is probably enough

Rainbow Roe

Many menus list a variety of caviars in an even greater variety of prices. Most caviar ranges from jet black to a dark brownish green, but gray and golden caviars are rare and highly prized. The best is marked *malossol*, which means slightly salted and refers to fresh (unripe) roe. (Actually, no caviar worth its name will be very salty.) Beluga has the largest grains; sevruga is the finest; and osetra is the most intensely flavored. Although you may see salmon, lumpfish (the red caviar often used in America), cod, or other kinds of caviar listed, the term "caviar" or "caviare" by itself can only mean sturgeon roe. Since the sushi boom, it has become easy to get the crunchy flying fish roe as well. Incidentally, true caviar is not kosher.

for two people to share; four diners should also order pelmeni or pierogi and borscht. For main courses, look for kulebiaka, roasted game, or wild-fowl; and beef lovers should take the chance to order Stroganov or steak tartare—nobody does it better.

Polish restaurants will also have a variety of stuffed dumplings and smoked or pickled meats and fish to start, and they may have smaller kulebiakis to be shared. Duck with apples is a classic dish, and there are many fine rabbit stews and ragouts as well; but the Polish are also mas-ters of frequently overlooked organ dishes, such as brains and livers. In a Hungarian restaurant you will probably find a soup with dumplings and some type of perogi; for a main course, look for a veal goulash or paprikash, wild game (particularly boar), and goose or duck.

These meaty cuisines are suited to the hearty red wines of the region (the Hungarian wines aren't called "bull's blood" for nothing). Russians like the stronger and sweeter fortified sherries and ports and brandies. They drink a great deal of tea brewed strong and diluted to taste with hot water.

COOKING AT HOME

A zakouski party is a great idea and can be the entire buffet if you like. Marinated mushrooms, pickled eggs, herring, cold ham or smoked turkey, and fish mousse or aspic is typical. And no party would be com-plete without at least some caviar.

Caviar should be kept cold until a few minutes before serving, and the entire container or bowl should be set in ice. You could even lay out a color wheel of caviars without going into bankruptcy if you are willing to pass on the very finest grades: Lumpfish roe is actually beigey-gray but is usually dyed either black or red, and it's not very flavorful. Cod roe is pink; salmon roe is orangey-red; whitefish is often golden (though not to be confused with the Iranian gold); flying fish roe is a deeper scarlet; and many new varieties from China and even the United States are pearly gray. (Unopened caviar will last several months and can even be carefully frozen; however, once opened, caviar should be contact-covered with plas-tic wrap and eaten within three or four days.)

Use small bone, lacquer, tortoise, shell, ivory, glass, or even wooden utensils to serve caviar, as silver gives it a metallic tang. Serve with toast triangles or fancy but not strongly flavored crackers and set out wedges of lemon, chopped hard-boiled egg, and sour cream. Other hors d'oeuvres that could be topped with caviar include small new potatoes cooled and cut in half or stuffed with sour cream; potato pancakes; beef or tuna carpaccio; or artichoke bottoms. The traditional beverages would be champagne, vodka, and aquavit.

Vodka is served ice-cold (it will not freeze, so the bottle can be left in the freezer compartment or even frozen inside blocks of ice in clean milk cartons), but not over ice, as the texture would be affected. You can buy vodkas flavored with hot pepper, caraway, saffron, anise, garlic, dill, lemon, cherry, even buffalo grass, but it's just as simple to pepper your own by dropping a jalapeño or even white or black peppercorns into the bottle and letting it steep anywhere from four days to two weeks, depending on your daring.

The Polish traditionally drink vodka with hors d'oeuvres but beer with dinner. Beer is served in small tumblers, not huge mugs. Coffee is served after dinner, never with.

Incidentally, although most U.S. restaurants serve beef Stroganov over rice or buttered noodles, it was traditionally presented over very thick, fried potato wedges.

BEEF STROGANOV

1 1/2 pounds sirloin tip or filet
salt and pepper to taste
1 1/2 tablespoons flour
oil for cooking
butter (optional)
1 medium onion, chopped
1 cup bouillon or beef stock
2 teaspoons Dijon or Pommery mustard
1 1/2 tablespoons tomato paste
1/2 cup sour cream
minced parsley for garnish

Cut the beef into longish strips about 1/4-inch thick, season with salt and pepper, and sprinkle with flour. In a heavy-bottomed skillet, heat 1 tablespoon oil and 1 tablespoon butter (if you are using it) and begin browning beef in batches—only one layer at a time in the skillet—and remove browned meat to a plate. (Do not cook through; leave rare or medium.) Repeat, adding a little oil and butter as needed, until all the beef has been sautéed; then add a little more oil and sauté onions until golden. Add stock, stir in mustard and tomato paste, and simmer until thickened; return beef to skillet and simmer for only 3 to 5 minutes. Remove from heat, stir in sour cream, adjust seasoning, and sprinkle with parsley.

Variations: Less expensive and/or leaner cuts of beef, such as rump roast or round steak can be used, but for these cuts you should increase the simmering time about 15 minutes or until the meat is tender. The oldest Russian recipes use less sour cream; Polish versions use more. Many people also like sliced mushrooms in their Stroganov; if so, sauté them with the onions to reduce liquid. Other optional seasonings include a splash of red wine or brandy and a dash of Worcestershire sauce.

BEEF SHASHLIK

1/2 cup dry red wine
juice of 1/2 lemon or 1 small lime
8 cloves garlic, minced
1 small onion, minced
1 tablespoon peppercorns, crushed
3 pounds boneless lamb or beef sirloin, cut in 1 1/2-inch cubes
3 small onions, cut into wedges
3 sweet peppers, seeded and cut into wedges
12–15 large mushrooms (optional)
12–15 cherry tomatoes or 3 tomatoes, cut into wedges (optional)
olive oil or vegetable oil spray
salt to taste

Combine wine, lemon or lime juice, minced garlic and onion, and peppercorns, and marinate meat in refrigerator for 8 hours or overnight. Return to room temperature before cooking. Toss onions, pepper wedges, mushrooms, and cherry tomatoes (if you are using them) with olive oil or spray to coat; pat meat cubes slightly and alternate meat and vegetables on metal skewers. Grill or broil skewers, basting with marinade; serve with rice.

PART II

AFRICA

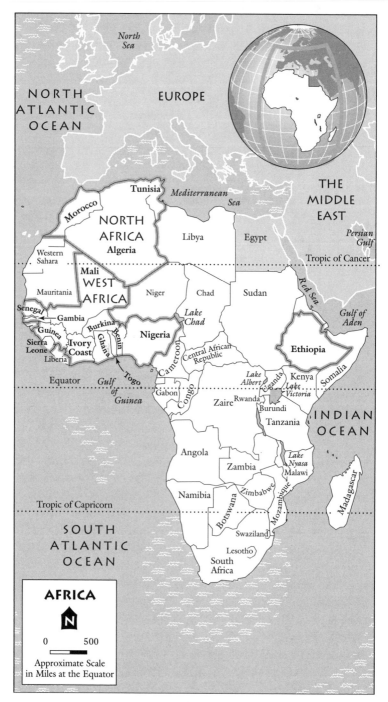

North
Sea

NORTH
ATLANTIC
OCEAN

EUROPE

THE
MIDDLE
EAST

Tunisia   *Mediterranean*
                Sea

Morocco

NORTH
AFRICA
Algeria

Libya

Egypt

*Persian
Gulf*

Western
Sahara

Tropic of Cancer

Mali
WEST
AFRICA

Mauritania

Niger

Chad

Sudan

Red Sea

*Gulf of
Aden*

Senegal

Gambia

Guinea

Burkina

Benin

Nigeria

*Lake
Chad*

Sierra
Leone

**Ivory
Coast**

Ghana

Cameroon

Central African
Republic

Ethiopia

Liberia

Togo

Equator   *Gulf
of
Guinea*

Gabon

Congo

Zaire

*Lake
Albert*

Uganda

Rwanda

Burundi

Tanzania

*Lake
Victoria*

Kenya

Somalia

INDIAN
OCEAN

Angola

Zambia

*Lake
Nyasa*

Malawi

Namibia

Botswana

Zimbabwe

Mozambique

Madagascar

Tropic of Capricorn

SOUTH
ATLANTIC
OCEAN

Swaziland

Lesotho

South
Africa

AFRICA

N

0   500

Approximate Scale
in Miles at the Equator

NORTH AFRICA

The most misleading thing about North African restaurants may be the name; for although Morocco, Algeria, and Tunisia are physically locked to the rest of Africa, they are culturally continents apart, their roots one-third in Europe and two-thirds in the Middle East.

These are Mediterranean countries, full partners in the creation of that cuisine, and their inhabitants speak French and Spanish as well as Arabic and Berber. Their rich food, served abundantly and enjoyed communally, conveys a panoply of civilizations. The Phoenicians brought in Lebanese wheat, Indian sugarcane, and Syrian olives and lentils and carried back Tunisian dates; they were also probably the first to sample nutmeg and cinnamon from Malaysia. The Carthaginians adopted West African okra and peanuts; the Persians tasted Afghani yogurt and mixed it with African honey and Asian almonds. The Greeks discovered Egyptian rice and traded it for lemons; the Romans transplanted Indian eggplants and dosed themselves with Indonesian garlic; the Moors planted orange trees in Spain. The Arabs imitated Mongol kebabs with Spanish mutton and Basque wildfowl and alternated Chinese tea with Ethiopian coffee.

In Tunis and Algiers, the North Africans exchanged Lebanese garbanzos and Armenian melons for Italian sardines and French carrots. The Arabs carried the date palm (and palm oil) to Indonesia and Southeast Asia. Once the Spanish returned from the New World with tomatoes, potatoes, and chilies, Mediterranean cuisine was nearly complete.

THE COUNTRIES

North Africa is topographically as well as historically part of Europe: The Atlas Mountains, which occupy most of the region, are part of the Alpine chain. Most of the arable areas are near the coast; the mountains and dune areas gradually give way in the south to the Sahara.

Morocco remains the most ethnically mixed area; the official language there, as elsewhere in North Africa, is Arabic (the Alamite dynasty, established in 1660, remains on the throne), but many residents also speak Spanish, French, or Berber. The main crops are olives, fruit, grapes, and grain, and there is some industrial fishing as well.

Algeria is larger than its two neighbors, but much of the arid Saharan south is suitable only for livestock grazing. Algeria's principal crops are wheat, barley, potatoes, citrus fruits, tomatoes, tobacco, figs, and dates, as well as olives and grapes. Tunisia, the most easterly of the three, has the lowest average elevations, and agriculture is successful enough there to drive the economy, although petroleum strikes have shifted the emphasis to industrial development. Livestock—sheep, poultry, goats, and cattle—are all common.

THE HISTORY

Beginning halfway across the north coast of Africa and stretching just around the curve of its left hip, Tunisia, Algeria, and Morocco were settled by Berbers. These are a mysterious ancient people variously said to be related to the Phoenicians, Celts, Basques, and Canaanites, and referred to in Egyptian wall paintings dating to about 2400 B.C.E. There are still several million Berber-speaking inhabitants of the North African region, and it is they who lent their name to the Barbary Coast, not the "barbarian" mercenaries of medieval pirate fleets.

The Phoenicians established trading ports along the coast in the twelfth century B.C.E., gradually extending their influence inland. The

Carthaginians, Phoenician "colonials" who created their own empire in Tunis about 700 years later, were also great sea traders and brought immense wealth to the region, eventually dominating most of the western Mediterranean. But beginning in the third century B.C.E., the Punic Wars (from the Roman term for "Phoenicians") turned the balance of power toward Rome, and by the time of Emperor Claudius, North Africa was Roman territory.

The Berbers had remained more or less unaffected by a millennium of Phoenician rule; they rather prospered under its Roman successors. Rome invested heavily in roads and aqueducts in the region and planted groves of olives and dates and citrus fruits. The Roman occupation was so successful that the Berbers were widely converted to Christianity— St. Augustine was Algerian—and remained Christian for several hundred years, through the division of the Roman empire into the European order and the Byzantine.

However, the great Muslim Arab invasions of the seventh and eighth centuries marked a sea change in the Berber culture. The majority of the Berbers converted to Sunni Islam, and they became so prominent a part of the great westward Islamic expansion that the Spanish term for their Islamic conquerors, Moors, actually derives from "Moroccan." (And despite Shakespeare's description, very few Moors were either literally Arab or even particularly dark-skinned.) During their centuries in Spain, the Moors transmitted so much of their agricultural and culinary knowledge to the Iberians that the ethnocentric French developed the saying, "Africa begins just south of the Pyrenees."

The Moors were finally driven back into North Africa, and after generations of invasions and counterinvasions, the empires finally settled into a somewhat uneasy coexistence. Beginning in the nineteenth century, the tactical importance of North Africa drew successive waves of British, French, Spanish, Italian, and Maltese colonizers. France and Spain ultimately agreed on a division of power, and French and Spanish people are still the primary European minorities in North Africa.

THE CUISINE

The formal cuisine of North Africa is almost an oxymoron, as it is primarily a matter of family recipes, handed down orally from mother to daughter (cooks are almost uniformly female) and still susceptible to melting-pot influences. The staple carbohydrate of North African food is *couscous*, a semolina or millet meal that is not only nutritious but also cooks quickly and is increasingly popular as a rice alternative in the United States. In fact, couscous (the word can refer either to the pasta alone or to a prepared dish involving chicken, lamb, and vegetables) is far and away the best-known regional dish, eaten at least twice a week in the average North African home and popular not only in France—so popular that many French restaurants in the United States offer it at least once a week—but also in Greece and Turkey and even as far away as Brazil.

Here, as in Ethiopia, the cooking technique defines the dish. Whether the main ingredient is lamb, chicken, or fish, it can be boiled (i.e., for couscous), steamed (in which case it is usually called *choua*), or stewed (into *tajines*).

Dishes are eaten by (the right) hand, using bread as a scoop and sauce mop, which explains why no place settings are needed, although restaurants in the United States will supply them on request. The one possible exception is couscous, which in some areas is eaten with a spoon. Because recipes are generally family variations passed down by word of mouth, there are almost no measuring cups or spoons, either. Large ladles, either worked metal or wood, are used for stirring the pot and turning the dish out on the table. Otherwise, North Africans basically get by with butcher and utility knives, a mortar and pestle for spices, perhaps a spatula or perforated spoon, and a charcoal brazier or plain open fire.

THE MAIN INGREDIENTS

SEASONINGS The most characteristic condiments are a pair of chili pastes: a wetter one called *harisa* (or *harissa*), which combines chilies, garlic, coriander, caraway, salt, olive oil, and sometimes lemon juice; and a dry paste, more popular in Tunisia, called *ras el hanut*, which uses roasted red chilies, black pepper, cinnamon, and cloves. Its Indian influence is striking, so on American menus it is often confusingly identified as curry—particularly in the case of "shrimp curry"—although some North African restaurants do make Indian-style cumin and lemon dishes. A slightly different dish may also be called *harisa* in Tunisia: Made of roasted tomatoes and chilies, onions, garlic, and coriander, it is usually served as a condiment or appetizer. (In recent years, North Africans have become quite fond of the bottled American and Mexican liquid chili pepper sauces.) However, not all peppers are that hot: Morocco is the source of a high-quality paprika made from a mild, tomato-shaped pepper that is milder than the Hungarian paprika cayenne.

Tewebil is a Tunisian mixed-spice paste of fennel and anise seeds, coriander seeds, caraway, red pepper, and salt. The other most popular flavorings are honey and sugar, wild thyme, coriander, parsley, dill, gray verbena, mint, and *za'atar*, which can either refer to the thyme itself or an intensely aromatic mix of thyme, sumac, sesame seeds, and perhaps marjoram and oregano.

As mentioned, both fruits and vegetables are used as condiments or seasonings, most prominently preserved lemons and limes, dried or brined olives, flower waters (especially rosewater, orange-flower, and verbena), and the oils of various fruits, these fragrant ingredients being among the most evocative remnants of Persian culture.

MEATS AND FISH   Ancient wall paintings show that there was a time, many millennia ago, when the Magreb and Sahara regions were covered by lakes and rivers; the early inhabitants used bows and arrows to bring down gazelles, ostriches, and buffalo. With the global climatic changes, the herds gradually migrated south; now, though the coastal regions are relatively fertile, North Africa's harsh climate—often frigid at night, even though sweltering during the day—make sheep the most adaptable meat source.

Not surprisingly, lamb is far and away the favorite meat, with poultry and other birds such as squab and guinea hen second, and goat a distant third. (Camel meat, once fairly common in the more arid regions, is less common now and not an issue in the United States.) Pork is almost unknown because of the overwhelmingly Muslim—and longtime Jewish minority—population. Game meats may be offered on special occasions. Organ meats, particularly lamb brains, kidneys, and livers, are popular in Africa but more hesitantly offered by restaurants here, although they occasionally appear as sausage; the spicy *merguez*, like a lamb andouille, has caught on not only all around the Mediterranean but with American chefs as well.

Like most seaside cultures, the North African peoples have dried and salted fish since the earliest times, but they are less popular in this region than almost anywhere else and are unlikely to be found in any restaurant. Some fish and shrimp and the occasional shellfish do appear on menus, but most often they reflect—or cater to—a more cosmopolitan attitude.

(The dominant role of meat is by itself a clue to the heavy Middle Eastern influence on this coastal diet.)

Both sheep and goat milk are used for drinking and making cheese, but these are not usually seen on menus in the United States. Eggs are used in making pastry and some stews, but when eaten are most often hard-boiled.

VEGETABLES AND FRUITS Vegetables are most frequently prepared as salads or marinated and served as appetizers or sometimes condiments. They include fennel, beets, and carrots and sometimes their greens; eggplant; red and green chilies; green peppers; squashes; onions; cucumbers; tomatoes; cauliflower; okra; garbanzos; fava beans; and lentils. (Mediterranean lentils, incidentally, are smaller and darker than Indian lentils and do not soften as much in cooking.) Among the fruits, far and away the most important are the olive and its oils and the date, which since earliest times has provided vital nutrients and fiber to the North African diet. However, citrus fruits, particularly lemons and oranges, grapes, figs, watermelons, and pomegranates are also prevalent. Among the nuts and seeds more commonly eaten are almonds, walnuts, chestnuts, sesame seeds, and poppy seeds.

COUSCOUS As we noted above, there are very few cooking utensils in North African cuisine, but the exception is for couscous. The traditional preparation of couscous requires its own dedicated steamer called, not surprisingly, a couscousière. It resembles a double boiler, with the stock (or in the more traditional manner, the main-course stew itself) in the lower pot and the grains in the upper bowl; perforations in the upper tray allow the steam to circulate and the couscous grains to absorb it. (One explanation for the name couscous is that it imitates the sound of steam escaping through the holes.)

Couscousières can be simple ceramic or iron pots or even elaborate copper; some cooks collect them in various sizes, as American cooks might acquire casseroles or saucepans. Interestingly, although Tunisians tend to cover the couscousière, Moroccans and Algerians leave it uncovered; hence, Tunisian couscous tends to be a little softer and moister and the others fluffier. Similarly, Tunisians more frequently mix the couscous directly into the stew before serving, whereas Moroccan and Algerian cooks tend to make a "bowl" of the cooked couscous on the plate and place the stew in the center.

The stew usually mixes lamb, chicken, and such vegetables as potatoes, carrots, onions, and greens; but there are as many variations as there are home cooks. Some are smoky-savory, such as the Djerba-style mixture with a jerky-like preserved lamb, dried sardines, and tewebil; some couscous versions are vegetarian, using fava beans instead of meat; and some are quite sweet, involving dates, raisins, and nuts.

The traditional drink with couscous is buttermilk; but more often these days you will be invited to select a North African wine or beer.

To eat couscous correctly, reach into the platter—everyone eats from a communal dish—using only the thumb, index, and middle finger of the right hand. Collect a small amount of the couscous, enclosing a bite of meat or vegetables if you wish, and roll the food into a ball by pulling it along the plate toward you, then pick up the ball and eat it. Do not touch your fingers to your mouth, however, as that would make the food seem unsanitary.

THE MAIN DISHES

APPETIZERS   Dinner often begins with a soup—a substantial one, not a consommé—and the most popular is *harira*, a lentil soup made with lamb stock and flavored with lemon, onions, parsley, coriander, cinnamon, and perhaps tomatoes. Sometimes it is prepared with noodles; occasionally it is thickened with eggs. The other most popular soup is a spicy and thick garbanzo soup with potatoes, ginger, and lamb or chicken stock.

The Arabic word for soaked bread is "gazpacho," and the Spanish learned it from the Moors, who used it for a version of the Persian *fettoush* of bread soaked in olive oil, lemon, and garlic. The Moors were expelled from Granada just as Columbus was running into North America, so they missed his triumphant return from the New World bearing tomatoes and peppers, which became the heart of Spanish gazpachos, and had to wait a few more decades for traders to tantalize them with chilies.

A family dish, popular particularly among Tunisians, is *brik*, a griddle-fried triangular pastry (or sometimes semolina crêpe) filled with potatoes, onions, harisa, and a raw egg before being folded up and fried or baked; the egg partially cooks inside, leaving the yolk soft and allowing it to play off the hot spices. To eat a brik without getting egg all over your face, in both senses, hold the pastry by two corners, nibble open the third corner and carefully suck the yolk out. (The griddled semolina versions are more likely to come out something like a quesadilla.)

SIDE DISHES Almost any vegetable, whether raw, marinated, or grilled, may appear during a North African meal as a salad. They are usually offered in combinations intended to arouse the palate with displays of color, texture, flavor, and sometimes spice. Carrots may be shredded or grated and tossed with cinnamon, lemon, and honey or slicked with sesame oil and dashed with orange-flower water. Green peppers and tomatoes might be roughly chopped, dressed with olive oil and lemon, and sometimes studded with chilies. Eggplant is usually grilled or baked and then stirred with coriander, lemon, garlic, cumin, and oil—a chunkier adaptation of the Middle Eastern baba ghanouj. Beets are roasted and then dressed with oil and sometimes sugar. The fruit and nut mixes, usually oranges with walnuts and lemon, may sound Persian but get a distinctively Mediterranean twist with the addition of olives.

Any of these salad/condiments, incidentally, may be offered as an appetizer or separate course as well.

MEAT AND POULTRY All meats in North Africa are cooked until the meat falls off the bone, and they can—must—be eaten with the fingers (see the section on couscous above and the section on "How to Order and Eat Like a Native" below). Lamb is most typically spit-roasted (called *mechoui*). Grilling—that is, the Turkish kebab—is a popular style of cooking and is used for chicken or game hens and sometimes skewers of shrimp or, in some of the larger cities or in the United States, beef.

One of the most popular dishes besides couscous is *bastilla* (one of the few dishes to receive varied spellings in America, showing up as *bisteeya* or *bestila*). It is a cross between pastry and chicken pot pie, a flaky phyllo-dough loaf stuffed with layers of squab, game birds or chicken, and a rich confection of ground almonds and sugar, all sprinkled with more sugar.

The most popular type of main-dish stews are *tajines* (or *tagines*), which are sweet-sour meat stews with fruit, a classically Persian combination. Chicken, for example, might be stewed with preserved lemons and olive oil; lamb with prunes or dates, garbanzos and carrots, or honey and almonds. Tajines are slow-cooked in earthenware pots with distinctive conical lids. (Vegetable tajines are common in North Africa, particularly on fast days, and in recent years, the growing interest in healthful eating has made vegetarian versions of both couscous and tajines a little more common in the United States.)

Moroccans in particular are fond of meat salads, really organ-meat appetizers of brains or liver, but these are seldom offered in American restaurants, which depend heavily on set multicourse dinners. Some chefs will, if asked, rustle up kidneys. These are most often grilled and may be skewered.

SWEETS AND BEVERAGES Dessert may be elaborate sweet pastries with almonds or dates or fried couscous drizzled with honey; more frequently, it is "home-style," meaning just a bowl of fruit and nuts.

North Africans most frequently drink a very sweet tea or mint tea with their meals; in Morocco it was considered essential for digestion, particularly of the richer dishes, to drink three glasses, very hot, at the end of dinner. The tea is prepared by the head of the household or his eldest son or even, as an honor, by a male guest; never by women. (Tea is a symbol of hospitality and community; it is drunk all day long, but with attention, not as Americans swig coffee.)

Observant Muslim restaurant owners may not even apply for an alcohol license; but wine is more popular in the United States, and many owners seem to be importing North African Cabernets in bulk.

HOW TO ORDER AND EAT LIKE A NATIVE

North African dining resembles Ethiopian in that bread is the sole utensil and the entire meal is served on a low, hourglass-shaped table. Rather than woven baskets, however, these tables may be elaborately carved and filigreed wood inlaid with mother-of-pearl and, especially at restaurants, may be surrounded by pillow-laden sofas, loveseats, and overstuffed ottomans rather than chairs. Typically, North African restaurants use fabrics in dark reds—burgundy, claret, maroon, brick, and rust—to evoke the traditional rugs and tent hangings.

As at Ethiopian restaurants, too, the use of the fingers for eating leads to an elaborate welcoming ceremony: At a Moroccan dinner, a servant or junior family member will pour water over each guest's hands into a basin and then offer the guest a towel; here, of course, the person performing these services is usually a waiter. In some cases, as in more casually Americanized restaurants, you may be offered a wet washcloth instead of the water cascade; frequently the towel or cloth will be left behind, so that you may use it (subtly) to dab at spills. A variation is the individual water bowl, into which you may dip your fingers between bites.

Meals are served communally; all dishes are placed in the middle of the table, and diners help themselves from the platters. Breads served with the meal may be flattish or roll-shaped pita, plain, anise-, or onion-flavored. Take a whole piece from the basket and put it on your plate, then tear off smaller pieces. You may scoop with it, use it as a palate cleanser, or just squeeze it with your fingers to wipe them clean. If you want to spice things up, reach for the ever-present bowl of harisa and mix it into your stew. (Remember to keep your fingers from touching your mouth.)

The great majority of North African restaurants here offer only a few à la carte dishes; most have set multicourse menus, perhaps a "large" and a "deluxe" as well. Such package meals generally begin with soup and various vegetable salads, followed by bastilla, then a choice of the first main dish (usually chicken or perhaps seafood); then a choice of the second, meatier entree (lamb stew, long-roasted meat, kebab, etc.); and couscous. Remember, there is no meat cooked less than very well done, and the chili adjustments are made individually.

If you can order specific dishes, get one grilled meat, perhaps a kebab platter; one tajine, preferably seasoned with olives or preserved lemons; and split a bastilla. For four, order a dip such as hummus, a vegetable salad, bastilla, one sweet stew, and one hot stew. For even larger groups, definitely order a family-style couscous with sausages or lamb and chicken, raisins, garbanzos, parsley, and carrots.

COOKING AT HOME

Because Moroccan food is generally cooked over braziers or grills—many North African cooks don't even own ovens—it is fairly simple to reproduce at home. Although you probably don't own a couscousière (like fondue pots and woks, they tend to be fashionable gifts every ten years or so and then disappear), you can use a colander over a pot; but if you prefer to buy quick-cooking couscous, you can make it in a regular saucepan. The eggplant salad that follows would traditionally be grilled over a brazier, but the oven will do just fine.

EGGPLANT SALAD, RABAT-STYLE

1 eggplant (about 1 pound)
1 clove garlic, peeled and slivered
2 tablespoons chopped parsley
2 sprigs chopped coriander (optional)
1/2 teaspoon paprika
1/2 teaspoon ground cumin
2 tablespoons olive oil
1–2 tablespoons lemon juice
Salt to taste

Use the point of a knife to make slits in the whole eggplant, then stud it with garlic slivers. Bake in 400°F oven until blackened, even blistered, and softened or "collapsed." Remove and let cool before rubbing off skin and squeezing pulp to release bitter juices (alternatively, scoop out pulp and drain in sieve). Discard liquid; mash or force pulp and garlic slivers through a food mill (do not blend or process—it would get too homogeneous). Add chopped herbs and spices and mix well; fry in oil over moderate heat, turning often with a spatula or perforated spoon, until all the liquid has evaporated and the eggplant is reduced to a thick, dark jam (15–20 minutes). Sprinkle with lemon juice, add salt, and adjust seasonings to taste. Serve warm or slightly chilled.

VEGETARIAN COUSCOUS

2 1/2 cups tightly packed fennel greens
(or fresh dill, or a combination)
1 cup tightly packed parsley leaves
1/4 cup tightly packed celery leaves
1/4 pound leeks, white and pale green parts
(substitute scallions or a combination)
1/2 cup chopped onions
1 cup chopped fennel bulb
1/4 cup olive oil
2 tablespoons tomato paste
2 teaspoons paprika
Salt to taste
1/2 teaspoon ground coriander seed

1/2 teaspoon ground caraway seed
2 teaspoons dried red chili flakes or pepper sauce
1 cup defatted chicken broth or vegetable stock
1 1/2 cups uncooked couscous (not quick-cooking or instant)
1 fresh green chili, minced
1 bell pepper, quartered
3 cloves garlic, peeled
1 small whole onion, studded with cloves
1 15-ounce can garbanzo beans, rinsed and drained
Harisa (available at Middle Eastern markets) or liquid pepper sauce

Wash, drain, and chop all greens; wash and chop leeks. Fill the bottom of a couscousière or double boiler with water and bring to boil; place perforated top, colander, or steamer dish over it and steam greens and leeks, covered, for 30 minutes. Drain, cool, and squeeze out excess moisture; set aside. Refill the bottom of the couscousière and bring back to a boil.

Meanwhile, sauté chopped onions and fennel bulb in olive oil in a large skillet until soft; stir in tomato paste, paprika, salt, coriander, caraway, and chili flakes and simmer until blended. Add chicken broth and simmer 15 minutes more. Remove from heat and add uncooked couscous, stirring well; repeat with greens and leeks; finally, add the green chili, bell pepper chunks, garlic cloves, and whole onion. Place top back over boiling water, add cooked vegetable and couscous mixture and garbanzos, and steam, covered, for another 30 minutes. Pour the cooked couscous mixture onto a tray, pick out the garlic cloves, bell pepper, and studded onion, and use serving fork to break up any lumps. Stir 1/2 cup water into couscous, cover with aluminum foil, and let rest in warm place for 10 minutes before serving. Serve with harisa or liquid pepper sauce.

Nonvegetarian variations: Add cubes of lean lamb to the skillet when adding the chicken broth and before adding dry couscous, then add raisins before steaming and add a cinnamon stick with clove-studded onion and garlic cloves (but remove it before serving). Add pan-browned chicken pieces to cooked vegetable mixture when it is placed in the top of the couscousière before steaming, or pan-cook chicken separately and serve on the side.

QUICK COUSCOUS WITH CHICKEN

1 3-pound chicken, cut into serving pieces
Salt and pepper to taste
2 tablespoons cooking oil
1 onion, sliced
1 large carrot, diced
3 garlic cloves, minced
1 28-ounce can peeled whole plum tomatoes, drained and chopped
(about 1 pound fresh tomatoes)
1 teaspoon ground cumin
1 teaspoon ground allspice
2 cups defatted chicken broth or vegetable stock, divided
1/4 cup dry white wine
1/2 teaspoon dried red chili flakes, harisa, or other hot pepper sauce
2 small zucchini, diced
3 tablespoons tomato paste
1 15-ounce can cooked garbanzos, rinsed and drained
4 tablespoons chopped fresh cilantro or
3 tablespoons chopped fresh parsley, divided
1 tablespoon butter or margarine (optional)
1 1/2 cups quick-cooking or "instant" couscous
Harisa or liquid pepper sauce

Rinse chicken, pat dry, and season with salt and pepper. Heat oil in large casserole or Dutch oven, brown chicken, and remove; add onion, carrot, and garlic and sauté until softened. Add tomatoes, cumin, and allspice and cook for 5 minutes, stirring; stir in 1/2 cup chicken broth, wine, and red chili flakes and return chicken to casserole. Cover and simmer 15 minutes; add zucchini and simmer until chicken is tender (20–30 minutes more). Stir in tomato paste, add garbanzos and half the chopped cilantro or parsley, heat through.

While chicken is simmering, bring remaining chicken broth (and butter if you are using it) to a boil and add couscous; stir well, cover and remove from heat. Let couscous stand 5 minutes, fluff with fork, and spoon onto serving platter. Arrange chicken and vegetables around it, pour some sauce over the top, and garnish with remaining cilantro or parsley. Serve with harisa or other liquid pepper sauce.

ORANGE AND OLIVE SALAD

4 navel oranges
2 tablespoons black olives, slivered
1 tablespoon pine nuts, toasted
1/2 cup chopped fresh mint
1 tablespoon olive oil
1 clove garlic, minced
Pinch sugar
Pinch salt
1/2 teaspoon dried red chili flakes (more to taste)
1 teaspoon lemon juice (if desired)

Peel oranges, removing all pith, and remove skin from segments, working over a bowl to retain juice. Cut segments into bite-size pieces and mix with olives and pine nuts. Whisk together mint, olive oil, garlic, sugar, salt, chili flakes, and reserved orange juice, plus lemon juice (if desired) to thin. Adjust seasoning, toss gently, and refrigerate until ready to serve.

ETHIOPIA

BASIC CUISINE

DINNER FOR TWO:
Doro watt, beef alecha

DINNER FOR FOUR:
Doro watt, lamb with
chili, kitfo, potato and
carrot alecha

GROUP DISH:
Mesob

STYLE:
Spicy, soft, slightly sour

KEY FLAVORS:
Red chili, sourdough

EATING UTENSILS:
Fingers

DISTINCTIVE DISHES:
Watts, alechas, injera

UNIFORMITY OF MENUS:
Good

NUTRITIONAL INDEX:
High carbohydrate, high
protein, medium fat

COST:
Inexpensive

"THANK YOU":
"Ama sekanada"

It's surprising that so many American diners let themselves be unnerved by the apparent difficulty of eating Ethiopian food. After all, in a country whose Big Three foods are hamburgers, pizza, and PB&J, eating with the hands is more familiar than using a fork. And unlike chopsticks, fingers require little practice.

Still, there is no denying that many first-timers feel extremely awkward faced with *kitfo* or *doro watt*. But any uncertainty can be erased in a matter of moments. Ethiopian food is simple—a breeze to order—delicious, nutritious, a rich choice for vegetarian diners, and a bargain as well. And the communal-platter style of service makes it a truly sociable experience. We only have one suggestion: Wear comfortable clothes, since you'll be leaning over the platter. And don't wear white the first time.

THE COUNTRY

Ethiopia is a roughly bell-shaped nation nearly twice the size of Texas, divided diagonally down the middle by the Great Rift Valley and sharply divided between desert and monsoon-drenched highlands as much as 18,000 feet apart in elevation. Its high plateaus are one reason it has been historically distinct from most of the rest of Africa. It's bounded by the Sudan to the northwest and west, Kenya to the south, and Somalia to the east. The northeast border, which meets the Red Sea, is the territory of Eritrea, which has struggled for independence against Italian, Egyptian, and Ethiopian forces all jealous of its coastal access: In fact, the name "Eritrea" comes from the Roman name for the Red Sea, *Mare Erythraeum*, and its ports were the region's earliest power centers.

(Although most restaurants in the United States refer to Eritrean and Ethiopian cuisine interchangeably, some are quite sensitive about the distinction. You can sometimes get a hint from the name of the establishment, since they frequently refer to the owner's original home: Axum, Asmara, and Massawa are all in Eritrea; Addis Ababa, Diredawa, the Blue Nile—or the Abbai, as it's known there—and Harar are in Ethiopia proper. In addition, Italy's long domination of Eritrea has left behind the odd culinary clue, usually lasagna and seafood pasta.)

Ethnically, Ethiopia is fairly diverse, predominantly Coptic Christian but with large Muslim and other recognized minorities and with identifiable Greek, Armenian, Italian, Saudi, and Indian and Pakistani populations.

THE HISTORY

In prehistoric times, much more of the African continent was fed by, or under, the Mediterranean Sea. Wall-paintings indicate that buffalo, antelopes, and even ostriches were hunted in what are now the Sahara and Magreb Deserts before the waters began retreating. In more modern times, meat has become much more of a luxury.

Ethiopia—the Abyssinia of mysterious allure—has many great civilizations in its past. According to legend, it was founded 3,000 years ago by Menelik I, offspring of the famous liaison between King Solomon and the Queen of Sheba (whose progenitor, the original Sheba himself, according to the Bible, was a direct descendent of Abraham). Ancient Egyptian records suggest that trade with Abyssinians stretched back a thousand years before that. And Ethiopia's great Lake Tana in the north is the fabled source of the Blue Nile, which drew so many oddly obsessed Europeans.

By the fifth century B.C.E., Ethiopia was a regular stop for Arab traders; 300 years later, the capital of Axum dominated Red Sea coastal trade and served as a juncture for the emerging Mediterranean civilizations, one source of the myriad ethnic minorities among its populace.

The country was officially converted to Christianity (Egyptian Coptic) in the fourth century. The first Jewish settlers probably arrived about 200 years after that, establishing a line of Beta Israel (children of Israel) or "Falashas" that to this day have remained rigorously observant; some 25,000 of them were airlifted to Israel during the mid- and late 1980s. However, with the increasing power of the Islamic nations, Axum's role declined, and its ties to the Byzantine Empire were effectively severed. Isolated from the vital trade routes, the country gradually turned feudal and fractious.

Europeans—the Portuguese, as usual—began trading there in the early sixteenth century, but Ethiopia held limited interest for the colonial powers until the opening of the Suez Canal in 1869, when it suddenly acquired strategic value. Italy bungled one invasion attempt at the end of the nineteenth century, the failed battle of Adwa, but in 1935 Mussolini succeeded in driving Emperor Haile Selassie (whose real name, Ras Tafari, became the password of his messianic cult) into exile. He was restored by British forces in 1941 and brought the country into the United Nations, but it remained poor and oligarchical, with power in the hands of the few landowners. Selassie was deposed briefly in 1960 and permanently in 1974, launching a period of civil strife that, coupled with repeated drought and famine, has devastated this once-prosperous nation. Selassie's most lingering influence, oddly, is in Jamaica, where his followers have developed not only a patois—and a religion of marijuana smoking—but a stringently vegetarian cuisine.

THE CUISINE

Though the main ingredients of Ethiopian cuisine are fairly straightforward and have remained almost unchanged at least since the importation of New World chilies, they are enhanced by intense and addictive seasonings that recall its years as the crossroads of the spice routes.

Introductory Ethiopian cuisine is as simple as one, two, three—one utensil, two stews, and three sauces. *Injera* is a spongy, slightly sour bread, made from fermented *tef*, that is napkin, plate, spoon, and starch all in one. *Watts* and *alechas* are the major types of stews, the first always spicy and the second either mild or hot. The three sauces—*berbere*, *awaz*, and *mitmitta*—are all hot; but the greatest of these is berbere.

THE MAIN INGREDIENTS

GRAINS AND STARCHES The Ethiopian economy is predominantly agricultural and rural; the vast majority of Ethiopians are subsistence farmers. The country's cultivation of an indigenous variety of oats, barley, millet, and sorghum stretches back long before recorded history (they are still among its primary crops), and the millet-like tef, which is extremely high in iron, remains the staple starch.

Tef, the grain used in the making of authentic injera, is the smallest of grains and difficult to harvest. It is grown only at high altitudes and is expensive to export, so those American restaurants that offer the real thing may have slightly higher prices than the others (though no Ethiopian restaurant is ever very expensive). However, transplanted chefs have become quite adept at substituting other grains, and many of the buckwheat and soured wheat versions are very tasty. Along with grains, Ethiopian farmers rely on potatoes, peas, and plantains for starch. The *ensete* or "false banana" is a root that is ground, fermented, and made into an alternative "bread" called *wesa*.

MEAT AND PROTEINS Ethiopian farmers raise a variety of livestock, depending on the region and rainfall: sheep and goats in the arid lowlands, cattle and poultry in the wetter highlands. Not surprisingly, they consume beef, sheep, some goat, and a great deal of chicken. Neither the Copts nor the Muslims consume pork, and many Ethiopians shun poultry and eggs as well. They raise animals not just for meat but also for eggs, milk, and a sort of clabbered cheese like sour cottage cheese. They are fond of organ meats, particularly tripe, though kidneys and livers do not interest them as much. (Many restaurants in the United States leave organ meats off their menus, as they are not popular here, but if you do like them, ask—they may be available anyway.) Those who either can't afford to or don't wish to eat meat get protein from peas, lentils, and peanuts.

Sometimes fish, and more frequently shrimp, are available, particularly in Eritrean restaurants. (Since Ethiopia proper is landlocked, a long list of seafood dishes is another clue to a kitchen's likely Eritrean background.)

DAIRY PRODUCTS Ethiopian cuisine is fairly rich in cheeses and butter, particularly the ghee-like clarified spiced butter called *niter kibbeh*. These various cheeses may be fresh or dried, salted or sweet, and are sometimes mixed with vegetables in stews.

FRUITS AND VEGETABLES Greens, particularly cabbage, collards, and kale, are common, as are garbanzos and split peas, beans, tomatoes, carrots, potatoes, and cauliflower; slightly less common are eggplant and sweet potatoes. Lentils are so popular that some version of them often appears on your table automatically, almost as a condiment. Onions, characteristically dry-fried, are a hallmark of Ethiopian cooking. Rape seeds, cottonseeds, and sunflower seeds are all planted for oil pressing, though niter kibbeh is the primary flavoring oil. Flaxseed is consumed as a grain. Eritrea has a slightly broader range of produce, including citrus fruits and tobacco, but many sects in the region avoid fruit.

HOT SAUCES Of the three prepared condiments, berbere is the most common and the most powerful. Berbere combines red chilies, cardamom, basil, and spices; like curry powders, it has a variable recipe but may include cloves, nutmeg, garlic, cinnamon, coriander, and ginger. (Because its resemblance to the North African harisa is so strong, one has to wonder whether berbere is, literally, Berber sauce.) Endorphin freaks in search of extra thrills will be happy to know that if a watt is somehow not hot enough, more berbere can usually be had as a condiment. Awaze is also a chili mixture but is heavily studded with garlic and onion, while the drier mitmitta combines chilies and cardamom with coarse salt.

OTHER FLAVORINGS Among herbs and spices, the most important are salt, cardamom, cumin, cloves, fenugreek, mustard, dill, carraway, ginger, turmeric, and the ubiquitous red and sometimes green chili peppers. However, varieties of basil and garlic are frequently used, and nutmeg and cloves are added not only to stews but also to the rich, powerful Ethiopian coffee. Honey is both used as a seasoning and eaten straight from the comb.

Ethiopians tend vast hives of wild and domesticated bees, and guests are often served honeycomb and curds and whey—milk and honey, in other words.

THE MAIN DISHES

APPETIZERS Since Ethiopians generally eat only (at most) two major meals a day, there are few distinct appetizers in the Western sense. However, fairly substantial snacks are eaten between meals, and those often appear on menus as appetizers. *Sambusas* are very similar to the Indian samosas; they come stuffed with either beef or lentils and perhaps potatoes and are usually spicy. Another popular snack is *quanta*, a salt- and berbere-cured beef jerky.

VEGETABLE DISHES Despite the relatively heavy presence of meat on menus, Ethiopians have also developed a fondness for meatless stews—a virtue of necessity, in fact, since more than half the traditional Ethiopian calendar is given over to fast days. The Ethiopian vegetarian dishes have become the mainstay of the Jamaican Rastafarians, who have made Selassie's native cuisine into a dietary requirement.

Yemiser watt is hot lentil stew; *yeduba watt* is pumpkin, and there is frequently a mildly spicy cabbage and carrot combination that may reconcile those whose taste for cabbage was demolished in elementary school cafeterias. Also, a variety of greens are usually available, particularly collards, kale, and spinach; occasionally there may be zucchini as well.

MEATS Ethiopians dearly love beef, perhaps because they were so often forbidden to eat it; and they love it not only stewed but also raw. Kitfo is the Ethiopian steak tartare, minced by hand and spiked with chili and kibbeh, the clarified butter. (In the old days, men often devoured whole slabs of raw meat around the table, biting into it and slicing off a chunk before passing it on. Americans are unlikely to witness this event; but if you do ever find yourself in such a group, dip the meat into the berbere dish first.)

Tere sega is similar, but the meat is served in cubes rather than hand-chopped (sort of like the difference between the chili in Texas and New Mexico). *Yesiga watt* is a braised beef stew. *Tibbs* is cooked meat, beef or sometimes lamb, and may be breast meat or ribs; *adulis tibbs* is usually charcoal-grilled. In comparison to watts and alechas, which are simmered, tibbs is more apt to be dry-cooked or grilled before being sauced—something like the distinction between "wet" and "dry" barbecue in the United States.

When meat is combined with a vegetable, it is more likely the flavoring than the primary ingredient: *Zilb* is collard greens with lamb; *bozena shuro* is yellow split pea stew flavored with beef. *Dulet* is tripe, which is frequently stuffed with spiced vegetables and braised with honey and may be offered as a watt; it may also be mixed with livers.

STEWS Again, there are two major types to choose from, the watts and the alechas (or alichas). This mnemonic may be helpful: "Watt" (also spelled "wat" or "wot") rhymes with "hot" and appropriately recalls "wattage," and it's the spicier version, thanks to the berbere mixed in. Alechas range from mild to moderately spicy. Almost any ingredient—meat, seafood, poultry, or vegetable—can be prepared as either a watt or an alecha. *Yebeg watt* is lamb. During fast days, lentils and garbanzos are sometimes mashed and used as "mock chicken" in much the same way the Chinese use tofu. And a *fitfit*, or *firfir*, is a watt with bits of injera stewed right in.

POULTRY Chicken dishes are extremely popular—particularly *doro watt*, which is probably as close to a national dish as there is; it's a stew of chicken pieces, hard-boiled eggs, and berbere. Chicken alecha is also very popular and is frequently sweetened lightly with honey. In some areas, other fowl such as quail may occasionally be offered.

BEVERAGES Both of the region's fermented drinks, beer and the honey-based mead called *tej*, are extremely old—but no less powerful for age, particularly the deceptively sweet tej. Ethiopia may also be the origin of coffee, which grows wild in the mountains; and "double-boil" is a strong version drunk after meals.

HOW TO ORDER
AND EAT LIKE A NATIVE

Ethiopian tables are fascinating things, large handwoven hourglass-shaped baskets with a lip around the surface and conical witches'-hat lids that make them look like the hives of huge African termites. (They may be representative of beehives, a symbol of fertility and richness.) The table surface is a little low by American standards, and the chairs are also

Made up in pizza-sized rounds and served (usually folded in fourths) in a basket, injera should be torn into small pieces and used to soak up sauce or pinch up bite-sized morsels of the other dishes; then you pop the whole tidbit into your mouth. As in most cultures, you must use only your right hand. If you are making a fuss over someone, or honoring a guest, you may prepare such mouthfuls and hand-feed your friend, in which case these tidbits are called *gurshas*. Do not pass them hand to hand, however. Whatever main dishes you order are poured out for you on a larger and perhaps thinner sheet of injera; you may tear off pieces of the infused injera and eat that, too. You may also lightly squeeze the injera to remove excess oil or seasonings from your fingers (don't wring it out, though) and eat it plain.

woven, with rounded backs for lounging, so that diners accustomed to pulling their knees up under the table—and having the tabletop safely between the mouth and the lap—may find that the distance between cup and lip leaves room for many a slip.

Most restaurants in the United States are furnished with the usual dinette table; but given a choice, you should really try the basket style; somehow, leaning forward to pick up your food and then leaning back in your chair reinforces the sociability of the occasion—it becomes part of the rhythm of conversation.

Traditionally, since diners will eat with their hands, restaurants provide a pitcher of water and a basin with a sort of colander in the middle. The waiter places the basin before you and pours the water over your hands while you rub them together and then dry them on the towel (remember, it is not a napkin) that is handed to you. Then a large round flat platter of injera, topped with mounds of the dishes you've ordered, is placed on the top of the table.

Most restaurants offer wine and beer (either Western-style or the wheat-based *talla*) along with tej, which is usually sold by the bottle or glass. However, if you order tej in a traditional-style restaurant, it may be served as it is there, in large, narrow-necked, and slightly tricky bottles called *bereles*, which are somewhere between a flask and a glass. In the traditional manner, the host may pour a little tej into his palm and taste it, just as a host or sommelier would taste wine; the custom in that case is for the taster to grimace, as if the quality is not up to the guest's due, and for the guest to protest and praise its flavor.

Ethiopian restaurants are among the best bargains in any case, but if you can't decide what you want, you might order the *mesob*, or sampler platter; most restaurants will have at least one mesob with meat and one without. The meals are surprisingly filling, so even if there are appetizers available, you may want to skip them (four people could order sambusas). Also, remember that meat dishes usually come with a vegetable on the side.

Two people should order one watt, preferably doro watt, and one alecha, beef or perhaps shrimp; if you don't like hot spices, order one alecha and one tibbs. (It may also help to know that most vegetable dishes are fairly mild.) If you have a group of four diners, one person should certainly order kitfo and another doro watt; with all the injera, a third dish may be all you need, but good additional choices would be chili-dressed lamb or shrimp and the potato-carrot stew.

COOKING AT HOME

To be honest, making injera at home is not hard—it's like making large crepes, using the bottom of a nonstick or well-seasoned cast-iron skillet—but unless you can find tef, it's not really the same. There are also imitation recipes involving pancake mixes (see below), but you should try to buy some real injera. Alternatively, serve doro watt with pita or Indian flat bread or even rice. Similarly, first- or even second-time Ethiopian chefs may wish to substitute harisa, available at many Middle Eastern markets, for homemade berbere, although the recipe below uses mostly familiar ingredients.

QUICK INJERA

3 tablespoons all-purpose flour
1 1/2 cups sourdough or buckwheat pancake mix
1/4 teaspoon baking soda
1 12-oz. bottle club soda
1 1/2 cups water

Combine flour, pancake mix, and baking soda in a large bowl. Whisking or stirring constantly, slowly but continuously pour in club soda and then water until the batter is smooth and fairly thin.

Meanwhile, heat a nonstick or seasoned cast iron 9-inch skillet over moderate heat. (Test the heat by dropping a spoonful of batter into the pan—it should solidify instantly but not brown.) Lift the skillet off the heat, pour in 1/4 cup of batter, and tilt the pan to spread evenly. Cover partly and cook just a minute, or until tiny air holes turn the top spongy while the bottom is dry (but not crisp or brown). Remove this piece to a plate and pour in more batter; you should end up with about 8 or 9 pieces altogether.

To serve, place 4 or 5 pieces around the inside of a basket, overlapping them like petals; fold the others into quarters and arrange them in the middle.

BERBERE PASTE

1/4 teaspoon ground allspice

1/4 teaspoon ground cardamom

1 teaspoon ground ginger

1/2 teaspoon ground coriander

pinch ground cloves

pinch ground cinnamon

1/2 teaspoon ground nutmeg

1/4 cup minced onion

1 tablespoon minced garlic

2 tablespoons salt, divided

1/4 cup dry red wine (not cooking wine)

1 1/2 cups paprika

2 tablespoons cayenne

1/4 teaspoon black pepper

1 cup water

dash vegetable oil

In a nonstick or enameled heavy saucepan, toast first 7 ingredients, shaking the pan to keep them from scorching, until hot and fragrant. Cool, then combine with onion, garlic, half the salt, and wine into a blender and process at high speed into a smooth paste. Return saucepan to heat and briefly toast paprika, cayenne, black pepper, and remaining salt, again shaking the pan to prevent sticking. (Don't lean over the skillet, because the aroma may burn your eyes or throat.) Lower heat, whisk in water in a slow stream, then add paste. Stirring constantly, cook on very low heat for 15 minutes. Scrape into jar, and tap the jar on the counter to remove air pockets. Let cool, then top with a thin film of oil. Cover and refrigerate. Always replace the oil film after use; this way the paste will keep for several months.

DORO WATT

1 3-pound chicken, cut into serving pieces
1/4 cup lemon juice
1 tablespoon salt
1 tablespoon black pepper
4 tablespoons (1/2 stick) unsalted butter
2 cups chopped onion
1 tablespoon minced ginger
1/2 teaspoon ground fenugreek or anise
1/2 cup berbere paste
1/2 cup dry wine, preferably white
1 cup chicken broth or water
4 eggs, hard-cooked and peeled

Rinse chicken and pat dry; rub with lemon juice, salt, and pepper and let marinate. Meanwhile, melt butter in a skillet and bring it to a boil; as soon as it is covered with white foam, reduce heat to the lowest setting and let it cook undisturbed until the milk solids separate at the bottom. Pour off clarified oil and reserve.

Spray heavy enameled or nonstick casserole very lightly with cooking spray; cook onion, ginger, and fenugreek over moderate heat for about five minutes, until soft and dry. Add clarified butter and berbere and heat to simmer; add wine and water or broth, bring mixture to a light boil, and let it bubble until thickened. Dry chicken again and add to casserole, turning to coat with sauce; reduce and simmer, covered, about 15 minutes.

With a fork, puncture the whites of the eggs in several places and add them to the saucepan; cover again and cook until chicken is tender (about 15–20 minutes). Turn out onto platter and serve.

WEST AFRICA

BASIC CUISINE

DINNER FOR TWO:
Akras or fried yucca,
grilled fish, chicken in
peanut or coconut sauce

DINNER FOR FOUR:
Grilled shrimp, yam
croquettes, chicken
yassa, bluefish chebjen

GROUP DISH:
Calaloo

STYLE:
Nutty, creamy, smoky

KEY FLAVORS:
Palm oil, hot chilies,
peanuts, okra, yam

EATING UTENSILS:
Fingers, spoons

DISTINCTIVE FOODS:
Gumbos, peanut stews,
spicy fish

UNIFORMITY OF MENUS:
Limited

NUTRITIONAL INDEX:
High starch, high
cholesterol

COST:
Inexpensive

"THANK YOU":
"Dieuredieuf" (Sene-
galese); "Odima,"
"Adupe," or "Avo"
(Nigerian); "Merci"
(French Mali, etc.)

The emergence of West African restaurants in the United States is a recent phenomenon—and oddly appropriate. For though West Africa was exhaustively exploited by European colonizers, West African cuisine absorbed virtually nothing from European food; the cultures remained intractably segregated. On the other hand, West Africans have had an indelible influence on American food; and now the United States is returning the favor by providing a wealth of ingredients and a hospitable market.

It was primarily transported Gambian slaves, long accustomed to cultivating rice in their swampy river valleys, who brought prosperity to the South Carolina and Georgia rice plantations and a whole new cuisine to the Caribbean, by transporting and transplanting rice, yams, peanuts, and black-eyed peas; they sent home corn, okra, coconuts, hot peppers, plantains, and string beans which had been gathered between South and Central America

148

and home. In some areas, West African cooking and words can be found almost unchanged after 300 years: The word "gumbo," used for one of the most famous Southern dishes, comes from *gombo*, a West African term for okra. Africans were literally sold for peanuts in South America; they returned good for evil by transplanting them in North America.

But Americans owe much more than peanuts to the West Africans. Homesick slaves not only preserved traditional "soul food" but also helped stew up the trendy Creole cuisine and a fair portion of Cajun as well. And just recently, with the development of an educated, entrepreneurial black middle class whose members are inclined to take advantage of modern techniques and trends, West African cuisine has begun to evolve in a calculated manner. Like West African textiles and music, the food speaks of home to thousands of black Americans who have never laid eyes upon Africa itself. To American southerners both black and white, the obvious resemblance between West African cuisine and soul food—"gitchee cooking," as it is called in the Carolina and Georgia island patois—can be eye-opening.

THE COUNTRIES

The West Coast of Africa—the area around and under the dip of ice cream on the cone of the African continent—is widely, if not densely, populated; more than 200 languages are spoken within Cameroon alone. The countries of the region include Ghana, Nigeria, Togo, Mali, Benin, Senegal, the Ivory Coast, Sierra Leone, Guinea, and Gambia.

The topography of the region swings from sandy beach to savannah, from plateau to forest, from swamp to desert. There are great networks of rivers whose names ring in history—the Niger, the Volta, the Gambia—and cities built entirely on stilts and traversed by canals rather than roads. The coastal areas, particularly Gambia, have become busy tourist attractions in the post-*Roots* era. But the region is still predominantly agricultural and thus susceptible to widespread famines.

West Africa is home to a mix of indigenous religions—the Yoruban tradition in particular remains influential, having taken root in Haiti (and hence Louisiana) as voudon and in Brazil as Candomble—and Catholicism and Islam, in various proportions. Consequently, a substantial number of vegetarian dishes are prepared, particularly during the Lentan and Ramadan fasting seasons. There are also identifiable Indian, Lebanese, and

Arab minorities, whose members have added to the mix their own bits of culinary variety (curries in particular, and the occasional fried samosa).

THE HISTORY

West Africa was the site of several great empires, beginning with the Nok in Nigeria; by 2000 B.C.E., they had mastered iron- and tinworking, and their terracotta work was highly sophisticated. In Ghana, a great trading power dominated the trans-Saharan caravan routes for some 800 years before declining in the thirteenth century; and in the fourteenth century, Timbuktu was a byword of Islamic scholarship.

The primary European colonial influences were the Portuguese, who were the first traders to heavily exploit the West African market, beginning in the mid-fifteenth century; the British, who established their influence particularly in Ghana, Nigeria, and Gambia; and the French, who maintained at least some control over "French West Africa"—2,000,000 square miles of it—into the 1960s. The region also endured colonial incursions by the Dutch, the Belgians, the Germans, and even the Danish, but it has one irrevocable historical tie to America: the slave trade. The introduction of sugar plantations by the Portuguese into Brazil required a substantial (slave) labor force; and the regular back-and-forth between continents produced so much food exchange—familiar foods being one of the best ways to "settle" immigrant populations, especially involuntary ones—that it is estimated to have resulted in the introduction of fully one-third of the foods now known in West Africa.

The slave trade had a triangular pattern: From Europe, ships filled with rum, textiles, jewelry, some money, and guns would sail south to Africa and buy slaves; then the slavers headed west to the Caribbean and American coasts to exchange the slaves for cotton, tobacco, molasses, and coffee, which were destined for Europe. The molasses was turned into rum, and the cycle began again. At the trade's height in the seventeenth century, Europeans were buying an estimated 20,000 slaves a year, and the general assumption that Africa existed entirely for commercial exploitation is reflected in the fact that maps of the times read like commodity exchange reports: the Slave Coast, the Ivory Coast, the Gold Coast. (It also says much about why hotels and "establishment" restaurants in West Africa still have French or Portuguese menus.)

THE CUISINE

Traditional West African food, although hearty and comforting, can seem heavy, starchy, and overcooked to some American palates—as veterans of southern U.S. soul food can testify. This is partly because the diet was heavily dependent on starchy foods and was often stewed with a small bit of salted pork or fish for flavor. (It also helps explain their free use of chilies and hot spices.)

In the poorer areas, cattle and goats had to be butchered conservatively, as milk was a much more reliable source of protein than meat. Black-eyed peas (or cowpeas), peanuts (groundnuts), and soybeans provided additional protein but not much flavor; hard-cooked eggs were often substituted as well.

It was also true that what meat there was, primarily mutton and beef, tended to be lean and somewhat stringy. Even in the more prosperous regions, where goats, lambs, and even oxen were raised for meat (depending upon the dietary restrictions of various religions), meat had to be tenderized, by either pounding, marinating, long cooking, or all three. Meat was also typically "stretched"—thickened with okra, manioc flour, or peanut butter.

In the coastal and river delta regions, there was protein aplenty from fish and shellfish. Like most coastal peoples, West Africans preserve their fish by drying, salting, and smoking: These may be used as an ingredient or occasionally as a soup base. One of the characteristics of coastal West African cuisine is that meat and fish are frequently stewed together. Yams and rice were always available, however, and revered for their reliability and versatility. In Ghana, the Ashanti use yams in the rituals that celebrate birth, death, marriage, and sometimes the survival of a serious illness or accident.

THE MAIN INGREDIENTS

SEASONINGS Although the introduction of New World chili peppers made an immediate and lasting impact on West (and North) African cooking, the cuisine was already somewhat spicy, thanks primarily to an aromatic seed called *malegueta* or Guinea pepper. Not a true pepper, it was widely used in Europe and, along with ivory and slaves, was one of the commodities the Portuguese exported from the coast. (It is sometimes referred to as "grains of paradise," which can be extremely confusing because that phrase is more frequently applied to cardamom.)

Among the most common herbs and spices are fiery habañero peppers (although many West African restaurants in the United States pull their punches on peppers), ginger, mint, and scallions. African chefs may be kind in easing up on the heat: For some reason, the capsaicin content of chilies grown in Africa is generally higher than elsewhere.

A common condiment is called "piri-piri" or "pili-pili" sauce, which is an incendiary mix of chilies, onion, garlic, lemon juice or vinegar, and occasionally horseradish. Some food historians believe that both these words and the Ethiopian berbere sauce—i.e., beri-beri—come from the same root word. Sorghum is widely raised, and its molasses, along with some wild honey and carob, provides the major sweetener.

Other less potent flavorings include a type of basil called partminger, lemongrass, coconut, ground peanuts, sesame seeds, turmeric, thyme, and various dried fruits. The characteristic red tint to many dishes is not the result of achiote or chilies, but comes from the liberal use of palm nut oil.

GRAINS AND STARCHES Rice is the major starch here, but maize, sorghum, yams, plantains, taro, baobab ("monkey bread") tree, and millet are also heavily planted. Manioc flour is pounded from the cassava root. All of these starches can be left to sour, thus providing greater variety of flavors. *Fou-fou*, which is the general name for a starchy paste, might be made from almost any of these.

MEATS AND SEAFOOD West Africans raise chickens, pork, goats, sheep, and some beef, ducks, and rabbits. (Not likely to appear on a restaurant menu are the "bush meats" such as bats, larger rodents, and wild pigs.) A fair variety of fish—primarily red snapper, croaker, and bluefish—are available; but shellfish, particularly shrimp, is far more common there than one would realize from reading American African menus: Cameroon, after all, was named by the Portuguese for its abundance of fine prawns, or "camarones." Giant freshwater snails are considered a delicacy there, and some restaurants in the United States do their best to recreate the dish using French-style escargots. To preserve and stretch these precious supplies, West Africans may pickle, salt, or dry meat for later use and stronger flavor.

POULTRY Along with chickens, which are prized for their eggs, West African farmers raise turkeys, ducks, and guinea hens. In some areas, small wildfowl and even songbirds are consumed, although you're not likely to see that on a menu, either.

VEGETABLES AND PRODUCE Tomatoes and onions are extremely popular and are used in the most popular sauces, either as a stew or sweetened and thickened into a sort of barbecue sauce. Okra's prominence is obvious, and other common vegetables include eggplant, greens (usually spinach or cassava in the United States but in West Africa encompassing more than 100 types of wild and cultivated greens), string beans, squashes and gourds, carob beans, carrots, cabbage, potatoes, sweet potatoes, and sweet peppers. Legumes, particularly lentils, black-eyed peas, peanuts, red peas, and some red beans are important alternative sources of protein.

FRUITS Though most Americans would be surprised to be reminded of it, many areas of coastal Africa are tropical in the truest sense, and fruits are plentiful, including a variety of bananas and plantains (both green and ripe), pineapples, oranges, papayas, and mangoes. The palm nuts and coconuts provide essential cooking oils and fats; we may have to limit those fats today, but they were essential to many West Africans, whose meat consumption was limited.

THE MAIN DISHES

FIRST COURSES Full-service restaurants are rare in West Africa. Outdoor vendors hawk barbecued turkey legs, beef brochette, grilled fish, or fried yam balls to be eaten while talking or shopping. Consequently, West Africans here enjoy lingering over appetizers, particularly fried sweet potatoes (one term for this is *patate sauté*) or fried plantains; peppery goat soup; or tomatoes dressed in a tangy turmeric-flavored "vinaigrette"—really, an emulsion thick as hollandaise or mayonnaise and served with almost everything.

Akras are salt cod fritters, the precursors of those popular in the Caribbean, served with a spanky green chili dip. Other fritters may be made of black-eyed peas and okra, spinach, or pumpkin. Smoked fish sometimes appears as a spread, and occasionally seafood is offered fried. Hard-cooked eggs and, among the more Americanized cafes, grilled shrimp and chicken tidbits are popular. *Kose* is a stew of black-eyed peas flavored with chicken gizzards; it appears either as a first course, like a heavy salad, or as a main dish.

BREADS AND STARCHES Rice still dominates in West African cuisines, although a few restaurants offer millet grains instead. *Jollof* rice is the African descendant of Middle Eastern pilafs and may be flavored with any sort of meat (ham, smoked fish, chicken, shrimp) or vegetable (cabbage, eggplant, pumpkin). There is almost no yeasted bread, but there are cornbreads, flatbreads, and the slightly sour fermented dough called *akassa* (corn) or *gari* (manioc). *Kpekple* is a cornmeal mush or farina frequently served with stewed fish. Most of the time, starches other than rice are incorporated into stews. A cassava-flour porridge is often served with eggs, sweet peppers, and tomatoes as a breakfast dish.

POULTRY Chicken and eggs are both extremely popular, and scrambled or hard-cooked and chopped eggs are often paired with beans and rice in place of meat. Poultry may be smoked, grilled, barbecued, or stewed. Among the most common dishes are chicken stewed with cassava and palm oil; chicken stewed with vegetables and ground peanuts or peanut butter (in Togo called *azidessi* and in Senegal called chicken *maffee*); and *moyo de poulet fumé*—smoked chicken braised with peppers, tomatoes, and onions. Grilled chicken may come sauced either with the barbecue-like sauce or a strong, lemony marinade often called *yassa*.

SEAFOOD Fish may be smoked or dried as well as fresh-caught and grilled, fried, or braised. Very fresh raw fish is sometimes filleted, salted, and then "cooked" ceviche-style in a mixture of coconut milk, lime juice, grated vegetables, and peanut oil, but it is rarely vinegar-cured as it is in the Caribbean. *Shika shika* is a lemon-flavored braised fish, often red snapper; croaker and other small fish are often fried and served with a hot sauce for dipping. *Cheb jen*, a spicy tomato-sauced bluefish, is a particular Senegalese favorite, served with rice. Some restaurants in the United States offer a sort of Americanized Africanized crab imperial—crab meat mixed with green onions, celery, garlic, and (here, at least) bread crumbs, but with the telltale addition of habañero peppers.

MEATS AND STEWS Since the majority of West African meals are still one-dish affairs, it is not surprising that stews are a significant class. Characteristic of these stews is the frequent combination of two kinds of protein, notably smoked fish and either beef or chicken, and the use of ground peanuts or peanut butter. Eggplant, okra, yams, and potatoes may be used as thickeners, and rice is usually served on the side. Another typical stew involves marinating chicken in citrus and chilies, barbecuing it, and then cooking it in the marinade.

Kpete (or *kepete*) is a stew originally prepared primarily for banquets and festivals (of which there are many); traditionally it features lamb, but sometimes cooks substitute goat or even occasionally duck. The lamb is butchered and the blood mixed with salt to prevent its coagulating; the meat is rubbed with garlic, bay, and pepper or grains of paradise and allowed to marinate before being stewed with the almost ritually scrubbed intestines (forerunner of the American chitterlings), the blood, chilies, and onions.

As we mentioned above, many stews combine beef, smoked fish, and okra, flavored with palm nuts or ground melon seeds. A particularly festive dish called *calaloo* combines spinach, lamb, shrimp, fish, and crabs and is served with cornmeal cakes; it sounds more like paella than Caribbean calaloo and may be the ancestor of jambalaya.

Although the average quantity of meat consumed in West Africa has increased, spit-roasting or grilling goat and lamb is still unusual, although kebabs are popular street fare. Whole roast suckling pig and whole roast lamb are available at many restaurants with advance notice. (Goat soup in Nigeria is a banquet dish reserved for the most important occasions.) Pork is often smoked and served with greens in a manner soul food aficionados will find extremely familiar. Organ meats and offal (the original chitterlings and ham hocks) are frequently included in stews.

BEVERAGES Traditionally, meals were eaten with water or palm wine, but West Africans of the boomer era—particularly in the United States—have shifted to cocktails and beer. (Among the most popular brands is the super-economy-sized Maruka.) *Gnamacoudji*, an Ivory Coast specialty, is a sort of mint-ginger ale mixed with pineapple juice and sugar.

HOW TO ORDER
AND EAT LIKE A NATIVE

In West Africa, many dishes—grilled fish, for one—are eaten by hand to prevent extraneous flavors from interfering. Consequently, it is traditional in West African, as in Ethiopia, restaurants to bring guests a basin of water to rinse their hands; as a matter of fact, guests are greeted this way even in private homes. However, most restaurants in the United States do not expect American patrons to eat with their fingers and will automatically set the tables with forks and spoons.

Two people will eat handsomely on an order of akras or fried yucca, a grilled fish dish, and chicken in peanut or coconut stew; four can probably consume grilled shrimp, yam croquettes, a chicken yassa, and Senegalese-style bluefish chebjen. If kpete or calaloo is available, by all means order one or both.

COOKING AT HOME

No particular equipment is needed to prepare these dishes; in fact, African kitchens are quite spare, and dishes prepared indoors are usually stewed, while larger roasted animals or grilled fish or chicken are prepared outdoors. If you wish to try eating finger-style, consider beginning with brochettes of beef or shrimp and warming your guests up to the idea of the chicken.

SMOKED CHICKEN STEW

1 medium smoked chicken, skinned and quartered
1 28-ounce can peeled tomatoes, chopped, with juice
2 onions, thinly sliced
1/4 cup chicken stock, broth, or water
1 tablespoon oil
1/2 tablespoon dark worchestershire-style sauce or soy sauce
2 habañero chilies, pierced two or three times with the tip of a knife

Place all ingredients in a dutch oven. Bring to a boil, reduce heat, and simmer uncovered for about 30 minutes. Serve hot over rice.

Variations: Add 2 tablespoons peanut butter and/or 1/2 cup tightly packed fresh greens.

VEGETARIAN GUMBO

1 cup fresh black-eyed peas
1 cup loosely packed dark greens (spinach, kale, collards, etc.)
1 pound small fresh okra, stems trimmed
2 ripe tomatoes, peeled, seeded, and chopped
(or 1 28-ounce can plum tomatoes)
1 habañero pepper or 2 jalapeños or bird chilies, halved and seeded
pinch ground coriander
salt and pepper to taste

Boil peas until almost done (time will depend on size, but test for tenderness after about 10 minutes); drain. Rinse greens, leaving water on leaves. In heavy saucepan combine peas, greens, okra, tomatoes, and pepper; simmer 15 minutes or until okra is tender. Add coriander, and season to taste with salt and pepper. Serve over rice.

Variations: This can be used as a sauce for fish, chicken, or crab, or a little smoked pork or smoked fish can be stirred in.

PART III

THE MIDDLE EAST, GREECE AND TURKEY, AND INDIA

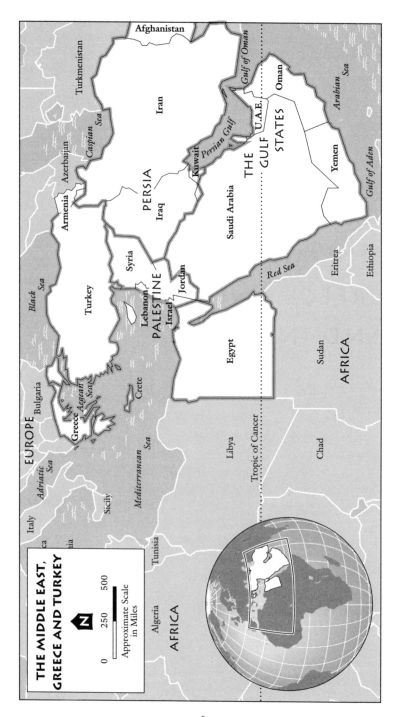

THE MIDDLE EAST, GREECE AND TURKEY

Approximate Scale in Miles

0   250   500

160

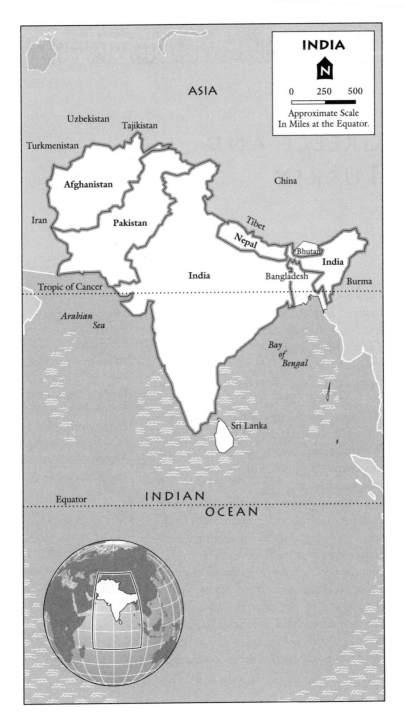

GREECE AND TURKEY

BASIC CUISINE

DINNER FOR TWO:
Taramosalata, grilled fish, souvlaki, or roast lamb

DINNER FOR FOUR:
Dolmas, baba ganouj, fried squid, roast chicken, moussaka

STYLE:
Simple, strong, tangy

KEY FLAVORS:
Olives, olive oil, goat cheese, lemon, oregano, honey

EATING UTENSILS:
Forks and knives

DISTINCTIVE DISHES:
Spanakopita, moussaka, souvlaki, baklava

UNIFORMITY OF MENUS:
Good

NUTRITIONAL INDEX:
High fat, moderate cholesterol, medium sodium

COST:
Inexpensive to moderate

"THANK YOU":
"Efharistan" (Greek)

On those old literary gazetteers of Western civilization, a great "X" must have marked this spot—the Aegean Sea between Greece and Turkey, where a pinwheel of road signs pointed toward Byzantium, Tyre, Mesopotamia, Macedonia, Persia, Egypt, Rome, and Jerusalem. Troy lay here, and Crete, with its bull dancers. Odysseus roamed this region, as did Xerxes, Alexander the Great, Suleiman the Magnificent, Barbarossa, and Lord Byron, who swam across the Dardanelles and died fighting for Greek independence.

This area, which has always had such an immense hold over our imaginations, has had only a secondary place in our culinary affections, probably because until relatively recently, the importation of many ingredients essential to Greek cooking—the grape leaves and goat cheeses and in particular the olive oils—was slow and unregulated and the quality was questionable. Greek restaurateurs only rarely prospered beyond the family-kitchen level, and Greek tavernas, with their hearty, village-tradition manners, were generally considered glorified greasy spoons.

Fortunately, both the cultural and commercial gaps have narrowed dramatically. Extra virgin olive oil is a staple even in chain supermarkets, and fine kalamata olives and grape leaves, kasseri and kefalotiri cheeses, and even the unmistakably resin-flavored *retsina* wine is available at many specialty markets and food boutiques. Improved refrigeration and storage has allowed for a lighter touch in the grilling of fish and meat, thus bringing Greek food more into line with the American palate. Greek chefs in the United States have also modified the amount of oils cooked into dishes and left more to diners' discretion, broadening its appeal even further.

Though this chapter specifically discusses Greek cuisine, it may also be used as a general guide to the eastern (European) section of Turkey; however, most Turkish restaurants in the United States offer Anatolian (Asian Turkish) and Persian fare. Historically, Crete fell under the domination of other civilizations, but there is no separate "Cretan" cuisine, at least not as practiced in the United States. The dishes of Macedonia are, like Bulgaria's, a mix of Turkish and Greek with a little Slavic influence thrown in; see the chapters on "Russia, Poland, and Eastern Europe" and "The Middle East" for more information.

THE COUNTRIES

Separated by a strait of water as thin as one mile in some places, Greece and Turkey together stretch from the Ionian Sea on the west to Iran and the Black Sea to the east. They literally "bridge" Asia and Europe: A small portion of Turkish territory lies north of the Dardanelles (the classical Hellespont) and the Bosporus in continental Europe. Though both have fairly large land masses, neither has much arable territory: Greece is three-quarters mountains, and although European Turkey is well drained by the Ergene River and fertile, it makes up only 3% of the nation. Greece has no navigable rivers, a situation that contributed to the early and jealous statism of its people.

Both countries produce corn, wheat, citrus fruits, olives, tomatoes, grapes and currants, beets, and potatoes; Turkey also produces a fair crop of rye, oats, and rice. Sheep and goats are plentiful in the entire region, but cattle, which require more grazing territory, are more common in Turkey. Pigs are popular in certain areas of the Greek islands. Chickens, of course, are ubiquitous; lemon-rubbed and rotisserie-grilled chicken was a Greek staple long before U.S. fast-food restaurants picked it up.

Greeks learned how to ferment and bake bread from the Egyptians in ancient times. As long as 4,000 years ago, Greek bakers were preparing dough from barley, wheat, millet, oats, rye, and spelt and topping it with poppy seeds, sesame seeds, and salt. (Records from the third century list 72 kinds of bread.) In fact, as in China, Greek foods were divided into grains, that is, breads, and others: olives, cheese, meat, fish, or fruit. Using bread as a plate, in what is recognizably the original pizza, is among the oldest habits in the world.

This is also one of the oldest wine-making regions of the world, although not one of the most famous; some wines are quite sweet (such as *mbrodaphne*) or literally turpentine-scented (like retsina, which contains pine resin and is definitely an acquired taste). However, there are many varietal wines produced in Greece, notably Merlot and Cabernet; and U.S. imports are increasing. *Ouzo* is the Greek equivalent of Pernod, a strong and potent anisette that is clear in the bottle but turns cloudy over ice.

Although Turkey as a whole is 99% Muslim, Eastern Turkey, with its proximity to Istanbul, the former capital of the Eastern Roman Empire and still the seat of the Greek Orthodox patriarch, has a much more diverse population, including Armenian Orthodox, Roman Catholic, Protestant, Jewish, and Sunni Muslim groups. Few of these communities abjure alcohol, and taverns are among the primary gathering spots. Still, strong, thick coffee remains a favorite stimulant and social medium all over the region.

THE HISTORY

Although so closely related in geography and experience, the Greeks and Turks are ethnically distinct. The indigenous Greeks were manufacturing and trading as early as 4000 B.C.E., and by 600 C.E. they had colonies stretching from the Black Sea to North Africa, and from Sicily to Mediterranean France and even Spain.

The first known civilization in Turkey was Hittite, dating from about 1800 B.C.E. Troy, which is just four miles from the Dardanelles in Asian Turkey, may have been one of its first great centers, and if so, the Trojan War set a pattern: It was from Turkey that the Persian armies repeatedly invaded Greece. By the eighth century B.C.E., Greece had established colonies along the coast into Asia Minor, where they came into contact with the Phrygians and Persians.

With the victories of Alexander the Great, however, the histories of Greece and Turkey began to intertwine. Although Alexander's empire dissolved soon after his untimely death, the rise of Rome had begun, and by the middle of the second century B.C.E., both Turkey and Greece were under Roman control. The eastern (Byzantine) half of the Roman Empire endured into the 11th century, but repeated attacks by Turks and Mongols from the east and European Crusaders from the west splintered it; Constantinople finally fell to the Ottomans in 1453, and despite Greece's crucial role in the rise of "Western" civilization, it became politically estranged from Europe—more an object of archaeological veneration than of cultural exchange. Consequently, the foods of modern Greece are clearly similar to those of earlier ages.

THE CUISINE

Two great physical features, and their greatest produce, laid down the primary laws of Greek cooking: the Mediterranean and Aegean Seas, and the steep inland mountains. The one provided seafood, the other the essential olive and the grapevine. No surprise, then, that ancient Greek myth has two powerful deities—Poseidon, representing the seas, and Athena, giver of the olive—battling for the primacy of worship. (Athena won, as "Athens" suggests; but both gods were frequently challenged by the cult of Dionysus, lord of wine.)

Nomadic, itinerant, warlike, and seagoing, the various ancestors of the Greeks and Turks didn't take the time for elaborate cooking or eating. The most prevalent form of cooking is grilling—a *souvlas* is a spit, hence *souvlaki*, the marinated kebabs that are Greek lunch shops' most famous offering—or the casserole-baking of one-pot dishes. Grilling over open coals is one heat-reducing maneuver, and in many Turkish homes, the coal fire is still preferred to the stove for cooking.

The other "air-conditioning" method is communal baking. In Greece it is still common for women to carry a casserole to the village bakery for cooking. This association of village market and family dinner is one reason that so many Greek restaurants in the United States are built around courtyards or employ flagstone flooring evocative of the old *tavernas*. Food is a social event, and you should be prepared to enjoy it.

Greeks are predominately Eastern Orthodox and pay allegiance to the patriarch at Istanbul. Both their religious beliefs and their convoluted shore line have made them masters of seafood—an obvious fact, perhaps, but one that might surprise Americans accustomed to thinking of Greek food only as moussaka, souvlaki, and stuffed grape leaves. The Muslim Turks, too, observe many fast days, but they rely less on seafood for alternatives than the Greeks do.

The main meal is midday dinner; feasts in particular are all-afternoon affairs. Portions are bountiful, particularly of the savory pies and roasted (frequently whole) lamb or kid. Eating utensils are basically the same as in the United States, at home and in restaurants. Unlike the Europeans, Greeks never considered the elaboration of cutlery a badge of civilization; hence, a salad fork is an entree fork is a dessert fork.

Incidentally, if you hear the cheer "Opa!," be sure to duck: A flaming platter is passing by.

There is little variety or fussiness to the food; it depends more on freshness. Menus are similar year-round, except that the emphasis shifts with the seasons; lamb is most popular in spring, as is suckling pig; hence their association with Easter feasting. Turkish dishes lean a bit more to the Persian style, with more yogurt, eggplant, wheat, and grains. Although special breads are baked for holidays, particularly sweet and fruit breads, both leavened doughs and flatbreads are daily fare.

THE MAIN INGREDIENTS

SEASONINGS The most characteristic flavors in Greek cooking are lemon, olives, and olive oil, which are used not only as ingredients but also as table condiments. Olives provide a wealth of different flavors, depending on whether they are dried, brine-cured, oil-cured, or green. Fresh herbs are essential, particularly parsley, mint, bay, rosemary, dill, marjoram, wild thyme, and the Greek oregano called *rigani*. To the south around the Aegean and in Crete, where Arab traders had more impact, Indian and Indonesian spices, such as cumin, cloves, cinnamon, and allspice, are more prevalent. Pine nuts, raisins, poppy seeds, sesame seeds, walnuts, and honey also recall the Persian influence.

A very characteristic condiment, made of nuts, soaked and squeezed bread crumbs, garlic, lemon and/or vinegar, and olive oil, is called *skorthalia*; it's often served with fish or vegetables.

VEGETABLES Greeks place somewhat more emphasis on greens than the Turks do, particularly spinach and wild leaf greens, which frequently appear in soup or combined with white beans or cheeses. Leeks, onions, garlic, and artichokes are particularly popular here, as are fava beans, lentils, and garbanzos. Although cauliflower did not grow naturally in the Middle East, it did flower in abundance in Greece.

MEAT AND POULTRY Lamb is the most popular meat, particularly when it comes to the organ meats, such as sweetbreads or liver. Farmers' treats, such as pig's trotters and jellied pig's head, are banquet food in Greece but not often seen in restaurants in the United States. Goat and lamb are both roasted; nearly any organ meat or offal—kidneys, livers, hearts, testicles, or brains—may be saved for use as *mezze*, the tapas-like dishes often served as appetizers.

Eggs are nearly always hard-boiled; the egg-dying American children associate with Easter is an ancient tradition in Greece.

SEAFOOD With its intricate coastlines, this region is rich in options: rockfish, pike, moray and conger eels, sardines, tuna, mullet, grouper, sea bream, bonito, monkfish, and sea bass. Shrimp, squid, oysters, octopus, mussels, sea urchins, limpets, and anemones are common as well, but of these only shrimp, octopus, squid, and shellfish are likely to show up on American menus.

STARCHES Rice is a regional staple (used for the famous Turkish *pilav*), but so are egg noodles and bulghur, and Greeks are particularly fond of a rice-shaped durum wheat pasta called *orzo*. Bulghur boiled in milk and then dried and stored for winter is called *tarhana*. *Phyllo*, the flaky butter-packed dough perfected by their Turkish neighbors, is used to wrap almost anything: meats, vegetables, cheese, or sweets.

DAIRY PRODUCTS Cheeses are usually fresh in the summer and salted or preserved in winter. The most famous Greek cheese is *feta*, a sharp, salty, semisoft cheese used in salads and phyllo pastries. *Kasseri* is a mild, Provolone-like cheese that is sometimes fried and served flambé; this dish is called *sagnaki*, but the word is now used as an adjective meaning "flaming," as in "shrimp sagnaki." *Mizithra* is a cheese that is soft when fresh but hardens as it ages; *kefalotiri* is another hard cheese. Yogurt is used as both ingredient and condiment. *Ayran*, made of yoghurt with water and a pinch of salt, is a popular drink, especially during summers.

THE MAIN DISHES

APPETIZERS Some of the most famous dips in the world are Greek and Turkish: *taramosalata*, the whipped carp roe/lemon juice/olive oil mixture; *baba ganouj*, the roasted eggplant spread; and *hummus*, the pureed garbanzo spread. The Greek version of mashed potatoes—called *skordalia*, it's pureed with olive oil and a great deal of garlic—is a dip rather than a side dish, as we would use it. *Tzatziki* is a dip or salad of shredded, drained cucumbers in garlic-flavored yogurt.

As mentioned above, organ meats left over from roasting meats are often used for *mezze* (see "The Middle East") or to flavor rice dishes or soups. Other appetizers include *keftedes*, small spicy meatballs; *dolmas*, those lemon-flavored grape leaves cigar-rolled around rice and ground meat (and, in Turkey, sometimes with raisins and pine nuts as well); and *tiropites*, cheese-filled phyllo puffs. *Spanakopita*, phyllo pie stuffed with spinach and feta cheese, may be offered as either an appetizer or a main course. *Lakerdes* and *bakaliaros* are salted and dried fish, respectively, often served as hors d'oeuvres. (Notice the relationship between the words *bakaliaros* and *bacalao*—the Portuguese salt cod that circled the globe.)

Squid is likely to be fried as an appetizer, as are smelts and baby octopus. Grilled sausages, such as the fennel-flavored lamb version called *loukanika*, may be served in appetizer portions.

SALADS Although the Greeks have adapted salads to American tastes (and in fact a "Greek salad" of greens, tomatoes, onions, olives, feta, lemon juice, and olive oil is a popular deli carry-out item), lettuce is not truly in their repertoire. Instead, they make *melitzanosalata*, an eggplant salad; and *patzari*, sliced or cubed beets in yogurt. Beets are also often mixed with oranges. Marinated baby octopus or squid are often served as salads.

Oil, Olé

Unless you pay close attention to what you order, it is difficult to have anything resembling a low-fat Greek meal. Olive oil is considered essential for flavor as well as lubrication, so there tends to be plenty in any baked dish (although, as we noted above, chefs in the United States have begun to lighten the dosage). Also, Greek cheeses tend to be fatty and salty and may "weep" more oil into a dish. Even grilled fish may have been coated with oil beforehand. The best bets are roasts—lamb or chicken—or kebabs, even those that have been marinated beforehand.

SOUPS *Avgolemono* is the Greek version of chicken soup, an egg-rich broth flavored with lemon and often thickened with rice; *kakavia* is a seafood soup with vegetables. The traditional Easter soup called *mageritsa* is a fringe benefit of all the lamb-roasting going on that time of year: It includes rice, lamb organs and intestines, and lots of herbs. You'll probably never see it on an American menu, even if it's lurking in the kitchen.

MEATS Most meats are marinated before being grilled: *Kelftiko* is the marinated roast lamb that is the mainstay of every Greek church picnic. Chicken is generally rubbed and stuffed with lemon before grilling. Kid and pork are also grill fodder, and livers and kidneys are increasingly visible on American menus. Occasionally, sweetbreads or brains will be stewed in wine or served as part of a mixed grill. Pork is also stewed with celery or onions; in some regions, the first two weeks of Carnival are an almost exclusively pork feast.

A particularly beloved and characteristically Turkish dish is *donner kebab*, in which layers of lamb, veal, and beef are marinated, layered, rolled, tied, grilled, and then sliced pinwheel-style and served with a tomato and yogurt sauce; because of the amount of work involved, many Turkish restaurants only offer this on weekends or by advance reservation. (In the United States, sadly, most donner kebab is solely lamb.) Turks also make a sort of ravioli called *manti*, related to the Persian aushak.

FISH AND SEAFOOD Grilling and frying are the two most common techniques used on both fish and seafood ("small fry" is a sort of pun, as tiny fingerlings or immature shrimp are often called "fry" and are treated just that way), but stuffing and baking whole fish and octopus or squid is also popular. Grilled or sautéed shrimp, roasted fish, or fish wrapped in grape or bay leaves may be available as well.

CASSEROLES The most common main-course casseroles include moussaka, an eggplant or potato dish layered with ground meat and noodles and set in béchamel custard; *pastitsio*, a Greek lasagna that may or may not have tomatoes; eggplant stuffed with rice, pine nuts, and tomatoes or with ground meat and mint; stuffed cabbage leaves; and various *kapama* dishes—shrimp, lamb shanks, or chicken—cooked with wine, tomatoes, and onions. However, hearty but unlayered dishes of goat or lamb with pasta and tomatoes are common comfort food.

Spinach/feta/onion stuffing is almost a seasoning in itself and may be used to pad whole fish, chicken breasts, breast of veal, or leg of lamb.

Artichokes are a fancier alternative: *Exobikon* is a lamb stew with artichokes, kalamata olives, and cheese wrapped in phyllo. Vegetable stews—artichokes with potatoes, carrots, and leeks, for instance, or the leek pie called *prasopita*—are often baked in or covered with phyllo.

SWEETS Greek and Turkish pastries are obvious carryovers from Persia and are extremely sweet and rich. The most famous is baklava, a phyllo pastry drenched in sugar syrup and nuts. (Unless you have a serious sweet tooth, one serving will generally be enough for two people.) Rice pudding is a lighter alternative and generally has a dusting of cinnamon or nutmeg.

HOW TO ORDER AND EAT LIKE A NATIVE

Most Greek menus are divided in the European fashion into hot and cold appetizers, soups, salads, and main courses. Two people should ideally test one dip—taramosalata or baba ganouj—and a finger dish, such as stuffed grape leaves; for four, add a platter of olives and red peppers, a large salad, or grilled or fried squid sprayed with lemon juice.

For the main courses, two people might consider one grilled and one roasted dish, perhaps fish and lamb; four people could have a lamb dish, roasted chicken, a fish or seafood dish, and either moussaka or pastitsio. Remember, the desserts are strong; ditto for the retsina and ouzo, both legendarily deceptive. Pace yourself.

Coffee is prepared in traditional Middle Eastern fashion and served with the powder-fine grounds mixed in. Be sure to give it time to settle: It may be served in a small cup or in a miniature pot, but in either case the bottom third will be sludge, and you only want to sip off the top half, at least until you get the feel of it. It's very rich (and speaking of deceptive, two cups of this stuff could wake a genie).

Greek food is generally inexpensive, particularly in the souvlaki shops, or moderate for roasted entrees and seafood. Rarely will an entree top $15 or $16.

COOKING AT HOME

You won't need any special equipment to prepare these dishes at home, although if you happen to have invested in one of those chicken-roasting racks that stands on its end, you'll come closer to replicating the original rotisserie chicken. If you want to roast a whole lamb, you'll have to dig a pit and install a spit; we leave that to your imagination.

MOUSSAKA WITH EGGPLANT

2 onions, finely chopped
2/3 cup olive oil
18 ounces minced (or coarsely ground) meat
2–3 tomatoes
1 bay leaf
1 garlic clove
salt and pepper to taste
4 or 5 eggplant
flour for dredging
oil for frying
2 cups béchamel sauce (see recipe below)
1/3 cup grated Parmesan cheese

Soften onions by cooking them in oil; add meat and sauté 10 minutes, then add tomatoes, bay leaf, garlic; salt and pepper to taste and simmer 1 hour.

Meanwhile, wash eggplant, trim stems, and slice into 1/2-inch rounds. Soak in salted water for 1 hour, drain, and pat dry. Dredge in flour and fry in very hot oil until golden; drain on paper towels. Preheat oven to 375°F. Layer a pan with half the eggplant slices, top with half the meat mixture, and repeat. Top the whole dish with béchamel sauce, sprinkle with grated Parmesan cheese, and bake approximately 25 minutes.

BÉCHAMEL SAUCE

2/3 cup extra virgin olive oil
2/3 cup flour
1 1/2 cups milk
2 eggs, beaten
salt and pepper
grated nutmeg
2/3 cup kefalotiri or Parmesan cheese, grated

Pour oil into pot, stir in flour, and cook over medium heat, stirring constantly, for about 5 minutes; meanwhile, warm milk in separate pan. Whisk warmed milk into flour mixture, then add eggs and seasonings, and simmer, still stirring, for 5 minutes. Add cheese; if the mixture becomes too thick, thin with a little more milk.

TZATZIKI (CUCUMBER DIP)

1 cucumber, grated and fluid drained
1 pint plain yogurt, drained
4–5 cloves garlic, finely minced
2 tablespoons olive oil
2 tablespoons vinegar
salt and pepper to taste

Combine cucumber and yogurt; add garlic. In alternating portions, add oil and vinegar, mixing constantly (preferably with a hand mixer). Add salt and pepper to taste. Serve with pita bread.

FETA SPREAD

1 clove garlic, minced
1 small red chili, seeded and minced
1 tablespoon extra virgin olive oil (more if needed)
2 sweet peppers, roasted, peeled, and seeded
1 1/2 cups fresh feta cheese
1 teaspoon lemon juice (optional)

Combine garlic, chili, and oil in food processor; puree, scraping down sides as needed. Add roasted peppers and repeat; add feta and puree, adding a little more oil if too thick or lumpy. Add lemon if desired, blend.

This spread can be used as a pita or vegetable dip; spread over cauliflower and baked; or stirred into garbanzos or other vegetables as a seasoning.

THE MIDDLE EAST

BASIC CUISINE

DINNER FOR TWO:
Fettoosh, baba ganouj, kebabs

DINNER FOR FOUR:
Dolmas, aushak, hummus, fessanjan, grilled chicken

GROUP DISH:
Mezze

STYLE:
Tangy, sweet-and-sour, nutty

KEY FLAVORS:
Sesame, lemon, yogurt, olives, honey

EATING UTENSILS:
Pita and other breads, skewers, spoons, and forks

DISTINCTIVE DISHES:
Kebabs, basmati rice, dolmas

UNIFORMITY OF MENUS:
Good

NUTRITIONAL INDEX:
High carbohydrate, medium fat, medium sodium

COST:
Inexpensive

"THANK YOU":
"Shukaran" (Arabic); "Tasha kur" (Afghani)

It is as much a metaphor as a geographical definition: The Middle East, midpoint of two worlds, cradle of civilization, source of mystery and religion.

Seeing photographs today of the region—the great deserts, vast steppes and mountain ranges, and caravans of camels and horses as well as more modern trucks—it's hard to imagine that this was once literally the garden spot of the world. The Garden of Eden, or its historical counterpoint, lay somewhere in or near Mesopotamia, the fertile delta region between the Tigris and Euphrates Rivers, in what is now southern Iraq. Many of the culinary basics were discovered here, none more important than wheat, but none more popular than beer, the earliest archaeological evidence of which dates to the fourth millennium B.C.E. Wine, too, probably originated in this region, as well as grain alcohol—and coffee, from Abyssinia, the nation founded by the son of Solomon and the queen of Sheba, was transformed from a berry to a stimulant here, in time to be brewed for Helen of

Troy. The first bread was baked here, and the molds piled up for rising; eventually the word for the stack, pyramid, would be applied to the great tombs as well.

But eons and empires pass. Nowadays, the Middle East is a region of problematic agriculture, and consequently depends either on laborious irrigation or periodic flooding—or, in the case of the aggressively modern Israeli kibbutzes, hydroponic techniques. Even Egypt, despite its long and intimate relationship with the Nile River, is only 5% cultivated.

The phrase "Middle East"—which for all its European bias has yet to be replaced by a better term—is generally taken to encompass Syria, Jordan, Lebanon, Israel, Egypt, Turkey, Iraq, Iran, and the Gulf States along the Arabian Peninsula. (The term "Palestine" or "Holy Land" comprises parts of Israel, Jordan, and Egypt). Libya is also in this region, but one is unlikely to find an advertised Libyan restaurant in the United States.

Each country has distinct preparations and specialties; but in the United States, Middle Eastern cooks tend to favor one of two broadly defined styles: Lebanese, Israeli, Egyptian, and Turkish restaurants have a somewhat more "western" or Mediterranean flavor; whereas Iranian (or, as they are more often referred to in the United States, Persian) and Arabian restaurants have a more exotic, "eastern" cast.

This generally reflects the rival historical influences of the region. Israeli, Lebanese, Syrian, and Armenian foods display closer ties to the Turkish and Greek cuisines (thanks to the domination of the Ottoman Empire), and the eastern cultures show the heavier stamp of the Byzantine Empire, which preceded the Ottoman, and Persian cuisine, which the Muslim revolution carried east to India and China and west across north Africa to Spain. (Although Afghanistan, Azerbaijan, and Armenia are not technically part of the Middle East, their cuisines, especially as they're available in the United States, were indelibly influenced by the Turks, so they are included in this chapter. Bulgaria, too, which shares many dishes, is mentioned as well.)

The rule of thumb in distinguishing the Persian influence from the Ottoman is that although the Persians enjoyed combining fruits and meats in the same dish and spicing the mix richly, even sweetly, the Ottomans tended to cook their meats separately and season more simply. But these distinctions are very general: It was the Turks who developed phyllo pastry, but it was the Persians who added the syrup and nuts for *baklava*.

THE HISTORY

The Middle East, lying at what was for millennia the center of the commercial world, has given birth to more civilizations (and been invaded by more upstarts) than any other region. Lebanon alone, which now looks back on its cosmopolitan history as a sort of golden age, was invaded by the Egyptians, Babylonians, Jews (fleeing Egypt behind Moses), Philistines, Assyrians, Babylonians (again), Persians, Greeks (under Alexander), Jews (this time under the Maccabees), Romans, Persians again, Romans again, Arabs, North Africans, Western European Crusaders, Marmeluk Turks, and, finally, the Ottoman Turks—and all that by the sixteenth century.

Consequently, although Americans tend to view Middle Easterners as a homogeneous group, they are quite heterogeneous, even within particular countries. For example, although Iran is 95% Shiite Muslim, it also has Sunni Muslim, Eastern Orthodox, Jewish, Roman Catholic, Protestant, Zoroastrian, and Bahaian minorities, speaking Farsi, Turkish, Kurdish, Armenian, Arabic, English, and French.

The earliest fossil records in the region date to about 10,000 B.C.E., when the town of Jericho, on the banks of the Jordan River, was growing domesticated species of wheat and barley, along with lentils and peas. Two thousand years after that, farmers were attempting to domesticate pigs, sheep, and goats. By 6000 B.C.E., virtually the whole region from Anatolia to the Mediterranean was raising wheat and earning the name "Fertile Crescent." Organized agriculture led to stock breeding for labor, metalworking for tools, and pottery making for storage.

The Sumerians, who moved out of India into Mesopotamia about 5000 B.C.E., developed not only one of the earliest writing systems but also produced the great saga of Gilgamesh, preserved in cuneiform on the oldest tablets in the world, which mentions wine and beer, ale and oil, cheese and butter. The Babylonians, who succeeded the Sumerians, left us actual recipes for barley and wheat beers, meats in sauces, and frescoes of dairy farmers milking and churning butter. (Crushing grains must have been considered women's work, however; Samson's labor in the mill was a special insult from the Philistines.)

By 3000 B.C.E., there were commercial markets all the way from Babylonia to Egypt, trading via the Caspian Sea and then over-land caravans, to India and China; from the Lebanese coast, the Phoenicians traded all around the Mediterranean, on both the European and African coasts.

Ur imported wine from the mountains to its north, the modern-day Iraq and Syria, and even from Armenia; eventually, it would send wine to China. Nebuchadnezzar was exporting olive oil across the Black Sea to Central Asia. The pharaohs' pantry included five kinds of cooking oils; their pens held ducks, geese, guinea hens, and songbirds. The Code of Hammurabi II, from the seventeenth century B.C.E., lays down imperial taxes for dairy and meat markets.

Around the mid-eighth century C.E., as the Uyghurs, who were strongly influenced by the Chinese, settled in Turkey, the *manti*, the stuffed dumpling of Asia—also known as "mandu" in Korea, "mantu" in Afghanistan, and "momo" in Tibet—became a regional staple. It was the Turks who transformed Persian rice dishes from desserts to main dishes, who used oil-frying, and who made yogurt and its derivatives central to seasoning. (Bulgarian Turks, intriguingly, were making sheep and cow's milk yogurt centuries before the Ottomans arrived.) As the centuries wore on, West African traders brought in okra and took back spinach, which is native to Iran. Pickled fig leaves, which had been used to wrap food, gave way to edible grape leaves. The Byzantines also appreciated salt roe, and by the twelfth century had picked out Black Sea caviar as the finest.

Sugar was a popular condiment in India from ancient times and had been used all around the Middle East from the time of Darius (the word *sakara* for sugar, from which *saccharine* evolved, is Sanskrit); but the Persians spent the time to purify and elaborate on it. By the end of the first millennium, Arabian chefs had become so sophisticated in the use and sale of sugar that they established a refinery on the island of Crete, which supplied a very lucrative trade to Europe. They popularized caramel as well, a delicacy that would later revolutionize European cuisine, particularly in Italy and Austria.

With the conquest of the old Byzantine Empire by the Ottoman Turks, beginning in the thirteenth century and culminating with the fall of Byzantium (Istanbul) in 1453, the Middle East became the richest and most diverse culinary civilization in the world—and one from which Italy's various city-states greatly profited. Elaborate imperial banquets featured Anatolian gazelles and sparrows. Tomatoes were introduced via the Moors, the African Muslims, who got them from the Spanish, who brought them back from the Americas. Coffee, which grew wild on the slopes of Abyssinia, had far more appeal to the sensual and physical Persians than the contemplative Chinese emperors' tea. Even the Portuguese, who briefly established settlements on the Persian Gulf in the sixteenth century, contributed chili peppers that they had picked up in the Caribbean. Nevertheless, not until the turn of the twentieth century did the European nations take serious note of the richness of the Middle Eastern cuisines.

THE CUISINES

Middle Eastern cuisine has been far more influential than is generally understood; the very word *gourmet* comes from the Farsi *ghormeh,* or stew, and was probably picked up by unsophisticated French Crusaders stunned by the lavish banquets enjoyed by their Muslim enemies in the Holy Land.

Long before the fabled Silk Route was established in the second millennium B.C.E., China and India were sending goods to Persia via the Caspian Sea, beginning with the essential rice. Five thousands years ago, Chinese apricots and peaches and Indian eggplants were already a luxury in Mesopotamia, where Babylonian fishermen were drying anchovies and grinding them into a paste that would still be a delicacy in the twenty-first century. A thousand years later, lemons had arrived from Kashmir. Babylonians imported Asian silks, spices, jewels, and perfumes in exchange for spinach, pomegranates, sesame seeds, garlic, fava beans, and honey. Spice Island riches—cumin, turmeric, and ginger—were transmitted via India, which in its turn adopted the *tanur* (in India, *tandoor*) oven and the Persian samosas and kofta. At its height, the Persian Empire stretched from Russia and India in the north and east to Greece and Egypt to the west and south.

Consequently, from the earliest of times, Middle Eastern dishes were fragrant with indigenous and Indonesian spices: thyme, cloves, cardamom, chervil, rosemary, and marjoram. Onions grow wild there, as does the invaluable olive; so do mint, saffron, parsley, frankincense, and myrrh. Figs and dates are native to the Middle East, as are cherries and pears; the Romans called pears "Persian apples." Plums and prunes were sealed up in Theban tombs as delicacies for the next life. Honey was an ancient discovery and was used to baste roast pork and duck. Simon Maccabeus, the first king of independent Judea, put the citron on his coinage in 142 B.C.E. Chicory covers the hillsides in Egypt; Caesar discovered it with Cleopatra.

From the mountains and plateaus of Iran came ice enough for summer cooking; the ancient sweet-and-spiced fruit drinks of the Middle East, cooled with snow and shaved ice, were called *sharbat*—the origin of our *sherbet.* Persians not only consumed rosewater and almond milk, they bathed in them. The Byzantines made puddings and marmalades and drank wines flavored with herbs, absinthe, rose, and anise—precursor of the anisettes and vermouths of the modern Mediterranean.

Between the Mediterranean Ocean and the Black Sea, fish were plentiful: mackerel, tuna, swordfish, anchovies, bluefish, bonita, sardines. The Arabs believed it was good luck to dream of fish, and amulets of fish meant long life in Egypt. A Byzantine recipe seasoned skate with caraway seeds. *Garos*, a condiment of fermented salted fish very like the nam pla and nuoc mam of Southeast Asia, was divided into the paste (for the wealthy) and the liquid that was poured off the top (which the poor used).

The Egyptians and Mesopotamians ate not only many types of fowl—adding domesticated chickens from China and peacocks and hens from Iran—but sheep, goats, donkeys, oxen, pigs, horses, and camels. They hunted from time immemorial. Nearly 12,000 years ago, Turkish hunters were using jackals to help them; eventually the Egyptians began selective breeding for a domesticated species. By 4500 B.C.E., the hunters of the Nile delta were bringing down buffalo, elephants, bulls, falcons, and gazelles. Two thousands years later, gazelles and antelope were being bred for food in the Sinai.

THE MAIN INGREDIENTS

Broadly speaking, the regional staples include wheat and rice, most famously the basmati rice of Iran, along with *orzo*, a rice-shaped pasta, and large-grain or "Israeli" couscous, the pearl-shaped semolina grain best known in Moroccan cuisine; legumes, particularly garbanzos, fava beans, and lentils (which have been cultivated in this region, according to some sources, for 8,000 years); fennel, purslane greens, and spinach; poultry, beef, and lamb; fish; vegetables; and citrus fruits. But from the Mediterranean coast to the Afghani hills, the soil and climate ranges widely; the great central plateau of Asian Turkey called Anatolia lies above 3,000 feet elevation, with only strips of coastal lowland.

The most common herbs and flavorings include tarragon, marjoram, saffron, sumac (not the poisonous American variety), garlic and garlic chives, oranges, a number of sweet and sour limes and lemons, turmeric, zatar (a kind of thyme), dill, mint and parsley (both fresh and dried), *tahini* (a sesame-seed butter), cumin, cinnamon, coriander, and poppy seeds. The ancient Spice Islands trade provided allspice, nutmeg, mace, black pepper, ginger, and cardamom. Hot and sweet peppers, fresh and dried, are extremely important, and most cooks make their own chili pastes from family recipes. In the eastern regions, bowls of fresh chopped herbs are placed on the table as routinely as salt and pepper might be in the United States, and swirls of herb-flavored oils are also used to finish soups and stews. Dried fruits, particularly cranberries, cherries, and citrus fruits, are also used as seasonings.

REGIONAL CUISINES

THE NORTHERN AND WESTERN COUNTRIES The Mediterranean coast, with its long, hot, dry summers and cool, rainy winters, remains one of the more fertile portions of the Middle East, and these nations have a wide variety of fruits and vegetables in their diets. The Jordan Valley produces citrus crops, bananas, and many vegetables; the higher regions are suited to olives, lentils, garbanzos, fava beans, and cereals, including corn and the bulghur wheat that was the staple in the millennia before rice was introduced. Lamb is the popular meat; but sheep and goats produce many cheeses, fresh and aged, and yogurt foods, also fresh and dried. Sesame seeds are pressed for oil.

Syria's primary crops are wheat, potatoes, sugar beets, barley, cotton, garbanzos, fruits, and dairy products such as cheese. Turkey's fruits and vegetables—particularly eggplant, okra, peppers, zucchini, onions, tomatoes, cherries, apricots, plums, and loquats—so-called Japanese plums—are highly prized. Israel has to import additional wheat and barley, as well as beef, but it has abundant fruits, including avocados, melons, bananas, peaches, eggplant, and tomatoes, plus olives, peanuts, grapes, and cotton.

Bulgaria is widely cultivated with wheat and maize, plus rice and lentils in the warmer south, and sustains large herds of cattle and pigs. Along the Black Sea and in the temperate regions, farmers raise apples, pears, cherries, almonds, chestnuts, figs, and peanuts. Unlike most Middle Eastern regions, Bulgaria does not raise olives, consumes relatively little fish (many Bulgarians eat seafood only in months with an R in the name, like the old saw about oysters), and still depends heavily on yogurt products. Bulgarians have also largely abandoned the use of animal fats in cooking, and even most nut oils have been replaced by sunflower oil.

Egypt's primary crop is not edible but exportable: cotton. Its subsistence crops include rice, corn, wheat, millet, onions, beans, barley, tomatoes, sugarcane, citrus fruits, and dates. Poultry, cattle, sheep, goats, donkeys, and even buffalo are also common.

THE EASTERN COUNTRIES   As you move east, there are fewer fruits and meat and more grains in the diet. Iraq's plateau regions and sandy soil make it ideal for growing dates, grains, and vegetables; Iran, most of whose cultivated territory is in the region of the Caspian Sea, produces primarily wheat but also rice, barley, and corn as well as fruits, nuts, and dates. Sheep and goats are the most common meats, and a little beef and camel; but poultry is the main animal protein. From the Persian Gulf come shrimp, tuna, and swordfish, which is eaten fresh near the water and dried in the central plateau. Iran also benefits from Caspian seafood, particularly salmon, carp, trout, pike, and the sturgeon that produces the world-famous Iranian and Russian caviar. Mountainous Afghanistan, with its Tatar and Mongol legacies, is much more heavily dependent on the grazing herds of fat-tail sheep, which provide not only meat and fats but also wool for clothing and rugs and skins for huts.

THE SOUTHERN COUNTRIES   The cuisine of the Arabian countries—Kuwait, Saudi Arabia, Qatar, and so on—is not widely represented in the United States and in general resembles that of Lebanon and Syria; but a few elements are notable for their obvious family connections. The closest thing to a national dish is probably *khouzi*, baked whole lamb stuffed with a mixture of chicken, rice, and eggs with such ancient spices as saffron and *baharat*, a spice mix of black pepper, coriander, cumin, cardamom, nutmeg, and *cassia* (false cinnamon)—the kind of combination that, thanks to the endlessly curious Arabian traders of early centuries, is popular from the Middle East all the way to Southeast Asia. Like its northern Indian and central Asian cousins, Arabian food is eaten either with rice or flatbreads, with salty pickles, yogurt, and green herbs such as mint, coriander, and parsley. Although Americans tend to envision these territories as all desert, they have extensive coastlines and consume large amounts of prawns and fish.

MEZZE

A good way to taste a lot of classic Middle Eastern dishes, especially at a Lebanese restaurant, is to order *mezze*—which, depending on the region the menu's author is from, may be spelled mezza, meza, mazzah, or some other variation. Mezze, a tableful of mini-servings or appetizers designed for sharing and conversation, is the Turkish tapas—or, more likely, tapas is the Spanish mezze, adopted during the Moorish occupation. It is the most sociable of meals, and some restaurants in the United States boast of offering scores of options, although most Americans will be lucky to experience one score. Unlike tapas, however, mezze platters—that is, preset combinations—are often served all at once, and some hot things may get cold, so consult your menu.

Among typical mezze dishes are the eggplant puree known as *baba ganouj* (or in some regions, *mutabbal*), the sesame-flavored garbanzo dip called *hummus*, stuffed grape leaves (*dolma*), cheese- or spinach-stuffed phyllo pastries called *borek*, fava beans or string beans with tomatoes, grilled sausages, fried smelts, goat and sheeps' cheese, marinated mushrooms, radishes, stuffed eggplant, shredded zucchini pancakes, brains in vinaigrette, hot peppers, dozens of types of olives, and *lamajun*, the pizza-style flatbread topped with minced meat (with or without tomatoes and onions) that is traditionally folded in half before being eaten, just as pizza is on the New Jersey boardwalk. *Tabbouleh* and *fettoosh*, the two most famous salads (described below), are almost standard.

Somewhat similar to the mezze is the *mokhalafat*, which also contains a number of small dishes, but these are served as condiments rather than appetizers: pickled garlic, stewed beets, and *boryani*, or yogurt with spinach. Such condiments can also be ordered as appetizers, in which case they are usually called *sabzee*.

THE MAIN DISHES

APPETIZERS The tidbits usually gathered up in mezze are often offered singly as hors d'oeuvres. The lamb-and-rice-stuffed grape leaves called dolmas are found throughout the region. Pita is particularly well known as the accompaniment to hummus and baba ganouj. Pastries and dumplings filled with ground lamb, spinach, and pine nuts or even zucchini and cheese are common.

What is sometimes called the national dish of Egypt, *ful* (or *fool*) *medames*, is used as a breakfast (or evening "break fast" during Ramadan), a mezze, or a meal. It's made of long-simmered fava beans or a combination of favas and lentils, mashed and mixed with lime juice and oil or a ghee-like clarified butter, garlic, onions, chilies, cumin, and sometimes sausage. What's referred to as the national dish of Israel is *falafel*—a small fried patty or croquette of fava beans or garbanzos; this ancient Egyptian invention now popular all over the Middle East is increasingly common as veggie fast food in the United States; it's been nicknamed the "Israeli hot dog."

SALADS The Lebanese salad called fettoosh (also spelled fattoush or fettoush) combines day-old toasted or fried bread, parsley, lemon, tomatoes, cucumber, green onions, and mint. In Syria, it generally includes cheese as well. Tabbouleh, the lemon juice-dressed salad of bulghur wheat and parsley, has been popular in the United States for a long time. In addition, vegetable salads featuring carrots, roasted sweet peppers, zucchini, tomatoes with hot peppers, beets, couscous, and any or all of these together are used as condiments and mezze.

SOUPS Although there are some broths, Middle Eastern soups tend to be thick, filling, and nutritious. Turkish favorites include lentil with purslane soup; chicken and tomato soup with plain dumplings; peppery broths with spiced meat and grain dumplings; and hearty lentil, white bean, and garbanzo soup with lamb broth. A common Persian soup combines bread and white beans—a dish transmitted to Tuscany and still popular there. Ful, the Egyptian stew of white beans or garbanzos, is sometimes offered as a soup, but *molokhia*, a soup made from the leaves of the mallow, is also symbolically popular. Israelis mix meat, vegetables, eggs, and rice into a stew called *cholent*, which is made a day ahead so it's kosher to serve on the Sabbath, when cooking is prohibited. Iranian soups have a characteristic sour element, usually from lemon or green fruit. In the summer, however, cooling cucumber and yogurt soups with mint and perhaps raisins and nuts are common.

FISH AND SEAFOOD Unlike the more western Mediterranean countries, Middle Eastern cultures are generally cool toward seafood. Shellfish is forbidden to kosher-keeping Jews, although they can eat fish—including, of course, the famous smoked and salted lox and nova salmon (see "A Note on Kosher Food," page 187). The Egyptians are also fond of mild fish like the carp and mullet that populate the Nile; they are often baked with tomato sauce or occasionally with curry spices.

MEATS *Kebabs* (or kebobs or kababs), grilled skewers of marinated chicken or lamb, have been common in the United States for a long time but nowadays may also include veal, lamb chops, filet mignon, quail, goat, and shrimp. (The Persian kebabs are the originals of the Greek souvlaki and the Indonesian satays; the word itself is Turkish.) A number of Iranian- and Afghani-run restaurants in America serve almost nothing but kebabs and the rice pilaf that accompanies them. *Donner kebab* is a fancier, Sunday-dinner version in which various meats (predominantly lamb) are sliced, marinated, layered, rolled, rotisserie-grilled, and then sliced pinwheel-fashion and topped with yogurt sauce. *Chowpan zheek* is a sort of Mongol answer to kebab-to-go: grilled rack of lamb and drippings served over thin bread. *Shawarma* is marinated spit-roasted lamb (or, in the United States, beef) sliced and stuffed into pita bread with tomatoes and pickles.

Kofta is ground meat, sometimes used in large meatballs and often stuffed. *Kibbeh*, finely minced or pounded lamb mixed with cracked wheat and mint into a smooth paste, can be shaped either into cakes and baked or skewer-grilled or, more frequently, stuffed with seasoned meat fillings and deep-fried to a crust. *Kibbeh kashkash* is shaped into sausages, grilled, and served with tomato sauce. (Kibbeh was traditionally sometimes served raw, as a sort of lamb tartare, but it is extremely rare, no pun intended, to find it served that way in the United States.) Occasionally these kibbeh balls are cooked in soup or vegetable stews. Other stews are flavored with a confit of lamb or mutton.

Stuffed meats, particularly lamb and chicken, are roasted in the tandoor oven or over open charcoal. Meats are also turned into various types of sausages, smoked and dry-cured hams, and pastramis. *Saniyeh* is a brisket of pot roast flavored with tahini. The more upscale kitchens may offer stewed or grilled brains or other organs as well.

POULTRY   Grilled or roasted chicken is a Middle Eastern classic, and Greek and Lebanese immigrants were among the first to jump on (actually, they probably built) the rotisserie-chicken bandwagon. *Fessanjan* (or *fessanjen*) is a classic Persian dish usually made of chicken but sometimes duck or even lamb stewed with walnuts and pomegranate.

Egyptians are particularly fond of fried hard-boiled eggs, a picnic staple since medieval times.

STEWS AND CASSEROLES   The eastern cuisines in particular are fond of richer meat and vegetable stews, or the classic meat and fruit combinations. *Koresh* (or *koresht* or *khoresh*) is the general word for a braised dish. *Ghormeh sabzee* is lamb shanks braised with garbanzos, scallions, onion, garlic, sumac, and dried lemon or lime. *Koresh bademjan* is lamb braised with eggplant. *Mizrah gasemi* is a variation of baba ganouj that includes tomatoes.

Among characteristic Afghan dishes are *korma-e-seib*, apples baked with tomato sauce, prunes, walnuts, split peas, and lamb; and *shalgram*, a stew of turnips baked in brown sugar and ginger and generally served alongside lamb. *Zardack palow*—sliced carrots and garbanzos stewed with walnuts and prunes and served over rice—is made with or without lamb (or beef). In fact, many Afghan dishes can be converted to vegetarian entrees, and eggplant, pumpkin, and spinach often appear as stews.

DUMPLINGS AND TURNOVERS Although the Middle East briefly fell under the spell of noodles (it was from Persia that the Chinese learned the technique for milling grains), they quickly fell well behind rice in popularity. Nowadays only a few remain, either as festival dishes or in the form of stuffed noodles, that is, dumplings. *Aushuk* (or aushak) is the best-known Afghani dish, a sort of inside-out ravioli or boiled dumpling stuffed with leeks or scallions and topped with a yogurt and mint sauce. The Turkish version is called manti and is stuffed or sometimes topped with ground lamb. *Boulani* is a vegetarian version, stuffed with leeks and potatoes and topped with yogurt. Afghan *sambosas* are usually stuffed with garbanzos and meat, rather than the Indian-style potato stuffing. A *knish* is a savory meat or potato-stuffed pastry brought to Israel by Eastern European immigrants along with *latkes,* pancakes of shredded potato and onion.

SIDE DISHES Vegetable dishes are generally rather simple, using familiar presentations but relying on freshness and visual appeal: grilled or sautéed eggplant, zucchini, and tomatoes in a sort of ratatouille but topped with yogurt; marinated green beans; sautéed chicory with caramelized onion; and spinach with yogurt. Middle Easterners stuff a variety of vegetables—zucchini, sweet peppers, artichokes, and pumpkins, as well as grape leaves—either with meat, rice, and raisin stuffings or rice and pine nut stuffings. *Shakshuka* is a dish borrowed from North Africa, but it sounds almost Central American; it's a hash of sautéed onions, tomatoes, and peppers with a fried egg on top. Stuffed cabbage often has a lamb and wheat bulghur filling, like unfried kibbeh, and a pomegranate sauce. The other common way to handle vegetables is to preserve them either by drying or pickling.

RICE Rice is so important, particularly in the eastern countries, that it is almost its own food group. Unlike most Asian cuisines, in which rice is first soaked, then boiled or steamed, Iranian rice goes through all three steps (plus, for special occasions, a three-day dry smoking), which produces a very light fluffy rice. The Iranian variety, called *basmati,* is considered by many—and not only Iranians—to be the best in the world. A firm, slightly nutty- or smoky-flavored long-grain species, basmati is grown only in the Middle East and portions of India ("Texmati" rice is an American imitation). Simply dressed with butter and saffron and perhaps a raw egg, it is called *chelo* or *chelou*, which is generally the way rice is served with stews or heavy sauces. This egg-thickened version is also sometimes crisped in a skillet and broken into pieces to be eaten with stew; then it is called *chelo ta dag*.

When rice is mixed with other ingredients it is called *pilau* or *polow* (i.e., pilaf): Pilaus may be flavored with meat or poultry cooked in almost any fashion, herbs, spices, vegetables or nuts. A classic rice dish, called "King of Persia," is intended to be served with saffron chicken: It's saffron rice mixed with candied fruits, nuts, and berries and covered in caramelized sugar.

Barley, wheat, and kasha (wheat bulghur), couscous, orzo, corn meals, and millet are also raised in various parts of the region.

BREADS AND DOUGHS   The Middle Eastern countries produce dozens of breads, nearly all from wheat, many of them flatbreads ranging from the Iranian *lavash* to the "pocket bread" or pita. Some are sweet and crisp, some sweet and thick, some herb- or salt-crusted. Iranian breads are nearly all leavened, but in most Middle Eastern countries, both leavened and unleavened doughs are common. The most famous Israeli bread, *matzo*, is ritually unleavened in memory of the flight from Egypt retold in the book of Exodus; the next most famous Jewish bread, *challah*, is the original egg bread. The rich, parchment-delicate dough called phyllo is a Persian invention. So is the tandoor oven, so that the puffed-up breads made from disks of dough slapped onto the sides of the oven are as familiar in Turkey as in India.

BEVERAGES   *Dooghs* are yogurt-based drinks flavored with mint. Coffee is still the stimulant of choice, particularly because alcohol is forbidden to most, though not all, observant Muslims. Some Middle Eastern restaurants may not offer beer or wine, but most have made a concession to American habits (and many are themselves becoming assimilated). Tea is drunk throughout the day. Lebanese and Israeli beers are becoming more common, as are wines from the region.

SWEETS   Middle Easterners have a very sweet tooth, particularly for honeyed phyllo pastries, candied fruit, and ice creams and sherbets. The word *candy* comes from the Farsi word for sugar, *qand*—probably another tribute from the Crusaders. Rice and rice flours, dates, and garbanzo or

Oil-Rich Regions

Middle Eastern chefs cook with quite a bit of oil, for flavor as well as texture. Even the sorts of dishes stocked in the refrigerators of health food stores, such as tabbouleh and hummus, tend to be higher in fat than many people realize, because the more visible ingredients, such as garbanzos and tabbouleh and parsley, are nutritious. Eggplant dishes in particular are deceptive, because that vegetable, like the potato, soaks up vast quantities of oil in baking. If there is a pool of oil on the bottom of your plate or on top of your hummus, it's only a hint of what you're consuming. But at least it's probably olive oil—the "right" kind of fat.

Interestingly, in some cases even more meat-dependent cuisines are becoming acclimated to U.S. standards and may be "better" to American tastes, because they use less oil. Most Afghani cooks in the United States use vegetable oils for cooking instead of the traditional mutton fat.

wheat flour pastries with nuts and spices are common. The most familiar in this country is baklava, phyllo dough filled with nuts and honey; *kataif*, wheat pastries, are less overwhelming. One such dessert is like a funnel cake; the batter is poured through a colander held over a hot griddle; then the strings of cake are bundled up and topped with cream.

HOW TO ORDER AND EAT LIKE A NATIVE

Most Armenian, Egyptian, Iraqi, and Israeli meals are served all at once, at a Western-style table. Jordanian, Syrian, Turkish, and Lebanese restaurants generally serve meals in courses. Iranians and Afghanis traditionally serve dinner on a carpeted floor—one reason they take such care in making rugs—and with plenty of cushions. Dishes are served in large bowls and eaten communally—even the soups (first a dumpling, then soup)—but nowadays diners are given individual bowls as well. Restaurants with a mixed clientele may even offer both Western-style seating and carpeting. In general, however, restaurants in the States have switched to table seating.

Ethnic Yemenis are the most traditional: They segregate the diners by sex, and the men frequently eat first. Conversation is also segregated: There is little talk over the meal but much over coffee and dessert, which is served in another room. Many Yemenis also retain the one-pot, communal dining tradition.

In the United States, most menus are divided into soups, salads, and main courses. Mezze may be a category, listing either a number of dishes or a preset tray of dishes. If mezze is not offered, two diners should order fettoosh and baba ganouj (and more dips if you think you can manage) and some kebabs. For four, order dolmas, aushak, a stew (preferably fessanjan), and a grilled marinated chicken.

Most Middle Eastern restaurants are inexpensive or moderately expensive, and fairly authentic.

A NOTE ON KOSHER FOOD

There was a time when only observant Jews even knew where kosher restaurants were. Nowadays there are not only a growing number of kosher (meaning "proper") Middle Eastern establishments but also a rather astonishing supply of kosher Chinese restaurants, with rabbi-certified kitchens.

According to dietary laws laid down in the Old Testament, observant Jews may not eat shellfish, lobsters, shrimp, or crabs; fish are allowed so long as they have scales and fins (no eels or sturgeon, meaning no caviar). Carrion is banned, as are birds of prey and animals that crawl on their bellies—such as snails and snakes, which have had a bad reputation since the time of the Garden of Eden. Only those animals that both chew their cud and have cloven hooves are acceptable, meaning that sheep, goats, and cattle are permitted but not pork, camel, or rabbit; and both meat and poultry must be purged of blood or pickled before cooking. In addition, meat and dairy dishes and utensils must be kept separate, and kosher cooks not only keep two sets of dishes but also, ideally, two kitchens. Milk or dairy products should be eaten first; in fact, if a meat dish is consumed first, the dairy foods should wait several hours.

There are requirements for kosher butchering as well. If you are concerned with keeping kosher, make sure the restaurant is not just "kosher-style" but *kashrut*, or observant in every way and so certified by a rabbinical board. (*Hallal* is the Muslim equivalent, incidentally, meaning that no pork or pork products have been involved.)

COOKING AT HOME

Most Middle Eastern kitchens are quite limited, perhaps with a small stovetop but most often with open fires or the large pit ovens that are built alongside the homes but kept separate, to limit the heat. Once these fire pits are lit, most of the dishes are cooked in quick succession so as not to waste heat or have to extend the fire.

LENTIL AND LAMB STEW

1/2 cup green lentils
3–4 cups Swiss chard, rinsed and drained
1 tablespoon olive oil
1/2 pound lean lamb, minced or processed with steel blade
1 medium onion, chopped
1 teaspoon hot pepper sauce or dried chili flakes (or more to taste)
1/2 tablespoon tomato paste
1 cup beef broth or water
1/4 cup bulghur wheat or kasha
1/2 cup canned or cooked dried garbanzos
1/2 tablespoon finely minced or mashed garlic
3 tablespoons lemon juice
salt and pepper to taste
dried mint leaves, plain yogurt

Rinse lentils, cover with 2 inches fresh water, and bring to a boil; cover, lower heat, and simmer until done (about 30 minutes). Drain, reserving cooking liquid. Blanch chard in boiling water, drain under cold water, and roll in a clean dish towel; squeeze dry and chop.

Heat 1 tablespoon oil in Dutch oven and sauté minced lamb until it loses its red color; lower heat, add onion, and cook just until they start to soften. Add pepper sauce, tomato paste, and broth or water. Bring to a simmer, cover, and cook 15–20 minutes. Increase heat and add bulghur, if using, lentils, and 2 cups of their cooking liquid (add water if necessary), and garbanzos. Bring to boil, then reduce heat to simmer and cook, covered, another 15–20 minutes. Add greens or kasha, if using, garlic, lemon juice, salt, and pepper. Simmer 15 minutes and transfer to serving dish; top with mint and yogurt.

TABBOULEH

1 cup bulghur wheat
3 cups cold water
1/2 cup chopped green onion
3 cups chopped fresh parsley leaves
1/2 cup chopped mint
1/4 cup extra virgin olive oil

3 tablespoons lemon juice
1 1/2 teaspoons salt
1 teaspoon allspice
1 teaspoon ground white (or black) pepper
3–4 ripe but firm tomatoes, peeled, seeded, and diced
lemon wedges for garnish

Soak bulghur in water 30 minutes; drain well, pressing out excess moisture, then spread on clean tea towel to dry for another 30 minutes. Pour into bowl, add onions, parsley, and mint, and mix well. (It's easier to mix with your hands: Rub a little olive oil between your palms first.) Whisk together olive oil, lemon juice, salt, allspice, and pepper; add to bulghur and mix well. Gently stir in tomatoes; cover and chill before serving; serve with extra lemon wedges for seasoning.

BABA GANOUJ

1 large eggplant or 4 small Italian eggplant
2 large ripe but firm tomatoes, peeled, seeded, and finely chopped
2 scallions, trimmed and chopped
2 tablespoons chopped fresh cilantro or mint leaves
2 cloves garlic or 1 clove mild elephant garlic, minced
salt and red pepper flakes to taste

Roast whole eggplant, skin generously pricked, on a cookie sheet in a 425°F oven until blackened and slightly collapsed or soft (usually 20–30 minutes, depending on size). Cool, remove skin, and puree in food processor. Stir in tomatoes, scallions, cilantro, garlic, salt, and pepper flakes to taste; serve with pita bread.

HUMMUS (GARBANZO DIP)

2 cans garbanzos, rinsed and drained
1/3 cup tahini (sesame paste)
1/2 cup lemon juice (more to taste)
2 cloves garlic
1/2 teaspoon salt (more to taste)
liquid pepper sauce to taste
1 tablespoon extra virgin olive oil
chopped parsley or mint for garnish

Combine garbanzos, tahini, and lemon juice in food processor and puree. Cream garlic with 1/2 teaspoon salt into a smooth paste, add to processor bowl, and blend. Add pepper sauce, additional lemon and salt if desired, and blend again. Turn dip into serving bowl and make a small depression in the center; pour oil into hollow, sprinkle with parsley or mint, and serve with pita bread.

INDIA

Almost everyone knows something about Indian food—curry with chutney—and almost everything they know is wrong.

Curry, the word the British casually applied to the spicy golden lamb and chicken stews they so enjoyed in Calcutta and Bombay, is probably a mistranslation of either the word *kari*, the generic term for sauce; or perhaps a confusion about the flavor of the kari leaf (actually a mild cross between citrus peel and bell pepper). The "curry powder" marketed in the United States, usually a rather flat blend of turmeric, cumin, and rice-powder filler, is something of a joke in India, where spices are not only roasted and ground fresh for each meal but nearly always in combinations of at least a half-dozen flavors. Curries aren't always spicy-hot and aren't always stewed: They might be fried, roasted, or grilled. Many curries aren't even yellow: They're green, red, and even white. The chutneys most familiar to Americans, like "Major Grey's," are cooked; but authentic chutneys, like real salsas, can be raw and fresh.

What we think of as "curry spices" are primarily those same Spice Island treasures that inspired virtually all the European colonial expeditions—coriander, cardamom, cinnamon, cloves, nutmeg, black mustard seed—plus homegrown kari leaves and peppercorns and the later addition of New World chilies. These same spices were available in Europe, of course, which had exploited the islands for just those treasures; but they had been passed along to the Persians and Arabs so far back in time and were so thoroughly assimilated into Moghul cuisine that the British (who, after all, have never been famous for their sophisticated use of spices or sauces) felt as though they were just discovering them. Although a few of the British were intrigued with "going native," like most European colonials in Asia, they only wanted to go so far.

This reduction of Indian cuisine to a single recipe robs it not only of its complexity—there are radical distinctions between northern and southern Indian cooking, and perhaps 20 regional cuisines—but of much of its opulent history as well. In fact, Indian cuisine is almost a perfect fusion of Middle Eastern, Mongolian, and Malaysian—with most of the healthier parts of each. Persian pilafs, Turkish flatbreads and samosas, Mongol kebabs, and Indonesian flavors are the mainstays of Indian foods; the high proportion of vegetarian and even vegan dishes makes this diet hospitable to every diner.

Not only that, but dining in the Indian culture is indivisible from hospitality and community. One ancient saying has it that "annam brahma"—"food is God." It is both a pleasure and a responsibility to provide healthful and delicious food to the family and to any guest or wayfarer.

Although this chapter refers almost exclusively to Indian food, it can be used as a guide to several related cuisines, especially as they are practiced in the United States: Bangladeshi, Nepalese, Ceylonese, and western-central Burmese, particularly the Mandalay region. Most Pakistani restaurants are indistinguishable from northern Indian establishments, although a few with chefs from the west (toward Afghanistan and Iran) may offer menus more reminiscent of Middle Eastern kitchens.

THE COUNTRY

A slightly cock-eyed, diamond-shaped, or toothy mass that juts into the Indian Ocean, India is the second most populous nation on earth, with nearly a billion inhabitants; two dozen cities hold more than a million people apiece. It is an extremely heterogeneous population, however, with anthropological roots in four races (Caucasoid, Mongoloid, Australoid, and Negroid) and 1,500 languages and dialects.

Four-fifths of the population is Hindu, 12% is Muslim, and the rest is a mixture of Christian, Buddhist, and Sikh (itself a monotheistic mix of Sufi Islam and Bhakti Hinduism). Most of them are employed in agriculture, either in subsistence farming or on the large tea, tobacco, and coffee plantations. Although the caste system, which placed the brahmins at the top and the "untouchables" irreversibly at the social bottom, has been officially outlawed, it continues to exercise considerable residual influence.

Physically, India is walled off along the northeast diagonal by the Himalayan crest, and along the northwest by desert; almost parallel to these lines, however, run two of the great river systems, the Indus River in what is now Pakistan, and the Ganges, below Nepal. The alluvial plain of the Ganges is the most arable territory in the country, along with the tropical east coast; the west is semi-arid and best suited to raising grains and livestock, but the entire country suffers from periodic drought, famine, monsoons, and floods.

THE HISTORY

Although much Indian archaeology is relatively recent, it is known that a flourishing and sophisticated civilization in the Indus Valley rose to its peak between 2500 B.C.E. and 1500 B.C.E. This civilization, which was already raising wheat and barley, was heavily involved in trade with the Mesopotamian societies, particularly profiting in the export of black and white peppercorns. The Khyber Pass was a crucial junction in the Silk Route; and India early on served as the exchange point for the two great staples of Asia, passing Chinese oranges, peaches, and rice to the Middle East and bringing back cumin, okra, almonds, roses, spinach, figs, and, most important, lentils. This set the pattern for centuries of intracontinental recipe swapping: The Syrians and Persians exchanged garlic, nuts, and oils for squashes and eggplant, which grew in India in dozens of delicious varieties, and then traders in the West Indies doused all these new foods with mustard, cinnamon, ginger, mace, and coconut milk. The Greeks and Romans offered fenugreek for black pepper; the Chinese, who first encountered saffron in Tibet, bartered textiles for this "flower of Tibet."

Large portions of India were several times part of Persia, and in conquering the Persian Empire, Alexander the Great also conquered the western regions of India. The dynasty that eventually wrested India free from Greece established a Buddhist society, but as the Indi and original Persian civilizations declined, two distinct influences emerged: Aryans, who were early Asiatic and Turkish Hindus, moved across the north as far as the Bay of Bengal, and the Greeks who had followed Alexander into Afghanistan and Turkey established a vital Indo-Hellenic culture. In the south, on the other hand, active trade was maintained with the evolving Roman Empire and the merchants of Malaysia and Indonesia; the culture, and the cuisine, looked farther east.

One significant principle of Indian culture dates to this early era: The Aryans were a beef-eating society, and brought cattle with them, but quickly discovered that the indigenous breed was better adapted to the hot climate; however, it produced less milk. As the amount of milk a cow produces daily far outweighs in nutritional value its one-time use as meat, cattle had to be protected from slaughter, and so the cow gradually became sacred. Eventually, with the spread of such pacifistic philosophies as Jainism and Buddhism, even barren cows became sacrosanct. And when the Moghul conquerors made no bones about eating meat, it only added insult to injury.

The Islamic influence crept in slowly with the Arab sea traders, but as the Muslim revolution spread, overland raids became more virulent, and in 1192 the Muslim army captured Delhi and established a vast sultanate that eventually ruled everything but Kashmir and the remote south. (Shahriar, husband of that Scheherazade who passed a "Thousand and One Nights" telling stories, was emperor of both Persia and India.) Tamerlane, the legendary Turk who claimed descent from Genghis Khan, marched in at the end of the fourteenth century; another Turk, Babur, who claimed descent from Tamerlane, established the great Moghul, that is, "Mongol," Empire, during which evolved the ornate Indo-Islamic art and architecture epitomized by the Taj Mahal. Nevertheless, Islam never won over the hearts of the Indian majority.

The Portuguese established their sphere of influence about the same time: Vasco de Gama landed at Calcutta in 1498, closely followed by Cabral. The British, French, and Dutch were close on their heels, as the route around Africa made importing West Indian spices much more profitable than it had been via the overland route. The British eventually dominated, but it was not until the mid-eighteenth century, when repeated Persian and Afghani insurrections weakened the Moghul rulers, that the British Empire actually claimed the entire territory.

Britain's withdrawal in 1948 reignited the historical Muslim-Hindu struggle, and an estimated 500,000 people died in the riots that accompanied the partitioning of Pakistan. Factional battles have continued sporadically ever since, leading to the establishment of the nation of Bangladesh (formerly East Pakistan) in 1972; Punjabi separatists continue guerrilla agitation for their autonomy as well. This ongoing unrest in central Asia is one reason that the dominant Indian culinary presence in the United States has for so long been Kashmiri and Punjabi.

REGIONAL CUISINES

The various European visitors and invaders made significant additions to Indian cuisine and culture. The Chinese introduced rice at least 5,000 years ago and somewhat later the wok, called in India the *kadhai* (and in India usually made of brass or copper rather than iron). The Portuguese brought vinegar, cashews, papayas, pineapples, tomatoes, potatoes, and chilies, which revolutionized the cuisine, particularly in the west and south; the Dutch organized rice cultivation, and the British did the same for tea.

> ### Milk of Kindness
>
> Intriguingly, the Aryans brought cattle with them, and beef was originally a common food in India. They quickly discovered that the indigenous breed was better adapted to the climate and began raising it instead, but that breed gave less milk, so it had to be protected from slaughter, because the amount of milk a cow produces daily far outweighs in nutritional value its one-time use as meat. Eventually, as pro-life religions such as Jainism and Buddhism spread, even barren cows became sacrosanct. And when the Moghul conquerors began eating meat, it only made the subject touchier.

Nevertheless, the two greatest influences on Indian cuisine are clearly Persian and Indonesian, and their spheres of influence extend roughly over the north and south, respectively. Loosely speaking, that means a greater emphasis on meat in the north and vegetables in the south; drier dishes and breads in the north, and wetter stews and rice in the south. In the cooler, drier north, wheat grows more plentifully than rice and is the primary starch for bread; in the south, the use of lentils and rice for flours and doughs is widespread. In the north, dishes are more likely to include Persian flavorings, such as nuts, sweets, rosewater, and saffron; whereas in the south the pantry is vibrant with ginger and garlic, chilies and peppercorns, cardamom, cinnamon, cloves, mustard seeds, and the distinctive use of coconut milk.

The other general rule of thumb is that the farther south you go, the hotter the food tends to be. This arises partly from the popularity of those Indonesian spices and partly because the North American chilies were introduced by the seagoing Portuguese rather than the overland traders and thus landed on the coasts, working their way into the interior more gradually. However, in this country, the boom in spicy cuisines, such as Southwestern, Szechuan, and Thai (and the expectation of American customers that all Indian food is very spicy) has encouraged many Indian cooks to heat up their own recipes, regardless of tradition.

Although in cities with larger Indian populations, some restaurants may define their cuisine more specifically—Punjabi, Kashmiri, Goan, Gujurati, Bengali, and so forth—the majority of Indian restaurants in the United States generally only describe themselves as northern or southern in style. (There is no historical restaurant tradition in India.) The first great wave of Indian restaurateurs in America were primarily from the north of India or from Pakistan; so that such mainstays of Moghul cuisine as tandoori cooking—that is, shish kebab—and basmati rice biryanis were among the first Indian dishes introduced to the American palate. (Not only is the tandoor oven Middle Eastern, but the traditional tandoori marinade—yogurt, lemon, ginger, turmeric—is classically Persian as well.) However, tandoori cooking is now fairly widespread even in India.

Kashmir, for instance, is in the far northern point, where Pakistan, Afghanistan, and western China come together, all regions in which Mongol influences remain strong. Saffron, the quintessential Persian spice, has been cultivated in Kashmir since at least the third century C.E., and its use, along with cloves, shallots, and mustard seeds, is characteristic of Kashmiri dishes. However, Kashmiri brahmins do not eat beef, garlic, or onions, so most Kashmiri dishes are lamb.

The Punjab is another of the major states in the northern neck, so "Punjabi" is often used as a synonym for tandoori cooking. But the Punjab is also the stronghold of the Sikhs, whose vegetarian cooking is fairly well known in the United States, thanks to their "Golden Temple" restaurants and cookbooks (and their distinctive white turbans and clothing). The Punjab is one of the richest grain-growing regions; it produces primarily wheat but also corn, millet, and barley, and Punjabi chefs are, not surprisingly, famous for their breads.

Goa, an Arabian Sea port in south-central India with a long history of Middle Eastern trade, was a Portuguese colony for nearly 400 years, and Goan cooking, particularly the hot-and-sour *vindaloo* style of curry, is distinctive for its use of vinegar, tomato, and garlic. (The word itself comes from the Portuguese term "vindalho," from "vinho" for vinegar and "aldos" for garlic.) Any pork dish is almost certainly Goan. Cashews and coconuts are also popular in this cuisine.

Just south of Goa is Udupi, an ancient shrine city on the coast particularly sacred to Vishna and hence rigorously vegetarian. A late-1990s boom in such restaurants, many of them with the word Udupi in the name to convey their observance, have made southern Indian food much more familiar to Americans, especially younger diners, than it was a few years ago.

Bombay is part of Maharashtra, and Maharashtran cuisine employs both rice and millet. Because it lies on the west coast and had the closest ties to Arab and African traders, Maharashtrans are fonder of peanuts, okra, and bananas than other Indians are. Along the southwest coast is Kerala, a tropical region rich in fish and shellfish and where goat and lamb are raised; but it also has a large Hindu population and thus a strong vegetarian tradition. Malabar is the region including Kerala.

The west point of the Indian diamond, between Bombay and the Pakistani border, is the state of Gujurat, which produces primarily vegetarian curries with tangy green chutneys. It is home to the Jainists, who reject slaughter of any sort and thus are entirely vegetarian; many even avoid root plants, such as onions, because insects may be displaced or killed in the harvesting. Though there are few meat dishes except among the Christians and Muslims, Gujurat's Persian heritage shows in the popularity of such flavors as cardamom, almond, saffron, and pistachio.

In the south, where the Hindu tradition is stronger, there is little meat served, but an abundance of tropical vegetables provides an almost endless supply of dishes. In the east, along the Bay of Bengal, fish is a major part of the diet. Bengali cooking (and the neighboring Bangladeshi cuisine) tend to be fairly spicy and more heavily mustard-flavored. Coromandel, a term

Heart-y Choice

Various cooking oils used lend particular flavors to Indian dishes—now all the more so, because the relatively neutral ghee, the clarified butter that was the common cooking fat in the north, has become much more expensive and is thus used less. Unfortunately, the replacements, while more aromatic, are not much less cholesterolic: The alternatives include sesame, peanut, coconut, almond, and mustard oils. The best of them is peanut oil, but you may not always get a straight answer from the waiter about which is being used.

However, aside from the oils and the foods that are fried in them, Indian cuisine has much to recommend it as a healthful choice: Many dishes are steamed, roasted, grilled, or baked; there is little meat and a high proportion of grains and legumes; in many regions there is almost no dairy except for the lower-fat yogurt. However, thickened or "wet" curry is apt to hide secret butter-fat from condensed milk, skimmed-off cream, or coconut. It is also a low-alcohol diet; most of the spirits served in Indian restaurants—gin, Pimm's cups, or beer—are remnants of the Raj.

familiar mostly from old novels, was on the east coast. Madras is also on the east coast, and "Madras-style" is usually a version of "hot!"

Off the southern tip of India lies Sri Lanka, formerly Ceylon; though its cuisine is similar to southern Indian food, it is even more "tropical," with a much wider variety of seafoods, including squid and crab. It also shows a strong European influence; it was under Portuguese control for 150 years, followed by the Dutch, who introduced butter and eggs and baking doughs. (One of the most popular dishes is a yeast-dough bun stuffed with curried beef and potatoes.) Sri Lankans like their curries extremely hot.

There is one other style of cooking worth noting: During the period of British imperial rule, known as the Raj, an entire Anglo-Indian subcuisine developed, including that version of curry and Major Grey's chutney described above. Raj-era dishes include mulligatawny soup, a chicken/rice/onion recipe from the Tamil phrase "milagu-tunir," or pepper-water; and kedgeree, a sort of Indian hoppin' john of lentils and rice. Intriguingly, it also includes Worcestershire sauce, which is believed to have been discovered when a cask of India-spiced sweet and sour vinegar, left to ferment in a British merchant's warehouse, unexpectedly and deliciously exploded.

THE MAIN INGREDIENTS

SEASONINGS The wealth of spices and flavorings in India, which has been at the crossroads of East-West trade for millennia, is overwhelming. The phrase "garam masala," which is closest to the spice combination Americans know as curry powder, actually just means "mixed spices," and every cook makes his or her own. The most common ingredients are fresh ginger, cumin, turmeric, coriander seeds, cardamom (called "elaichi," the "seed of paradise"), cinnamon, mace, nutmeg, cloves, star anise, and fennel seed. Adding dried red chilies or chili powder, peppercorns, and ginger to this household concoction provides the heat.

Other frequently used spices and flavorings are cilantro, coriander leaf, bay, dill, fresh green chilies, mint, white poppy seeds, sesame seeds, sorrel, anise seed, onion seed or asafeotida (a garlicky-flavored herb that replaced the onions proscribed by many ethnic groups), saffron, lemon, tamarind, rose hips, and oregano. Jaggery, a raw palm sugar, is similar to unsulfured molasses and particularly common in Gujarat. Madras cooks are particularly fond of fenugreek, Bengalis of brown mustard seeds and mustard oil, and Keralans of raw cashews, which they grind and use as a condiment. Garlic is fairly common in the north, but it is not as widely used as in most Asian cuisines; many Indians believe it inflames the passions. The kari leaf, incidentally, is used the way bay leaves are used in European cooking—whole, but removed before eating.

Not all "seasonings" are just spices, however; slowly caramelized onions, further enriched by cinnamon, jaggery, star anise, and cardamom, are the basis for many sauces, particularly the eggplant stew called *banghan bharta*. Similarly, many stews begin with tomatoes cooked down to a dry paste, with or without hot spices. (For "dry" curries, the garlic, onions, and spices are usually slow-fried together before other ingredients are added to the oil; for "wet" curries, the seasonings are added at the end of the cooking.) Pumpkin seeds, roasted rice, and toasted coconut are also used as flavorings.

VEGETABLES In India, lentils and beans are such a large part of the diet that they are often a menu category in themselves. *Dal* or *dahl* is the generic word and may refer to any of a half a dozen kinds of lentils (black, red, yellow, orange, white, green), garbanzos, pigeon (black-eyed) peas, green peas, red kidney beans, mung beans, split peas, and sometimes tiny black beans. Lentils are used not only as protein but as starch; lentil flour and fermented lentil doughs are frequently used for breads and crêpes and as a thickener for curries. Garbanzo flour, or *besan*, is also important and is used to make the batter many appetizers such as pakoras are fried in.

Among the other vegetables, the most important are the greens (categorically, *palak*), especially mustard, spinach, and kale; okra, eggplant, potatoes, cauliflower, cabbage, broccoli, carrots, gourds, squashes and pumpkins, green beans, beets, and onions and tomatoes.

FRUITS Indians have mangoes the way Indonesians have bananas —dozens of varieties—and think the mangoes available in the United States a rather poor alternative. They also grow oranges, lemons, limes, pineapples, pomegranates, tamarinds, plums, peaches, guavas, grapes, musk melons, quinces, and bananas. Papayas are used both as a fruit (and medicine) and, dried and ground to a powder, as a tenderizer for meat or fowl. *Kodumpuli* is a sour fruit used to take the "fish odor" away from fish.

The most versatile fruit, however, is the coconut, which is one of the building blocks of Indian life as well as cuisine. It provides not only milk and meat but also wood for buildings and fronds for roofs, rope, fibers, and oil. Indian cooks use two sorts of coconut milk, in fact— what's called the "first milk," which is the heavier, creamier fluid taken from the first squeezing of grated fresh nuts; and the "second milk," a thinner, remnant pressing. First milk cannot be boiled, as it will curdle, so it's added at the end of the recipe; second milk can be used throughout the cooking process.

Perhaps the most common way fruit is served in Indian cuisine is as a chutney, the sweet-spicy conserve; as a relish; or as a vegetable pickle, such as lemon pickle, a salted lemon condiment that recalls the preserved lemons of North Africa.

MEATS Considering the size of the country, there is less to say on this subject in Indian cuisine than almost anywhere else. Between the Muslims (and west Indian Jews), who eat no pork, and the Hindus, Buddhists, and Jains, who eat (or are supposed to eat) no meat at all, pork is virtually unknown in India. Beef is limited, but goat and lamb, the Persian and Moghul favorites, are plentiful and easily the most popular, especially in the north.

POULTRY AND SEAFOOD Chicken is surprisingly expensive in most parts of the country, though in the north and central territories game birds are fairly common. (Chicken, of course, is extremely popular in Indian restaurants in the United States, where it is not expensive.) Duck is a west coast and Bombay specialty.

Freshwater fish include grouper and pearl spot; saltwater favorites include salmon, Spanish mackerel, pomfret, and "Indian" salmon, which is not a true salmon but tastes similar. (In the United States, true salmon is the fish most commonly offered in Indian restaurants.) Shrimp or prawns (*jingba*) and shellfish, particularly mussels and clams, are abundant in the coastal regions but are rarely offered in American restaurants.

EGGS AND DAIRY The most important dairy products are *ghee*, cheese, and yogurt. Ghee is a clarified butter, melted and slow-cooked until all the water boils away and the milk solids turn light brown; it's an ancient way of preserving the primary cooking oil in a hot climate. Cheese is frequently used in curries, usually in combination with a vegetable, such as peas or spinach. The yogurt in India is quite thick, almost curdlike; goat's milk and sheep's milk yogurts are said to have more authentic flavor, but the restaurants in America are pretty likely only to have cow's milk yogurt, so sometimes it is drained to make it thicker. Yogurt is stirred into many curries as an alternative to coconut milk or cream, but it is more frequently seasoned—either with hot spices or chilies or simply mint or spinach— and served as a condiment, called *raita*. Some menus refer to "yogurt curries," but those are generally raitas rather than entrees.

Buttermilk (*moru*) is popular in the south, where it is used both to marinate and to cook. However, Indian cooks also boil milk and condense it, or allow it to separate and then skim off the thick cream, called *koa*; both condensed milk and koa are also used to thicken sauces.

Eggs are used as a main course but very rarely as a sauce ingredient or binder. The most common way to serve eggs is to hard-boil and halve them, then top them with a curry sauce; in the south it's usually a coconut curry. Eggs are also scrambled, frequently with fish, a memento of the British breakfast habit.

GRAINS AND STARCHES Breads of India—*nam* in general— are made from a variety of flours: white, whole wheat, lentil, and occasionally rice, although potatoes are not often used for doughs. These breads, flat, puffy, and even stuffed, are more common in the north, where rice grows less easily and is savored as a main dish. Indian chefs also employ different varieties of rice for different purposes: The fine Middle Eastern basmati grain is used in biryanis; a long-grain, red-bran rice called rosematta is usually blended with other grains; and the shorter, stickier Asian grain (not the sweet sticky rice common in other parts of Asia) is popular in the south. In general, a fluffy, dry consistency is preferred; rice is cooked with salt. Indians even make a cream of rice that is very similar to the cereal made in the United States.

One striking anomaly about Indian cuisine is that it is the only country between Mongolia and the Middle East never to have adopted noodles in any serious form.

CURRIES

Like other inhabitants of hot climates, Indians adhere to the theory that spicy food makes you sweat and thus cools you off; it also excites the appetite and aids in digestion. Perhaps that's why there are such an abundance of "exciting" dishes.

Curries come in a variety of colors: red, which has a tomato base (more common in the south and along the coast, where they were first introduced by the Europeans); yellow, which has the heaviest concentration of the turmeric and cumin flavors Americans traditionally associate with "curry powder"; green, which can either mean spinach, mint or cilantro, or green chilies; and "black," from the Sri Lankan habit of roasting the spices until they are the color and richness of coffee. Coconut-based stews, particularly common in south India and Sri Lanka, are referred to as white curries (though in Malaysia, a "white curry" also contains ground kemiri nuts). Confusingly, it's not the addition of coconut milk that turns a curry from "dry" to "wet," but the timing of the seasoning: If the dish is cooked first and the spices only added at the end, it's "wet"; if the spices are fried in oil first, and the other ingredients cooking in it, it will seem "dry." Coincidentally, coconut milk will likely be added last.

Because the word curry has such a broad meaning in India, many restaurant menus use it erratically, and there are several types of dishes that Americans would tend to include in that category. Most of the terms have to do with the manner in which the main ingredients are prepared: A *korma* is a meat curry, a *keema* a minced-meat curry, and a vindaloo a stew of vinegar-marinated meat. These all have sauces and are closest to what Americans think of as curries.

However, many dry dishes also involve curry spices: *koftas*, the Middle Eastern–style minced meats (or lentils) formed into meatballs or sausages; *raan*, which means a roast that was probably spice-rubbed; and tandoori dishes, which have been marinated in lemon, yogurt, and (usually mild) spices. *Josh* refers to a curried meat in a yogurt or cream-thickened sauce. The term *bhuna* refers to a stir-frying technique in which all the liquid is cooked out and the spices left behind—ultra-dry. Kebabs can be curried as well, especially those with the word *tikka* (pieces), which means the meat or poultry has been cut up and marinated.

Fish curries may have a distinctively sour note, because some cooks use the juice of the sour kodumpuli, fenugreek, or green tamarinds to erase the "fishy" character of the meat.

Vegetables curries are generally called *bhaji* and are relatively dry; curries in which the vegetables are mashed or cooked into a puree-like consistency are *bhartas*. The words *takari* and *sabzi* just mean vegetables, either raw or cooked; these dishes may include curry spices, too. Some things you just have to take for granted, like samosas, the stuffings of which are almost always lightly spiced.

THE MAIN DISHES

APPETIZERS The word for snacks in Indian is, pleasantly, *chat*, and most of the dumplings and fritters listed on American menus under "appetizers" are really snacks. (*Mathai* shops, which may be found in cities with established Indian communities, are combination convenience stores and bakeries and sell dozens of varieties of chat and sweets.) Among the most popular are samosas, triangular fried pastries stuffed with either curried potatoes and peas or minced lamb or beef; *kachori*, lentil-stuffed samosas; *pappadam*, the crispy lentil-flour cracker bread; *vadas*, garbanzo or lentil dumplings served with raita; pakoras, sometimes called *bhajias*, batter-fried vegetables, meat or sometimes fish; *dosa* or *dosai*, fried patties of fermented rice and lentil flour; *idli*, fermented rice dumplings eaten with chutney; and *bondas*, fried mashed potato balls, the Indian knish. *Pani puri* are deep-fried puffs filled with chutneys or split peas or spiced potatoes. *Chakli* (or *chakri*) are fried spirals or "rounds" of lentil or rice-flour dough, pressed out through a special tool into hot oil. Rice pancakes and potato straws or even baked potato slices, cooked and seasoned, are also popular.

Occasionally restaurants may offer miniature versions of main courses, such as single skewers of chicken tikka. *El maru* is a sort of north Indian trail mix, combining rice, nuts, and crispy noodles. *Oothapam* is a south Indian crêpe stuffed with sautéed onions, tomatoes, and peppers.

SALADS There is no separate course or real menu category here. What raw vegetable mixtures there are resemble Middle Eastern or North African salads and condiments: cucumbers with lemon and mint; eggplant with tomato, shredded carrots, and raisins; even a sort of gazpacho of raw onions, tomato, chilies, coriander, and a touch of sugar. Cold spiced potatoes, cucumber in yogurt, and occasionally cold spiced eggplant may be used as a combination condiment and appetizer.

SOUPS Mulligatawny soup is probably the best-known Indian soup, but like curry, the Anglicized version is the one most familiar to us. The original milagu-tunir has been thickened with beef and soup bones, coconut milk, onion, and curry spices. The other most popular soups feature lentils, split peas, lentils with mixed vegetables, and occasionally pumpkin or squash. *Sambor* is a curry-seasoned soup thickened with pureed lentils.

VEGETABLES Again, there are dozens of lentils and beans, and any of them may be offered as a stew or puree, spiced or mild; so may squash, potatoes, beans, cabbage, pumpkin, mushrooms, okra, or any of the greens. Potatoes were only introduced toward the end of the eighteenth century but quickly became extremely popular; potato and pea is a very common combination (called *alu mattar*), as is cauliflower and potato *(alu gobi)*, spinach and cheese *(sag paneer)*, and pea with cheese *(mattar paneer)*. Thickly stewed eggplant, mixed baked vegetables *(tandoori sabzi)*, stuffed cabbages or green peppers, and fried eggplant slices are purely Middle Eastern carryovers. Stir-fried vegetables, on the other hand, are clearly Chinese.

RICE AND GRAINS Biryanis and pilaus are central to the Indian diet, the first being a richer (more Persian-influenced) version of the second. Biryanis are cooked as casseroles, baked in the oven so the flavors blend; while pilaus, or pilafs, are cooked very slowly in an open pot so that the rice grains remain separate. Add cream or yogurt and they become kormas. Both are considered main dishes. Pilaus may be mixed with vegetables (peas, garbanzos, lentils) or spices (cinnamon, almonds or pistachios, lemon, dill), minced meat, yogurt, and even a little shrimp or coconut. Biryanis are highly aromatic, flavored with mutton or lamb or chicken, nuts, cinnamon, cardamom, chilies, even rosewater, and particularly saffron. Rice and lentils cooked together is called *kitchri*.

SEAFOOD Prawns are quite popular, either in coconut-flavored curries, in vindaloo stews, or skewered satay-style. Tandoori-marinated fish, particularly salmon, has become extremely popular in the United States. Fish (generically, *machi* or *machli*) is curried, stuffed with seasoned rice and broiled or baked, deep-fried, minced and fried, steamed in banana leaves Malay-style, curried with tomato (both fish and tomato are southern specialties), simmered in coconut milk, or grilled. Where shellfish is available, it is usually steamed.

POULTRY "Murgh" (chicken) may be marinated and tandoori-roasted, prepared in dry or wet curries, in a vindaloo sauce, with coconut milk but without hot spices, chopped and fried, or mixed with vegetables. Tikka are small skewered morsels like satays. Chicken (or shrimp) *kadai* is stir-fried, usually with tomatoes, onions, and green peppers. Chicken Mahkanwala is a twice-cooked dish, tandoori-roasted meat sautéed in butter and tomatoes. Chicken is also used to flavor biryanis, curried with cashews, stewed with lentils and vegetables and occasionally deep-fried. Although organ meats are not generally considered edible in India, chicken livers are sometimes served, even curried.

Small game birds are cooked the same ways as chicken. Duck, which is fattier, does not respond as well to tandoori preparations (the marinade cannot penetrate the fatty layer), so it is more frequently prepared with a vindaloo sauce or in some other offsetting, tangy manner (with tamarind, ginger, papaya, etc.). "Bombay duck" is not poultry at all but a dried fish that is fried and served as a salty seasoning, the way Americans use bacon bits. (Oddly, "Polish duck" is also fish—a substitute for the more expensive item.)

MEATS Lamb is the most popular meat, followed closely by goat and distantly by beef; mutton, the stronger flavor of which is often mellowed by marination, is also popular. Lamb is rubbed with spices and roasted, rubbed with spices and skewered, soaked in vinegar, and stewed with tomato and yogurt (*rogan josh*, which might be the national dish if more Indians ate meat). *Badami gosht* is pure Persian: lamb spiced with saffron, cinnamon, ginger, almonds, and yogurt, but little or no heat. Lamb is made into meatballs (called, as in so many Persian-influenced regions, kofta), kebabs, coconut curries, and biryanis; in a few extravagant Goanese dishes, it may even be combined with pork. *Ghourma* is the Farsi word for "braise"—"gorma" in the north toward Afghanistan—a creamy, mild sort of curry. Sometimes meat is twice-cooked, boiled with spices until tender, then stir-fried.

Most other lean meats can be cooked in the same ways; however, because meat fat (and fat meat) are not common in India, meat is not made into sausages or cured. Organ meats and offal are discarded. Buffalo and horse are considered meats in India, though camels and dogs are "unclean"; none of these last is apt to appear on an American menu.

CONDIMENTS Chutneys, like salsas, are mixed fruit and vegetable or spice mixes eaten alongside and sometimes with main dishes; *sambals*, also a feature of Indonesian cooking, are flavorings—onions sautéed with lemon and chilies, for example, or perhaps highly seasoned vegetables. Raitas are yogurt-based condiments and can include simply cucumber mint (the version most familiar in the United States) or bananas, tomatoes, spinach, and so on. Chutneys may feature coconut, mango, papaya, chilies, eggplant, mint, coriander, and lemon or pineapple.

There are also a variety of sweet-and-sour pickles: lemon pickle (which is widely known here), mango, green coconut, tomato or green tomato, and so on. The table may be set with small dishes of dried coconut, nuts, banana chips, tiny dried fish, and so on for customizing your meal.

BEVERAGES The spiciness of most curries has made beer the most common American accompaniment, though some people believe the carbonation makes the spice burn hotter. There are both sweet and savory yogurt drinks (called *lassis*) and mint drinks and spiced teas. *Faludas* are jelly-like sweetish drinks flavored with rose syrup and milk; fruit and milk drinks are sometimes called "fools," from the English fruit and cream desserts. Rice beers and a sugarcane and melon alcohol are popular among the rural people, but if they are available here, it's only under the counter.

DESSERTS Like their Persian forebears, the Indians like sweets and generally serve a couple at the end of a meal. (In some areas, dinner begins with a sweet dish, and in the west, one of the main dishes may be sweet.) Rice puddings, banana puddings, bread, vermicelli, nut and raisin puddings, fried sweetened nut doughs or cookies, honey- or syrup-covered sweetmeats *(laddu)*, or fruits or cheese balls are common. *Halva*, a honey-flavored semolina confection, comes in a variety of flavors. Ice cream and frozen fruit sherbets are also popular, particularly in the United States.

HOW TO ORDER AND EAT LIKE A NATIVE

A typical Indian meal consists of five or six dishes, and traditionally, meals are served family-style, all at once, on a platter called a *thali*, which somewhat resembles those indented deviled egg plates: It's a circular tray with a number of small bowls or cups nestled around the outside and a pile of rice or chapati in the middle.

It is customary to eat with the hands, using the fingers for the meat or vegetable and the chapati or rice to absorb sauce. As in other countries, only the fingers of the right hand are used, but be warned—it's considered bad manners to drop food, particularly rice. There is one more curious difference between northern and southern Indian dining: In the north, it is considered bad form to dip more than the first joint of the fingers into the food; northerners look down on those in the south, who use the whole hand to eat. Of course, it's easier to eat neatly in the north, where they are more likely to use bread to pick up stews. Most restaurants that serve in the traditional manner will bring a pitcher of water and a basin to the table, or at least supply fingerbowls; a few use wet cloths.

In most cities in India, as well as the United States, Western-style service—that is, plates and forks—is now common. However, the arrangement of dishes is similar: Rice should be put in the center of the plate, with various curries and condiments around it, and only one dish at a time should be tasted. The rice should also be the predominant part of the meal.

Two people might split an order of samosas and some paratha or a crêpe, tandoori chicken, and rogan josh. Four people should share samosas, pakoras, lentil soup, benghan bharta, chicken Makhanwala, lamb vindaloo, and a pilau or biryani. A group might ask about a thali: Although such "sampler" platters are now often served for one or two people, a real family-style dinner may be forthcoming.

Spell Check

Menu spellings in the United States are irregular but rarely confusing: Vindaloo may be "vandaloo" or even "bandaloo," kebabs may be "kababs or "kebobs," and tandoor spelled "tandur," but they will be easily identifiable. In a few cases, the difference in intonation makes for "harder" or "softer" transliterations, so you might see "machi" instead of "machli" for fish or even "karhai" for "kadai."

COOKING AT HOME

Except for a tandoori oven, for which a broiler or grill will have to substitute, most Indian utensils and techniques can be reproduced fairly easily in an American kitchen. The most important pan in Indian cooking is the karhai, a slightly deeper version of a Chinese wok, used for stir-frying (hence the descriptive phrase "karhai" on menus). But if you don't have a wok, any deep skillet will do. Although roasted spices are traditionally ground in a mortar, a small nut grinder or mini food processor works fine.

There is no standard recipe for garam masala, and even those available in Indian groceries vary from brand to brand; but it's simple to make your own, and the flavor (and the house aroma) will be better. You can make up your own version, and in a pinch, ground allspice plus a little chili powder will get you by.

GARAM MASALA

1 tablespoon black peppercorns
1 1/2 tablespoons cumin seed
1 tablespoon black mustard seed
1 tablespoon cardamom seed
2 tablespoons coriander seed
2 teaspoons whole cloves
2 teaspoons whole allspice berries
2 sticks cinnamon, broken in smaller pieces
2 teaspoons ground nutmeg

Using a small skillet or Japanese sesame-seed pan, toast all the spices except the nutmeg one at a time; as the seeds become fragrant, turn them into a bowl to cool. When they have all cooled, grind them together. Keep in an airtight jar.

CHICKEN MOGHULI

1 3-pound roasting chicken, cut into serving pieces
2 tablespoons canola or peanut oil
1 large onion, thinly sliced
2 cloves garlic, minced
2 teaspoons fresh ginger root, minced
1 tablespoon ground turmeric

1 teaspoon salt
2 tablespoons garam masala
1 cup thick yogurt
1/4 cup chicken broth or hot water
1/4 cup cream (optional)
1/4 cup cashews or slivered almonds
chopped coriander for garnish

Remove skin and fat from chicken pieces, rinse, and pat dry. In a large heavy pan, heat oil and sauté onion until soft, then add garlic, ginger, turmeric, salt, and garam masala and fry gently until spices are softened (10 to 15 minutes). Add chicken pieces and cook, turning frequently, until lightly browned on all sides. Stir in half the yogurt, the chicken broth, and the cream (if you are using it); cook gently until chicken is tender.

Meanwhile, grind about two-thirds of the nuts. Remove chicken pieces to a warm platter; add remaining yogurt and nuts to skillet, adding a splash more water if necessary, and heat through. Return chicken to sauce, coating evenly, then serve, sprinkling remaining nuts and coriander on top. Serve with rice and chapatis (or whole wheat pita bread).

Note: To thicken commercial yogurt, drain in yogurt strainer or strainer lined with cheesecloth so the whey separates.

TANDOORI-STYLE LAMB

1 half leg of lamb, sirloin section, trimmed of excess fat
2 cloves garlic, minced
2 teaspoons fresh ginger, minced
1 teaspoon salt
1 tablespoon garam masala
pinch chili powder
pinch turmeric
1 tablespoon lemon juice
1/2 cup thick yogurt
2 tablespoons cashews or pistachios, ground,
or 1 tablespoon nut butter

With the point of a sharp knife, make 1-inch slits all over the lamb. Combine the next 7 ingredients (garlic through lemon juice) into a paste (use more lemon juice if needed) and rub it over the meat, pushing spice mixture into slits. Combine yogurt and nuts and coat lamb; marinate, covered, in the refrigerator for at least 8 hours, though 24 or even 36 would be better.

Preheat oven to 450°; place lamb, still covered, in oven and cook 30 minutes; reduce heat to 350° and cook another 40 to 45 minutes or until cooked through but not dry. Serve with rice and tomato-cucumber salsa or chutney.

BANGHAN BHARTA

2 large eggplant, or about 2 pounds of the smaller variety
2 tablespoons mustard or peanut oil
1 onion, chopped
1 small Thai or bird chili, chopped
1 teaspoon fresh ginger, chopped
1 tablespoon garam masala
2 tomatoes, chopped (peeling optional)
1 teaspoon lemon juice
salt (optional)

Cut eggplant in half and cut slits in meat; place cut side down on oiled foil in oven and bake at 350°F until skin mottles and partially collapses; remove, cool, peel, and discard any liquid. Coarsely chop or mash meat.

Meanwhile, heat oil and sauté onion over medium heat until soft; add chili, ginger, and spices and cook 5 minutes; add tomatoes and cook 5 minutes more. Add eggplant, stir, and simmer until the dish resembles a puree. Season with lemon juice and salt if desired.

PART IV

SOUTHEAST ASIA, INDONESIA AND MALAYSIA, AND THE PHILIPPINES

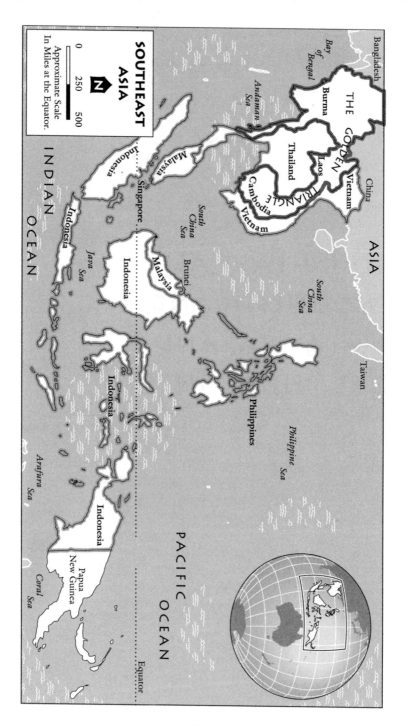

SOUTHEAST ASIA

N

Approximate Scale
In Miles at the Equator.

0   250   500

THAILAND

Thai food has become tremendously popular in the United States, and for several reasons: Like many Asian cuisines, it is relatively simple, low in fat, and high in flavor. On the other hand, it is quite distinctive, reflecting far less Western influence than most of its neighbors. Among Southeast Asian countries, Thailand alone has never been colonized; in fact, the Thais' own name for their nation, Prathat Thai, means "Land of the Free." And although not all Thai dishes are as hot as rumored, many are, so Thai restaurants have also been picked up by the hot-chili and Cajun-spice bandwagons.

Unlike some of their neighbors, the Thai people "do" restaurants, and they do them up in style. Eating out is a national pastime, and there are garden restaurants in Bangkok that will seat a thousand people at a time. The names and styles of Thai dishes are relatively standardized, so ordering in a Thai restaurant is easily mastered; and since the Thai people use chopsticks only when eating noodles (which, like the chopsticks themselves, are Chinese imports), the fork-dependent—or rather, the spoon-dependent—can feel perfectly at home. (See "How to Order and Eat Like a Native," page 221.)

THE COUNTRY

Thailand, known for centuries (and in American theatrical history) as Siam, is at the heart of the Southeast Asian peninsula. It forms the base of the region's "flower" part and stretches partway down the stem, toward Malaysia to the south. Myanmar (Burma) borders it on the west, Laos lies to the north and east, and below Laos, Cambodia curves around the east and southeast.

Thailand is permeated with water, both fresh and salt. It is criss-crossed by streams and canals; the Mekong River provides much of the Cambodian-Thai border, and the southern peninsular region is squeezed between the Andaman Sea (part of the Indian Ocean) on the west and the Gulf of Siam (the South China Sea) on the east. Not sur-prisingly, the great central plateau of the country is all but turned over to rice paddies; rice is not only the staple food but also the largest export commodity. Thailand is in fact the world's leading exporter of rice, ship-ping out nearly seven million tons a year, which is even more amazing when you consider that the average Thai eats the cooked product of three-fourths of a pound of dry rice a day.

The northern region, however, is hilly and difficult to farm, and in many areas has been denuded by the harvesting of teak, another primary export. The southern peninsula is mountainous, too, but thickly jun-gled. It served the United States as a major staging area during the Viet-nam War; consequently, Thai immigrants have had a relatively easy time relocating (and establishing restaurants) here.

THE HISTORY

The Thai have always had a fiesty, independent streak. Their own his-torical "exodus" out of south-central China occurred near the end of the thirteenth century, when they migrated to the hill country rather than live under Kublai Khan's Mongols; and although Thai speech is related to Chinese and other Southeast Asian languages, its alphabet was bor-rowed from the Cambodian Khmer and is written left to right, rather than right to left as Chinese is.

Ever since its establishment as a nation, Thailand has knocked elbows and frequently worse with Burma, Cambodia, Laos, France, England, and

Japan. It was first exposed to Western culture in 1511, when the ever-adventurous Portuguese traders and missionaries first explored what were long called the East Indies; the Dutch and English were shut out for nearly 200 years, and after the French financed an abortive coup in 1688, Europeans were locked out again for another century, which they whiled away by colonizing and influencing Malaysia, Burma, and Indochina. In the decades just after the American Civil War, Thailand was gradually reopened and then determinedly "Westernized" by King Mongkut, or Rama IV (the King of Siam memorialized in *The King and I*), and his son, Chulalongkorn, also known as Rama V. Except for the period between 1930 and 1950, when the newly named Thailand—then renamed Siam, then renamed Thailand—was pulled in and out of the Communist Chinese orbit, Thailand has remained Western-oriented.

Although the greatest religious influence is Buddhist—members of the royal family also serve as religious figureheads, which partially explains the almost shrine-like portraits of Thai rulers seen in many restaurants here—there are Hindu, Christian, and Muslim minorities, and a wide variety of religious holidays are observed in the country. Interestingly, despite the long and otherwise pervasive influences of Buddhism on Thai society, it did not produce a dominantly vegetarian cuisine.

THE CUISINE

Thai food has only one rule: balance. Thai meals, and even single dishes, are supposed to combine the four essences: hot, sour, salty, and sweet, or *prik, preeo, khem,* and *wan.* Thai food has room for creativity and adaptation—another reason Thai restaurants have flourished in the West—so long as the essential quality and balance are preserved. (Thai restaurants may also have done so well so quickly because unlike Cambodia, for example, Thailand does have a fairly formal culinary tradition: Bangkok is one of the great restaurant cities of the world.) And the Thai eat, or at least snack, round the clock: They've been "grazing" for centuries.

The two great influences on Thai cuisine have historically been China and India—stir-fries and curries. On Thai menus, curry dishes are often listed in a sort of color chart: red, green, yellow, and "country style," usually referring to the northern-style dishes without coconut milk. Curry paste is usually indicated by the word *panaeng,* also spelled *pakaeng* or even *kaengpaa. Kaeng* (or *gaeng*) by itself means both curry and the sauce itself, so it can also be used for any soupy or heavily sauced

Thai cooking is not regionally distinct, at least as practiced in the United States, but it does have regional tendencies. Generally speaking, the northern dishes are simpler and include more meat; and the preferred rice is the sweet or "sticky" variety. Southern dishes are creamier—the use of coconut milk, in particular, demonstrates this area's ties to the Malay nations—and tend more heavily to seafood. These Malay-style southern dishes can be high in fat, because both coconut milk and the peanuts used in satay sauce are fatty; in some restaurants, satays of marinated and skewered meat or poultry are served with a sweet-sour dipping sauce made of corn syrup.

In general, though, except for fried foods such as soft-shell crabs and whole fish, and the somewhat high sodium content, Thai cuisine is quite healthful. In fact, Thai stir-fried dishes are lighter and less oily than the Chinese versions, with little if any starch; even sauces are thickened through slow simmering rather than with cornstarch. They are also heavy on vegetables, except at restaurants trying to cater to Americans' excessive reliance on meat.

dish. *Kaeng mussaman* (i.e., Muslim curry) is a thicker, milder version with Middle Eastern aromatics such as cloves, cumin, fennel seed, cinnamon, and cardamom.

Cooking styles are also simple; indeed, in most traditional Thai houses, the kitchen is a separate shack out back, with woks, steamers, strainers, and assorted utensils hanging around a gas or wood stove. Even in the United States, many restaurant kitchens are surprisingly basic, depending on cleavers and mortars and pestles in place of grinders or food processors, and centering on the gas flame. Curries are usually simmered, meats and fish grilled over charcoal, and whole fish sometimes fried or wrapped in banana leaves and grill-steamed. Vegetables are generally julienned or chopped (or even grated) and served raw or lightly stir-fried. In fact, the presence of often decoratively carved vegetables is a characteristic of even the most basic Thai recipe.

Another distinction has to do with rice and its preferred cooking style. Like the Vietnamese and Indonesians, the Thai prefer their rice cooked without salt, so that the grains are almost dry. This allows the rice to absorb sauces, which are frequently salty themselves.

THE MAIN INGREDIENTS

SEASONINGS The most characteristic flavors in Thai food are *nam pla* (the nuoc mam of Vietnam), a fermented anchovy- or squid-based fish sauce that is to the Thai what soy sauce is to the Chinese; shrimp paste; chilies, ranging from fairly mild (the yellow *prik num* or banana chilies) to very hot (dried red *prik* *baeng* and fiery multicolored *prik kee noo* or bird chilies); coconut milk; curry pastes, also ranging in heat from mild to incendiary and either prepared at home or available in markets; and basil, lemongrass, lime juice, and tamarind. Thai chefs frequently grind garlic, peppercorns, and coriander root into a paste that is used in cooking as an instant marinade.

Common herbs and spices include lemongrass, only the lower stalks of which are used (bruised or flattened to break the woody fibers, then sliced or minced), kaffir lime leaves, the Thai basil known as *gaprow* (also called "holy basil"), cilantro (also called coriander or Chinese parsley), turmeric, cumin, cinnamon, cardamom, cloves, paprika, and mint. The most prevalent flavors are basil, black pepper, galangal and its near cousin ginger, and garlic. Next to the Koreans, in fact, Thais have the greatest per capita consumption of garlic in the world—about a pound per person per year.

The major condiments are chili-vinegar dipping sauce, a sort of Thai vinaigrette, called *nam som kratien*; a chili-soy-shrimp paste mix called *nam prik*; and the peanut sauce used for satays. Bottles of nam pla, both light and dark soy sauces, and rice vinegar are usually set on the tables with the salt and pepper. Dried minced shrimp is often used to punch up salads and noodle dishes; so is roasted ground rice.

PASTAS AND STARCH Rice is the basis of all meals: In welcome, the Thai say "*Kin khao!*"—"Eat rice!" In comparison to the Thais' consumption of three-fourths of a pound every day, Americans average less than a half-

Hot, Hot, Hot

In some cases, ordering is as simple as picking beef, chicken, or shrimp and then "color-coding" the sauce. Green chilies are the hottest and tend to announce themselves immediately; red chilies move to the back of your tongue and then gradually take hold. Yellow chili pastes usually get their color from the addition of turmeric, suggesting more Burmese or Malay influence. "Dry curries," which sound to American ears as if they ought to be spice rubs but look much like yellow curries, omit the coconut milk in favor of a tamarind paste.

This is probably the time to point out that while northern or Isaan (sometimes transliterated as "Eesan") cooking, with its green and red curries, is notoriously hot, many Bangkok-style dishes are just as powerfully and persistently incendiary. If you see a listing for something like "tiger steak," remember that the dipping sauce or marinade served with grilled steak is called *seua rong hai*—literally, hot enough "to make a tiger cry." However, not all Thai dishes are hot; and most menus have stars or asterisks (or even little chili pods) to indicate the degree of spiciness. To be sure, ask your server.

pound a month, and even that average has gone up in the years since Asians began immigrating in such numbers. The preference in the north is for "sticky rice," called *kao nio* and related to the sweet rice of Japan; in the south, the longer-grained and intensely fragrant jasmine rice is standard. However, both are eaten everywhere.

Like other Asian cuisines, Thai cooking features a range of noodles—thick and thin, flat and round noodles, made of rice, wheat, and buckwheat, and those so-called cellophane or glass noodles made from mung bean starch—but even many noodle dishes are served with rice alongside.

MEAT AND POULTRY Pork and beef are the most common livestock, providing steaks and roast sections for grilling along with a variety of organ meats and offal; but the Thai rarely eat lamb, which is considered an Asian—that is, Mongol—import and too strong-smelling. Chicken is popular, and to a lesser degree, so are duck and quail.

SEAFOOD Though most Thai restaurants in the United States tend to offer only a couple of types of fish, particularly flounder and red snapper, at home they prepare a wide variety of salt- and freshwater fish, such as catfish and bass. Squid and shrimp are the most common shellfish, followed by mussels. Soft-shell crabs are becoming a staple in Thai restaurants in the United States, at least on the East Coast.

VEGETABLES Thai markets are frenetic places, and they stock many kinds of produce rarely seen (or prepared) here. There's a catalogue's worth of eggplants, for instance, from pea-sized bitter plants often found in curries, to white or pale green golf ball–sized "Thai eggplant" used in stir-fry, to the so-called Japanese eggplant, which are small, nearly seedless, and so sweet they do not require the pretreatment big European eggplants do. Other staple vegetables include bok choy and related cabbages, "yard-long" green beans, fresh bamboo shoots, onions, carrots, broccoli, sweet potatoes, and both fresh and dried mushrooms.

FRUITS Although they are infrequently included on menus, except perhaps as desserts, more than 30 varieties of bananas alone are available in Thailand, along with lychees, mangoes, pineapples, papayas, longan, star fruit, the red hairy rambutan, custardy mangosteen, coconut, the sour-appleish and smelly durian, and the even more pungent jackfruit, which is the Limburger cheese of the fruit stand—delicious but so odiferous that many hotels won't allow it in. It almost never appears on an American menu, but some Thai kitchens that cater to other Thai diners—and know you well—may admit to having some in the back.

THE MAIN DISHES

NOODLES AND RICE Probably the most famous Thai dish is the straightforwardly named *pad thai*—Thai noodles—which is served by street vendors in Thailand the way hot dogs are in New York City. Pad thai combines rice noodles stirfried with bean sprouts, chicken, pork, shrimp or tofu, dried shrimp, egg, green onions, and chopped peanuts, along with whatever else takes the chef's fancy (or happens to be at hand).

Among other major noodle dishes are *mee krop*, flash-fried and puffed noodles tossed with a sweetish dressing and chicken or seafood; and *rad nar* or *guay tio rad nar*, fat rice noodles stir-fried with broccoli and chicken, pork, or beef and dressed with oyster sauce or fish sauce and a pinch of sugar. *Joke*, or *jooke*, is a thick rice porridge related to Chinese congee.

Among the most popular curries are *nam prik num*, a thick green vegetarian stew, and *nam prik oong*, made from ground meat and probably as close to American chili as Asian cooking gets. Both are northern in origin and should be eaten with sticky rice, using your fingers.

SOUPS Although Thais traditionally eat all their "courses" together, restaurants in the United States generally serve soups first. The most common are lemongrass-flavored broths with chilies, mushrooms, green onions, cilantro leaves, and either chicken (*tom yum gai*) or shrimp (*tom yum goong*). Don't try to eat either the woody lemongrass stalks or pieces of galangal themselves—they're strictly for flavoring. The other most popular soup is chicken with coconut milk (*tom kah gai*), which is also sparked by chilies and galangal. *Gaeng jud taohoo* is a bean curd soup with minced chicken, shrimp, and/or pork. Other fine options include hot-and-sour soups made with either shrimp or chicken; thickish rice soups made with meat or chicken; or the hearty *guay tio rangsit*, a rice noodle-and-beef soup often enriched with organ meats.

APPETIZERS Like the soup course, the separate hors d'oeuvre course doesn't actually exist in Thailand; the ones listed on menus here generally started out as light meals or *kanto*. Among the most popular are fried chicken drumsticks or "drumettes" pulled inside out and stuffed with pork or shrimp; pork or beef or chicken satay; and crab and meat dumplings, sometimes called "puffs" or even "balls." Although it is rarely seen in the United States, butterflied raw shrimp layered with chopped chilies and garlic is a seafood revelation, even to sushi addicts.

SALADS The Thai would be baffled by the mounds of iceberg lettuce that most Americans associate with the term "salad." Theirs are light entrees. The most popular feature squid or shrimp "cooked" ceviche-style in lime and chilies (in America, they are sometimes blanched or poached) and tossed with onion, chilies, cilantro, and cellophane noodles: The shrimp version is called *pra goong* (sometimes *pla gung*) and the squid salad is *pra pla mug* (or *moog*). Grilled marinated beef (*yum nam tok* or *yam nua*) and roasted duck (*yum ped yang*) are also often served atop salads, seasoned with red onion, cilantro, mint, ginger, ground roasted rice, lime juice, and fish sauce.

Meang kom is a sort of finger salad that involves mixing together dried shrimp, roasted coconut, minced onion, sweet pepper, and a little sauce, all served in little dishes, on a spinach or lettuce leaf and rolling it up to nibble on.

MEATS The most common ways of cooking beef and pork are to grill them (usually thin-sliced and skewered) or to stir-fry them in one of the curry sauces. Minced raw meat salads may be available in really authentic restaurants; called *larb* (or *labb*), they are a northern regional dish made of pork or beef or even water buffalo. In the United States, however, most larb is chicken, *larb gai*, and it's cooked. Larb is served with sticky rice, which should be formed into a patty or flatted ball and used to snag a bite of meat—something like the way Ethiopian injera is used to eat kitfo. *Nem* is a sausage made of raw meat and roasted rice and then cured—really pickled—in chili and garlic; *sai krog* is a pork sausage, usually served grilled. *Siklok* is a pork and seafood sausage packed with curry paste, fish sauce, coconut milk, and peanuts and then grilled.

SEAFOOD The Gulf of Thailand is extremely rich in shellfish and prawns as well as flesh fish, hence the high quality of seafood dishes. Shrimp, squid, and soft-shell crabs are particular favorites and are offered in a variety of sauces, usually including a curry, a ginger-and-scallion sauce, coarse black pepper and vinegar, chili paste and scallions, or black bean sauce, or in the almost universally applied *kra prou* style—basil and chilies. Small whole squid may be stuffed with ground pork (a dish called *pla muk sod sal*). Tiger shrimp and prawns are commonly grilled and served with sauces on the side, while mussels and seafood stews (more and more often listed on American menus as "Thai bouillabaisse") are usually prepared with coconut milk. Whole fish are often fried and offered with either black bean, ground pork, chili sauce, or sweet-and-sour sauce or steamed with ginger.

POULTRY   Chicken may be grilled or skewered and served with the same choice of chili, black bean, or sweet-and-sour sauces, as well as with the curries described above. Chicken is also frequently offered in a peanut or cashew-flavored sauce; and duck may be fried or roasted. In restaurants with stronger Indonesian influences, you may see duck breast with mango and cashew or with tamarind sauce. Quail, either marinated and grilled or fried, is also common.

BEVERAGES   You will probably find that the sweet-sour vinegars and nam pla spoil the taste of wine (and those "exotic" cocktails with umbrellas are the potable equivalent of bermuda shorts and black socks). Your best bet is beer; the Thai Singha ("Tiger") brand is widely available. The primary nonalcoholic drinks are iced coffee and iced tea, both served with sweetened evaporated milk; hot tea (though not hot coffee), lemonade (rather salty to Western tastes), and perhaps soft drinks. Rice whiskey, which is rarely listed but frequently available, is highly potent.

SWEETS   Desserts may be fruits (fried bananas, plain fresh melon) or a combination of sticky rice and coconut milk with mangoes or bananas. Mangoes are a particular favorite in any form, even green with a bit of salt, dried chilies, and sugar—very similar to the way it is eaten in the Philippines. Sweet custards, mung bean cakes, and a sort of coconut fudge are enjoyed, though less common in the United States. Coconut ice cream (particularly in the United States), lychee nuts, and sweet cakes or jellies called *kanom* are also popular.

HOW TO ORDER
AND EAT LIKE A NATIVE

Thai restaurants in the United States are making fewer and fewer concessions to Western tastes, for several reasons. One is the increasing interest among American diners in real ethnic food and fresh ingredients. Another

As with all menus transliterated from other alphabets, there are spelling differences among Thai menus (sate vs. satay, pad vs. pud, etc.). The knottiest problem for English speakers is the consonant that in most Southeast Asian languages, along with Korean and to a lesser extent Japanese, falls halfway between the English "r" and "l" and is apt to be spelled either way. (Asians tend to be soft with all consonants as a matter of style and think Western languages somewhat rude and abrupt because they have such "harsh" sounds.) There is also a rather fluid vowel that ranges between "ow" and "uh" and "ah," but most other syllables are fairly clear, and you will probably have no difficulty spotting your favorite dishes.

is the greater number of fresh Thai spices and vegetables available. (In the usual circular fashion, greater demand leads to more and fresher ingredients being made available, which leads to more interest, and so on.) Spicy cuisines are more than a rage; they've become standard.

The one concession Thai menus have made is in classification. Although Thai meals are served simultaneously, Thai restaurants here have adopted the Western scheme: appetizers or soups first, then salads, main dishes, and desserts. You can ask to have them all served at once, however, as the Thai do, and use a spoon to dish up the rice and top it with a little entree. You will come to appreciate the soups more if you have them alongside entrees—for one thing, you'll be able to eat a bite of rice now and then to cool off!

Generally, menus here split up dishes into appetizers, soups, salads, meat dishes, poultry dishes, seafood dishes, curries, and noodle and rice dishes. Two diners will probably want two dishes and a soup—say, lemongrass soup with shrimp; larb; and beef curry. Four diners should order a soup (maybe hot and sour), squid or grilled beef salad, pad thai, chicken curry, and either soft-shell crabs or whole fish. Some rice will be served automatically, but you may find yourself ordering more; they would.

Thai cooking, like many Asian cuisines, is relatively quick and inexpensive, putting it high on the office-lunchers' list: You can expect to have a good meal for $10 a person and a great one for $20.

Rice, the mainstay, is the only dish served hot rather than comfortably warm or even room temperature, often in lidded woven baskets (particularly in the case of sticky rice) or covered porcelain bowls. Each diner takes a large portion of rice and then small portions of the main dishes, supplementing them as the meal progresses. Again, there are two main types of rice, the glutinous sticky or "sweet" rice and the unmistakably fragrant jasmine rice. You may even come across a third type during your meal—uncooked rice that has been roasted and then ground into a spicing powder that tastes a little like malt or Grape Nuts. Altogether, a Thai diner may consume three to four cups of rice at a sitting, treating what we consider the main dishes merely as gloried condiments.

In Thailand itself, especially in the north country or informally at home, many people still eat with their fingers, rolling bite-size balls of sticky rice with their fingers and then dipping them into the curry or other sauce. Otherwise, they tend to use spoons, sometimes pushing food into the flattened bowl of the spoon with forks. Noodles are eaten with chopsticks.

Traditionally, the dining table is round, with a short pedestal, and diners sit around it on the floor; but while some Japanese and Korean restaurants in the United States maintain traditional floor seating, few if any Thai establishments do. And although it is considered polite to remove your shoes before entering Thai homes, as it is with Japanese homes, that is not necessary in a restaurant.

COOKING AT HOME

Little special equipment is required to prepare Thai dishes at home; if you don't have a mortar and pestle, a spice or coffee grinder will do, or even a food processor. A wok, a skillet, and a couple of bowls will just about do it; a bamboo steamer is helpful, but a wok with a rack and steam-proof dish will do just as well.

CUCUMBER SALAD

1 cucumber, peeled, seeded, and chopped
1 tablespoon onion, minced
2 tablespoons dried shrimp, pounded into pieces
1 teaspoon granulated sugar
3 tablespoons lime juice
2 tablespoons fish sauce (nam pla)
8 lettuce leaves
2 tablespoons roasted peanuts, coarsely crushed
1 teaspoon red chili flakes

Line a bowl with paper towels. Place chopped cucumber in the bowl and gently squeeze out moisture. Remove paper towels and add onion, dried shrimp, and sugar. Sprinkle with lime juice and fish sauce and toss gently. Line a serving dish with lettuce leaves and mound cucumber mixture in the middle; top with peanuts and chili flakes. Chill and serve.

MINCED BEEF (LARB)

1 1/2 tablespoons long- or short-grain rice
4 small dried red chilies, seeded
1 pound top round steak, finely minced
juice of 2 limes
3 stalks lemongrass, finely minced
1 large red onion, finely chopped
1 large bell pepper, cored, seeded, and chopped
30 mint leaves (approximately)
2 tablespoons fish sauce (nam pla)

In a small dry frying pan over medium heat, roast rice and chilies, shaking until the grains have browned and chilies darkened. Pour this mixture into mortar and pestle or electric grinder and grind to the consistency of coarse sand.

Place minced steak in a bowl and with your hands mix in ground rice and chili mixture, lime juice, lemongrass, red onion, and green pepper. Chop half the mint leaves and stir into the meat; reserve the rest for garnish. Season the mixture with fish sauce and transfer to serving dish. Garnish with remaining mint or decorate with lime wedges, cucumber slices, etc.

Note: You may modify the recipe by lightly poaching the minced meat in boiling water until it just changes color, then proceed.

CHICKEN, COCONUT, AND GALANGAL SOUP

4 cups chicken stock or canned unsalted broth
4 lime leaves, chopped
4-inch piece lemongrass, chopped
2-inch piece galangal, split lengthwise into several pieces
6–8 tablespoons nam pla (available at Asian markets)
6 tablespoons lemon juice

8 ounces chicken breast, thinly sliced
1 1/4 cups coconut milk
4 small red chilies, slightly crushed
cilantro leaves for garnish

In a saucepan, heat stock, lime leaves, lemongrass, galangal, nam pla, and lemon juice. Stirring thoroughly, bring to a boil and add chicken and coconut milk. Continue to cook over high heat, stirring constantly, until meat is cooked through (about 2 minutes). Add crushed chilies for the last few seconds, pour into small bowls, and garnish with cilantro.

SHRIMP CURRY
3 tablespoons oil
3 large garlic cloves, finely chopped
2 tablespoons red curry paste (available at Asian markets)
2 cups coconut milk, divided
4 tablespoons nam pla (available at Asian markets)
2 teaspoons sugar
24 large raw shrimp, deveined and peeled
but with small tail shell intact
4 lime leaves, thinly sliced
2 small red chilies, thinly sliced lengthwise
20 leaves holy basil

In a wok or skillet, heat oil and sauté garlic until golden brown. Add curry paste and cook briefly, then add half the coconut milk, the nam pla, and the sugar, stirring briskly after each addition. The mixture will thicken slightly. Add shrimp and cook until they start to become opaque, then add remaining coconut milk, the lime leaves, and the chilies. Continue to turn shrimp in the sauce until cooked through. Using a slotted spoon, remove shrimp to serving dish, add basil leaves to sauce, stir, and pour over shrimp. Serve with rice.

VIETNAM

BASIC CUISINE

DINNER FOR TWO:
Cha gio, grilled beef in lettuce leaves, caramel chicken, stuffed squid

DINNER FOR FOUR:
Stuffed chicken wings, pho, banh xeo, soft-shell crabs, steamed fish, roast quail

GROUP DISH:
Bo Ban Mon

STYLE:
Light, crisp, spicy

KEY FLAVORS:
Cilantro, nuoc mam, chilies

EATING UTENSILS:
Fingers, chopsticks

DISTINCTIVE DISHES:
Pho, spring rolls, banh xeo

UNIFORMITY OF MENUS:
Good

NUTRITIONAL INDEX:
Low fat, high protein, medium sodium

COST:
Inexpensive

"THANK YOU":
"Cam ahn"

Perhaps the deceptive simplicity of Vietnamese cuisine has kept it from achieving the wide popularity one would expect of a style so clean, light, and healthful, yet so satisfying. Maybe diners lost sight of it in moving away from the more familiar, heavily sauced Chinese cooking to the spicier Thai restaurants.

However, it is an easy cuisine to like—fresh, low in fat and calories, and inexpensive, particularly in the case of the *pho* kitchens that specialize in one-pot soup meals. Where some cuisines emphasize variety of flavors (such as Thai) or simplicity and purity (Japanese), Vietnamese cuisine concentrates on texture, mixing cooked ingredients with raw ones, spicy or sour ingredients with mild ones, and cold foods with hot. Cold soft noodles are topped with grilled meats and chopped fresh herbs; minced pork and shrimp are mixed with crunchy bean sprouts, chopped peanuts, and mint and wrapped in paper-thin sheets of rice flour; and marinated chicken is tossed with grapefruit sections and served over cabbage slaw. And since nearly all foods are dipped in sauce after cooking, the contrasting flavors are exaggerated even further.

THE HISTORY

Shaped like a gracefully extended "f" from some old love letter, never wider than about 45 miles, Vietnam stretches down the east coast of Southeast Asia along the South China Sea and up under the southern tip of Cambodia. Just larger than the state of New Mexico, it is home to 40 times as many residents—more than 65 million.

Settled more than 4,000 years ago and culturally linked to the Chinese, Vietnam was actually conquered by China about 100 B.C.E. and remained a subject nation for another thousand years before establishing its independence and stretching south into what had been ethnic Khmer (Cambodian) territory. Its division into north and south has long historical precedent; from the mid-sixteenth through the mid-nineteenth centuries, C.E., the country was ruled as two separate kingdoms, centered at Hanoi in the north and Hue near Da Nang in the central plateau, but for most of its history, as its cuisine shows, it has been three nations.

Beginning in the sixteenth century, various European powers—starting, as usual in this part of the world, with the Portuguese—attempted to establish first commercial and then political connections. The French began aggressively attempting to colonize the area in the nineteenth century, and by the 1880s French Indochina included not only Vietnam but also Laos and Cambodia. The region remained under French domination until World War II, when it was occupied by Japanese forces; it was "returned" to the French after the war and did not achieve independence until the mid-1950s, but French influence on the cuisine, though superficially strong (because so many restaurant menus were translated into French), is actually fairly limited.

THE CUISINE

Vietnam has three geographical regions, each with its own produce and recognizable culinary style, although in the United States the regional cuisines are less distinctive.

The cooler, mountainous north has fewer foods available—the plateaus are largely turned over to tea, coffee, and sugar plantations, with a few starches such as sweet potatoes, corn, and beans planted in between—so the cuisine depends heavily on spices for variety. Dried and preserved ingredients are common here, too, including mushrooms and other fungi and dried jellyfish. Much use is made of the seafood found in colder water, such as crabs; but the plateaus are good for raising cattle, and the northern Vietnamese prize beef somewhat more highly than their southern counterparts do. The North's proximity to China shows in its more frequent use of stir-frying, though Chinese cooking techniques remain prevalent throughout the country. It is also here that black pepper (as opposed to chilies) and ginger provide much of the "heat."

The central lowlands—whose old capital, Hue, was once considered particularly sophisticated—reflect the typical courtiers' assumption that more is better: "Court cuisine" consisted of many highly and imaginatively spiced dishes served in small portions. Specially fed and fattened pork were a Hue delicacy, and pork is still highly popular here; but game, often pursued in or purchased from the highlands, is common. A thicker, more assertively fermented fish sauce is used in cooking in this region.

And the south, with its humid climate and the rich alluvial soil deposited by heavy rainfall in the Mekong Delta, produces the widest variety of vegetables and fruits, as well as the sugarcane that is used in both grilling and candying. The Indian influence is seen here in the fondness for curry spices; the French occupation is evident in the popularity of asparagus, pâté, and potatoes (and wine-braised meats); and the Indonesian trade is visible in the use of peanut-based dipping sauces and coconut milk and the tendency to use sweet-sour citrus fruits to refresh food, particularly seafood dishes.

Despite its strong Chinese ties, Vietnamese cooking remains remarkably distinct. The most obvious differences are a preference for cooking with water or broth rather than oil; the taste for raw rather than cooked vegetables; and the use of nuoc mam, the fermented fish sauce that is cousin to condiments all over Southeast Asia, instead of the domineering soy sauce (except in dishes that are actually borrowed from Chinese recipes). While stir-frying, boiling, steaming, and roasting—all traditional Chinese techniques—are very common, the Vietnamese also have two very characteristic styles of cooking: grilling over charcoal and simmering in "caramel" sauce, either mild or spicy. However, the Vietnamese remain the only Southeast Asian people that commonly use chopsticks. (For more on how Vietnamese food is eaten, see "Merrily We Roll," on page 236.)

The Portuguese arrived in 1535 bearing the New World's revolutionary foodstuffs: corn, tomatoes, peanuts, potatoes, watercress, peanuts, and chilies, and in return carried away peppercorns and other spices. The Dutch, French, and English arrived a few centuries later, along with a steady influx of Catholic missionaries; today Vietnam's population is divided between Buddhists and Catholics. The many fast days and the strict vegetarianism of Buddhist philosophy contributed to the number of vegetarian dishes common among Vietnamese restaurants.

Among prominent mementos of French colonization are French bread (eaten in addition to, not instead of, rice and noodles); strong French coffee (usually iced and sweetened with condensed milk, in deference to the climate); and a fondness for such vegetables as asparagus (usually canned, since cultivation is difficult) and artichokes (grown in Vietnam but most often dried and turned into tea). The French language is still spoken throughout Southeast Asia, but menus in the United States, which used to use French terms for most dishes, are increasingly in Vietnamese and English only.

THE MAIN INGREDIENTS

SEASONINGS Nuoc mam, which is both ingredient and condiment, is a fermented anchovy sauce. Mixed with fresh lime juice, vinegar, garlic, chilies, and a dash of sugar it becomes *nuoc cham*, the dipping sauce provided for most finger foods (which are numerous) and salads. Mixed with peanuts, a little tomato or chili paste, and soybean or hoisin sauce, it becomes *nuoc leo*. At least one of these three, if not all, will be served at some point during the meal.

The most distinctive flavorings in Vietnamese cooking, after nuoc mam, are cilantro, parsley, *ngo gai* (the "saw leaf herb" used in hot-and-

---

Delicious and Nutritious

Although some dishes, particularly those made with *nuoc mam* or *mam nem*, may seem slightly salty, Vietnamese food in general is unusually healthful. The Vietnamese prefer to use only a small amount of oil even when stir-frying; most dishes are either grilled (the charcoal brazier is the most important element in Vietnamese cooking), simmered, braised, or steamed. Although skewered meat and poultry are as popular here as they are in the Middle East, Vietnamese marinades are much less likely to be oil-based, and vegetables and rice far outweigh meat in the diet anyway. Soups and sauces are simmered and reduced rather than thickened with starch as in China.

Main exceptions are the whole fried fish (and unfortunately, the Vietnamese version can be addictive), the fried stuffed chicken drumettes, and the Malay-influenced dipping sauces, whose fat double-whammy of coconut milk and peanut butter can turn an otherwise lean satay into a diet-buster. Also, some restaurants have a pretty heavy hand with the oil when making *banh xeo*, the giant crepes.

Vietnamese cooks in the United States have made accommodations to American tastes—and toning down the chili heat is just the first. At home, the Vietnamese buy all their poultry live (whatever they don't raise themselves, that is) and have it killed, bled, and cleaned on the spot; they prefer their poultry slightly pink, which the freshness allows for. Here chicken is cooked throughout, as most Americans prefer; on the other hand, the beef and pork that we might cook less is also well done. Contrary to popular wisdom, Vietnamese like spicy food almost as much as the Thai, but restaurant chefs here don't generally cook with as much garlic or chilies as they do at home. Also, dishes that in Vietnam would be hand-wrapped in rice papers are frequently either prewrapped by the kitchen or served with steamed rice instead unless you specify a preference first.

sour soup), lemongrass, vinegar, ginger, garlic and garlic chives, sesame seeds and sesame oil, shallots, black and especially white pepper, tamarind, annatto (the aromatic orangy seed also used in Latin American and Philippine cooking), five-spice powder, star anise, curry spices (coriander seed, fennel seed, turmeric, cumin, cloves, and cardamom), fresh coriander, dried shrimp, flower waters, rice vinegar, rock sugar and sugar cane, coconut milk, a variety of basils (purple Thai basil, green basil, and perilla), mints, and hot red and green chilies, particularly the tiny Thai or bird peppers.

Sweetened or sweet-and-sour tomato sauces and barbecue sauces are popular particularly on street snacks or dishes commonly cooked on the waterfront, such as whole fried fish. Peanut sauces borrowed from Indonesia are served on the satays learned from the same source. There is also an unfermented anchovy sauce, called *mam nem;* and the Chinese staples hoisin sauce and oyster sauce are also used, along with soy, in those recipes that reflect the Chinese influence. Interestingly, strict Buddhists are forbidden to consume either garlic or scallions; and since they believe that all living things, including fish, have a soul, nuoc mam is also forbidden, so on Buddhist holidays it is replaced by soy.

RICE AND OTHER STARCHES The two delta regions—the Red River and its extensive canals in the north and the Mekong in the south—are among the world's most productive rice fields; the Vietnamese sometimes compare their bone-shaped country to a porter's pole with buckets of rice hanging from either end. The everyday rice is a fragrant jasmine or basmati, but for special occasions and as comfort food, they cook the more glutinous type, called "sweet rice" by the Japanese, "sticky rice" by the Thai, and called *gao nep* by the Vietnamese. (There is also a black glutinous rice, but it is still fairly rare in the United States.) Like the Thai and Indonesian peoples, the Vietnamese prefer their dining rice to be fairly dry, not as clinging as Chinese or Japanese rice.

Much flour is made from rice, but tapioca flour and potato flour are also produced. The variety of flours results in a wide range of noodles and pastas as well as rolls and dumplings.

MEAT AND GAME Beef (*bo*) is the favorite meat, although it is scarce and therefore expensive in some places. Organs are fairly common—particularly liver, kidneys, tripe, and brains—but are not as specifically popular as in China or Singapore. Pork (*heo*) is more expansively consumed, because it is cheaper and easier to raise, and its leftovers and fats are turned into either mild or spicy sausages. (While dried Chinese sausages, or lap chuong, are somewhat sweet, boiled Vietnamese sausages, *gio*, are savory.) Vietnam is also surprisingly rich in game, such as buffalo, wild oxen, elk, and deer; one of the delicacies sold in markets is a sort of candied venison jerky with sesame seeds. Mutton is not eaten.

POULTRY There is almost as much wildfowl as game meat in Vietnam, including pheasant, thrush, and waterfowl; quail is a particular favorite. Almost all families raise chickens and ducks, but the eggs are not a major dietary item.

FISH AND SEAFOOD Restaurants here may play up the meats, because they assume Americans prefer them to seafood, but their cuisine is rich in both saltwater and freshwater fish: carp, red snapper, perch, catfish, and the anchovies essential for the making of nuoc mam. Vietnam is even richer in river creatures and shellfish—shrimp, crabs, clams, oysters, langoustines, lobsters, snails, eels, jellyfish, rays, sharks, squid, and even frogs.

VEGETABLES For any pro-fiber nutritionists looking for paradise, Vietnam might be the place. Among the common vegetables are radishes, cauliflower, artichokes, assorted cabbages, carrots, cucumber, jicama, lettuce, spinaches, watercress, eggplant, bean sprouts, bamboo shoots, long beans, daikon radish, lilybuds, lotus root, leeks, scallions, snow peas, and a wide variety of mushrooms. Preserved vegetables, primarily Chinese cabbage, are often used as condiments. As with all Chinese-influenced cuisines, Vietnamese fare also features tofu, both soft and firm; it is the essential protein for many observant Buddhists. They also use taro root and cassava (tapioca) both as a vegetable and as flour.

FRUITS AND NUTS   Vietnam is a thousand-mile-long fruit market, and one need never be without fruit in hand. Although they appear primarily as desserts on American menus, the Vietnamese enjoy many citrus fruits (lemons, oranges, and the very popular tangerines), papaya, mango, coconut, the sweet-sour mangosteen, the rambutan (nicknamed the "hairy cherry" because of its erect fuzz), persimmon, the molasses-flavored sapodilla (imported from the Americas to the Philippines by the Spanish), breadfruit, carambola, jackfruit, bitter melon, the legendarily odiferous durian, pineapples, and plums. Pickled plums—actually salted, dried, and then sugared—are simmered into many meat sauces and called *xi mui*.

Surprisingly, however, the national fruit of Vietnam is the banana, which grows in greater abundance than any other fruit. As elsewhere in Southeast Asia, the whole plant is consumed: The stem and flowers, and sometimes the bulbs, are eaten as vegetables, the leaves are used for wrapping food and for impromptu weather gear, and the trees for housing.

Vietnam not only relies on peanuts for seasonings but also on cashews, which though originally American, are widely grown there (and consumed much as they are in the States, fried and salted and with beer).

THE MAIN DISHES

FIRST COURSES   What are usually listed as appetizers in restaurants here are called *do nhau*, or "little bites," in Vietnam. They are the sort of fresh-off-the-grill finger foods that vendors hand out from food stalls in the marketplaces in Vietnam: tiny crab cakes, spring rolls, shrimp toast (minced shrimp paste spread over grilled French bread), barbecued spare ribs and meatballs, chicken wings or drumettes stuffed with crabmeat and chopped rice vermicelli, minced shrimp paste wrapped around sugarcane or crab claws and then grilled, grilled or fried squid, stuffed fried shrimp, curry-flavored turnovers, beef grilled in grape leaves, grilled meatballs, or lemon chicken. A lot of these items may be served with lettuce leaves or rice papers for wrapping up, and you could easily "graze" through a whole meal of them. (*Banh trang*, the "rice papers," are really rice-flour pancakes rolled very thin, then dried, then reconstituted by soaking in water—something like Vietnamese tortillas.)

More formal sit-down first courses might include "happy pancakes" (usually, but not always, called *banh xeo*), rice-flour omelets or heavy crepes filled with mushrooms, pork, and shrimp; artichokes stuffed with crabmeat; squid stuffed with pork; or Indonesian-style grilled beef satays with peanut sauce.

Cha gio (pronounced "zhah zhaw"), the justly famous spring rolls, are rice-paper wrappers filled with pork, tree ear mushrooms, shrimp, herbs, and the translucent "cellophane noodles" or "glass noodles" (also called bean threads); they are fried and, like almost all these appetizers, are meant to be dipped in nuoc cham. (Adherents of cha gio shudder at the term "egg roll.") *Goi cuon*, sometimes referred to here as "imperial rolls" or summer rolls, are unfried rolls with noodles, pork, shrimp, scallions, and herbs dipped in plum sauce; *bi cuon* are similar but with pork fat added.

SALADS Raw vegetable dishes are part of nearly every meal, but they go far beyond what we think of as salads. They are more likely seafood (shrimp or squid) or grilled meat with raw carrots, cucumbers, lettuce, scallions, and fresh herbs all composed on a plate and presented with the rice papers for wrapping them all up and a saucer of nuoc cham for dipping. (Be sure to read the menu carefully, however: In the United States, Vietnamese restaurants frequently attempt to hand out salad bowls of iceberg lettuce and tomato, assuming that's what Americans want.) Seafood and citrus combinations are also popular, such as lobster with papaya or shrimp with oranges or lemons.

SOUPS Particularly in the case of the North Vietnamese favorite called *pho* (see page 235), soups can be whole meals, but they may also be offered as appetizers, served either individually or in large family-sized tureens. Soup is frequently served as breakfast, which makes sense in a climate that may be blisteringly hot by midday. Among the popular first-course soups are crab and asparagus, chicken and rice, chicken and corn, or chicken and noodle soups; hot-and-sour soup with shrimp (sometimes called "Vietnamese bouillabaisse") or pork; crab dumpling soup; meatball soup; beef-noodle soup; and dried squid stew. Non-noodle soups are known collectively as *sup*.

PASTAS AND PORRIDGES Noodles are extremely popular, particularly rice vermicelli and cellophane or mung bean noodles (*mien*), and are most often served cold. The word *bun* refers to rice vermicelli, *banh hoi* to extra thin noodles and *banh pho* to what are called in the United States, "rice sticks." Noodles are frequently fried into crispy baskets to hold seafood or beef stews, or are stir-fried with tomato and vegetables under seafood. Egg noodles are often used in soups, as are the

Japanese *somen* made from alimentary paste. However, rice (*com*) is still the most popular starch and is anything but dull: The deceptively plain-looking "Perfume River rice," for instance, is flavored with lemongrass, dried shrimp, and sesame seeds. *Come tay chao* is a familiar dish to fans of Chinese mom-and-pop kitchens, a sort of congee or rice porridge topped with anything from duck to tripe. There are also a number of rice stews cooked in clay pots: *Con tay cam* is flavored with duck broth, crabmeat, shrimp, and vegetables; *come tay cam ga* is the chicken version.

MEATS Beef is relatively rare and thus more expensive—hence the tradition of presenting "Beef Seven Ways" at celebrations and banquets. Beef is often "stretched," either as part of a salad, soup, or stir-fry or as meatballs. It may also be "stuffed" or rolled around vegetables and cut in pinwheel slices; among these dishes are fragrant "cinnamon beef" with orange peel; wine-and-honey-marinated beef pinwheeled around grilled onions; and flank steak rolled around caramelized carrots. Wine-flavored bouef bourguignonne–style stews, sometimes called "Saigon beef," are often padded, with the potatoes and bread stewed right in. Pork is barbecued, turned into meatballs, sauced sweet-and-sour, roasted, braised, or "caramel"-simmered in a sauce of coconut milk and nuoc mam.

Other common meat entrees include pork chops, short ribs, and venison in red wine.

POULTRY Roast duck is extremely popular over salads and rice congees, usually with the skin and fat (where the smoke or spices linger) intact. Quail is very popular, marinated and grilled and served with the coarse salt-and-pepper dip or marinated in coconut. Chicken (*ga*) is roasted, marinated, stewed in coconut milk and ginger sauce, satay-grilled, braised with a caramel sauce (in the United States sometimes made from the sweetened condensed milk the Vietnamese favor in coffee but more authentically with coconut milk, brown rock sugar, and nuoc mam), fried, or stir-fried with chilies and lemongrass. A chicken and rice casserole is a home-cooking favorite; although it is not often on restaurant menus, it is frequently available for the asking.

FISH AND SHELLFISH As mentioned, whole fish are extremely popular, particularly fried or steamed. (In the United States they most often steam the snapper and fry flounder.) Mixed seafoods are popular too, either steamed, grilled, poached, or stir-fried; and they are frequently presented in fried rice-noodle "nests." Mussels and oysters are often steamed with ginger and garlic or scallions; squid often appears stuffed with pork or shrimp or even crab. Shrimp are most often grilled, but they are popular in curry and coconut milk sauces. Soft-shell crabs are a particular Vietnamese specialty, and in season many restaurants will offer them four or five ways a day.

ONE-POT MEALS   Some restaurants offer beef or even fish fondues called *lau*, which are Chinese hot pots recalling the Mongol invasions of the thirteenth century; however, the "broth" may have a very un-Mongol flavoring of coconut milk or vinegar. Similar dishes are cooked in the kitchen in clay pots. Tofu frequently is stir-fried not just instead of meats but in addition to them, flavored with roast pork or smoked duck.

BEVERAGES   With meals—particularly with "little bites" such as crabs, satays, and barbecue—the Vietnamese like beer or coffee, along with soft drinks (including a soy milk, club soda, and egg yolk "cream" called *soda sua not ga*), teas (green, black, or floral), French-style wines, or a rice wine called *ruou de* that is similar to sake.

SWEETS   The Vietnamese themselves do not serve sugary desserts—they tend to eat them in the late afternoon with hot tea or coffee, following the post-lunch siesta—and generally prefer fruit, either fresh or perhaps caramelized, after dinner. However, since most customers in restaurants here do expect dessert choices, menus are likely to include a least a simple flan, bananas flambé, or rice or taro pudding. (You may also see less predictable pudding choices; some are even made with black-eyed peas.) Vietnamese iced coffee—espresso with sweetened condensed milk—is very sweet and serves as a sort of combination coffee and dessert.

PHO

Pho, the most famous Vietnamese soup, is a whole meal in a bowl and is just about the only dish *not* served communally; the word *pho* actually means "one's own bowl," because you don't share it.

Pho is a beef broth and noodle soup with raw bean sprouts, fresh green herbs, and usually a choice of up to eight or ten various cuts of beef (occasionally, but not traditionally, chicken or seafood) placed on top and served with various condiments on the side. Like most beef dishes, it was most popular in the north—some restaurants advertise it as "beef noodle soup, Hanoi-style"—but it became almost a staple in the south

Merrily We Roll

The great majority of Vietnamese dishes—salads, satays, barbecues, and even the flesh of whole fish, pulled by chopsticks away from the bone—are traditionally eaten by hand. Meats, along with a few of the green herbs and noodles that will be served on the side, are wrapped in rice-paper crepes and dipped into sauce; this rolling and dipping rhythm blends effortlessly with the natural rhythm of chatting, and makes Vietnamese dining even more sociable.

The best way to make a roll is to use the chopsticks to transfer food into the rice-paper sheet about a third of the way up, then, using your hands, turn the short flap of crepe over the filling and fold in the two remaining "long sides" butcher-paper style before tightly rolling from the filled end toward the open side. That way the food won't fall out the ends. The first few times, try putting only a morsel or two of each ingredient into the paper—they add up, and then the roll gets hard to hold together. Also, rice-paper crepes are much thinner than the Chinese pancakes you may have had Peking duck or moo shi pork in, and they tear more easily.

after the fall of Saigon and the influx of northerners. In the United States there are an increasing number of "pho houses" that offer only pho. From $4 a bowl for the basics to about $10 with all the deluxe toppings, these meals are budget bonanzas.

When you order pho, the soup bowl will arrive nearly full of hot broth and noodles with whatever meat you have chosen on top; the bean sprouts, fresh green herbs, chilies, and flavoring sauces (vinegar, soy or nuoc mam, and hoisin) will be served separately. You will be given chopsticks, a soup spoon, and a small sauce dish. Stir the raw vegetables into the soup and put the dipping sauces (which are for the meats) in the small saucer. Then using the chopsticks in your stronger hand and the spoon in the other, draw up some noodles out of the broth to cool, resting the lower part of them in the bowl of the spoon. You may blow on the noodles or make a slurping noise without being impolite. In between noodles and sprouts, use the chopsticks to bring out the meats or seafood and dip them in the sauce. Although most Americans pronounce the soup as "fo," the true pronunciation is somewhere between that and "fee," "fi," and "fum"—*fuh*.

HOW TO ORDER AND EAT LIKE A NATIVE

Dining is a lively social exercise in Vietnam, either out (at the food stalls that are the very heart of the markets), in restaurants, or at home, where everyone is served at once and a great hubbub arises while the dishes are passed.

In traditional Vietnamese homes, diners sit cross-legged on bamboo mats on the floor around a low table, but this practice is almost never seen in the United States. Each place is set with a bowl, a small saucer for nuoc cham or other dipping sauces, chopsticks, and a flat-bottomed Chinese porcelain spoon; here a plate is almost certain. You may also be offered wet washcloths or towels for your hands. There will probably be bowls of cilantro, mint, and lettuce leaves on the table, and perhaps cold noodles on the table as well. After the salad and soup, all the dishes—generally three or four entrees—are served at once, and when the big bowl of rice appears, the noise (and pleasure) level rises appreciably.

Each diner puts rice in his or her bowl, then takes a small portion of each entree and puts it on top of the rice; it is polite to take only as much as you can manage, because the rice and dishes will go around again and again. Use the larger ends of the chopsticks to serve yourself rather than the eating ends.

Incidentally, if any of the dishes are served with sticky rice instead of banh trang, you should use the rice itself as a spoon, molding it with your fingers; see the chapter on Thailand for hints.

"Bo Bay Mon," the Beef Seven Ways banquet, is obviously a whole meal, but in the United States restaurants frequently offer customers the choice of ordering only two or three of the courses. However, if you have the full dinner, the last course will be *chao thit bo*, a beef-rice soup cooked in the broth created by previous courses of hot pots, etc. Like the pho, these

Say It Again, Sam

Menus here are logistically predictable but linguistically problematic. Although traditional Vietnamese meals do not include "appetizers" as we know them, and have "salads" we'd consider light meals, most Vietnamese restaurants have managed to arrange the menus in a way that is more familiar to American diners.

On the other hand, recognizing the names of dishes—which can be difficult in any Asian restaurant, because the words have to be spelled phonetically—seems especially tricky in this case because the phonetics themselves seem mysterious: *Pho*, for instance, is pronounced with almost any vowel you can imagine. The most undependably translated word appears to be *banh*, which literally means "cake" but which refers frequently to rice-noodle patties, sometimes to French bread, and most often to a sort of thick omelet. Fortunately, though they are unobtrusive and deferential, Vietnamese waiters are very helpful and will tell you what you want to know about your food and often show you how to eat it.

dishes are served with varieties of green herbs, chilies, and lime to flavor just as you like.

Pho is also a whole meal, but you might want to save it for a second (or solo) visit. To order from a full menu, two people should try cha gio, grilled beef in grape leaves, and, if you have fairly hearty appetites, extra appetizers such as shrimp grilled on sugarcane or the so-called shrimp beignets (minced shrimp and eggwhites quick-fired and puffed up), then caramelized or coconut milk chicken and stuffed squid. For four people, order stuffed chicken wings; either beef noodle soup or hot-and-sour soup; banh xeo; fried soft-shell crabs; a whole steamed fish (remember to ask for rice papers so you can roll it); and roast quail.

A few Vietnamese restaurants serve more modern street food, some of it imported by homesick French soldiers and some probably traceable to the American servicemen stationed there: cheeses, pâtés, hero-type sandwiches on French baguettes, etc.

COOKING AT HOME

Vietnamese kitchens are among the simplest in the world. Usually they are annexes to the house, partly open to the outdoors to let the heat out, and they depend on charcoal braziers. A wok, some skillets, a mortar and pestle (or grinder), a colander, a bamboo steamer, a cleaver, chopsticks, and a couple of spoons are almost all you need either there or here; a rice cooker is helpful, but a regular saucepan will do, of course. You can either cook outdoors on a grill or use the broiler inside. (If you will be grilling on bamboo skewers, be sure to soak them in water 30 minutes beforehand.)

Dishes should be served at least warm or room temperature, but the rice should be hot, so make up all the dipping sauces and set out the condiments (lettuce leaves, dipping sauces, cold rice noodles, chili peppers) in advance.

NUOC CHAM

1/4 cup sugar
1/4 cup rice vinegar
3 cloves garlic, peeled
1 Thai or bird chili
1/2 cup fish sauce (nuoc mam)

1/4 cup lime juice
1 medium carrot, finely shredded (optional)

Combine sugar and vinegar in blender and mix until dissolved. Add all other ingredients except carrots, if desired, in blender and puree; stir carrot in last. Serve at room temperature.

GRILLED MEATBALLS (NINH HOA)

1 pound ground pork (or mixed pork and beef)
1 teaspoon freshly ground white pepper (or more to taste)
3 cloves garlic, peeled and finely minced (or more to taste)
1 tablespoon sugar
1 scallion or green onion, finely chopped
3 leaves mint or basil, finely chopped (optional)
1 tablespoon fish sauce (nuoc mam)
3 teaspoons cornstarch or potato starch
oil for rolling meatballs
lettuce leaves for wrapping
nuoc cham (recipe above)

Combine ground meat, pepper, garlic, sugar, scallion or onion, mint or basil, and fish sauce; sprinkle with starch and mix again. Cover, place in refrigerator, and let flavors blend several hours.

Prepare grill or preheat broiler. Rub a little oil on your hands, then make meatballs about one inch across; place on skewers, if you are using them, and grill or broil until crispy on all sides (2–3 minutes per side). Serve with lettuce leaves for wrapping and nuoc cham dipping sauce.

RICE WITH CHICKEN IN CLAY POT CASSEROLE (COME TAY CAM)

2 tablespoons fish sauce (nuoc mam)
1 teaspoon sugar
2 teaspoons sesame oil
4 cloves garlic, peeled and finely minced
salt and white pepper to taste
6 chicken thighs, skinned, boned, and cut into bite-sized pieces
8 dried shiitake mushrooms
1 tablespoon cornstarch or potato starch

1/2 cup dry sherry or Chinese cooking wine
2 tablespoons peanut oil, divided
4 shallots, peeled and finely minced
1 small white onion, chopped
2 cups uncooked long grain rice
2 1/2 cups chicken or vegetable broth

Mix together fish sauce, sugar, sesame oil, 1 clove garlic, and salt and pepper; add chicken and stir to cover with sauce. Meanwhile, soak mushrooms in warm water until soft; dispose of tough stems and julienne the caps. In a separate bowl, dissolve cornstarch in sherry.

Heat 1 teaspoon peanut oil in a skillet, sauté shallots and remaining garlic cloves for 1 minute, and add chicken mixture. Sauté, stirring, about 8 minutes or until thoroughly cooked. Add mushrooms and stir 1 minute; add sherry mixture and continue to stir another 5 minutes. Set aside.

In a heavy casserole or enamel-coated pot, heat the remaining peanut oil and sauté the onion until golden; increase heat to high, add rice, and stir-fry about 3 minutes. Add broth, stir once, and cover; reduce heat to medium, cook about 5 minutes or until liquid has been absorbed, and then reduce heat to low. Continue to cook, stirring once or twice, another 10 minutes, then pour chicken mixture over rice and cook another 10 minutes. Serve hot.

FRIED CHICKEN WITH LEMONGRASS

1 stalk fresh lemongrass (or 1 tablespoon dried)
2 tablespoons rice wine vinegar or white wine
3 tablespoons fresh ginger, peeled and finely minced
2 tablespoons fish sauce (nuoc mam), divided
1/2 cup water
1 teaspoon cornstarch or potato starch
1 teaspoon sugar
3 chicken thighs, skinned, boned, and cut into bite-sized pieces
freshly ground white pepper
1 tablespoon peanut oil
2 cloves garlic, peeled and minced (or more to taste)
1 medium onion, cut in eight wedges
2 scallions, green parts only, cut in 2-inch lengths

Trim away outer leaves and upper half of lemongrass stalk; slice tender bottom as thinly as possible (soak dried lemongrass for 2 hours, drain, pat dry, and chop). Combine vinegar and ginger and set aside. Combine 1 tablespoon fish sauce, water, starch, and sugar and set aside. Season chicken with remaining fish sauce and ground pepper, add lemongrass, and mix well.

Heat oil and sauté garlic and onion; add chicken and scallions and cook, stirring constantly, about 5 minutes. Cover, lower heat to medium, and cook another 5 minutes. Add ginger-vinegar mixture and starch mixture and stir well; recover and cook 5 minutes more. Serve with rice.

THE GOLDEN TRIANGLE: CAMBODIA, LAOS, AND BURMA

Even though there are growing Cambodian, Laotian, and Burmese communities in the United States, particularly on the coasts, they have established only a few restaurants here—and in fact are having to learn the business almost from scratch. Unlike Thailand and Vietnam, where dining out was an established and sociable tradition, Cambodia had no real restaurant tradition outside the royal court; most families cooked and ate at home, and the few restaurants were generally owned by expatriate or ethnic Chinese. In Laos, which is rugged, mountainous, and thickly forested, farming is mostly for subsistence, and home-style cooking is heavily borrowed from the Thai. In both countries, French food is quite popular and is mainly served in restaurants, but it has not been hybridized with native dishes. And although Burma has an intriguingly hybrid cuisine, influenced by India and Malaysia and Indonesia and China, there has been as yet little emigration from Burma to the United States.

Nevertheless, these countries offer intriguing side trips into Asian cuisine. Cambodia, which shares many ingredients with Thai and Laotian cuisines, shows a greater Chinese influence than its neighbors. The food of Laos is probably the plainest of the region, emphasizing freshwater fish and some wild hogs for protein. It is also unusual in that it relies almost exclusively on glutinous or "sticky" rice, even in main dishes (all three cuisines rely heavily on fish or shrimp pastes for flavor and nutrition). The Burmese have developed a fondness for curries, though not as aromatic as Indian versions, and use a distinctive flavoring created by the fermenting and cooking of green tea leaves.

THE COUNTRIES

Cambodia (also known as Kampuchea) is the most fertile of the three, half tropical forest and half a network of rivers and lakes that annually floods and enriches the earth. During the rainy season, the Mekong River backs up all the way to the Tonlé Sap ("Great Lake"), turning the whole center of the country into a natural paddy. Laos, which is landlocked, is entirely dependent on the Mekong River but is plentifully supplied through a system of lakes and paddies.

Burma (known today as Myanmar) borders on Bangladesh and India as well as Laos, Thailand, China, the Bay of Bengal, and the Andaman Sea. The heavy marks of Indian, Chinese, and Indonesian trade show in its cooking, suggesting that at various points in its history, Burma served as a docking point for the various trading fleets. Like its neighbors, Burma is a rice-growing country; the Mekong River defines most of its western border, and the Irrawaddy River runs down the spine of the country, through the legendary Mandalay to Yangon (the former Rangoon). Formerly the "Rice Bowl of Asia" in the British days, Burma has seen its rice crops decline drastically in recent years under military rule.

THE HISTORY

Although the entire peninsula has much history in common, and much conflict, the countries are ethnically and often religiously distinct. Cambodia is 90% Khmer, descended from a great empire that prospered for nearly a thousand years, with its capital at Ankgor, until it fell prey first to the constant regional battles between the Thai and Vietnamese and later to the French colonials.

The Laotians are descended from the Tai tribes that in the twelfth and thirteenth centuries C.E. pushed south from China into Khmer territory; though it was also part of French Indochina, its cuisine remains closely related to Thai food (see the chapter on Thailand). The Burmese still slightly resemble their Mongol ancestors; they are descended from tribes that roared out of Tibet in the ninth century, and they picked up a fresh infusion of blood a few centuries later, when Kublai Khan's armies swept in.

All the countries in the Golden Triangle are primarily Buddhist, but Burma (which was a British rather than French colony) has a large Christian population as well. The Japanese occupied the entire subcontinent during World War II but left little if any mark on the cuisine.

THE CUISINES

More than half the population of Laos lives along the banks of the Mekong River, which runs through the heart of the country; farmers depend on rice, corn, and vegetables, supplemented by river fish. Although many of the dishes are Thai in origin, and the Laotians use the Thai-style glutinous rice rather than paddy rice, the meats are gamey and the seasoning is much plainer; Laotian cooks depend heavily on wild herbs and leaves, notably the mild ginger-flavored *romdeng*.

Eggplant has a peculiar and very distinctive role in Laotian cooking: It is highly prized as a vegetable, particularly grilled; also, it is reduced to a paste, then used as a thickener in stews. Laotian cooking, incidentally, is frequently a communal event, a leisurely gathering of family and neighbors pooling ingredients and making a whole day of the process.

Both Cambodian and Laotian cuisines depend heavily on garden herbs and spices; since only fresh foods, including meat, are eaten (there are few refrigerators, and eating just-killed animals is a matter of safety as well as flavor), meals depend on seasonal availability.

Cambodian dishes are defined not so much by main ingredients—they may include meat, poultry, fish, or prawns—as by cooking style: A typical meal will combine one sautéed dish, one grilled, and one fried.

Burmese cooking is veggie-heavy and uses proteins mostly for flavoring. They too like eggplant, but as a vegetable; they prefer to grind or puree garbanzos or roasted rice to thicken dishes. However, although proteins are not a large element in the dishes, they are quite varied—beef, poultry, shrimp and fish, and beans, plus peanuts, eggs, and tofu—and one of the characteristics of Burmese recipes is that they frequently combine several proteins in a single dish. Burma has plenty of coastline, but so accustomed to the flavor of freshwater fish are Burmese cooks that sea fish are served only reluctantly, and then with strong seasonings to mask the taste. While Cambodians and Laotians serve vegetables raw, the Burmese generally cook theirs, even for salads, and the vegetables are often made visually more exciting by sprinklings of turmeric and fried onions.

Burmese cuisine offers more variety than the other two in style as well as substance: The Indian-style curried dishes are often served alongside and in contrast to the tart vinegar-flavored, or fish-sauced regional dishes. (Curries actually come in two styles, "wet" and "dry." The presence or absence of coconut milk is one of the major differences, but it is not the only distinction; some curries get their liquid from the ingredients themselves.) Other common cooking techniques include braising, frying (in peanut and occasionally sesame oil), and stir-frying.

THE MAIN INGREDIENTS

SEASONINGS Cambodians have a strong "sour tooth": Among the most popular flavorings are lime juice, tamarind, and lemongrass. Where the Chinese use soy sauce and the Vietnamese use nuoc mam, the Cambodians prefer a fermented fish sauce called *tak trey* (or *tuk trey*). Made of minced or ground grilled fish, it is used as either condiment or cooking ingredient. Mixed with lime juice, basil, ground peanuts, and chilies it becomes a dipping sauce called *tak kruen;* and mixed with coconut milk and ground meat, it becomes *nataing.*

Another important sauce is called *prahok katih* (*prahok* is dried anchovies and *katih* is ground pork flavored with coconut); often served with rice or raw vegetables, this sauce is essential for flavoring a popular homestyle dish of eggplant and shrimp. Other characteristic flavorings include galangal (a variety of ginger), Kaffir lime leaves, tamarind, basil, mint, black pepper, chili powder, garlic, spring onions, sesame seeds, dried mushrooms, cumin, coconut milk, ground fennel seed, turmeric, and the rarely imported but irreplaceable banana blossoms. Indonesian aromatics, including coriander, cardamom, cinnamon, nutmeg, cloves, and star anise, are blended with ginger and lemongrass and shallots to produce an important spice blend called *kroeung.* Added flavor is supplied by bits of ham, powdered shrimp or fish, and, occasionally, preserved citrus. Chinese-influenced dishes often include fermented soy beans, soy sauce, and five-spice powder.

Laotian condiments are relatively plain: Eggplant, peanuts, lime juice or pickles, malty-roasted rice, chilies, mint, green tomatoes, lemongrass, coriander, dried tamarind, fennel, soy sauce, sesame seeds, and bitter greens are the most common flavoring agents. Though all these cuisines long ago absorbed chilies into their diet, the chili may have more individual importance in Laos than any of its neighbors other than Thailand: Here they are apt to be an unadulterated ingredient, not just an element in a sauce. Laotian cuisine also depends on dried shrimp paste, fermented fish sauces, soy, and sesame oil.

The Burmese have been heavily influenced by Indian food and have adopted curry spices and sauces; these are typically dark red sauces, made by sautéing onions, garlic, chilies, and ginger in oil until they brown and reseparate from the oil. The Burmese also prefer a little more oil (peanut for cooking, sesame for flavoring) in their dishes than most Americans do and may even use the Indian-style clarified butter called ghee to make the curry base.

The most common flavorings are the pickled tea leaves, shallots, garlic, dried fish paste, fish sauce (generally the Vietnamese nuoc mam), dried shrimp, lemongrass, cilantro, coconut milk, vinegar (pickled condiments are important for contrast), and citrus or fruit-pickle chutneys. *Balachuang* is a major seasoning sauce, made of shrimp paste, garlic, ginger, turmeric, and sesame oil. However, there are a few more Western flavorings, including garbanzo flour and roasted garbanzos and paprika. The roasted rice powder used in Thai and Laotian salads is used here as well.

MEATS By Asian standards, Cambodians are extremely fond of meat; they raise cattle, buffalo, pork, and some goats and rabbits, but like most of their neighbors, the Cambodians abjure mutton. Laotians depend on the countryside to supplement their rice and somewhat limited vegetable crops: buffalo, venison, some elk, and the occasional boar replace beef and pork. Meat in Burmese cooking is most often beef or pork.

POULTRY AND EGGS Cambodian cuisine includes quite of bit of chicken, duck, squab, guinea hen, and even tiny paddy birds or rails; in poorer areas they are generally used as flavorings rather than main ingredients, but most cooks grill or roast them. Laotians raise ducks, chickens, and turkeys but seldom eat eggs. The Burmese like both and frequently add eggs to dishes that already include meat, poultry, or even fish.

FISH AND SHELLFISH   The Cambodians are particularly adept at the use of both fresh- and saltwater fish, shellfish, and even snails and frogs. Laotians prize freshwater eels, and the huge *pa boeuk* fish supplies a delicate roe that is often salted like caviar. The Burmese prepare quite a bit of shrimp; they also serve fish whole or minced into a paste.

VEGETABLES AND FRUITS   The Cambodians are able to raise corn, peanuts, squash, long beans, cabbage, cucumbers, greens, pumpkins, and sugar palms. The Laotians depend heavily on eggplant, beans, mustard and other wild greens, some forest mushrooms and fungus, and some corn. The Burmese enjoy lentils, greens (mustard, chrysanthemum, and tea among them, along with some sea vegetables), Chinese cabbage, bamboo shoots, carrots, onions, bean sprouts, squash, okra, cabbage, cauliflower, eggplant, and garbanzos. Melons, bananas, papayas, lemons, limes, and oranges are the most common fruits in the region.

STARCHES   As we mentioned above, Laotians are much fonder of sticky rice than steamed rice. The Burmese prefer long-grained steamed rice, as do the Cambodians, but the Burmese, like their Indian neighbors but alone among the Southeast Asian peoples, prefer to cook their rice with salt, producing a drier, fluffier grain. Corn is the second most popular grain, but dough wrappers and noodles are almost solely made from rice flour. Cambodians often make stir-fried noodle dishes with obvious Chinese origins, but they also make chilled rice noodle dishes, familiar to customers of Vietnamese restaurants, tossed with crunchy grilled beef, peanuts, cucumbers, mint, and basil. The Burmese especially love noodles, soft or fried, and serve them almost as frequently as rice.

THE MAIN DISHES

SOUPS AND CASSEROLES   Cambodians are fond of soups (*samla*), which are served at every meal. *Samla mchou banle* is a tart, tamarind-flavored fish soup, and *machu kroeng* is a hearty eggplant and beef soup. Seafood hot pots, another legacy of the Mongols, get a twist here—the broth is flavored with coconut milk and lemongrass, and the cooked seafood is wrapped in lettuce leaves for eating in the Vietnamese style. A really hearty one-pot meal called *khao phoune* is a combination of thin rice noodles, raw salad vegetables, chili and nataing sauces, and banana blossoms, plus dried meat or meatballs.

Like Cambodians, the Laotians take soup at every meal. Most of these everyday soups are mild and vegetarian; the meats are reserved for special occasions.

At lunch and dinner the Burmese nearly always serve soup, along with little fried snacks such as chopped shrimp or meat patties, fried sprouts or calabash "fingers," and lentil cakes. However, to the Burmese soup is not just a first course but a beverage that is sipped throughout the meal; consequently, many of them, such as black-pepper soup, have palate-priming roles of their own. And some are extremely hearty: "Twelve varieties" soup combines chicken or duck with pork, liver, cabbage, cauliflower, green beans, mushrooms, onions, and so on.

The Burmese national dish is *mohinga* (sometimes *moo hing nga* or *mohhing gha*), a thick, spicy fish stew or chowder flavored with chili paste, coconut milk, fish sauce, and shrimp paste; it's served over rice noodles and flavored with roasted rice and slices of young banana greens. Mohinga is so popular that no street market would be without vendors dishing it up.

SALADS The Cambodians often top shredded vegetables with grilled or shredded meat or chicken. Laotians also like the meat salads, eaten by hand in the Thai fashion; sticky rice is rolled into small balls or patties held in the fingers and dipped in the central dish—food and utensil in one.

The Burmese make salads of raw or cooked vegetables and even fruits. *Lapet thoke* is a dish uniquely Burmese, combining green tea leaves, fried lentils, peanuts, onions, limes and chilies and often mixed at the table; the tea leaves, which may also be added to shrimp, chicken, or pork salads as well, lend a smoky and just slightly sour taste. Frequently the onions are caramelized and the tea leaves "pickled" for even greater contrast. "Ginger" salad is a hearty mix of cabbage, beans, dried shrimp, and chilies.

MEATS Indonesian-style satays are common in Cambodian and Burmese restaurants in the United States, and grilling is a popular style of cooking almost anything, from marinated pork or boneless duck to whole fish or stuffed boneless chicken. The Laotians like Thai-style ground meat mixed with spices and powdered roasted rice, but with a slight twist: The Laotians prefer to pound their meat into a paste with a mortar and pestle rather than mince it with a knife. *O lam* is eggplant with buffalo meat and fresh beans.

One unusually meat-heavy Laotian meal is a type of Sunday dinner dish called *lap* or *koy;* it is a sort of venison tartare, with the meat of the leg and liver finely sliced or chopped and seasoned with lime juice, ground roasted rice, chilies, mint, and bitter greens, all to be eaten with sticky rice. Since "lap" also translates as "luck," it is a common dish at weddings, housewarmings, etc.

POULTRY Fowl, especially the smaller ones, are frequently grilled. *Larb gai*, the chopped chicken dish, is common throughout the region. Chicken often shows an Indonesian influence, but somewhat inside-out—stuffed, rather than sauced, with a peanut-coconut mixture and then steamed.

FISH AND SEAFOOD Deep-frying is a style usually reserved for whole fish, but in general seafood is either grilled or wrapped in herbs or banana leaves and then steamed; it is often seasoned with tangy sauces featuring tamarind, pineapple, and chopped nuts or even black beans. The Cambodians often grill fish over charcoal or steam it in a wok; the grilled fish may be wrapped in a salad leaf with vegetables and dipped into sauce, much as it is in Vietman. Another hand-pureed Laotian dish is *tom pohn*, a fish and eggplant mixture spread over lettuce leaves.

RICE AND NOODLES Rice is essential for every Burmese meal, often in addition to noodles, which may be soft or fried. In fact, some dishes have both rice and noodles; a popular homestyle dish called *htamin lethoke* (literally "rice mixed with the fingers") is a sort of mix-your-own platter of rice, egg and rice noodles, vegetables (seaweed, bean sprouts, potatoes), and flavorings.

Rice is served hot, even when the other dishes are lukewarm. It is accompanied by a number of small and pungent side dishes or condiments, called *toolee moolee*, usually including coriander, chutney, fried garlic and shallots, chilies (sometimes even fried whole chilies), and fish sauce; they are primarily intended to allow every diner to, in effect, design his or her own recipe; informally, with rice, they become a meal. The most popular accompaniment is balachaung, the mixture of dried shrimp paste, garlic, onions, and chili powder.

Kaukswe thoke is a noodle dish tossed with dried shrimp, cilantro, chilies, and peanuts.

Cambodians cook their rice to a glossy but not dry state and eat it all day; in the hottest season, dinner may be simply a bowl of rice, with or without seasoning.

The Laotians also serve rice for all three meals. For breakfast, it is soaked overnight, steamed until soft, and eaten with mango, coconut, and perhaps pickled fish.

DESSERTS The Cambodians and Laotians most often serve fresh fruit, though sometimes they simmer rice in coconut milk and then add the fruit. The Burmese traditionally serve fruit or digestifs (marinated fresh ginger slices) after a meal, but between meals they are fond of Indian-style desserts such as spongy cakes, flavored jellies, coconut milk sweets, and semolina, rice, or tapioca puddings.

BEVERAGES Tea and beer are the most common beverages in Burmese restaurants. Laotians prefer tea. Cambodians also drink mild tea but more often drink warm or hot water with meals to aid digestion.

HOW TO ORDER
AND EAT LIKE A NATIVE

In a Laotian restaurant, be sure to order a meat salad (a larb), which will come with the sticky rice to roll with your fingers. Two of you will need a soup and either a stew (eggplant-thickened if possible) or a chicken dish; four should order a fish-paste appetizer, a seafood stew (or large lobster salad), and a second stew, particularly a meat or game stew if available.

The Cambodians eat much as their neighbors do, pulling off small pieces of grilled fish or meat, wrapping it in a salad leaf with herbs and bean sprouts, and then dipping the roll in hot sauce. In a Cambodian restaurant, four people should order rice, curry, a vegetable entree, soup, and a duck or fish dish (preferably grilled). If it's offered, try a hot pot; if hot pots for two are available, this should be the first choice for a duo as well. Cambodians serve all dishes at once.

As we mentioned before, the Burmese prefer curries, and almost any entree—beef, poultry, pork, fish (and minced fish *kofta*), shrimp, or tofu—may be offered as a curry. A full Burmese dinner traditionally involves a half-dozen dishes, including a salad (raw vegetables or fruit); soup (milder if the curries are very hot, stronger if they are mild); several curries of beef, fish, eggs, or pork; fresh vegetables; and perhaps lentils.

Burmese eating customs, like the foods themselves, derive from India rather than from China or Thailand; originally neither chopsticks, sticky rice, nor spoons were used, and lethoke must, as its name suggests, still be eaten by hand. In Burma, diners sit at tables set with individual plates; the dishes are served communally in bowls with serving spoons, but only the fingers of the right hand are used to eat. Diners serve themselves a little of each of the six or eight dishes, beginning with the rice and using only the left hand for the serving spoons. The food is left separate on the plate, in small piles. Then little bites are taken up with the fingers—using only the right hand, remember, and only the fingers; the palm must not be used as a scoop. As in many Asian countries, it is considered rude to put more on the plate than you can eat, but second and third helpings are fine.

If you do order a dish such as lethoke (pronounced "letho"—the interior k is silent in Burmese), it will be preceded by a bowl of hot water and soap for washing the hands; after the meal, the hands are washed again. However, although any Burmese restaurateur will be delighted to see you eat in their traditional way, most establishments here set out forks and spoons.

Again, the Burmese meals consist of many dishes. For two diners, look for something with the green tea leaves, probably a salad; and order two curries, perhaps one wet and one dry. Four people should try one of the mix-your-own dishes, such as lethoke, or perhaps the fish-curry stew mohinga; add to that fried turnovers or fried prawns and a dry chicken curry.

COOKING AT HOME

Although many Laotian, Cambodian, or Burmese dishes are labor-intensive, few are actually difficult—primarily since kitchens in the region tend to be limited. Wood or charcoal fires are the main source of heat, and most dishes that are not simply grilled are prepared in pots (or woks). Mortars and pestles are desirable for authenticity, but grinders will do nicely.

To serve a Burmese meal, set out plates for rice as general trays, and serve the rest of the meal in bowls. Laotian and Cambodian meals are traditionally served on a large tray set down on the floor in the middle of a circle of diners; all the dishes are set on the tray, and baskets (or bowls) of rice are placed between diners. Serve weak tea or beer.

LAOTIAN PORK SOUP

1 pound lean pork chops
5 cups beef broth (or water)
4 cloves garlic, minced

1 teaspoon oil
1 tablespoon fish sauce (nuoc mam)
1 tablespoon sugar
1 tablespoon lemon juice
1 tablespoon fresh ginger, julienned
chopped fresh cilantro for garnish

Bone the chops; cut or coarsely chop pork into small pieces and enrich broth or make stock from the bones. Sauté garlic in oil over medium heat until soft, but not brown, then increase heat and add pork; sauté for a minute, then pour in stock and add all other ingredients except cilantro. Reduce heat to low; cover and simmer 20–30 minutes; top with cilantro and serve.

LAOTIAN CHICKEN

1 3-pound roasting chicken
1 teaspoon salt
2 cloves garlic, crushed
1 teaspoon oil
2 medium onions, chopped
1/2 pound lean pork, minced or ground
salt and pepper to taste
1 fresh red chili, finely chopped
2 tablespoons fresh cilantro, chopped
1/2 cup uncooked rice
2 1/2 cups coconut milk, divided
1 teaspoon fish sauce (nuoc mam)

Wash and dry chicken, then rub inside and out with salt and one of the garlic cloves. Heat oil in a large skillet, sauté the other garlic clove, the chopped onions, and the pork, and season with salt, pepper, and red chili. Add cilantro, rice, and 1 cup coconut milk and bring to a boil, then cover, lower heat, and cook at bare simmer until liquid is absorbed (about 10 minutes). Use pork and rice mixture to stuff chicken. Mix remaining coconut milk, 1/2 cup water, and fish sauce. Place stuffed chicken in a deep saucepan, pour coconut milk mixture over it, cover, and simmer until tender (about 1 hour).

STEAMED FISH WITH GINGER

4 6- to 8-ounce fish fillets or steaks
4 ounces fresh ginger root, preferably young
juice of 1 lemon
4 large cloves garlic
1 1/2 tablespoons cooking oil
1 tablespoon sesame oil
3 tablespoons toasted sesame seeds
2 tablespoons soy sauce
banana leaves for steaming (or foil wrap)

Wash fish, removing any remaining scales, and pat dry. Scrape rough skin off ginger and julienne. Cover with lemon juice and set aside. Slice garlic thinly and sauté in the combined oils over low heat until golden; pour garlic and oil into ginger mixture and add sesame seeds and soy sauce. Place fillets on banana leaves (or in foil packages), sprinkle with ginger mixture, wrap tightly, and steam 15 minutes.

BURMESE "DRY" SHRIMP CURRY

1 pound large or jumbo shrimp
1 onion, chopped
3 cloves garlic
1/2 teaspoon turmeric
1 teaspoon grated ginger
1/2 teaspoon chili powder
3 tablespoons sesame oil
dash of coriander
2 tablespoons spring onions (thin green parts only), chopped
2 tablespoons cilantro, chopped
salt to taste

Shell and devein shrimp. Put onion, garlic, turmeric, and ginger in blender or food processor and puree. Add chili powder and blend again. Heat oil to smoking point and add ground onion mixture (it may splatter); reduce heat, stir, and simmer covered for 15 minutes, stirring often to prevent sticking. When the paste turns deep red and the oil begins to separate to the sides, add the shrimp and stir. Sprinkle with coriander and cook just until opaque, then add green onions and remove from heat. Serve with rice.

INDONESIA, MALAYSIA, AND SINGAPORE

Though there are few authentic Indonesian or Malay restaurants in the United States, they are in one sense the universal common denominator: They made virtually every other cuisine possible.

Here lie the legendary Spice Islands, the Bandas and Moluccas, whose riches permeated Byzantine culture; whose incalculable commercial value drove the European nations to sea and frequently to war; whose aromatics inspired the first truly worldwide trade. It was their spices—nutmeg, pepper, ginger, cloves, cinnamon, and allspice—that allowed cooking to become cuisine, not only serving as preservatives and masking the odors of spoiling meat but also inspiring the *creation* of actual dishes and flavorings. Like the vegetables of the Americas, which revolutionized European food, the spices of Indonesia and Malaysia made possible the curries, pilafs, stews, sautés, and salads of China, Southeast Asia, and the Middle East.

They also made possible a boom in home medication: Many of the most popular spices were used as pharmaceuticals long before they

BASIC CUISINE

DINNER FOR TWO:
Satays, chicken in coconut milk, beef sambal

DINNER FOR FOUR:
Satays, soup, gado-gado, sambal, shrimp sayur or fried fish

GROUP DISH:
Rijsttafel

STYLE:
Hot, spicy, aromatic

KEY FLAVORS:
Curry, coconut, chilies, peanuts

EATING UTENSILS:
Fingers, spoons, forks

DISTINCTIVE FOODS:
Rijsttafel, gado-gado, satay

UNIFORMITY OF MENUS:
Fair

NUTRITIONAL INDEX:
High fiber and protein, medium fat, cholesterol, and sodium

COST:
Moderate

"THANK YOU":
"Terima kasih" (Indonesian)

became flavoring agents, and the Europeans and Arabs who began trading in the powders also began boasting of their healing powers. Garlic was prescribed for migraines and menstrual cramps, lemongrass for intestinal disorders, peppers for fever and flu, cloves for toothache (clove oil is still used by many dentists to soak surgical dressings), and virtually all the hottest spices, including chilies, cinnamon, cumin, ginger, onion, and turmeric, were used for stomach disorders, dysentery, and diarrhea—all of which were endemic before refrigeration or sanitary handling.

THE COUNTRIES

Indonesia is almost like a watery galaxy—more than 15,000 islands, fewer than a third of them populated (though even at that there are 180 million people and hundreds of languages), flung along the equator between Southeast Asia and Australia. They form a natural barrier between the Pacific and Indian (i.e., Atlantic) oceans, so the early explorers who believed they were at the edge of the world were almost right: Indonesia is the seam of the world. Its territories are synonymous with adventure—Java, Sumatra, Borneo, Bali, the Moluccas, New Guinea, and the catastrophic Krakatoa—and tigers, elephants, crocodiles, and surreally brilliant wild birds still roam them. Earthquakes are frequent, and more than 100 active volcanoes attest to the islands' turbulent origins.

Malaysia, like Turkey, comprises two parts divided by water. Eastern Malaysia, which is mostly rainforest, forms a slightly cockeyed lid over the large island of Borneo, with the tiny but independent and extremely wealthy kingdom of Brunei as a handle. Western Malaysia is actually on the Indochinese peninsula, south of Thailand. Topographically, western Malaysia resembles a fish skeleton, with a mountain range down its spine and tiny rivers, like ribs, running east and west, and at its southern tip is the city-state of Singapore—which itself actually comprises some 60 islands.

Most of the region is quite fertile along the coasts, thanks to the volcanic soils and tropical climate. (Singapore is the exception: Only about 5% of its land is turned over to raising fruits and vegetables, and it devotes more attention to raising pork and poultry, including ducks.) Fish are the major source of protein, and rice the primary crop, but several other starches—cassava, yams, and soybeans—are cultivated, along with sugarcane, coffee, tobacco, peanuts, palm oil, cinchona (the source of quinine), cacao, coconuts, and, of course, spices.

THE HISTORY

Malaysia, particularly the contiguous part, was settled about 4,000 years ago by Malay tribes from southern China, who drove the aboriginals into the mountains and jungle islands where many of them still live. Throughout its history, it has been subject to invasions by and intermarriages with Thai, Indian, and Javanese peoples; of its modern population, about 59 percent is ethnically Malay, 32 percent is Chinese, and another 10 percent is Indian, especially Southern Indian, or Pakistani.

Most Indonesians are either from Papuan or Malay groups, and although one of the 300 Malay dialects is the official language, English is the second. The largest ethnic minority is Chinese, and there are sizable Arab, Indian, and Pakistani communities as well. For 600 years, from the seventh to the thirteenth centuries, Sumatra was the seat of a prosperous Buddhist empire, and the kingdom of Java was Hindu; but beginning in the fourteenth century, the increasing influence of Arab traders spread Islam through the islands, and by the end of the sixteenth century, the region was overwhelmingly Muslim. Only Bali remains predominantly Hindu.

Religion is one reason (geography obviously being the primary one) that so many meals are based on fish and rice: The Malay are primarily Muslim and do not eat pork (or drink alcohol); the Indians are Hindu and do not eat beef; and the Chinese, who are primarily Buddhist, have a strong vegetarian tradition as well, though they do enjoy pork. Singapore, founded by the British in the early nineteenth century, has the heartiest and least restricted diet; meats and eggs, which are expensive and not too common elsewhere, are served relatively lavishly here.

It is impossible to explain the lure of the Spice Islands without comparing the craze for nutmeg in Europe to the modern-day drug traffic. It was marketed not as a flavoring but as a hallucinogenic, an aphrodisiac, a cure for dysentery, and effectively as money. A dealer could sell his cargo in Western Europe for 60,000 times what he paid for it.

However, while the spice trade made many European nations fabulously wealthy (and occasionally bankrupted their rivals), it was anything but a boon to the native peoples. Incursions by Portuguese, British, and most brutal of all, Dutch East Indies Company officers resulted in forced labor, a caste system, and in 1621 a massacre that cut the population of the Bandanese in half.

THE CUISINE

There are two underlying principles in Indonesian/Malaysian cuisine, both related to the tropical climate. One is that the excessive heat can kill the appetite (thus ultimately weakening the body), and the other is that food spoils rapidly. So chilies and spices are essential both for preserving the food and for stimulating the palate; and meals tend to center on "market availability," so to speak, for both reasons. In general, the cuisine is not terribly fancy or varied but is fresh, bright, and colorful.

Cooking methods are fairly limited. In the old days, wood stoves were kept away from the house, in small shacks clustered together in the common back courtyard; and most dishes could either be left to themselves or cooked very quickly. Heavy woks, called *kualis*, are used for stir-frying, steaming, frying, and braising; flat iron griddles are used not only for grilling but also for baking flatbreads. The most important kitchen utensil is a heavy bowl or mortar called a *ukelan*, which is used for grinding spices into powder or paste; it is similar to the old Mexican metate.

The P-Nuttiest

There is much about Indonesian food that looks healthful—the seafoods, the satays and salads—but in fact, this is one of the world's highest-fat cuisines. Palm oil, coconut oil, and coconut milk are all at the top of the fat-level list, and peanuts are not far behind, so grilled and steamed dishes are better nutritional bets than sweet coconut curries and peanut-based satay dipping sauces. The Sumatran and Singa-pore-style dishes are often less fatty, because they depend more on chili sauces than on sweet ones; and the Indian-influenced rice birya-nis are pretty good bets, too. If you're trying to limit fat, eat lots of rice and try to avoid the dishes that have oil puddling in the bottom (eat off the top if you must).

The most obvious element of Indonesian cuisine is its hodgepodge of influences. Rice arrived at least 2,000 years ago with immigrants from Southeast Asia—but distinctively in this part of the world, both taro and cassava are preferred as starches. The first Europeans to reach the Indian Ocean were the Portuguese, who captured Molucca in the early sixteenth century and introduced the natives to the power of the chili pepper; but the Dutch, who took advantage of Portugal's internal troubles (i.e., the "Spanish captivity") to wrest away its colonies, established a hold over what came to be known as the Dutch East Indies. Their control of Indonesia lasted until the turn of the twentieth century.

Hence there are some regional specialties and stylistic differences, notably the rich and sweetish dishes from Molucca, where the Portuguese influence was strongest; the simple but powerfully spicy curries from Sumatra; the relatively elaborate, Europeanized meals of Java; and the long, slow-simmered and more mellow clay-pot stews from Penang. (Note, however, that Penang-style barbecue can be eye-wateringly spicy.) In addition, Malaysian cooks preserve many Indian-style recipes, particularly biryanis and kormas. The popular *rijsttafel*, or "rice table," is a Dutch adaptation of a village feast. And one of the most famous Indonesian dishes, *nasi goreng*, is (Chinese) fried rice topped with a (Dutch) fried egg.

The most distinctive dishes of Singapore come from the Nonya style, a mixture of Chinese ingredients and Malay spices that evolved in the nineteenth century, when Chinese labor recruits married Malay women. (According to a more romantic explanation, the Nonya culture dates from the sixteenth century, when a Malaccan sultan married a Beijing princess, and its name derives from the Mandarin phrase *nan yang*, or "southern ocean.") Only women are called *nonyas*: The men are called *babas*, and collectively the people are known as *paranakan*. Nonya dishes are hot and spicy, most often based on a chili-onion-turmeric paste called a *rempah*, and tend to a hot and sour character, emphasizing tamarind sauce and shrimp paste. Unlike most of the region's cuisines, Nonya has retained the pork dishes and noodles of its Chinese past. Chili crabs are so ubiquitous in Singapore that they might be called the national dish.

THE MAIN INGREDIENTS

SEASONINGS Like the Cambodians and Burmese, Indonesians have a sour tooth (although the Javanese prefer sweet elements). The most important spices are ginger, pepper, cumin, curry (turmeric), cloves, lemongrass, limes, rice wine and vinegar, tamarind, cinnamon, coriander, coconut, galangal, sugar (frequently brown sugar), cilantro, basil, cardamom, sesame oil, soy sauce, garlic, nutmeg, dried fish or shrimp pastes, dried red chilies, and fresh chilies, both green and red. *Terasi* is a fermented shrimp paste, with a slightly more pungent flavor than the fish sauces of the region. *Ketjap*, or "sweet soy"—the tomato-less ancestor of ketchup—is a blend of dark Chinese soy sauce, sugar, onions, and spices. The *kemiri* nut, also called a candle nut, is a characteristic flavoring something like macadamia.

RICE The Balinese are among the world champions of rice consumption; they eat the cooked equivalent of a pound of raw rice every day (and also leave small rice piles on windowsills and pathways, for the spirits). The most famous meal of Indonesia, ordered up (and christened) with pleasure by the Dutch, is the rijsttafel, or "rice table"—a sit-down buffet, in effect, with rice in the center and 15 or 20 toppings (ceremonially, up to 50) and side dishes laid out around it. The rice is the main dish here, not the accompaniment, and although there may be meat dishes or vegetable curries as well, they are flavorings rather than entrees. A smaller version, with fewer side dishes, may be called a *nasi rames* (*nasi* is the word for rice).

Like the Vietnamese and Thai, the Malay and Indonesians tend to prefer a dry, unsalted rice. Both steamed rice and the sweeter glutinous or sticky rice are common, and sticky rice is frequently used to wrap sausages, vegetables, or meats into a finger food. Rice is often fried as well. As a meal base, noodles are the only alternative to rice (and whatever their shape, they are almost always rice noodles); they are among the most obvious Chinese contributions, along with dumplings.

FISH AND SHELLFISH Seafood—particularly crabs, cockles or clams, squid, and shrimp—and fish, both fresh- and saltwater, provide the primary proteins: *Ikan* is the generic word for fish, *cumi-cumi* is squid, *udang* is shrimp. Milkfish, catfish, carp, pomfret, and tuna are among the most common. The basic diet of many Indonesians is still plain boiled rice, a few vegetables, a bit of fish, and a handful of chilies. Here, as all over the region, anchovies are dried and fermented into sauce.

POULTRY AND MEATS Beef and pork are not uncommon, particularly among Chinese families, but because of various religious prohibitions, they are served less frequently than they are in the United States. Organ meats—brains, liver, kidneys, and so forth—are also particularly popular among Chinese families. Buddhists get most of their proteins from tofu and tempeh, the mold-fermented soy variant, which are widely used in vegetarian soups and stews; they also appear in addition to meat or seafood in "fancy" recipes.

VEGETABLES AND FRUITS The Portuguese were responsible for bringing in the New World squashes, tomatoes, corn, chilies, and sweet potatoes; they may also have been the first to transport peanuts from Africa and eggplant from Turkey. The Dutch supplied the broccoli and cauliflower that the Chinese taught them to stir-fry with their own

Many Indonesian and Malaysian menus categorize dishes not by the entree—beef, chicken, shrimp, whatever—but by the style of cooking. *Sambals* are usually dishes fried with chilies but can also refer to powerful chili pastes; *sayurs* are dishes with plenty of sauce to dip rice into (see "How to Order and Eat Like a Native," below). *Kalio* sauce is heavily flavored with coriander and coconut; *bumbu* is another spice paste, usually mixed with coconut milk. *Croquettes* (or, from the Dutch, *krokets*) are just what they sound like—fried balls or dumplings—but may be fish, shrimp, or potato or some other vegetable.

bok choy. Other vegetables include bean sprouts, bamboo shoots, a wide variety of mushrooms, and okra (from Africa, courtesy of the Arab traders). Fruits include mangoes, papayas, jackfruit, and oranges (also a Middle Eastern contribution).

THE MAIN DISHES

MEAT AND POULTRY Almost any meat or fowl can be curried or braised in coconut milk; chicken in coconut curry with ground kemiri nuts, called *opor ayam*, is particularly popular. Satays, which evolved from the kebabs of Persia and became more delicate, are among Indonesia's most famous foods: marinated meats (beef, lamb, pork) and chicken are skewered, broiled or grilled, and served with dipping sauces of ground peanuts, coconut milk, and chilies. Eggs are rarely served as the main protein but often act as a medium for vegetables (in a sort of stir-fried "scramble") or seafood (like Singapore's oyster omelets).

Rendang, which originated in Western Sumatra but is now common all over Indonesia, is a sort of "dry" curry, usually beef or water buffalo brisket cooked in coconut milk with ginger, galangal, garlic, turmeric, and chilies; after long simmering, the coconut milk browns, relapses into oil, and nearly dries up.

SEAFOOD Shrimp and squid can be curried or coconut-stewed, too, but flesh fish are more frequently deep-fried whole, steamed in banana leaves, or rubbed with chili paste and grilled. In some places, shrimp is skewered and served up like a satay. Also, mixed seafood stews are fairly common.

SALADS AND VEGETARIAN DISHES *Gado-gado* is a very popular mixed-vegetable salad with peanut sauce that is often used to illustrate the region's melting-pot cuisine, since it combines European vegetables, African peanuts, and indigenous spices. *Urap* is a coconut-vegetable salad usually reserved for fancier occasions. Otherwise, vegetables (green beans, carrots, potatoes, cauliflower, etc.) tend to be served as curries and stews and may not be any "lighter" than the meat dishes.

Sambals are both condiments and dishes: A hot fried-chili paste or the meat, fish, or vegetable dish cooked in such a sauce. Some sambals are raw—chilies, salt, and lime or lemon juice crushed in a mortar. Some are cooked (i.e., fried), some include terasi, and some coconut milk.

BEVERAGES AND DESSERTS   The most popular drinks are tea and coffee, coconut milk (often served in the shell with a flavoring of lime or nutmeg and cinnamon), beer, rice wine, or fruit juices. Sweet desserts are almost a requirement here—not just fruits but thick coconut puddings, bean flour buns, sweetened rice cakes, and so forth.

HOW TO ORDER
AND EAT LIKE A NATIVE

Indonesia and Malaysia are, like Central America, crowded with outdoor food vendors, many specializing in only one dish—even a single type of fish—and others laying out a spread of curries and sambals. In larger cities, such as Singapore and Kuala Lumpur, not only markets but also parking lots and parks at night become al fresco taverns for progressive dinners; when you sit down at a table, serving boys from nearby stalls, each representing a different chef, trot up and sing out the menus. Warm water and soap are offered as a matter of course, and larger clusters of stalls may have a sort of communal washroom. More formal restaurants differ not so much in the menu as in the presentation: They provide such items as carved vegetable garnishes and extra side dishes.

All dishes are served at the same time—even soup, which is sipped with food rather than eaten beforehand—and food is traditionally eaten with the fingers. Fingerbowls are standard tableware.

Most Indonesian restaurants here, of course, are full-service establishments; but even if they have separated their menus into what appears to be courses—soups, curries, satays, and noodle and rice dishes—remember that all dishes may be served simultaneously.

Like many other cultures, the Indonesian and Malay societies dictate that only the fingertips and the thumb of the right hand may be used for eating. (The left hand is customarily used for bathing, etc., and is thus considered unclean.) As elsewhere, the rice is formed into small balls and dipped into the sauce or curry. However, spoons are quite common, particularly for wetter dishes, and are becoming even more so, particularly

Dining in Indonesian restaurants is not so much tricky as chancy. Menu spellings are not too diverse, but actual recipes, which depend so heavily on the individual chef's spice mixes, are anything but standardized, so it's possible that a dish you order in one restaurant will be quite different from the "same" dish from another chef. The Americanized versions of Indonesian and Malaysian food in smaller cities can be extremely disappointing, about as authentic as meals in "Polynesian" huts used to be; but there are good restaurants in larger cities, particularly along both coasts.

among younger diners; and forks are increasingly common as well, so if you would rather not eat the traditional way, you need not. (Dishes that are eaten with a spoon and fork, modern-style, are known as *lauk pering*—"food served on a plate.") Chopsticks are generally used only for Chinese dishes.

A typical meal consists of rice; at least two curries; one fish and one meat or poultry (or all three); two or more vegetable dishes, one soupy (a sayur) and one stir-fried or in salad; and dishes of chilies, green onions, and other condiments. Many Indonesian establishments serve fixed-price rijsttafels (some with a choice of vegetarian, seafood, or meat side dishes) as well as individual curries, fish, or satays. The rice table is the most fun and allows you to taste the most dishes, but if you don't want a rijsttafel, two diners should order satays, chicken curry, and beef sambal; for four, add gado-gado and either shrimp or chicken sayur or a fish. If chili crabs are available, by all means order them, but don't wear your best clothes; you pretty much have to eat them with your fingers, and a dainty method hasn't been invented yet.

COOKING AT HOME

Many Indonesian and Malaysian dishes are easy to re-create at home with just a blender (for spices) and a deep heavy skillet, although woks are also useful. Satays can be grilled indoors or out and are particularly well adapted to small tabletop grills or hibachis. Set out fingerbowls with lemon slices for those who want to try eating with their fingers.

PAN-FRIED FISH IN COCONUT MILK

5 spring onions, chopped

2 cloves garlic, peeled

2 dime-sized slices of ginger root, peeled

2 small hot chilies, seeded
1 stalk lemongrass, thinly sliced
4 kemiri nuts or 6 unsalted, unroasted macadamia nuts
1/2 teaspoon shrimp paste
1/2 to 1 teaspoon sesame oil (optional)
2 tablespoons vegetable oil
4 fillets of mackerel or other firm fish, about 1 inch thick
juice of 1 lime
1 cup condensed coconut milk or thick portion of separated canned milk
pinch salt

Combine onions, garlic, ginger, chilies, lemongrass, kemiri nuts, and shrimp paste in mortar, blender, or food processor; blend into a smooth paste, adding a dash of sesame oil or coconut milk if needed. Meanwhile, heat vegetable oil in a skillet and sauté fish 2–3 minutes on each side; set aside. Add spice paste and cook until "spicy" smell fades; add lime juice and coconut milk and simmer about 10 minutes; add fish and heat through. Serve with rice.

SINGAPORE-STYLE CRABS

2 large or 4 medium live crabs
1/2 cup vegetable oil
1 tablespoon ginger, peeled and minced
2 cloves garlic, peeled and minced
4 fresh green or red chilies, seeded and minced
1/3 cup tomato-based chili sauce
1 tablespoon light soy sauce
1 tablespoon sugar (or substitute 1 1/2 tablespoons "sweet soy"
or katjap for both soy and sugar)
1/4 cup flat beer, defatted chicken broth, or water
pinch salt

Scrub crabs well; remove top shell, stomach, and lungs (or have vendor clean them); and chop into quarters. Heat oil in wok and stir-fry crabs, turning them constantly, until they turn red; remove. Add ginger, garlic, and chilies to wok and stir-fry 2 minutes; add chili sauce, soy, sugar (or ketjap), and beer and bring to boil. Return crabs to sauce, lower heat, and simmer 5 minutes; serve with rice.

GADO-GADO

2 medium potatoes
1/2 cup fresh bean sprouts
3/4 cup Chinese or green cabbage, sliced
1/2 cup green beans, cut on diagonal into 2-inch pieces
1 carrot, julienned
1/2 cup small cauliflower florets
1 small bunch fresh watercress
1 small cucumber, seeded and julienned
1 hard-boiled egg, sliced
1 ripe tomato, peeled, seeded, and chopped
1/2 cake firm silken tofu, cut in 1-inch cubes
peanut sauce (see below)

Boil potatoes, let cool, and slice. Blanch bean sprouts and drain; repeat with cabbage. Cook green beans until crisp-tender; drain. Repeat with cauliflower and carrot. Remove watercress stems and chill leaves and cucumber until crisp. Arrange vegetables either in large bowl or on platter; make sure all vegetables are visible in layers or in separate piles. Place egg slices around top and scatter tomato and tofu on top. Peanut sauce may either be poured in a circle over the salad or served on the side or in a smaller bowl in the center of the platter.

QUICK PEANUT SAUCE

1/2 cup smooth or crunchy peanut butter
1/2 cup coconut milk
1/2 cup water
1 fresh red or green chili, chopped
1 teaspoon garlic, minced
1 teaspoon dried lemon peel or 1/2 teaspoon fresh minced peel
1 teaspoon dark brown sugar
2 tablespoons dark soy
1/2 teaspoon shrimp paste or anchovy paste
2 teaspoons lemon juice

Heat peanut butter, coconut milk, and water in a saucepan until blended. Meanwhile, in a mortar, blender, or processor, combine chili, garlic, lemon peel, and sugar into a paste; add soy and shrimp paste and blend again. Add to saucepan, along with lemon juice; add more coconut milk if mixture is too thick. This sauce can also be used for dipping satays.

SWEET-SOUR SATAY MARINADE

1 tablespoon coriander powder
1/4 teaspoon cumin
1 tablespoon garlic, minced
1 teaspoon fresh ginger, minced
1 fresh red or green chili, coarsely chopped
2 green onions, chopped
1/2 teaspoon salt
2 teaspoons lemon juice
2 tablespoons dark soy sauce
2 teaspoons dark brown sugar
1 tablespoon peanut oil
(Lean pork, beef, lamb, chicken breast, or shrimp)

Combine all spices except oil in blender and process until smooth. Pour into bowl, whisk in oil, and marinate meat 3 hours or longer in refrigerator. (At the same time, if using bamboo skewers, soak them in water so they won't burn.) When ready to cook, thread meat on bamboo skewers and grill until browned.

THE PHILIPPINES

Given its geographical location—as an outrider to China between Japan and Indonesia—one would expect cuisine in the Philippines to be thoroughly Asian and largely dependent on seafood. But despite a long history as an Asian and Arab stopover, over three centuries of Spanish occupation and 50 years as a U.S. colony have produced a meat-heavy cuisine that mixes Indonesian flavorings, such as ginger and coconut; Spanish-imported cooking methods, including frying, marinating, and barbecuing; Chinese noodles, egg rolls, and soy sauce; American omelets and lettuce-and-tomato salads; and the African and Middle Eastern dishes—chicken with garbanzos, pork with greens, satays, and shish kebabs—that the Arab traders left behind.

THE COUNTRY

The culture of the Philippines is truly creole, in that it retains clear but complementary strains from all the outside cultures that have attempted to impose themselves on it: Malay, Chinese, Spanish, and American, plus the odd German

---

BASIC CUISINE

DINNER FOR TWO:
Kilawin, sio mai, chicken adobo, roast pork

DINNER FOR FOUR:
Lumpia, pancit guisado, chicken guinataan, pork adobo, kare-kare

GROUP DISH:
Turo-turo

STYLE:
Meaty, tangy, rich

KEY FLAVORS:
Coconut milk, vinegar, tamarind

EATING UTENSILS:
Forks and knives

DISTINCTIVE DISHES:
Adobo, puchero, lumpia

UNIFORMITY OF MENUS:
Good

NUTRITIONAL INDEX:
High fat, high protein, high starch

COST:
Moderate

"THANK YOU":
"Salamat"

and Dutch additions absorbed from Java and Indonesia. An archipelago of 7,000 islands, most of them very tiny (11 of the islands comprise 95% of the land mass), the Philippines is slightly larger than Great Britain and supports about the same size population. Like Indonesia, it is a country of myriad languages, about 70. The official language is Pilipino, though Tagalog is more common; a large number of Filipinos speak English. (Only a small number speak Spanish, intriguingly.) It remains overwhelmingly Christian—only about 5% are Muslim, most of them residing in the Western regions—and thanks to the Spanish, pork is still the most popular meat in the Philippines.

Like its equatorial neighbors, the Philippines is volcanic and richly forested, subject to constant earthquakes and studded with hot springs. There are navigable rivers and large lakes, providing freshwater fish and shellfish as well as irrigation for crops. Rice, corn, and coconut cultivation takes up four-fifths of the cropland; the rest is given over to sugarcane, yams (including a particularly sweet purple yam used in desserts), manioc, bananas, coffee, tobacco, and hemp.

THE HISTORY

The Philippines' first residents were Negritos, a Malayo-Polynesian people, who crossed over from Sumatra and Borneo when the islands were still connected by dry land. These first Malays, who moved in 30,000 years ago, have living descendants among most aboriginal tribes; later waves of more sophisticated Malay and Indonesian immigrants evolved into the people now called Filipino.

The first Javanese and Chinese ships arrived around 300 B.C.E., and by the end of the first millennium, the islands were a regular port along the Chino-Malay trade route; but it was not until the fourteenth century, with the arrival of the Arab traders and their Muslim evangelism, that much cross-cultural evolution took place. Then, in 1521, the Spanish appeared—captained by the Portuguese explorer Ferdinand Magellan, whose dream of a passage to the East had been laughed off by his own king—followed shortly by another Spanish fleet sailing west from Mexico, which claimed the islands in the name of the Infante Philip, who would grow up to be the pious and rapacious Philip II.

(The papal bull by which Pope Alexander VI "divided" the New Worlds between Spain and Portugal—implicitly claiming it all for the Catholic Church—had been promulgated in 1494, presumptively awarding India and Africa to Portugal and most of the Americas and unknown islands to the west to Spain. One of the most visible legacies of the Spanish annexation is that the Philippines remain the only Asian country that is primarily Catholic.)

The islands were a rich find, supplying gold, silver, timber, spices, coffee, and sugar to the Spanish empire. They were also vulnerable to attacks by Chinese and English pirates, fanatically anti-Christian Moors, and the Dutch, who already controlled the rest of the East Indies and were eager to cement their monopoly of the region. Nevertheless, the Philippines remained in Spanish hands until the Spanish-American War, when, despite their declaration of democratic independence, the Filipinos (and Puerto Ricans) found themselves in the "protective" custody of the United States.

On December 7, 1941, the same day they attacked Pearl Harbor in Hawaii, Japanese forces invaded the Philippines. Filipino-American forces suffered terrible losses at Bataan and Corregidor, and the Filipino government went into exile in Washington. In October 1944, the Gulf of Leyte became the site of the greatest naval engagement of all time; over the course of three days, American forces destroyed the Japanese fleet. On July 5, 1945, General Douglas MacArthur was able to declare the Philippines entirely liberated; almost exactly a year later, on July 4, 1946—the American Independence Day—the autonomous Republic of the Philippines was finally recognized by the United States.

THE CUISINE

As noted above, Filipino cuisine pulls together threads of all its ethnic "visitors" over the centuries. The Malay style is most obvious in such dishes as *kare-kare*, a meat and vegetable stew in peanut sauce; and *pinakbet*, which is a kind of slaw in shrimp paste. The noodle dishes, called *pancit*, are Chinese, as are the steamed dumplings (called *sio mai*, a direct pick-up), tofu (which is usually firm or even dried rather than soft), and egg rolls (*lumpia*). A century or so of American domination shows up in such homey favorites as hamburgers, canned corned beef sautéed with rice, and macaroni and potato salads. In recent decades, an influx of Japanese tourists and the "export" of Filipino business and labor has produced a boom in sushi bars and noodle shops.

However, it has been estimated that fully 80% of Filipino recipes reveal the lingering influence of the Spanish, starting with the sheer amount of meat consumed, the sautéed tomato and onion sauces, the vinegar marinades, and the preference for olive oil over peanut or palm oil. (The names of so many Filipino dishes are still in Spanish that you can almost count the exceptions on your fingers.) It was the Spanish who established the bread bakeries and dairies, cured sausages and hams, turned coconut milk into flan, and even insisted on brewing up menudo, no longer necessarily a tripe stew but a recognizable variant of pork and pork liver and still recommended as a hangover remedy.

The most famous Spanish import is the unofficial national dish, adobo, derived from the spicy adobo sauce that the Spanish absorbed in the Americas. In fact, adobo is

> ## Fat Watch
>
> Eating a light meal in a Philippine restaurant requires careful planning, since many of the most popular ingredients—pork, olive oil, peanuts, and coconut and coconut oil—are all high in fat. A surprisingly high percentage of dishes, including dumplings, meats, fish, rice, and tofu, are fried. If possible, stick to the grilled foods. Also be prepared to drink a lot of water; many dishes may seem very salty.

both the dish, when it generally means a pork roast, and the sauce, so that it can actually refer to any meat, chicken, or even seafood marinated in garlic, vinegar, and soy marinade. Bacalao, the salted dried codfish that European sailors carried around the world, is an expensive delicacy here and is often the centerpiece of Good Friday dinner. Greedily absorbing dishes from all their dominions, the Spanish also passed along Mexican tamales (steamed Chinese-style in bamboo leaves) and Cuban ground meat stews with peas, olives, and raisins.

Other ingredients that the medieval Spanish administrators, then based in Mexico, sent over to their outposts here were bay leaves, chestnuts, oregano, annatto seeds (achiote, here corrupted to "achuete," which adds a distinctive orange tinge to a dish), the exorbitantly expensive chocolate, chayote, and jicama, and of course hot chilies. They also imposed the tradition of serving dinner in courses—soup, fish, meat, fruit, dessert—though home-style meals may still be served all at once.

Not surprisingly, in a nation of so many smaller groups, there are some major regional distinctions. To the north, particularly on the large island of Luzon, where Manila is located, the standard starch is rice, the spicing is mild, and vegetables are often steamed or boiled; on Mindanao, the major southern island, cassava is preferred to rice. Indonesian and Malay influences are particularly strong to the west and south, emphasizing curry spices, coconut milk, and hot chilies. The west, being primarily Muslim, is beef-heavy. The area around Manila in south-central Luzon shows the most intense Spanish influence, particularly in the sauces, sausages, and the stuffed dishes that are a regional specialty. In the area south of Manila, the cooking has an emphatic tang that comes from heavy doses of garlic and salt, as well as the lavish use of vinegars, tamarind, and guavas and broths made from them; to play off that potent splash, home cooks delve into melons, the many kinds of bananas, and coconuts.

Throughout the country, however, characteristic flavorings come from fermented fish or shrimp sauces, generally called *guinamos*, which are not unlike Thai nam pla or Vietnamese nuoc nam. *Buro* is a mixture of raw fish and raw rice that ferments for several months and takes on a characteristic pink color. *Bagoong* is a very strong version, half salt, half fish or shellfish, that ferments for a year; eventually the fish collapses and settles to the bottom. Bagoong is actually the sediment, which is used as a paste; *patis* is the liquid that rises to the top. These sauces may be made from a variety of proteins: anchovies (like nam pla), oysters, clams, shrimp, small fried fish, fish eggs, small native flat fish, and so on. In the south, dried salted fish are boiled in vinegar until the mixture is dry.

When the Filipino chef uses coconut, it isn't just the milk and meat; it's the pith, the blossoms, the leaves (as wrappings), and all. The Philippines are the largest producers of coconut oil and use it as a flavoring rather than a cooking oil.

THE MAIN INGREDIENTS

SEASONINGS Filipinos still prefer the flavor of Spanish olive oil and use it fairly generously. They often combine it with coconut milk, and the resulting rich sauces are only partially tempered by vinegar, tamarind, ginger, or fish sauce. Among other prevalent flavors, besides the guinamos or patis and coconut, are garlic and chilies, black and white pepper, lemongrass, oregano, curry powder, cilantro, ketchup, sweet pickles, Chinese black bean sauce, raisins, and soy sauce. A citrus fruit called calamansi or Philippine lime is actually a hybrid of the mandarin orange and the kumquat; it has a particular sour taste that is very characteristic of Filipino food.

MEAT AND POULTRY The Filipino diet is extremely meat-heavy, especially in comparison with other neighboring cuisines. Even breakfast is apt to consist of leftover rice sautéed with garlic, eggs, and a meat such as fried canned corned beef or the air-dried jerky-style beef called *tapa*. Livestock farmers raise hogs, water buffalo, and goats (which are generally eaten as kid); there are also dairy farms around the larger cities. All types of meat turn into sausages, particularly Spanish-style chorizos, and stews. Organ meats and offal, such as tongue, ears, tails, tripe, liver, and especially hocks and bellies, are common fare. Not surprisingly, the richer ducks are favored over chickens, though in the United States chicken is generally substituted.

NOODLES AND RICE The generic term for noodles, pancit, is believed to derive from the Hokkein phrase "pian i sit," or "something conveniently cooked"—that is, fast food. *Bihon* are rice vermicelli, *miswa* are thin wheat noodles, *lomi* is the Chinese rice noodle, and *sotanghon* are bean thread noodles. "Luglug" means dipped in boiling water, and *pancit luglug* are thick rice noodles lowered several times into boiling water, much like Japanese udon. However, in typical Filipino fashion, the Chinese noodles are likely to get Spanish treatments and wind up with bilingual names; thus, a dish of rice noodles sautéed with onions, garlic, and tomatoes (and then shrimp, pork, and vegetables) is called *bihon guisado*.

Both white and glutinous or sticky rices are used in cooking. What is called black rice in some other Asian countries is called "purple rice" here—a dark, unmilled rice whose husk color leaches into the grain when it's cooked. Several different types of rice are raised, including so-called hard grain and the very small-grained *milagrosa;* particularly prized are aged varieties, which fluff up when cooked. Rice, or rather rice flours, are used to produce a vast number of rice cakes and buns, usually sweet but variously steamed, baked, fermented, or even filled with meat or cheese. Sticky rice is used in rice cakes, but so are purple and white rices. Rice is turned into other sweets, too, especially cooked like rice pudding.

VEGETABLES AND FRUITS Although it is not a diet that emphasizes vegetables the way many other Asian cuisines do, the Filipino pantry includes a hodgepodge of Asian, American, and Latin American vegetables: not only potatoes and the various cooking veggies, such as onions, garlic, and tomatoes, but assorted greens and watercresses, lotus roots, peas and pea shoots, kalabasa squash and squash blossoms, bamboo shoots, asparagus, beans, many sorts of mushrooms (fresh and dried), sweet potatoes, cassava root, cucumbers, radishes, water chestnuts, chayote, jicama, the cucumber-like sponge gourd, sweet and hot peppers, eggplant, Chinese okra, and a few indigenous species such as the *saluyot* (which resembles a squash and is sometimes called "okra leaf" because it releases a slick, viscous juice) and *alugbati*, a red vine with edible green leaves. Vegetables are frequently used as salads rather than as side dishes and combined in idiosyncratic ways.

Fruits, which are often used as soup or stew ingredients and parts of the extremely sweet desserts, include papaya (which is also cooked as a vegetable when green), guava, bitter melon (which Filipinos prefer green and very bitter), mango (which they eat both ripe and green, often with sweet-and-sour sauce or shrimp paste with pork), various citrus fruits, the two-foot-long jackfruit (which is also cooked when unripe), and a range of bananas, including plantains, the white-fleshed Latundan, the flat round Saba, and the tiny fingerling banana called the Senorita.

Both fruits and vegetables are turned into pickles and relishes, from green tomatoes and mangoes to mustard greens, cucumbers, and jicama. One common relish is called *atsara*, which is something like sauerkraut—a dish the Europeans actually learned from the Chinese—but using green papaya rather than cabbage. Sea purslane is often used as a pickle.

SEAFOOD Among the most common freshwater fish are catfish, tilapia, and a cultivated whitefish greatly beloved in the Philippines but unavailable here called "*bangus*" or "milkfish." Ocean favorites, depending on the region, include pompano, grouper, snapper, rays, sharks, sea urchins, the misnamed sea slug called sea cucumber, tuna, sardines, and mackerel. *Tinapa* is a smoked fish, most often mackerel, sardines, or milkfish, used as a topping for rice or noodle dishes. The Filipinos also enjoy shellfish, particularly the delicate Manila clams, mussels, shrimp, squid, and several species of clawless spiny lobster like those found in the Caribbean. Dried, salted fish probably predates the arrival of the Spanish, but the cod, *bacalao*, is the most desirable.

THE MAIN DISHES

Filipino foods are often referred to not by ingredients but by cooking style. By far the most popular dish in the country is adobo, which is usually pork or chicken but can be beef or goat, chicken, vegetables, or even shrimp or fish. It can even be stuffed into buns, like empanadas. It refers to any sort of dish that involves marinating and braising the meat in a mixture of vinegar, garlic, chilies, and soy sauce; after that, the chef adds plantains, potatoes, greens, bamboo shoots, or whatever else comes to hand.

The ornate "stuffed" dishes mentioned above are generally called *rellenos*, just as in the familiar chili relleno, but when Filipino cooks do stuffed bell peppers, they frequently substitute native ingredients for the European ones. For example, relleno dishes include such recognizable Spanish colonial leftovers as baby squid stuffed with pork and the intact skins of chickens stuffed with chorizo, vegetables, and a filling of ground chicken, ground pork, raisins, and spices; but they also refer to pork hocks stuffed with ground seasoned meat, chickens stuffed with crab, pork shoulders stuffed with sausages and cheese, and even fish skins stuffed with the fish meat, soy, vegetables, raisins, and a sweet relish.

Another common method of cooking produces *guinataan*, stewing in coconut milk. Gisado is just what it sounds like—cooked in oil (that is, sautéed or fried). *Inihaw* refers to grilled foods, and *sinigang* is a type of stew, again either meat or fish, given a particularly sour bite by tamarind. Chinese-style stir-frying is also popular.

GRAINS AND STARCHES   As in many Asian cuisines, rice is served at every meal (including breakfast), usually boiled but frequently fried. It's mixed with all sorts of sausages, shellfish, and vegetables in classic rice recipes, still called, in Spanish, *arroz*, from all over the one-time empire: *arroz à la Catalana*, *arroz à la Cubana*, *arroz à la Valenciana*, and of course, *paella*. When glutinous rice is used, such multi-ingredient dishes are often called *arroz à la Filipina*. *Turo-turo*, which also refers to a kind of restaurant, is a relative of the Indonesian rijsttafel: It literally means "point, point," and what happens is that you get a bowl of rice and point to the various toppings you want. Rice is also boiled to a soupy consistency, like the Chinese congee (called simply "arroz caldo," hot rice), and topped with tripe or sausages or chicken or whatever.

Rice, glass, and wheat noodles are used almost interchangeably, especially in soups and classic noodle and vegetable stir-fries familiar as lo mein or even pad thai (though, not surprisingly, these noodle dishes tend to include pork cracklings, smoked fish, and fish sauce). As in China, noodles represent "long life," and are served for special occasions. The Filipinos have also adopted and adapted the Chinese dumpling and the spring roll. As with the originals, *sio mai* are open-faced dumplings with a pork stuffing; but *lumpia*, the spring rolls, have a little different twist—thin rice crêpes (which is what the word "lumpia" actually refers to), rolled around a stuffing that may include not only pork, vegetables, shrimp, and tofu but also perhaps garbanzo beans. These deep-fried rolls may be either large or bite-sized (*lumpianita*), easier to pick up, dip in sweet-and-sour sauce, and pop into the mouth.

SOUPS Soups are major menu items and tend to have sour broths, to stimulate the appetite; beyond that, almost anything goes. They may be meaty soups, with chorizo or spareribs; fish soups, particularly milk-fish and vegetable soups with coconut milk or tamarind broth; chowders, coconut creams, Chinese-style chicken-and-noodles or chicken-and-greens soups—nearly all given Filipino character with the addition of fish sauce. *Sinigang*, a shrimp and vegetable soup in calamansi broth, is one of the most characteristic remnants of "native" cuisine. Many Spanish-style recipes still have their old names, including meatball soup (*almondigas*), garlic soup (*sopa de ajo*), and *migas*, the bread-and-oil soup usually spiced up with sausage.

FISH AND SEAFOOD The Filipinos not only like seafood, they also like it in combination with meat; the Philippine arroz à la paella, with chicken, pork chops, prawns, mussels, chorizo, lobster, and even saffron, would do any Spaniard proud. Fish is most often pan-fried or braised, or even stuffed with tomatoes and onions (purely Spanish) and steamed in banana leaves (just as distinctly Asian). A very Catalan-like dish is a stew that mixes squid and shrimp with raisins and peas.

Shrimp are fried, deep-fried, sautéed, grilled, stir-fried, and simmered. Shrimp, crabs, and some fish may be braised in coconut milk with ginger, peppers, onions, and garlic. What's called "stuffed shrimp" on menus is often just the opposite—the "stuffing" of ham, pork, and vegetables is wrapped around the shrimp and then the whole thing is deep-fried. As in Spain, shellfish are often marinated in lime or lemon juice, like ceviche, then mixed with chilies, tomatoes, and coconut (called *kilawin*); in the south (where it's called *kinilaw*), it's even more pungent, marinated in vinegar, garlic, onions, and salt. This is not a colonial import, however: Evidence shows that kinilaw is at least 1,000 years old.

MEATS To say that there are numerous recipes for pork is an understatement. The Filipinos eat pork literally "barbe à queue"—nose to tail. Even the blood is saved for stews. It's almost as if a cook can't pick up a pan without the pig, often using pork as a flavoring in dishes that supposedly feature seafood or other meats. Pork is commonly combined with squid, beef, sausages, shrimp, chicken, and, well, more pork, as in the pork liver and kidney soup with pork tenderloin in broth. Besides the more familiar presentations—whole roast pig, called *lechon*, roasted loin, and barbecued chops, butts, and satays—and the reasonably tame grilled livers and kidneys, there are offal soups (*dinuguan*), congee-style rice gruels with tripe (*goto*), fried hocks and cracklings, and recipes for jowl and snout and belly, not to mention bacon, ham, and sausage.

This cuisine gives soul food a new dimension. Even the fat by itself gets fried, as do the knuckles, which are little more than fat and tendon. Nor is one piece of pork enough: Braised pork is paired with chitterlings; ribs or oxtail and tripe combine in peanut-coconut soup; and menudo is a pork stew seasoned with liver. In some areas, even pork and beef are doused with fish sauce before being boiled in coconut milk. Then there are the pork fried rices and pork pieces stir-fried with shrimp and noodles and so on. In some cases these overwhelmingly rich (at least, to American tastes) dishes are tempered with tamarind or vinegar or tomatoes, but not often.

The Filipinos eat beef and water buffalo as well as pork, including a beef marrow soup called *bulalo* and a braised roast called *mechado*; almondigas are, as they are in Spain, ground meatballs. Beef gets the pork treatment, too, in earthy liver-tomato sauce stews with carrots and potatoes. *Pochero*, sometimes called *cuchido*, is another thick stew, often beef and chicken paired with sausage and lots of garlic, that can be served in two parts—meat and vegetables in one bowl and broth on the side. Thin-sliced round steak is marinated and then dried or stuffed, rolled up and braised. Kare-kare, a popular stew, is a trading-circuit (Asia to Africa to Middle East) dish of oxtail, peanut butter, and eggplant. Goat is usually stewed or barbecued; like suckling pig, it's popular roasted whole. But one startlingly Euro-Indonesian hybrid recipe calls for braising goat with pimientos, stuffed olives, garlic, canned peas, hardboiled eggs, and liverwurst—not a dish likely to show up on American restaurant menus.

POULTRY AND CHICKEN   Poultry and chicken can be adobo-barbecued, sweet-barbecued, Asian barbecued, deep-fried, roasted, cooked in coconut milk, doused in peanut sauce, or combined with a second meat, usually sausage or pork. The wings may show up in a sweet-and-sour sauce—that wonderful Chinese precursor to buffalo wings. It is also stewed in a sauce of its own blood, the liver, and lots of garlic. Duck is popular and widely raised. *Balut* are duck eggs, allowed to fertilize and then salted.

Eggs are popular in omelets, but these are often more like Korean paijun or Vietnamese golden pancakes than American omelets, in that they may contain a number of vegetables, shellfish, or meat together.

VEGETABLES AND FRUIT In general, vegetables are considered only mildly interesting, but eggplant, called *talong*, is the obvious exception; it is the one constant ingredient in a sort of ratatouille-like stew called *pinakbet* that otherwise may include almost any vegetable. As mentioned above, any vegetable may be used in a "salad," whether it would be associated with the term in America or not.

SWEETS Again, thanks to the Spanish, the Filipinos crave sweets —concoctions of yams and rice, coconut flans, corn puddings, cookies, and sherbet-like coconut and mango ices; but rather than being served as desserts, they are more often mixed in with the dinner to complement the other flavors. *Agar-agar*, the jelly-like seaweed extract, is very popular, and comes in a rainbow of colors; it is often turned into fruit salads. Nut brittles, fried or candied bananas, and chocolates are also popular.

BEVERAGES About a few things, the Filipinos are stubbornly traditional. Despite the otherwise pervasive Spanish influence, the Filipinos only rarely drink wine or sherry; nor, despite the Chinese, do they favor tea, which is consumed medicinally rather than socially. Instead, they prefer to drink water with meals and at other times, coffee, hot chocolate, or beer (San Miguel is a Filipino brand widely available in the United States). *Halo-halo* ("mix-mix") is a sort of fruit shake or cooler with sweet red beans.

HOW TO ORDER
AND EAT LIKE A NATIVE

Like their old squatters the Spanish, the Filipinos customarily eat four times a day, with a late-afternoon meal between lunch and dinner (and frequently a late-morning break for coffee and sweet cheese pastries). Breakfast is either rice and fish or a spicy sausage called *longaniza*, fried in a skillet and accompanied by rice cooked in the sausage grease. The afternoon meal is called *merienda*, a cross between English high tea and dim sum: lumpia, sandwiches, sweets, and cakes are all offered together.

A classic Filipino meal consists of rice, a crispy or chewy dish (a fried fish, for instance), something salty (a soy sauce or fish sauce dish), something sour with vinegar or tamarind, a noodle dish, and, almost inevitably, some sort of adobo. As noted above, Spanish-style dinners are often served in courses, but the communal native dishes, such as adobo or guinataan stews, and their accompaniments are offered all at once to point up the various flavors and textures. (Admittedly, these may be subtle distinctions to the American taste.) Traditionally, Filipinos eat at tables with lazy Susan–like turntables in the center, and some restaurants in the United States are equipped with these. Turo-turo restaurants, the pick-your-topping rice joints, are sometimes just glorified steam tables with stools.

Although a few Filipinos in rural areas continue to eat with their fingers, nearly all have become accustomed to forks and spoons. A semi-Westernized way of dining is to use the fork in the left hand and the spoon in the right; the fork is used to hold the meat and the spoon pulls a bit loose; then that bite is pushed into the spoon with the fork and eaten. However, if you are intrigued by hand-dining, which is generally reserved for those communal dishes, the traditional manner is to use the fingers to press rice against the plate into balls surrounding pieces of the meat or fish.

Adobo is a must-try, and two diners might split chicken adobo and roast pork after appetizers of kilawin and sio mai dumplings. Four people should start with lumpia and a fish soup before going on to try an adobo (preferably pork) and a guinataan stew (probably chicken), with a third dish of pancit guisado or kare-kare. A group might ask whether the restaurant has a turo-turo menu; if not, paella would be a good alternative.

COOKING AT HOME

Most ingredients for cooking Filipino dishes at home can be bought at the local market; the most important would be *patis* (the fish sauce), tamarind sauce, and coconut milk. Thai nam pla may be substituted for patis but should be slightly diluted; likewise, the vinegar generally used in making adobo is a palm vinegar much milder than the cider or wine vinegars Westerners are accustomed to, so you should either buy some or dilute rice wine vinegar with water. Rice was traditionally cooked in an earthenware pot but is now usually boiled Western-style. The Philippine version of a wok is called a *carajay* (pronounced, in the Spanish style, "cara-hai") and is good for stir-frying, though a skillet will do fine.

PORK ADOBO

1 1/4 pounds pork butt or 4 meaty chops
6 cloves garlic, sliced
1/2 cup diluted rice or wine vinegar

3/4 cup water
2 bay leaves
2 tablespoons soy sauce
1 teaspoon black peppercorns, crushed
1/2 teaspoon salt
olive oil (or rendered pork fat or lard)

If using pork butt, cut into large chunks; trim fat on chops to 1/4 inch. Combine all ingredients except oil in a heavy casserole or saucepan and marinate at least 1 hour. Turn on medium heat, bring to a boil, and simmer until pork is tender. Remove meat and reduce marinade to a thick sauce; pour through strainer into a small bowl or juice separator and return fat to pan. Add oil to cover pan bottom by 1/4 inch. Return pork to pan and fry until evenly browned. Remove meat from pan, serve with rice, and top with sauce.

Variation: Use 3/4 pound pork or small leg chops and add a small chicken, cut into serving pieces. For chicken only, omit precooking marinade and just cook in the adobo sauce. After cooking, remove meat and brown as above, or with the livers if desired, and add 1/2 cup coconut milk to reduced sauce.

LUMPIA

2 tablespoons olive oil
1 cup chopped green onion
5 cloves garlic, peeled and minced
1 cup chopped raw shrimp
1 cup diced pork, cooked
1/2 cup diced ham or sausage
1/2 cup diced chicken, cooked
1 carrot, peeled and julienned
1/2 cup bamboo shoots or water chestnuts, chopped
1/2 cup bean sprouts
2 cups shredded Chinese cabbage
salt and pepper to taste
soy sauce (optional)
spring roll or egg roll wrappers (about 2 dozen)

20–25 small romaine or flat lettuce leaves
vegetable oil for frying (optional)

Heat oil in wok or deep skillet and cook onion and garlic over medium heat until soft; add shrimp, stir-fry until just opaque, and add pork, ham, and chicken. Stir-fry 3 minutes and add carrot, bamboo shoots or water chestnuts, and bean sprouts; stir-fry 3 minutes more and add cabbage, sprinkling with salt and pepper. Continue cooking, tossing frequently, until cabbage is tender but still crisp. Season to taste with more salt or soy sauce and pepper, then drain off excess liquid and set aside to cool.

Place a spoonful of cooled stuffing mixture on egg roll wrapper, about two-thirds of the way up; tuck in sides and roll tightly from top. Wet last edge to seal. If crisp-fried lumpia are desired: Heat oil in a skillet until shimmering and fry rolls until crisp.

To serve, place a roll on a lettuce leaf, fold two edges in, then roll to enclose lumpia. Serve with dipping sauce (below).

DIPPING SAUCE

1 cup chicken stock
2 tablespoons soy sauce
5 tablespoons brown sugar
2 tablespoons cornstarch
salt to taste
3 cloves garlic, finely minced

Place stock, soy sauce, sugar, and cornstarch in small saucepan; simmer, stirring constantly, until thickened. Salt to taste and pour into serving bowl (or bowls) and sprinkle with garlic.

PART V

ASIA

CHINA

It could be said that China's version of King Tut was a woman—and a gourmet chef.

In the 1970s, when archaeologists in the Hunan region excavated a 2,000-year-old tomb from the Han dynasty era, they discovered a room nearly as well-stocked as that of the Egyptian pharaoh—but instead of toys, tools, and ornaments, the woman was surrounded by bamboo and pottery dishes, cooking utensils, woks, steamers, and more than 300 recipes for cooking duck, quail, mutton, pork, pheasant, chicken, and even dog. Like Tutankhamen's tomb, it was covered in murals and bas-relief; but instead of showing court scenes of hunting and warfare, it depicted cooks, bakers, winemakers, and dinner parties. Other Han-era tombs have yielded information on butchering, organ meats, and curing. In other words, while the Egyptians desired comfort in the next world, the Chinese wanted comfort food.

The Chinese may not have established the first civilization, but theirs is the oldest existing society, and its culinary roots range far and wide. The Chinese were growing rice at least as far back as 8,500 years ago—some estimates are as much as 12,000 years—and barley, wheat, and millet soon thereafter. The soybean is native to the region and has served them as protein, preservative, and flavoring for at least 5,000 years. Chinese farmers all across the continent were breeding pigs 4,000 years ago and cattle, sheep, and goats 3,000 years ago. Chickens, geese, game birds, venison, boar, rabbits, and horses were common fare. But food is one area in which the Chinese have always been open to outsiders: A great many of the foods and spices we think of as Chinese were originally imports from the Middle East, Malaysia, India, and the Americas—often via the seagoing Europeans and Arabs.

Like the French, the Chinese are fascinated by technique: They conceived of "recipes" 3,000 years ago and had court nutritionists and cooking professionals even then. (One deity, Cao Jun, has exclusive duty as Lord of the Stove.) Some estimates put the number of Chinese dishes at 80,000. And like the French, the Chinese consider cooking a great profession; high-ranking chefs are expected not only to lord it over their subordinates but to cook only for the most important clients (who, in the United States, are more often *not* the Americans). The approved course for learning to make Beijing duck is a full year long.

However, just because Chinese cuisine is so old and so accomplished does not mean that it is (or ever was) terribly rich outside of the great palaces. Only about 10% of the land is arable, and the tending of that fraction is so intense it requires the labor of 60% of the people. China is a land of limited wood and natural fuels, which is one reason that so many dishes are cooked quickly: Compare the relative cost of baking bread in one of those Italian ovens at 1,500° with steaming a whole dinner in stacking baskets over a single pot. Dairy products are scarce because arable land has always been too precious to serve as pasture. There were many periods of famine and warfare—several within relatively recent memory—that had to be survived as well.

Nevertheless, the Chinese can legitimately lay claim to those two crucial foods, rice and soy, and two of the most important culinary inventions in history: Chopsticks, the most versatile eating utensil known, and the wok, the deep, sloped-sided Chinese frying pan/stockpot/braising dish that is their equal.

THE COUNTRY

China, long the most populous nation in the world, with over a billion people, covers some 400 million square miles and, in the central and southeastern regions, has 4,000 miles of coastline and scores of rivers and lakes. The primary dialect of the Chinese language is Mandarin, which evolved from the koine used by the officials of several foreign groups (namely those that formed the Liao, Jin, and Yuan dynasties) during the thirteenth century, and is spoken by about 70% of the population. However, there are many other dialects—108 in the province of Fujian alone.

China is physically as well as spiritually at the heart of many cultures: At the northeast corner of the coast, Manchuria meets the peninsula of Korea; moving around counterclockwise, China is bounded by Russia, Mongolia, several former Soviet republics (such as Kazakhstan and Tajikistan), Afghanistan, Pakistan, India, Nepal, Myanmar (Burma), Laos, and Vietnam.

The country itself is shaped, appropriately, like a high-rimmed wok or hot pot tilted slightly to one side, with the more populous region in the base, Tibet in the western part of the "bowl," Manchuria cocked up on the eastern part, and the now-independent Mongolia as the lid. The Huang He (Yellow) and Yangtze Rivers cut roughly across the bottom of the bowl above the fat base; they are the cradles of Chinese culture.

Northern China is semi-arid; the Gobi Desert rises into the Inner Mongolian steppes. The Tibetan plateau runs at 3,660 feet high between the Himalayas and the Kunlun Mountains, and Manchuria is mostly plains and highlands. Hence, wheat is the primary grain in the north, rather than rice. Only central and southern China, from the great Huang He and Yangtze basins to the sea, are suited to broader agricultural production.

THE HISTORY

Chinese cooking could be said to go back to Beijing Man, who was using fire to cook meat nearly half a million years ago (though he may not have had salt with which to season it). A more recognizable "man" appeared in northern China after the last Ice Age—about 20,000 years ago—and one well-documented culture, the Yangshao, was established in the north around 5,000 B.C.E. Yangshao farmers already raised rice, millet, wheat, and barley; fished and netted seafood; and were the first to domesticate the pig, still the "first meat" in the hearts of Chinese diners.

Chinese civilization on a broad geographical level coalesced about 4,000 years ago. Its resemblances to the first Mesopotamian civilizations are strong, leading to some scholarly debate about which actually originated first. Regardless, the exchange of information and ingredients is so ancient—and required the traversing of so great a distance and difficult a terrain—that the similarities are a tribute to both.

Thanks to the preservation of so much Chinese literature, and to the ongoing excavation of paleolithic and neolithic settlements, we have a fairly complete sense of the evolution of Chinese culture and cuisine. In classical Chinese, the word for rice was also the word for agriculture, suggesting that rice was known back when the language was actually being formed; in many of the Southeast Asian languages influenced by Chinese, "rice" is synonymous with "food" or "meals." (The etymology also reminds us that irrigation and drainage were invented to support rice cultivation.) A 3,000-year-old book of poems speaks of farmers raising rice and brewing wine from it; planting wheat; harvesting melons, gourds, and chives; boiling celery and soybeans; and picking dates and wild asparagus. A Chu ode written about 500 B.C.E. lures back the souls of the dead not with love, as the Greek Orpheus would have, but with promises of rice with honey, lamb roasted with sugarcane, and braised beef tendons. (The Chinese always knew that the way to the heart was through the stomach.)

The first crucial trade, many millennia ago, was probably in grains, as the millet and wheat that were the staples in early northern China were cultivated (and in some cases, worshipped) in ways clearly inherited from Mesopotamia. In return, ancient Middle East people were introduced to Chinese peaches and apricots.

The next great wave of foods also came from Persia via an imperial spy named Zhang Xian (or Chang Hsien), who marked what became the Silk Road into Central Asia in the second century B.C.E. Zhang Xian brought back grapes, pomegranates, squash, peas, figs, sugar beets, pears, eggplant, spinach, coriander, garlic, walnuts, pistachios, and sesame oil, which remains essential in northern Chinese cooking. More important, he or one of his contemporaries also disclosed the Persian technique of milling, which made the production of flour (and so noodles) easy and cheap.

Almonds arrived through Turkestan, cardamom from India, saffron from Kashmir, and oranges from Indonesia. Meat stews became more common, flavored with mustard seed, cinnamon, ginger, galangal, soy sauce, and fermented black beans.

Soybeans were fermented, seeds were pressed for oil, and curry spices became popular. Meanwhile, in southern China, poets were writing of oranges, coconuts, lotus seeds, dates, bananas, and mangoes, and the northern aristocrats paid heavily for such delicacies. The wok was in general use by the sixth century B.C.E., and Turkish spirits had been discovered; a few centuries later, residents of Sichuan were distilling alcohol. In Vietnam, a faster-growing strain of rice was developed, and agriculture boomed.

By the end of the first millennium, distinct regional cuisines had taken shape, such as Sichuan cuisine, already spicy but then using peppercorns rather than the chilies imported after the exploration of the Americas. Lamb, kid, and mutton were prominent in cookbooks of the time, but after the invasion of the Mongols, who ate a lot of lamb, these meats became politically incorrect and their rejection a form of cultural and political protest.

By the fourteenth century—still before much of the European trade was established—a cookbook listed 43 different techniques for cooking, covering 68 varieties of fish and seafood, 42 meats, 50 grains and legumes, and so on.

The dynastic history of China is quite intricate, but in general, the empire had a sort of heartbeat; it would expand, often toward the west; then it would relax, become decadent, and deteriorate. Territories at the fringes would be lost, the "heart" would contract, and then a tide of new "barbarian" blood would flow in—usually from the north, as if through an artery—to conquer and eventually to be assimilated. Then the empire would expand, grow fat and content, and the whole cycle would repeat itself. Genghis Khan's Mongols first conquered the northern ranges and then, in 1279, put Marco Polo's idol Kublai Khan on the Celestial Throne. A century later, rebels overthrew the Khans and set up the Ming dynasty; they were conquered by the Manchus, also from the north.

It was during the Ming reign that the Portuguese established the colony of Macau (1514), the Spanish conquered the Philippines (1565), and modern Chinese cuisine took shape. International trade brought in snow peas (called "Holland peas") from the Dutch, watercress from Portugal, tomatoes ("foreign eggplant") and chayote, tobacco, jicama, limas, and chilies from the Americas. More important for the subsistence farmers, the Spanish traders also supplied New World corn and white and sweet potatoes, which flourished in areas where rice could not.

THE CUISINE

As ancient as Chinese cuisine is, many of its basic tenets are just coming into mainstream thought in the United States. Food should be prepared and consumed to maximize health and the body's natural balance by taking advantage of the ingredients' intrinsic medicinal properties—the basis for many contemporary health-food plans. Grains should be the firm base of the diet, as they are of the so-called food pyramid. Foods should be consumed in season: lamb and suckling pig in spring, chicken in summer, venison in fall, and fish and game in winter. (This very modern menu style was formulated some 3,000 years ago, during the Zhou dynasty.) Sauces should enhance the dish, not smother it (i.e., nouvelle cuisine.) Food should not be gulped, but eaten slowly and with attention and pleasure. An old proverb has it that "food should be eaten first with the eyes, then with the mind, then with the nose, and finally with the mouth."

Finally, although no food is forbidden, nothing should be eaten or drunk to excess. "Everything in moderation." Who knew Julia Child was a Confucian?

Chinese culinary philosophy divides all foods into two categories: "Fan," which really means rice but in this case includes grains and breads; and "t'sai" or "cai," simply everything else. (Classical Chinese thought also divides foods into "hot" and "cool," referring not to their preparation but to their effect on the body; hot is "yang," cool "yin." It's the same concept—that onions and garlic inflame the senses—that causes many devout Buddhists and Jainists to abjure them altogether.) Individual foods are believed to have specific medicinal properties, and though eating fried scorpions sounds like a tough way to keep hair from going gray (especially in the age of Grecian Formula), many scientists now agree that ginger eases digestive troubles, and the palliative effects of gingko on memory loss are still being debated.

Rice and wheat were among the very first crops, and China remains the world's largest producer of both. They are symbolic of the country's divided economies: In the north, wheat is the primary starch, and noodles and *mantou* (steamed buns) the preferred manner of consumption; in the southern and central regions, rice is the staple. As on the Indian subcontinent, this is a matter of geography and climate. Similarly, in the north, pork and lamb are still the favorite meats, and fish and seafood the primary proteins in the south.

As we have already seen, the essential seasonings came from all over—Persia, India, Malaysia, the Americas—and were absorbed over many thousands of years. However, the methods of cooking have remained relatively unchanged in all that time, simple and fast and fuel-efficient: boiling, braising, steaming, roasting, stir-frying, and deep-frying. There are many refinements of each: simmering, steeping, smothering, pan-sticking, and smoking, for example. Each cooking method has even further degrees of variations—there are probably a dozen ways to boil chicken, depending on exactly the texture desired for a particular dish—and the Chinese often double-cook dishes, boiling and then frying; but few methods require both long cooking and high heat. Marinating, which in addition to flavoring meats and poultry preserves and tenderizes them, thus shortening cooking time, can be adjusted to permeate, crisp, or even "velvet" a dish, giving it a silky coating.

Many of the aesthetic elements in Chinese cuisine were at least partially inspired by the need to husband resources. The Chinese use contrast, color, texture, and cosmic "harmony" to make every dish seem more elaborate and to make eating it a more fulfilling experience. A 2,500-year-old book of etiquette speaks not only of seasonal foods but seasonal seasoning, so to speak: spices in autumn, salt in winter, sour flavors in spring, and bitter in summer, offsetting all of them with sweetness. It also prescribes the correct fat to be used in frying various meats. Although dishes in a meal may not be rich, they are varied to exaggerate the diner's sense of proportions: seafood, poultry, pork, tofu, and vegetables are each offered in a different sauce and, ideally, cut or sliced in different ways.

The use of ornate, metaphorical names for recipes works the same way, demanding the diner's attention to the creation of the dish and slowing its consumption. The dragon and phoenix are both considered propitious animals, so they are often invoked symbolically—the dragon usually represented by lobster and the phoenix by white chicken meat.

Authentic Chinese food is unusually healthful, and for some unusual reasons. For one thing, it is virtually free of dairy foods—milk, butter, or cheese—which not only limits the diet's cholesterol content but makes it an especially attractive choice for lactose-intolerant diners. It also explains the large number of kosher Chinese establishments in large cities. Despite its popularity, meat, especially pork, is used as a flavoring for vegetables and grains, not generally as the main dish, limiting cholesterol even further. (In fact, there is no real "main dish" in a Chinese dinner, variety being the key to stretching the meal.) Grains and beans of various types are important in all regions of the country, as is tofu, a first-class form of protein.

Because so much of the agricultural land in the central and southern regions is either regularly flooded for rice-growing or naturally marshy, a surprising number of the vegetables consumed are watery and low in calories: lotus and bamboo shoots, lily buds, water chestnuts, bean sprouts, cabbages, and so forth. For the same reasons, many are fibrous, adding another healthful element to the diet. Other "vegetables" are actually marine life, such as algae and sea cucumbers, which supply nutrients that macrobiologists venerate.

The exceptions are dishes that are fried, of course, including dumplings, buns, wontons, and fried rice as well as deep-fried fish and what are called "twice-cooked" dishes; but even these are not too fatty if correctly prepared.

Unfortunately, Chinese cuisine has until recently been poorly represented in the United States, partly because the first immigrants couldn't find the ingredients they wanted and partly because few of them had been professional cooks back home. American stir-fried dishes tend to be overly greasy and, in the cheaper establishments, may be cooked in oil that has been reused and become rank. Corner-cutting "Sichuan" carryouts often use hot pepper oil to flavor dishes rather than taking the time to incorporate real chilies. Cornstarch, sugar, and salt, all used sparingly in China, are loaded on in America; and MSG (monosodium glutamate), once so dominant in American Chinese dishes that menus now advertise its absence, is almost unknown in China. Americans have demanded that their pork and beef be raised to be fat and rich, whereas Chinese meat is traditionally lean and more flavorful.

Consider the menu carefully. Poached, braised, and steamed dishes, particularly those that include seafood and mixed vegetables, are good bets; but even these dishes can be deceptive: Many meats used in soups and stews are stir-fried first, to add flavor, and noodles can also be pre-fried. The telltale sign is the oil on the surface of the dish or in the bottom of the plate.

Finally, Chinese food is fairly high in sodium, much of it hidden, as food is traditionally seasoned during the cooking rather than at the table.

REGIONAL CUISINES

There are many regional distinctions in Chinese cooking, and luckily for Americans, more Chinese restaurants in the United States are specializing in regional cuisines. (It's probably more accurate to say that they are beginning to advertise their specialties in English and list them on the menus; for many years, the only way to get real Chinese food was to ask for the Chinese-language menu, wait for the host to come over and try to convince you that you *didn't* want to order the tripe in chili oil that you were pointing to, and then order precisely that.)

Intriguingly, there are Chinese writers who fear that the same instruments of "progress" that made authentic Chinese food in America possible—swifter and more reliable transport, better communication and education—may work against regional cuisines back home and that Chinese cooking may be becoming increasingly homogenized. The two greatest changes in recent decades have probably been the protection of many rare and exotic animals previously used for meat and the adoption of some international dishes, particularly around Shanghai, which was for many decades an international mecca and is gradually reclaiming its cosmopolitan image

The five main regional styles available in the United States, which reflect historical as well as topographical and climactic differences, are Cantonese, from the southeast; Sichuan, from the southwest; Beijing, from the east; Hunan, from the central regions; and Fujian, from the east coast.

CANTONESE Generally speaking, Cantonese cuisine is the most simple-flavored, characterized by minimal seasonings (coriander, black beans, oyster sauce, bean cheese, and shrimp paste), the use of chicken broth as a cooking medium, and a heavy dependence on stir-frying and steaming; most dim sum, the variety of steamed dumplings and tidbits rolled around on carts, is Cantonese. In the mid-seventeenth century, when the Manchus swept into the Imperial City, many of the royal chefs fled south to the Guangzhou region. There they turned their practiced hand to new ingredients, particularly seafood, and to such imports as okra, peanuts, tomatoes, and eggplant.

The Cantonese generally prefer both fish and poultry slightly pink at the bone, but because they are bought live and cooked only at the last minute, there is no danger of food poisoning. In the United States, meats and fish are usually cooked more thoroughly to satisfy perceived American tastes. (The Chinese do occasionally eat raw fish, i.e., sashimi, called "yue shang"; sliced while the fish is stunned but still nominally live, it is generally reserved for wedding parties and birthdays.) Cantonese cuisine is also full of delicate fruits and vegetables, such as lychees, cashews, coconuts, pineapples, papaya, apricots, kumquats, watercress, pea leaves, chrysanthemum petals, squash, cilantro, and water chestnuts.

Because the port of Canton was the first major East-West crossroads, and the Cantonese were the first group to travel widely in Europe and the United States, theirs was also the first cooking style most Westerners were introduced to, and it remains the most common here. (Historians have pointed out that the Chinese laborers' healthier diet and abstinence from cheap rotgut whisky helped them survive the crippling working conditions of the transcontinental railroads, whereas the Americans, downing spoiled beef and beans, suffered chronic illness.) Hong Kong is off the coast of Canton, and many Hong Kong dishes offered in Cantonese restaurants closely resemble Singaporean Nonja cuisine (see the chapter on Indonesia, Malaysia, and Singapore, page 254).

BEIJING (Formerly spelled Peking.) Beijing was one of the sites of the Imperial Court and thus the site of many elaborate banquets, so Beijing cuisine is among the most consciously sophisticated of the regional cuisines. It is also light and fairly delicately seasoned but uses much more garlic (as much as its neighbors in Korea) and scallions and other green onions. Rice is used less frequently in the north than elsewhere in the country; wheat, millet, and soybeans are the staples. Because of the harsher climate, root vegetables and dried and pickled ones were common; partly because of the more limited choices, powerful and simple seasonings,

Chop Shop

Most "Chinese-American" dishes are just unfortunate adaptations of classic recipes, the best that impoverished nineteenth-century Chinese immigrants—most of whom were not professional chefs but mom-and-pop cooks—had to do with what they could get here. Because they didn't have the time or ingredients to make flavorful Supreme Stock (described on page 297), they doused fried rice with soy sauce. Since Americans were unaccustomed to delicate egg roll wrappings and disliked most seafood anyway, egg rolls became thicker, with pork instead of shrimp. Unable to get fresh fruit, they improvised sweet-and-sour sauces out of canned pineapples and ketchup, and so on.

There is one dish that *could* be termed "authentic" Chinese-American and that is chop suey. According to legend, Ambassador Li Hong Zhang, who represented the Manchu court here at the end of the nineteenth century, once forgot to warn his chef that he had invited company over for supper. At the

such as garlic and onions, were favored. Northerners also tend to prefer dark soy sauce almost exclusively over light soy. Wine is used as a cooking liquid, especially for meats, and so is vinegar. Soft-fried foods are a hallmark.

Most so-called Mongolian dishes are northern Chinese in style, but because of the great grass steppes there (and the Muslim influence in the northwest), lamb, mutton, and goat are still more common than pork, and some fermented dairy products (such as yogurt) are common. On the other hand, Beijing and the closely related Shandong dishes used to be called "Mandarin" as well, referring to the aristocrats of the court and many far more ornate recipes. (Court cuisine could be very demanding: In the sixth century B.C.E., the duke of Jin is said to have executed his chef for undercooking braised bear's paw—still a northern Chinese specialty, though it is now illegal.)

The "hot pot" and various casseroles that were characteristic of the swift-moving Mongols are still common, though they were probably reintroduced from Inner Mongolia sometime after the Khans had been evicted. "Mongolian barbecue" restaurants are almost like Japanese teppanyaki houses, where sliced meat and vegetables are quick-grilled with a flourish of chopsticks and then stuffed into little rolls—wheat again, rather than rice—and eaten by hand. The Shandong version is a lamb stew with dunked buns. The city of Tsingtao (or Qingdao) was once occupied by German troops, which is how it came to make such good beer.

SICHUAN (Also spelled Szechuan or Szechwan.) Sichuan cuisine has become increasingly popular in the United States over the last 20 years and probably laid the groundwork for the boom in Thai restaurants as well. Sichuan food is spicy and peppery and tends to be oily (partly the influence of nearby India and Pakistan); many ingredients are fried, wrapped in dough, and then fried again. The cooking fat may be lard or chicken fat as well as oil. Even "lighter fare" may be boiled, then stir-fried, such as Twice-Cooked Pork. Beef is more common here than in some other areas; lamb and chicken are also readily available. Roasting is a common technique, as is smoking; both tea-smoked and camphor-smoked duck are Sichuan in origin. China's western region has less fish than some areas, because the rivers race down from the mountains too fast for leisurely breeding, so "fish-flavored" in Sichuan cuisine refers to a rich, slightly sour barbecue sauce with vinegar, hot bean paste, ginger, garlic, and onions. Ironically, though Chung King is one of the major names in homogenized, thoroughly unspicy American-Chinese fare, "Chung-king" (or Chongqing) cuisine is another name for Sichuan cooking.

HUNAN Hunan cuisine, which in the United States is frequently confused with Sichuan, is also spicy but richer; dishes are more likely to be marinated in or sauced with sweet-and-sour compotes. Meats may also be dried and preserved. Though the chili peppers used now in Sichuan and Hunan cooking originated in the New World and were not known in China until the seventeenth century, both styles were already characterized by generous doses of black and white pepper and ginger; the chilies just upped the ante.

FUJIAN (Fukien.) This cuisine is just beginning to be available in the United States and is extremely healthful: It emphasizes "wet" dishes,

---

Chop Shop
continued

last minute, the chef combined all the leftovers and seasonings he could find into what we would call refrigerator roulette, and when his guests asked him the name of the dish, the ambassador answered honestly, "Tsap seui"—an amalgamation of scraps. A related story has Li serving tsap seui at a diplomatic dinner at the Waldorf Astoria, of all places. A third credits the ingenuity of a San Francisco cook faced with a rowdy crowd of drunk and hungry miners. A few scholars scoff at such tales and call it an old country dish. Nevertheless, a Shanghai restaurant in the 1930s advertised "Genuine American Chop Suey."

That silliest of "Chinese" specialties, the fortune cookie, is definitely native to the United States—invented in 1916 by a California noodle maker named David Jung. Ironically, not long ago a Brooklyn fortune cookie firm was hired to build a factory in Canton. As Confucius say, "There's no accounting for taste."

particularly soups (which are filling and not fatty) and soupy dishes, stocks, wine braising, and especially seafood. Chicken and duck are favorites, and pork is more popular here than lamb or beef. Because Fujian is on the east coast of China and has perhaps had more exchange with Japanese cuisine, Fujian cooking uses more soy sauce and vinegar than some of the other regional styles and features more "fish and rice" dishes; Fujian restaurants in the United States may have sushi bars. The thin crêpes called *poopia* are almost Vietnamese in style; as many as 20 julienned or shredded meats and vegetables are laid out, and diners fill and roll their own crêpes. Oysterette pan-fry is a sort of omelet.

Salted and preserved duck, crabs, the original fried rice (made with Supreme Stock), and many dim sum dishes originated in the eastern regions as well. Shanghai cooking can be heavily Europeanized (cold meat aspic, for instance) but also includes such specialties as "red-cooked" pork shoulder with rock candy. (Sweetness is a hallmark of Shanghai cooking.) Taiwan is off the shore of Fujian province, so Taiwanese-style cuisine is primarily Fujianese.

Most recently, Chinese food in Hong Kong and on the West Coast of North America has begun to evolve in a new direction, reflecting both the international outlook of young upwardly mobile Hong Kong professionals—called, inevitably, "chuppies"—and the increasing pride Chinese Americans have in their dual heritage. Chop suey is back, in a snappier, fresher fashion; and some new-wave Chinese restaurants are even experimenting—as are Japanese sushi bars—with such familiar American dairy products as mayonnaise and cheese. And the fine, cosmopolitan dishes of Shanghai, which absorbed traditions and ingredients from all over China as well as from foreign trade, are beginning to reappear.

THE MAIN INGREDIENTS

SEASONINGS The most prominent flavors are soy sauce, sesame oil, peanut oil, sweet wines, garlic, ginger, various onions, bean pastes, sesame paste, fermented black beans, "Chinese" chives (garlic chives), coriander, star anise, and mustard. Salt, pepper, cinnamon, curry spices, anise, galangal and ginger, chilies, brown sugar, vinegar, honey, and various dried and pickled ingredients, such as dried shrimp, dried mushrooms, and pickled cabbage, are characteristic. "Five-spice powder" may not always have only five ingredients—the usual combination is star anise, fennel seed, cinnamon, cloves, and ginger, with anise root, nutmeg, and Sichuan peppercorns as alternatives—but five is a propitious number, and because it was originally a medicinal mixture, the name emphasized and even increased its potency. (Sichuan peppercorns are not true pepper, incidentally, but a small dried berry with a slight numbing effect.) Dried orange peel is a particularly old and treasured flavor; the orange is native to China.

A number of already prepared sauces are used as condiments or seasonings, including hoisin sauce (a mix of soybean paste, five-spice powder, chili, and a bit of brown sugar), chili paste with soy sauce, vinegar-chili mixes, plum sauce (often called "duck sauce" because it was usually served with duck in American restaurants), bean sauce (fermented soybeans flavored with ginger and orange peel) and a chili-fired version, and oyster sauce, which is especially valued in Buddhist circles. Tea is also an important ingredient: Tea is used as a broth, particularly for hard-boiled eggs; and the leaves are used for smoking duck and chicken and occasionally stir-fried.

One of the most important ingredients in Cantonese cooking is called Supreme or Superior Stock; each chef has his or her own version, but it is generally a rich broth made from a combination of chicken and perhaps duck or squab, ham, and pork. Like sourdough starter, this stock, once made, is then replenished, expanded, and continually re-created for years; in some epicurean circles, it is the stock that separates the ordinary cooks from the culinary stars.

Chinese soy sauce is a little less sweet and more salty than Japanese shoyu, which mixes more wheat with the soy. Dark soy has a little molasses in it and is used more with meats; light soy is more suited to seafoods, dipping sauces, and soups. *Shaoshing* (or *shaoxing*) wine is a cooking wine something like Japanese mirin or sherry. Sesame oil is a flavoring, not a cooking medium; it cannot withstand the high temperatures required for stir-frying and will smoke and break down.

VEGETABLES Thanks to those thousands of years of trading, the Chinese eat nearly all of the vegetables that any other culture eats, but a few—bamboo shoots, bean sprouts, water chestnuts, mung beans and soybeans, lotus roots, and lily bulbs—are purely Chinese. Among the most common vegetables are mushrooms (especially "black" or shiitake mushrooms, straw mushrooms, and wood ear and cloud ear fungi), greens (spinach, mustard, the bok choy and celery cabbages called in this country "Chinese" and "Napa" cabbages, celery, watercress, the collard-like snow or "Shanghai" cabbage, and many lettuces), seaweeds, cucumbers, several eggplants, snow peas and pea shoots, lima and fava beans, string beans, radishes, gourds and squashes, winter melons, sweet potatoes, taro root, turnips, okra, Chinese and Western broccoli, asparagus, sweet peppers, and corn. Among the most popular gourds is the native American chayote, called in Chinese *fat su*, or "Buddha's hand," because of its shape. Lotus leaves and bamboo leaves are used for wrapping and steaming, but are not eaten. Red beans are primarily used for coloring and to make a sweet paste used in buns and treats.

Soybeans provide more protein per acre and per pound than any other crop (or animal); the Chinese consume soy not only as tofu but as plain boiled beans, dried beans, bean sprouts, fermented bean paste, and soy milk. In fact, soy is the most widely eaten plant in the world—and, as nutritious as it is as a food, it simultaneously feeds the earth: its roots disperse nitrogenous bacteria, and soy can even be planted to refresh fields exhausted by other crops.

FRUITS AND NUTS Melons, grapes, kumquats, loquats, bananas, apples, oranges, dates, mangoes, apricots, and plums are common. So-called lychee nuts are really a fruit. Many fruits are candied or preserved to eat as snacks and occasionally as desserts, but they may also be used in sauces. Walnuts, chestnuts, lotus seeds, cashews, almonds, coconut, gingko nuts, peanuts, and sesame seeds are also prominent; and many of these may be ground into a flour or oil as well.

RICE AND NOODLES Rice originated in China, and it remains at its heart. (It's even, as Eliza Doolittle might say, as mother's milk to them: White rice powder in sugar water is often used as baby formula.) Here, as in most of the cuisines of Asia, rice is synonymous with food. The first lesson Chinese cooks (and most children) learn is to make perfect rice, well-rinsed to remove excess starch, steamed to a fluffy but distinct state—and absolutely lump-free.

Chinese cooking calls for many types of rice: long-, medium-, and short-grain white (the longer and older, the better, because they cook up fluffier) as well as an "extra-long" grain white rice, a long-grain red rice and a shorter one from the Thai border area, sweet glutinous rice, and a rarer black glutinous rice. The region near Thailand also produces a jasmine rice with an extra-long grain that is highly prized. Sweet rice is generally used as an ingredient, not as the main starch, especially in stuffings and sweets; similarly, the red rice is most often used as a decorative touch. Brown or unmilled rice is considered lower-class, though some Chinese restaurants in the United States, particularly those specializing in vegetarian or promoting "healthy" menus, now offer it.

Noodles, generically called mien (not so broadly pronounced as the American version, "mein") have been known in China for more than 2,000 years—as have breads and dumplings, because it was the technique of milling that made doughs readily accessible. (If you are ever lucky enough to see a noodle maker "hand-pull" noodles, twirling and stretching the sliced dough into ever-longer, thinner elastic skeins, you will understand why mass production was important. But the real feat is amazing to watch. If you have a VCR, you can rent Jackie Chan's movie, Mr. Nice Guy, and watch him play chef.)

According to the stereotype, all Chinese food comes with rice, either steamed or fried; but that is a slight exaggeration. What is true is that all meals include "fan"—grains—and in the north, where rice was originally scarce, other grains were needed to fill out the diet. Wheat is the major grain there (in fact, "mien" originally implied wheat flour), but barley, buckwheat, maize, and millet are also cultivated, and all five of these are used to make not only noodles but breads, buns, pastries, and the tortilla-like pancakes used in Beijing duck and moo shu pork. In the north, noodles are more often served in soup than dry. In the south, where rice is so readily available, rice noodles are more common, but even sesame seeds, mung beans, and soybeans can be turned into noodles.

In Italy, pasta is defined by its shape, but in China the distinction is material. In addition to the grains mentioned above, there are garbanzo starch noodles, "cellophane" or mung bean thread noodles (fen si), and pale white "rice sticks" (mi fen). Wheat noodles may or may not have egg in them; they may be colored or flavored with shrimp, tea, or vegetables; fresh or dried; wide, "regular," thin, or extra-thin.

Noodles are consumed in the south, too, but more as a snack or on special occasions; because of their length, noodles are considered metaphors for long life. (Some old-fashioned southerners still consider noodles rather low-class.) In China, as in Korea and Japan, rice is cooked without salt; and the preferred consistency for rice is fluffy and glossy, with distinct, firm grains but clinging enough for chopstick use. Sticky or glutinous rice is used mainly for stuffings and desserts. Short-grain rice is roasted and used to coat meatballs or pork. As in Persia, the crusty rice left in the bottom of the pot is a special treat.

What are often called "egg roll wrappers" do not include eggs; they are solely flour and water. Actually, there is no such thing as an egg roll, either; it's an Americanized version of the spring roll—and, in typical American style, swollen up to twice or three times traditional size. So-called rice noodles are frequently sheets, also used for wrapping.

Gluten is a wheat protein and is used instead of tofu by some monks; it is also beginning to show up in health-food stores in the United States.

TOFU   As mentioned above, soybean curd and other soy products are vital to Chinese cooking, including a variety of soy sauces, light, dark, and mushroom-flavored; fresh and dried tofu and thin tofu skins; and fermented soy bean pastes similar to Japanese miso.

FISH AND SEAFOOD   China is rolling, or roiling, in both fresh- and saltwater foods: bass, bluefish, bream, carp, catfish, cod, dogfish, flounder, halibut, herring, mackerel, mullet, perch, pike, shad, sardines, shark, snapper, sole, sturgeon, trout, and tuna—plus, to abandon the alphabet of fish, lobster, crab, abalone, scallops, oysters, clams, eels, shrimp, and squid. Nori (seaweed sheets) are used to enrich soups and sometimes to wrap fish and rice, Japanese-style; kelp is eaten as a source of iodine. Many fish, shrimp, abalone, and scallops are dried and used for flavorings. "Sea cucumber," incidentally, is not a vegetable but a marine slug, also known as bêche-de-mer. It is also dried and has to be long-soaked and simmered before being added to a dish.

POULTRY AND GAME BIRDS   Duck, rather than chicken, is the first choice in poultry in the Chinese diet, and a Chinese clipper ship that sailed into the United States in the 1870s brought with it the ancestors of all those Long Island and Beijing ducks here now. However, chicken is considered one of the most healthful foods available and is often referred to as the immortal phoenix in classic dishes. Like the geese fattened for foie gras, ducks are force-fed for weeks before slaughter. Many Chinese restaurants smoke, dry (all poultry is well-drained of blood), and roast whole ducks and chickens and hang them in the windows as a sort of advertising, just as sushi bars display plastic fish. The Chinese also enjoy many other birds: squab, quail, partridge, wild duck, pheasant, goose, and occasionally turkey.

Duck eggs, fresh and salted, are extremely popular, again followed by hen's eggs, quail, and pigeon eggs. (Duck eggs have a slightly oilier texture than hens' eggs, and some French pastry experts claim they are essential for making cordon bleu pastry dough.) So-called thousand-year-old eggs tend to be more like a hundred days old, duck eggs preserved in a mix of salt, tea leaves, and rice husks; the whites turn brown and the yolks green.

MEATS Pork is the first meat in Chinese cookery, in both senses: The pink pig we know was domesticated in China thousands of years ago, and it is also the most popular meat in the diet. If the meat in a recipe is not specified, it's assumed to be pork. Pork is made into bacon, a Smithfield-like ham, and sausage—although it is hard to guess what constitutes leftover offal for sausage, given that the Chinese eat pork kidneys, livers, hearts, tripe, stomachs, brains, ears, tails, tongues, blood (in pudding), pigs' feet, suckling pig skin, and even snouts and spleens. Some sausages are described as all-pork, some as pork and pork liver, and some very rich ones have duck liver as well. All-liver sausages are called "gold and silver," and are served for luck for the New Year.

Beef is only gradually becoming common outside the western regions (it is used far more frequently in American Chinese restaurants than anywhere in China itself), but again, little is wasted: The Chinese consume organ meats and even the shinbones. On the other hand, veal, so highly prized in European cuisines, is not considered interesting. Lamb, along with some goat, is eaten mostly in the northern regions, where the steppes are best suited to sheep grazing; in the south, a Muslim specialty is paper-thin horsemeat cooked with rice noodles, like a fondue or shabu-shabu.

THE MAIN DISHES

Perhaps the most famous banquet dish in China is a banquet in itself: "Buddha Jumps Over the Wall," a huge pot-au-feu so fragrant that it would supposedly cause even the devoutly vegetarian sage to abandon his principles and climb a wall to taste it. It involves some 25 or 30 ingredients, takes days to prepare (it requires shark's fin broth, reconstituted dried scallops, several fresh abalone, a whole chicken and a whole duck, lamb, pork and pork's feet, ham, quail eggs, mushrooms, vegetables, and herbs, all cooked separately and then layered and simmered together and served in huge bowls. If you are ever fortunate enough to taste it, you may feel blessed yourself.

There isn't room to list all the 80,000 recipes, and fortunately, most menu listings are fairly self-explanatory ("shrimp and scallops in black bean sauce"). However, there are some dishes so common that they are referred to by their Chinese names, which we'll describe.

APPETIZERS Spareribs, even barbecued ones, are more authentic than you might think; but they aren't generally served as appetizers except at formal dinners or banquets. Traditionally, appetizers are cold and are more likely to include cold chicken, ham or sausage, meatballs, smoked fish, shrimp toast, pickled or parboiled vegetables, and even peanuts or preserved eggs. Most of what we consider appetizers, particularly hot ones, are transplanted dim sum—teahouse meals (see page 310). Spring rolls are the original egg rolls, but smaller, more delicate than the modern version; they were originally Chinese New Year snacks. Wontons are stuffed dumplings (the things tossed on top of soup in cheap restaurants are just fried wonton skins); they can either be boiled in soup or served a dozen to a plate, deep-fried or steamed, as a light meal.

SOUPS The Chinese consider soup as a part of the meal, to be drunk throughout rather than only at the beginning, and so most are served (to Chinese patrons, anyway) in large tureens and may be replenished. Among the standards are hot-and-sour soup (as popular in China as in the United States), egg-drop soup, wonton, chicken with bean-thread noodles, crab meat with asparagus, mixed seafood soups with bok choy and rice noodles, pork with winter melon, meatballs and vermicelli, and flavored broths with fish. These are relatively light soups; the simplest is merely boiled water poured over freshly minced greens. Thicker soups are generally long-simmered and more likely to be served as lunch or light meals. Meat is usually limited to flavorings or even garnish, although "crossing the bridge" noodle soup has slices of pork and shrimp as well as noodles. (It supposedly refers to a dish carried by his wife to a scholar secluded in his distant study.) The "bird's nests" used in soup are not twigs but a gelatinous protein produced by a certain type of swift to bind the nests together; it looks more like toasted coconut. Shark's fin is just what it sounds like.

There are also sweet dessert soups, usually made of fruit and seen primarily at banquets. Because the appetizers at a formal dinner often include peanuts or walnuts, a Chinese banquet can be said to go from nuts to soup.

RICE AND NOODLE DISHES The classic fried rice is a dish of cooled cooked rice, shrimp, eggs, scallions, and barbecued pork, seasoned with soy, oyster sauce, sesame oil, ginger, garlic, sugar, and rice wine. In America, fried rice dishes, named for the majority ingredient (shrimp fried rice, pork fried rice, and so on) may or may not include eggs; *subgum*, which sometimes appears in the name, too, just means "many ingredients"—a sort of deluxe version. There are regional versions that use glutinous rice; one Taiwanese favorite, called green rice, gets its name from the spinach with which it's stir-fried.

Fried rice is eaten as a meal rather than ordered as a entree among others. "Sizzling rice" dishes use the rice crusts that are left in the pan when rice is boiled; these crusts are deep-fried, and stir-fried seafood is poured over them, producing a popping or sizzling sound.

Congee or *jook* is a rice porridge that by itself is very bland but is usually the base for a variety of toppings, humble and exalted: wontons, sliced duck, pork kidneys, lobster, sliced fish, preserved eggs, meatballs, and so forth. Noodle restaurants often work the same way, only the toppings arrive on a large bowl of noodles in broth (called *yakkomein*) like the Vietnamese pho. *Wo mein* noodles are fine egg noodles in soup. Wonton shops specialize in chewy noodles and water crescents (really soup dumplings or soft wontons). "Lo mein" means simply "mixed noodles," that is, noodles tossed with mixed vegetables and meat.

"Soft-fried" noodles are parboiled then lightly stir-fried; "crisp-fried" noodles are used as garnish. Real "chow mein" (*ciao mien*) means fresh pan-fried noodles, not the hard (canned) noodles familiar in the United States; the noodles are boiled and then stir-fried until crispy on the outside and tender inside, then topped with an assortment of meat and vegetables that were stir-fried separately. Lo mein is similar, but the noodles are parboiled and then added directly to the meat and vegetable mixture. *Dan-dan* noodles are Sichuan-style, fresh wheat noodles with ground pork and cabbage; they were originally street fare, sold in pails that vendors balanced on their shoulders, and got their name from the clanging of the pails. Singapore noodles have curry powder in the sauce; they traditionally include shrimp and barbecued pork as well as vegetables.

VEGETABLES Because observant Buddhist monks didn't eat meat, the classic mixed-vegetable stir-fry, which may have as many as 10 or 12 ingredients, is often called Buddha's or Buddhist Delight. Dishes with names such as "Hard Immortal" and "Soft Immortal" or "Food of the Forest" are also vegetarian. "Mock chicken" is tofu; so is mock duck, mock goose, and so on. "Yellow birds" are thin tofu skins filled with vegetables.

Incidentally, vegetable dishes, even those served cold and resembling Southeast Asian vegetable salads, are almost never eaten raw; for safety, they have traditionally been boiled, salted, or pickled. Sauerkraut, intriguingly, is Chinese.

FISH AND SEAFOOD Fish is traditionally served whole, not only because it looks nicer but also because the meat of the cheeks is a delicacy and because the fish stays moister if it is cooked whole. The way a fish is cooked (steamed, simmered, fried, pan-fried, braised, etc.) is dictated by its relative thickness and oiliness.

Cantonese-style steamed fish, marinated with sesame, soy, and rice wine and steamed with julienned scallions and ginger has become so popular that it is likely to be available in almost any Chinese restaurant, whatever the regional specialty. Sea bass is especially delicious this way because it has a layer of fat that keeps the meat moist. "Emperor's fish" has long slits cut in the flesh, which are filled with shiitake mushrooms and then steamed.

You can also get fried whole fish with sweet-and-sour or black bean sauce. (The traditional Hunan version is served with the fish propped upright, as if it were preparing to swim away.) In better restaurants, you may be able to order fresh scallops with their coral intact steamed with ginger. Mixed seafood is frequently served in a basket of quick-fried noodles. "Vinegar-slipped" fish is a northern Chinese specialty; the fish is quick-fried and then slipped into a sweet-and-sour vinegar sauce.

Crabs are not seen often on American Chinese menus, but are very popular along the Chinese coast, usually served with other meats and seafoods rather than separately. Spicy clams are more common there than in the United States, but scallops and shrimp are available in almost every conceivable style: fried, stir-fried, in ginger and garlic, in black bean sauce, *kung pao*, salt-baked, chopped and boiled as balls in broth, stuffed into dumplings, tossed in noodles and rices, and so on. Lobster is becoming more common as well.

POULTRY Northern duck dishes, such as Beijing duck, have extra-crispy skin because the carcass is inflated before roasting to separate the layer of fat from the meat. In the United States, this is a one-course meal: The duck is presented whole at the table, the meat is sliced off by the waiter (with the skin attached), rolled in tortilla-like pancakes with a sliver of scallion and a dollop of hoisin sauce, and eaten by hand. However, the traditional presentation of Beijing duck is a three-course affair: The skin, which is coated with wine and honey, is sliced away from the meat, and it is the skin that is rolled up, sauced, and scallioned and eaten as the appetizer. The meat, meanwhile, is stir-fried with a smattering of vegetables for the next course, and the carcass goes right into the stock pot to make a rich broth that is served last.

Cantonese-style duck—the type that is often seen hanging around in windows—is marinated with wine, filled with a thick marinade, and then roasted. Roast duck may be coated with honey, orange juice, or sherry; boned and braised with five-spice powder and hoisin; or chopped into two-inch pieces and simmered with fruit. Nanking-style duck is rolled in coarse salt and crushed peppercorns, steamed, chopped into bite-size pieces, and served cold.

"Eight-treasure" duck (or chicken) is originally a dish from the Hakka people, China's version of gypsies, who were driven from their northern territories by the Mongols and wandered for centuries before finally settling in the south. The ingredients, which are stuffed into a whole boned carcass, are highly symbolic, representing the eight signs of Buddha, his eight organs, the eight "Immortals" of Taoism, and the eight ways to eternal joy: They include shiitake mushrooms, water chestnuts, ginkgo nuts, pork, ham, shrimp, and lotus seeds.

Chicken and other birds can be poached, steamed, smoked (over tea or herbs), deep-fried, braised, curried, roasted, soy-marinated, salt-roasted, shredded, stir-fried, turned into soups and salads, boned and stuffed whole, and double-cooked; "white-simmered" means cooked without soy sauce, "red-simmered" with. "Drunken chicken" is steamed whole and then marinated, not surprisingly, with wine. Kung pao (or *gung pao*) chicken with peanuts and hot peppers is named for the "guardian of the palace" who is supposed to have invented it (the original version had the chilies, but used corn kernels rather than peanuts). *Moo goo gai pan* is stir-fried chicken with button mushrooms. "Jade tree chicken" combines steamed chicken slices with ham and broccoli, the broccoli stalks being the trees; "jade flower chicken" has florets.

"Beggar's chicken," which is rolled in lotus leaves and roasted, got its name from a story about a beggar who stole a chicken and, having no pot or stove, made a hole in the ground, covered the bird with mud and baked it. However, this Beijing-style dish is anything but poor: It involves stuffing the chicken with mushrooms and such aromatics as sesame oil, five-spice powder, and fat; rubbing it with wine and more aromatics; swaddling it in lotus leaves; and then rewrapping it all in dough. (Neither the dough nor the leaves are consumed.)

And the famous General Tso's chicken is traditionally thigh and leg meat in a sweet-tangy hoisin-ginger sauce with hot chilies.

Eggs are rarely eaten alone; instead, they are combined with meat or seafood and vegetables. The original *egg foo yung* was a soufflé of egg white and minced chicken breast, but in the United States, it has become a much heartier, frittata-style pancake, either pan-fried or, more commonly, deep-fried.

MEAT   Chinese cuisine offers more pork recipes than anything else, but American diners rarely have a chance to order such delicacies as "five-flower pork" (belly bacon with alternating strips of fat and lean); Chairman Mao's favorite, fatty bacon with bitter gourd and chilies; or deep-fried roast pork squares with crab meat. More common is "happy family" (sea cucumber, chicken, pork shoulder, ham, and vegetables in sweet-and-sour sauce), barbecued spareribs, really broiled in soy, hoisin, and honey; and "drunken pork" (boiled, then marinated in sherry for about a week, as apparently pigs are less susceptible than chickens).

Moo shu pork—stir-fried julienned pork with lily buds, cloud ear mushrooms, cabbage, and scrambled eggs, rolled up in Beijing duck pancakes with hoisin sauce—is one of the most popular traditional dishes, both in China and the United States. "Red-cooked pork" is a Shanghai classic, braised in soy and spices. True sweet-and-sour pork gets its flavor from sugar, rice vinegar, soy, and tomato sauce, not canned pineapple. "Gold coin pork" is skewered deep-fried squares of pork, bacon, and black mushrooms in sesame and anise; Chinese coins are, as this description suggests, square. Ground pork cooked in a Sichuan chili sauce and tossed with noodles becomes "ants climbing a tree." Fresh ham is often boiled, then sliced, and given a spicy sauce; fresh bacon is braised with a spicy, sweet-and-sour broth. Pork is also the basis for most dumpling stuffings.

Sichuan beef is thin-cut, double-cooked, and glazed with a sweet-hot sauce; "orange beef" is a similar dish, but with fresh orange slices. Crispy beef, also a Sichuan recipe, is actually triple-fried with spicy sauce. Cantonese steak is stir-fried with brandy and tomatoes. "Beef roll" is usually stuffed with shrimp and pine nuts—a change from the usual surf and turf—and flavored with soy and brown sugar. Five-spice beef is served cold, usually as a first course; it's shin beef, long simmered in a broth with star anise, ginger, soy, and wine. Pepper beef is not hot; it's marinated beef sautéed with (rinsed) fermented black beans and sweet peppers.

Lamb is still popular in the north (and in this country, among Muslim immigrants): Common dishes include stir-fried lamb with leeks, and lamb stew in a clay pot with sweet-and-sour citrus broth. Many beef recipes are also prepared with lamb.

TOFU   One of the most popular tofu dishes everywhere is the original Sichuan tofu, which is stir-fried with ground pork and chili sauce and stirred into noodles; in the United States, the dish is usually prepared without the noodles and served with rice. Hakka-style stuffed tofu has a tangy filling of both fresh and dried shrimp, ginger juice, oyster sauce, soy, sesame oil, and scallions.

DESSERTS   The Chinese do not have pastries or confections; they prefer fresh fruit or lychee nuts and sometimes preserved plums and even olives. On special occasions, apples and bananas may be battered and fried and drizzled with caramelized sugar called "silken threads," or you may be served buns filled with sweet bean paste or almonds. Restaurant desserts in China may also include almond-paste or sponge cakes. In the United States, most restaurants bring around sliced oranges after dinner, but many offer ice cream and the ubiquitous fortune cookie.

As with eight-treasure duck, which is considered propitious because of the Eight Immortals (Taoist figures) and Eight Portents of Buddha, there is an "eight-treasure cake" made of sticky rice filled with such treats as lotus seeds, almonds, red dates, candied ginger, and so on. More like a cake, it is also used as a banquet sweet.

BEVERAGES Shaoxing wine is often referred to as if it were a specific wine, but as in France, it actually describes a region in which the best Chinese wines are produced; and so is the only wine Americans are likely to be offered. Wines are usually drunk warm but not hot. Some Chinese wines are made from glutinous rice and taste more like sherry than sake; like sherry, they vary in depth and dryness.

The Chinese also ferment a variety of liqueurs from sorghum and flavor them with plums, oranges, lychees, apricots, kiwi fruit, ginseng, and other fruits and herbs. One of the most famous is made with rice petals. *Ng ga pai*, or "five companies" wine, is almost like a whiskey. *Fen*, which is 130 proof, is often used for cooking. *Kaoling* is a rice spirit that suggests vodka or the Korean shochu. These stronger spirits do not need warming.

Beer is increasingly popular in Chinese restaurants, particularly in the United States, where a full bar is almost standard.

TEA

With the exception of rice, no Chinese discovery has taken on greater social and emotional importance than tea. Though there is no tea ceremony or etiquette quite as elaborate as those in Japan, the tea ritual is a constant in Chinese life, representing a moment of calm, of rebalancing the body's yin and yang, and of reconnection with family and with the cosmos. Chinese teahouses bear little resemblance to the pastry and sandwich shops of Europe; they are places of commerce and elevated conversation that is encouraged to last for hours—a bit like the cafes of Paris are supposed to be, but more formal.

Tea (originally referred to as *ch'a*, from which the Japanese *cha* derives, and later *tei*) has been known in China for perhaps 2,500 years, and been the universal beverage for at least 2,000. Like rice, it was first cultivated in the Yangtze river valley, and, like rice, quickly became a favorite of the imperial court. One Sung dynasty (960–1279 C.E.) emperor deeded to himself nearly 48 private tea gardens. Tea's history is full of crowns: Ninth-century Buddhist monks carried tea seeds from China to Japan, where it quickly became intertwined with samurai society. Over the centuries it spread into parts of India and Ceylon (Sri Lanka). In the sixteenth century, the Portuguese took it back from Macao to Lisbon, the Portuguese princess Catharine of Braganza married Charles II of England and carried it with her, and eventually it became so profitable that the British East India Company decided to plant it all over India and later Kenya.

Although Chinese restaurants in the United States rarely offer much choice, the Chinese are connoisseurs of teas and consider a broad knowledge of the subject as much a part of a sophisticated upbringing as the French would wine. The differences in flavor, color, and strength are partly a matter of the type of tea bush and partly the method of curing. Green tea is unfermented; black tea (referred to as "red" by both Chinese and Japanese) is fermented and roasted. "White" teas look silvery when dried, and produce a pale yellow tea. "Gunpowder" tea, called by the Chinese "pearl tea," has a tiny gray-green leaf that is formed into bullet- or pearl-shaped pellets and has a smoky flavor. Oolong teas are lightly fermented or semifermented. The famous Lapsang Souchong from Fujian is first fermented, then smoked—the single malt scotch of teas. There are even deeper-flavored double-fermented teas used as digestives.

Teas with small leaves are considered the most desirable. "Green snail spring" tea, so named for the spiral twist its dried leaves develop, has leaves so tiny that it takes an estimated 80,000 leaves to make a pound of tea. Dried tea leaves should be whole; unlike the Japanese, the Chinese have pretty much abandoned powdered tea.

The names for Chinese teas are far more poetic than simply "English breakfast." *Pekoe* means "white hair," because young leaves have a pale fuzz and make a pale tea; *oolong* means "black dragon." Other teas have such names as Cloud Mist, Iron Goddess of Mercy (which has a metallic flavor), Dragon Well, and Water Fairy.

Teas are also brewed from any number of flowers and herbs, often in combination with true tea leaves, including jasmine, rose, gardenia and chrysanthemum leaves, ginseng, and ginger. Dozens of other herbs are prescribed medicinally.

Chinese tea experts also believe that, as with wines, certain teas are more complementary to specific foods. Green teas are said to be best with seafood, white with vegetarian dishes, oolong with game, and black with roast pork.

The Chinese drink tea at the beginning of the meal and at the end (to aid digestion); in the middle they prefer to stick to the soup or sip warm rice wine (except when eating dim sum, which calls for copious consumption of tea.) In any case, they do not drink iced water, which they believe is hard on the digestion; that belief is now held by many Western doctors as well.

DIM SUM

My father used to say he needed "a little something for the inner man," that is, something that was as warming for the spirit as for the stomach. *Dim sum*, sweetly, means "touch the heart"—satisfy the inner man.

In Canton, where dim sum originated nearly 1,500 years ago, businessmen traditionally used teahouses as their offices, often staying 12 or even 15 hours at a time. Consequently, teahouses began to specialize in snacks, particularly dumplings, both to accommodate the customers and to pad the bill. (After all, even dozens of pots of tea is not highly profitable.)

Although there are literally hundreds of types of dim sum, the most traditional are *sui mei* (or *shu mai*), which when made correctly are nearly fat-free and gossamer-thin open-topped steamed dumplings filled with crab, shrimp, coriander, and freshwater chestnuts. "Sui mai" means "cook and sell," because the minute they come out of the kitchen, they disappear. *Har gau* are tiny pleated shrimp dumplings; pork-filled buns are *char siu bau*. Pot-stickers are dumplings stuffed with meat and vegetables, first steamed and then pan-browned on the flat side to an almost caramelized crust that "sticks" to the pan. "Soup dumplings" are not dumplings in broth, but dumplings filled with a semi-solid flavored gelatin that melts when the dumpling is steamed and bursts in the mouth.

Many other snacks, some of them originally street fare or appetizers from banquets, have come to be included in the dim sum repertoire, such as scallion pancakes, duck's feet, boned chicken wings, and the Chinese sausage called *lap cheung*. One type of steamed bun is called *mantou; shizi tou*, or "lion's head," is an extra-large meatball. Fried or steamed sticky rice may be wrapped in lotus leaves and filled with shrimp, pork, chicken, sweets, or pickles; bean curd might be stuffed with mushrooms or mixed vegetables and steamed or fried. Steamed spareribs are called *pai kwat*. Flaky pastries and sesame buns are filled with curried chicken, minced beef, or sweet bean paste. Though many of these dumplings sound similar, and in the United States may be similar, traditionally each had a particular dough, size, shape, and method of cooking (steaming, simmering in broth, steaming in wraps, pan-frying), and a complementary dipping sauce, that gave each its distinct flavor.

In the traditional fashion, carts covered with dim sum hot out of the kitchen are wheeled through the dining room, and you stop the waiter and point to what you want. At the end of the meal, your bill is calculated by how many empty plates you have accumulated. However, dim sum has become so popular in recent years that many restaurants in the United States have a special dim sum menu to order from; its increasing popularity also explains why dim sum, which for decades was available only on Sundays and usually only to Chinese-reading diners, is now frequently offered on Saturdays or even seven days a week.

HOT POT MEALS

The Chinese firepot, also called the Mongolian hot pot, is a festive one-dish meal like a mixed fondue; it is related to the Japanese shabu-shabu, among other things. The firepot is something like a wok with a chimney in the center; the "moat" is filled with a rich stock (one recipe includes a whole chicken, a ham bone, dried scallops, abalone, a pound of roast pork, pints of oysters and clams, and scallions) that is brought to a boil and then poured into the pot.

Meanwhile, each diner has custom-blended condiments—soy, sherry, hoisin sauce, sesame paste, vinegar, mustard, soybean paste, sugar, sesame oil, raw eggs—in a small bowl. Platters of paper-thin sliced beef, pork, duck, chicken, ham, lamb, chicken livers, pork kidneys (parboiled), fish, shellfish, shrimp, lobster, squid, greens, bean curd, mushrooms, tofu, and nearly anything else are arranged on the table along with bowls of pickled ginger, leeks, scallions, garlic, parsley, and so forth.

Once the stock begins to simmer, each diner picks up a single piece of food with chopsticks, dips it into the stock until it is cooked, and then returns it to his or her flavoring bowl, dips it and eats it. (In some restaurants with a large northern Chinese clientele, there may be bowls of cornstarch-water paste at the table as well, so that customers can "velvet" the meat before cooking.) About halfway through the meal, noodles are added to the broth. At the end, the broth is ladled into the condiment bowl until balanced to taste; some noodles are added, and perhaps an egg is swirled into it; the diners drink this "soup."

Mongolian barbecue works the same way, with a similar mixture of ingredients and a bowl of seasonings, but the meats and vegetables are quick-grilled and stuffed into buns for eating.

However, most of the new Mongolian barbecue restaurants in the United States are like a cross between a real Mongolian grill and a Japanese teppanyaki house: The customer fills a bowl with meats or seafoods and vegetables, hands it to a cook who quick-fries it on a huge grill, and then gives it back to the customer for eating.

HOW TO ORDER AND EAT LIKE A NATIVE

Column 1, Column 2

Chinese menus suffer from the same transliteration problems as other Asian cuisines, and the "official" respelling of many names during the 1980s, such as Peking (now Beijing) or Szechwan (now Sichuan), doesn't help much. Nevertheless, most dishes are themselves translated, and after a while, you will begin to recognize the various spellings.

There are several reasons to insist upon seeing the "Chinese" menu in addition to the American one. Not only will it include dozens of dishes probably not listed on the general menu (particularly the organ meats and offal), it is also more likely to put you in the hands of one of the more experienced chefs—and hopefully, one who won't dose your food with the extra sauce he assumes Americans prefer. If there is no other menu, or it's entirely in ideographs, talk to the waiter or manager about recommending dishes. If you see a party of Chinese diners eating something you don't recognize, order that. You might be surprised at how good it tastes. But whatever you get, treat it with respect. If you don't like it, don't make faces. Try a little and take the rest home—with feigned if not sincere pleasure.

Chopsticks are about 4,000 years old and, with a little practice, can be used for almost everything in the kitchen except chopping: mixing, stirring, turning, serving.

Chopsticks are most often made of bamboo (in the United States), but they may also be jade, silver, ivory, fine woods, and even silver; and in the last several years, antique and artisan-crafted chopsticks have become widely available in the United States as well. (Intriguingly, though the Koreans believed that silver would betray poison by turning dark, the Chinese attributed that power to ivory.) If you have them, flaunt them; why waste trees? Besides, plastic chopsticks are slippery, and cheap wooden sticks have a scent that may distract from the food.

Chinese chopsticks are shaped somewhat differently from Japanese chopsticks; Chinese chopsticks are almost always square at the top, where they're held, and rounded in the lower half, the eating part; Japanese chopsticks tend to be either squarish all the way down or even pointed, which many people find easier to master. However, since the Chinese find it acceptable to raise the rice bowl to the lips and shovel with the sticks, it is fairly easy either way.

It is considered unlucky to cross the chopsticks or to let one fall to the floor, and a mismatched pair is said to predict difficult travel. It is considered rude to stick your elbows out, because you may inhibit a neighboring diner. Unfortunately for southpaws, it is also considered less polite to eat with your chopsticks in your left hand, because families traditionally ate gathered around a table with all reaching for food from the middle.

Nearly all Chinese dishes are eaten with chopsticks, and for some dishes, this requires a little practice. Noodles are picked up, bitten off, and allowed to gently slide back into the bowl. For poultry or beef chopped into small pieces with the bones intact, hold onto the bone with the chopsticks and then return it to the plate. Some texts say that when you eat shrimp in their shells, you should pick them up with chopsticks and pop them whole into your mouth, squeeze the meat out with your teeth, and return the shell to the plate with the chopsticks. However, it's easier and just as neat to pick up the shrimp near the tail, squeeze the meat out with the teeth, and replace the shell. Fingers are not allowed in either case. Similarly, bones in fish should be transferred to the plate using the chopsticks.

The Chinese believe that variety in a meal means variety in the preparation styles as well as the ingredients; so a traditional family-style meal would include appetizers; one dish per diner—fish or seafood, meat, poultry, and vegetables, stir-fried, roasted, broiled, steamed, and baked—plus continually replenished soup and rice; and, finally, fruit. Except for the appetizers and fruit, everything is served simultaneously.

When ordering, remember that pork is the favorite meat and so is apt to be offered in the most interesting ways; duck is the second choice. In the Chinese order of courses, incidentally, fish follows the meat and poultry rather than preceding it in the Western fashion. Two people might try hot-and-sour soup and egg-drop soup, tea-smoked duck, and Hunan-style pork. Four people should order a family-size soup with noodles, steamed fish with ginger and scallions or kung pao shrimp, red-cooked chicken,

In Like Yin

According to Taoist philosophy, the entire world is divided into two elements, the feminine (yin) and the masculine (yang). These correspond to "cold" and "hot" humors—in food, in the human body, in animate and inanimate matter. "Hot-humored" food increases energy and circulation; "cold-humored" food is relaxing and cleansing. Lamb is considered hot, beef is warm, and most other meat is neutral; yellow vegetables and beans are neutral, green vegetables are cool, bean curd and mung beans are cold. Peppers are hot, garlic is warm, fruit is cool. Shrimp is hot, crab is cold.

The theory is that foods should be chosen to help balance the body in the cosmic scheme—that is, hot-humored foods should be consumed in the winter, and cool and cold foods in the summer. Consult your Chinese grocer.

twice-cooked pork or beef in five-spice powder, and Sichuan-style green beans or Hunan-style tofu.

Chinese restaurants in the United States are (not surprisingly) somewhat ambivalent about serving meals in the Western fashion, a course at a time, or traditionally, all at once. For the best results, ask to be served Chinese-style. All dishes are shared except rice; each diner has his or her own rice bowl, which may be refilled at any time. Food is taken from the main platter with the chopsticks and either eaten directly or placed in the rice bowl; it can be dipped into a sauce or seasoning in between.

COOKING AT HOME

Although a wok is the easiest way to cook almost any Chinese dish—and addictively adaptable to other cuisines as well—it is perfectly possible to re-create Chinese recipes using casseroles, skillets, saucepans, and so forth. Automatic rice cookers are a great time-saver, and the texture of their rice is more like that of authentic Chinese rice, but they are not essential.

If you are stir-frying a dish, it is important to remember that you cannot simply double a recipe, because the heat will be insufficient and the dish will be thin and soggy. Recipes for four or perhaps six is about the maximum; for more than that, cook in batches.

When entertaining, remember that a meal should consist of at least four elements—meat, seafood, vegetables, and poultry—and varied seasonings and flavors. The table setting should include a soup bowl, rice bowl, plate, flat-bottomed porcelain spoon, small wine cup (like a Japanese sake glass), a teacup, and chopsticks.

CHINESE COOKED RICE

4 cups extra-long-grain rice
3 3/4 cups water

Combine rice and water in pot. Bring water to boil and cook, stirring, about 5 minutes or until water is absorbed. Cover, turn heat to very low, and continue cooking 10 minutes, stirring once or twice. Remove from heat, stir lightly to fluff grains and keep covered; just before serving, fluff again.

RED COOKED PORK

2 tablespoons peanut oil
3 scallions, cut into fourths

3 (1/4-inch) slices peeled fresh ginger
2 cloves garlic, crushed
3 1/2 pounds boneless pork loin, butt, or fresh ham
4 tablespoons dark or mushroom-flavored soy sauce
1/4 cup rice wine or dry sherry
4 tablespoons crushed rock candy crystals (or brown sugar)
1 whole star anise or 2 teaspoons five-spice powder
1 stick cinnamon
pinch salt
3 cups boiling water
1 pound fresh water chestnuts (or large can)

Heat oil in heavy pot or casserole dish; quickly sauté scallions, ginger, and garlic, push aside, and sear meat on all sides. Add soy, wine, sugar, anise, cinnamon, and salt; stir; then add boiling water. Simmer, covered, for about 2 1/2 hours, turning meat every 30 minutes. If using fresh water chestnuts, prepare by boiling 30 minutes and peeling off shell and membrane; add after 1 1/2 hours. If using canned, rinse and drain and add for last 30 minutes. (Add boiling water as needed.)

HONEY-ROASTED DUCK

1 4–5 pound duck, rinsed and patted dry
coarse salt
3 cloves garlic, crushed
3 scallions, minced
3 tablespoons dark soy
3 tablespoons rice wine or dry sherry
2 1/2 tablespoons honey

Preheat oven to 350°F. Rub duck lightly, inside and out, with salt; with the point of a sharp knife cut small slits in the skin without piercing the meat. Combine garlic, scallions, soy, and wine. Mix 1/4 cup of mixture (about half) with honey and rub the combination into skin; let dry, then repeat. Pour the rest of the reserved spice mixture into duck cavity and place, breast side up, on a rack in a roasting pan with about 1 inch water (add more as needed). Roast about 1 1/2 hours (check beginning at 1 hour), frequently basting with any remaining honey mixture thinned with hot water.

JAPAN

BASIC CUISINE

DINNER FOR TWO:
Sashimi, shrimp tempura, beef negimaki

DINNER FOR FOUR:
Sushi, soft-shell crabs, tempura, grilled fish, yakitori

GROUP DISH:
Shabu-shabu

In Japanese culture, the greatest art is that of understatement. The two guiding principles of Japanese life and design are *wabi* (quiet and simplicity) and *sabi* (understated elegance). Poetry, painting, music, manners, fashion, even food preparation, all are polished to a concentrated purity. The observer is meant to contemplate the simplicity of any object and "see" not just the result but also the intricate process by which it was created. It wasn't a Japanese artist who defined sculpture as cutting away all the stone that was not the statue within, but that is a philosophy any Japanese chef would understand. In most cuisines flavors are blended, but in Japanese cuisine flavors are distinct and meant to be appreciated individually—in harmony rather than in concert.

Another great tenet of Japanese culture is also alluded to in the cuisine: All of nature is interrelated. In the most formal traditional meals, called *kaiseki*, nature determines not only the menu but also the metaphors. Nothing

STYLE:
Light, subtle, austere

KEY FLAVORS:
Soy sauce, vinegar, wasabi, ginger pickle

EATING UTENSILS:
Chopsticks, spoons, fingers

DISTINCTIVE DISHES:
Sushi, sashimi, teriyaki, tempura

UNIFORMITY OF MENUS:
Good

NUTRITIONAL INDEX:
Low fat, high protein, high carbohydrate, high sodium

COST:
Moderate

"THANK YOU":
"Domo arigato"

should be eaten out of season, lest the harmony of the diners be disturbed; live flowers or foliages are used for garnish; even kimonos and table decorations are changed to reflect the seasons. Although it is a fading art, sushi chefs (or *itamae*) trained in the old-fashioned way—with apprenticeships lasting for 10 to 15 years—can create landscapes and seasonal symbols using masterfully cut fish, shellfish, vegetables, and seaweed. Translucently thin sheets of daikon radish, themselves a marvel of knifework, are cross-hatched into "fishermen's nets" in which tiny shrimp or smelts are hopelessly tangled. Squid may be cut into matchsticks, fashioned into a bird's nest, and served with a quail egg yolk inside. More common are roses formed of sashimi petals—white blooms of flounder or blushing red snapper, red roses of tuna—that appear on mixed sushi-sashimi platters.

THE COUNTRY

Although it is often referred to as an island, Japan is actually four large islands and nearly 4,000 smaller ones. This island chain stretches 1,750 miles, from the snow-covered mountains of Hokkaido almost to the Tropic of Cancer—a latitude stretch roughly matching that from Montreal to the Yucatán. Much of the land is either mountainous or forested, with heavy rainfall in the summer and monsoons from late June to early July, particularly on Hokkaido, a scenic wilderness with vast areas for hiking, skiing, and fishing.

The largest island is the intensely developed Honshu, just smaller than the state of California but with a population three times as large—93 million. Honshu includes Tokyo (formerly Edo), as well as Yokohama, Osaka, Hiroshima, and Kyoto, which was the capital of Japan for most of its history. Honshu is agriculturally as well as politically the "big island," as it contains many of the productive rice fields. These fields remain a prickly issue: Because rice is a unique symbol of Japanese traditional culture, Japan is still reluctant to allow Western imports; however, growing sufficient rice for its own consumption requires the cultivation of vast parcels of land, the one resource Japan can least afford. At the same time, younger Japanese no longer consume rice as previous generations did, having absorbed the McFries habit as well as toast for breakfast; and the agricultural economy is increasingly overshadowed by manufacturing and high-tech interests.

THE HISTORY

Not much is known about Japan's aboriginal inhabitants, called the Jomon after a particular style of pottery they created, but they may have emigrated from Siberia and the Korean peninsula and concentrated in the area north of what is now Tokyo. An animistic culture, they considered the relatively bounteous islands a paradise and introduced the worship of nature that would eventually evolve into the Shinto faith.

Honshu is a long thin crescent, squeezed between the Pacific on the east and the Sea of Japan on the west, so it is not surprising that the Japanese developed such a fine distinction for fresh fish. Because there was so great a variety and so constant a fresh supply, there was less reason to preserve proteins than in countries more vulnerable to seasonal shortages: There was some pickling and a bit of salt-curing—sushi actually evolved around the seventh century from a method of curing meat and fish by salting it and storing it in rice until it fermented—but little smoking, hard-curing, or drying. (This old-fashioned fermented sushi, called *narezushi*, is still served in a few places, but it's definitely an acquired taste.)

Rice itself took hold in the third century B.C.E. with the Yayoi (also named for their pottery), who brought with them the dredging and flooding techniques of rice cultivation. Rice provided not only food but also drink (the potent *sake*).

Sometime in the mid-sixth century, Buddhism—which entered Japan via Korea—became the official religion of the Japanese court. Although Buddhism in Japan gradually blended with secular Confucian and pantheistic Shinto practices, it remained a pervasive influence. It is the reason that meat dishes are so few and so relatively simple, since the Japanese were (at least officially) forbidden to eat meat for some 1,200 years (see the description of *sukiyaki* below). It was the Chinese Buddhists, incidentally, who introduced the soybean into Japan, where it quickly was recognized for its healthfulness and versatility.

Two of Those . . .

How can you tell whether a restaurant serves sushi? If it's not on the sign—and frequently even if it is—there is likely to be a display of plastic but quite realistic sushi in the window, hearkening back to a time when most ordinary customers could not read. If the plastic delicacies are not visible, there will be a poster or picture menu instead. And you are entirely welcome to use the picture menu as a "cheat sheet" or even to point to what you want.

In the middle of the sixteenth century, the evangelical and commercially ambitious Portuguese fleet stumbled onto Japan and attempted to establish a monopoly on Japanese trade—and, being as aggressively Catholic as mercantile, to convert the country as well. The equally ambitious but Protestant Dutch traders soon followed, however, and fearing both the influence of the ecclesiastical orders and a war over trade routes, Tokugawa Ieyasu, the shogun made famous by James Clavell's novel, effectively sealed Japan off from the outside world for nearly 250 years.

Before their expulsion, however, the Europeans left their marks, and not just among the baptized. *Tempura*, or batter-fried fish and vegetables, was a Portuguese contribution to Japanese cuisine; the name comes from "quattuor tempora," the "Ember Days" during which observant Catholics had to abjure meat and so turned to ways of making fish a more varied substitute. Ieyasu became so fond of this "foreign delicacy" that he died of a surfeit of tempura, according to some historians. Sugar, corn, chicken, and potatoes, along with the tobacco that remains a Japanese staple, were all New World items then newly discovered and quickly passed along the trade routes by these avid colonizers; more gradually pork and beef entered the general repertoire.

When Commodore Perry forced the reopening of Japan to trade in the mid-nineteenth century, Japanese professionals and scholars were stunned to discover how far Western medicine and science had progressed. To symbolize his desire to become part of the "civilized world,"—or perhaps to surrender to it—in 1872 Japan's emperor ate beef in public for the first time in more than a millennium. This was the first step toward breaking the meat-eating taboo in Japan.

THE CUISINE

Rice, miso soup, *sashimi* (plain raw seafood), and seaweed are all staples of the Japanese diet, but first among equals, as in so many Asian diets, is rice—so much so that the common words for breakfast, lunch, and dinner are *asagohan*, *hirugohan*, and *bangohan*—literally, morning rice, midday rice, and evening rice. In fact, *gohan* by itself can mean either rice or a meal. Rice is believed to have been given to the Japanese directly by the goddess Amaterasu, and as her direct descendent, it is the emperor's duty—even today—to cultivate some small plot of rice himself.

Although vastly bastardized versions of sukiyaki and tempura have been made in the United States for 50 years, sushi has been the breakthrough for most Americans, overcoming a widespread cultural squeamishness over raw fish to become the most popular ethnic lunch since pizza. Sushi bars, or *sushi-ya*, are only one type of Japanese restaurant, however. Among the other major varieties are the *robata* grills, which cook meats, fish, and vegetables over hot charcoal; noodle houses, also called *soba-ya*, which offer the hot, cold, wet, or dry noodle dishes that are the fast foods of Japan; and (in the United States) *teppanyaki* restaurants, those with the huge, hot, steel grills for tables. There are also the more traditional *shokuji dokoro* establishments, which serve a variety of traditional or semi-formal entrees; *nomi-ya*, neighborhood taverns; tempura kitchens, which like the Calabash buffets of North Carolina lay out reams of fried shrimp and vegetables; and occasionally the single-style specialty houses that quick-fix *yakitori*—literally, grilled chicken, but also including skewers of grilled shrimp, tofu, and vegetables.

Yoshoku-ya, the restaurants specializing in Japanese adaptations of Western dishes, such as fried oysters (*kaki furai*), beef stew, curries, croquettes (*korokke*), and even spaghetti, date from that first era of European fleets and remain popular today. In fact *tonkatsu*, the Japanese version of Wiener schnitzel or country-fried pork, is so popular that some expensive restaurants are devoted almost exclusively to its production. Other originally Western dishes include *hayashi-raisu*, a version of hashed beef that includes fried beef and onions, soy sauce, ketchup, and Worcestershire sauce; and *omu-raisu*, a sort of omelet stuffed with chicken pilaf and topped with ketchup. There is even a version of hoppin' john, called *sekihan*, which is sweet rice mixed with black-eyed peas; it is a sort of pinkish color and is usually served at weddings for luck.

Sushi bars may well have robotayaki food and probably traditional one-pot meals as well. Shokuji dokoro restaurants may well have a small sushi bar, or just a "service bar" in the kitchen; teppanyaki steakhouses, responding to the sushi craze, now are likely to have at least a small sushi bar as well.

In passing we should note that these "Japanese steakhouses" are only minimally authentic. The inventor of the knife-juggling routine was a publicity-savvy sportsman and adventurer named "Rocky" Aoki, one of those corporate millionaires who tried several times to circle the globe in a hot-air balloon and who believed (correctly, obviously) that Americans would pay more for prime flesh if it came with some prime-time flash. However, few of the chain restaurants in America actually employ Japanese cooks—which scarcely matters, in any case—and the beef is usually not Kobe or any other Japanese specialty.

You should also remember that at a teppanyaki house, where each grill (and cook) serves up to a dozen customers at a time, you are almost certainly going to be seated with a group of strangers, which can be fun as long as you're prepared for it. In fact, it's a great way to spend the evening if you're traveling by yourself.

THE MAIN INGREDIENTS

The "holy trinity," as Emeril might say, of Japanese cuisine are rice, tea, and sake; the names of these three receive the honorific prefix "o-" generally reserved for social superiors. Rice is called *gohan* once it is cooked ("go-" is a Chinese remnant form of "o-"); uncooked, it is called *kome* or *o-kome*. Rice for sushi, tossed with seasoned vinegar, is called *shari*. Gohan is traditionally served at breakfast as well as lunch and dinner— a combination of cereal, bread, and potato. The Japanese prefer a short-grained rice, which clumps a bit and so is easy to pick up with chopsticks; they also prefer a sweet grain for making sushi rice.

O-sake is also a rice product, and although it is primarily for drinking, it is also used for marinating, simmering, and flavoring food. *Mirin* is cooking wine; *kasuzake* is the mash left from the fermenting process and is used for marinades. *Su* is rice vinegar, essential for sushi rice. Tea is *cha* or, more politely, *o-cha*. You may also hear tea referred to as *agari*, but that is a slang term to be used only when sitting at a sushi bar.

SOY PRODUCTS The second most important food in the Japanese diet is the soybean. Although most Americans only recognize soy in soy sauce, it is perhaps the most prolific of vegetables. Among the other most common ingredients are *tofu* (bean curd cakes, either firm, silken, or fried) and *miso*, the fermented soybean paste that comes in a range of qualities, from the sweeter "white miso" (really yellow) that is used in *miso shiro* soup to pungent, saltier dark red and even brown pastes used to marinate fish and meat. (Miso can also be made from soy with the rice mold *koji* or with barley.) *Natto*, a fermented soybean paste, is pungent and sour and is the sort of flavor many Americans find too strong—and their Japanese friends find funny.

Shoyu, or soy sauce, also ranges from light (and now "lite") to dark. Japanese soy sauce, unlike the Chinese and American varieties, is fermented for up to two years before being bottled, and some particularly fine shoyu is even older. Soybeans are also eaten fresh; boiled in their pods and lightly salted, they are called *edamame* and are frequently offered as a snack food or appetizer—the beer nuts of Japan.

SEASONINGS Monosodium glutamate (MSG), or *ajinomoto*, used to be habitually included in Japanese dishes; in fact, though the English language only defines four kinds of flavors—salty, sweet, bitter, and sour—the Japanese have a fifth term just for that MSG taste, which occurs naturally in seaweeds. However, in deference to the increasing dislike many Americans have for MSG (what we used to call Accent and throw on every piece of meat in the kitchen), more Japanese and even other Asian restaurants are eliminating it from the pantry. The tiny shaker on your table today is more likely to be *sansho* or *togarashi*, the Japanese equivalents of ground black or chili peppers (*akatogarashi*). These are not true peppercorns but a minty, lemon-scented plant; the dried red chilies are for real, however. Other familiar seasonings include garlic, ginger (both the familiar type, called *shoga*, and a milder, more oniony "mountain ginger" called *myoga*), cinnamon, cardamom, cloves, and sugar. *Shishimi*, literally "seven-spice powder," is a blend of poppy seeds, akato chilies, sesame seeds, hemp seeds, sansho, finely ground *nori* (see "Life in the Sushi Lane") and dried orange peel.

The most distinctive herb is *shiso* (called perilla in other Asian cuisines), which is usually translated as "beefsteak plant," though it tastes like a cross between its cousins, basil and mint. A slightly fuzzy, saw-tooth-edged green (or, more rarely, purple or red) leaf, it is frequently served whole or julienned with sashimi. Occasionally, it is served tempura-fried. Sesame seeds and sesame oil are also popular flavorings, and so are the pickled green plums used to produce a vinegar (umeboshi) that is among the major sour elements.

Incidentally, one of the apparently odder, very Western additions to the Japanese menu, Worcestershire sauce, which is frequently served with fried dishes such as oysters and tonkatsu, isn't as strange as it seems. After all, it's believed that the original Lea & Perrins sauce was discovered when an Indian spice vinegar, probably containing shoyu, was left to ferment at the merchants' office in England and exploded. So the Japanese were probably dipping into a similar dish long before we were.

CONDIMENTS Pickled vegetables, called tsukemono, are an essential part of the Japanese diet, and among the most common are cucumbers, eggplant, cabbage, lotus root (renkon), and daikon and daikon greens. The daikon is the radish world's giant, frequently reaching three feet in length and weighing several pounds. It is extremely popular in Japanese recipes and may be grated into sauces or shredded as "salad" under sashimi or sushi as well as boiled, braised, and grilled. Its peppery-flavored sprouts are also popular as garnishes. Pickled ginger (wari) is the invariable complement to sushi, and with sushi also comes the hot grated or powdered green "horseradish" called wasabi.

FRUITS AND VEGETABLES Despite the popular emphasis on seafood, Japanese cuisine includes plenty of vegetables: burdock (gobo); squash (kabocha); gourds (kanpyo); the mild small eggplant (nasu); the small, warty Japanese cucumbers (kyuri); bean sprouts; snow peas; and carrots, all of which may be served alongside broiled meats, in soups, or as the ubiquitous pickles. Sansai, or "mountain vegetables," are spring greens, including ferns and ground wort; boiled to remove bitterness, they sometimes substitute for spinach. What is frequently called Chinese cabbage in

---

Fat Is Beautiful

In this Buddhist society, meat-eaters (i.e., Europeans) were considered not merely unclean but completely soulless—which only goes to show that the Japanese have displayed their usual dispatch by turning Kobe beef into a byword for quality. For price, too: Real Kobe beef comes from steers that are fed and even overfed a rich diet so that they develop a high degree of fat; then they are massaged and pounded so that the fat marbles all the way through the meat, making it even richer—and more expensive. Kobe beef, in other words, is the sumo wrestler of the meat-packing industry.

America (or Napa cabbage in California) is called *hakusai* in Japan and is most frequently used in soups or for pickling. There are several kinds of yams, including a small sweet potato that worked its way from North America via the Spanish empire to the Philippines to China and finally Japan; and the so-called mountain potato, which has a sticky, tapiocalike juice and is served either boiled or raw. Scallions are common, particularly a large variety called *negi* (as in *negimaki* or *negimayaki*, marinated beef rolled around braised onions); white bulb onions are used in soups, casseroles, and tempura. Among the sweet peppers is the green *shishito-garashi*, literally, "Chinese lion's head pepper," because of its curly mane shape.

Mushrooms are a treasured ingredient and range from the tiny, white, bulb-headed *enoki* to the familiar *shiitake* or "forest mushrooms" to the large, meaty, and briefly available *matsutake* (usually found in autumn), which grow on pine trees (*matsu*) and are served broiled like a steak or simmered with rice. *Nameko* are orange or yellow and have a rich, almost rot-sweet, earthy smell; *shimeji* have plump white stems and brown tops, like cremini; wood-ear mushrooms (*kikurage*) are sold dried and then reconstituted; they are sometimes called jelly mushrooms because of their consistency.

Mizuna, the deeply serrated leaf now popular in the salad mix called mesclun, is a Japanese favorite, as is *mitsuba* ("three leaves"), something like celery greens. Among other greens frequently seen are fiddlehead ferns, chrysanthemum greens (*shungiku*), and pepper-tree leaves (*kinome*), similar to cilantro or watercress.

But next to pickles, the most important traditional vegetables in the Japanese diet, and an essential source of nutrients dating back thousands of years, come from the sea—seaweeds. The most common varieties are *nori*, which is actually leaver or algae; *kombu*, the giant kelp, which is used to make the basic broth called *dashi* as well as *kobucha* (a sort of health tea) and is used in salads and soups; *nonia*, which provides vitamins A, D, and B_{12}; the brownish green *wakame*, which supplies vitamins C and iodine; the blackish *hijiki*; and the reddish, frilly *tengusa*.

The Japanese don't eat a great variety of fruits, but they are particularly fond of persimmons (*kaki*), which isn't surprising, considering the number of poems and paintings in which they appear; golf ball–sized grapes; various melons; pineapples; and a hybrid citrus fruit called *yuzu,* not unlike the citron in flavor. The astringent *ume*, or green plum, is prized primarily for cooking rather than eating.

NOODLES The Japanese are notoriously addicted to noodles: fat, skinny, doughy, ethereal, white, brown, or green. They eat them morning, noon, train commute, and night. (The most popular fast-food version, those skinny little *ramen* noodles sold either dried in waves or in instant-soup cups, is another Chinese invention: *Ramen* is the Japanese transliteration of "lo mein.") The generic term is *menrui*; among the most popular are *udon*, the soft, fat, friendly noodles used in *nabeyaki udon* soup; *somen*, the thin vermicelli served chilled in summer; *harusame,* called bean threads or cellophane noodles; *soba*, the buckwheat noodles that are an entire cuisine in Japan, where they are still handmade and where there are still restaurants devoted to their service; and *cha-soba*, buckwheat noodles flavored and colored with green tea. At soba-ya, some particular combinations of noodles and toppings are very old and specific: One, the *okame*, is actually laid out so that the vegetables resemble the face of a beautiful woman ("okame") of the Heian era.

DAIRY PRODUCTS Although these are clearly Western imports and come relatively late into the Japanese pantry, dairy products are becoming more common (just as, ironically, Japanese-style soy milks are becoming more popular in the United States). Mayonnaise, cream cheese, and even homogenized cheese show up in sushi occasionally; more commonly, mayonnaise is the condiment of choice on the crêpe or omelet called *otonomiyaki.*

LIFE IN THE SUSHI LANE

Stepping into a sushi bar, especially for a novice, can be one of the most atmospherically transporting experiences in dining. As you duck through the printed blue cloth "doors" called *noren,* which are hung out as the "open" sign, you hear the formal welcoming cry, "*Irasshaimase!*" A waitress in kimono bows before you, the sushi chefs nod their bandana'd heads, and you are truly in another world. Some would consider it heaven.

The difference between sashimi and sushi is the presence (or presentation) of rice: Sashimi is served by itself, whereas sushi is either draped over a bite-sized roll of seasoned rice (the style called *nigiri*), rolled with rice and nori sheets into logs and sliced (called *maki* or rolled sushi), or served as a "hand roll," *temaki*, an ice cream cone–shaped nori sheet half-filled with rice and then topped with fish. (Nori is a sheet of dark green "paper," usually referred to as seaweed but actually composed of algae.)

Some of the more fluid shellfish, such as sea urchin, salmon roe, and scallops, are cradled in a sort of sideways nigiri: A strip of nori is wound around a small ball of rice, leaving a lip like a soufflé collar, and then the seafood is spooned in.

Oshizushi, or "pressed sushi," is a sandwich affair prepared in a wooden box; seasoned rice is placed in the bottom, layered with assorted fish, topped with more rice, and then pressed and sliced into what looks like petit fours. *Chirashizushi* is an assortment of sushi left unassembled, in effect—a box or bowl of seasoned rice topped with sliced raw fish, ginger, a dash of sugar (dyed festively red), and wasabi, the water-grown herb usually compared to horseradish—and you can eat the items in whatever order you choose. There are also many kinds of formal and decorative sushi carefully arranged to form flowers or cranes, rolled and sliced to reveal fillings that swirl like waves, flower petals, or checkerboards, and so on.

Not all sushi involves raw fish, incidentally; novices with qualms might prefer to start with shrimp, crab, eel, octopus, salmon, or egg-omelet sushi (*tamago*), which are all precooked, or one of the vegetable or American-style rolls. (*Surimi*, or "crab stick," is what we know in this country as "sea treats" or crab-flavored fish bits; made of a variety of white fish seasoned to taste like crab, they are used in California rolls and are also a safe bet even for those allergic to real crab.) What might be called new American sushi, in fact, is a burgeoning field: Virtually every Japanese restaurant has at least one "signature" roll that incorporates American ingredients (mayonnaise, chili sauce, or even Cajun spices) or mixes and matches seafoods for a bigger-is-better effect.

There are many sorts of vegetarian sushi rolls featuring asparagus, cucumber (*kappamaki*), umeboshi, burdock root, spinach, and various pickles. (You might enjoy knowing that kappamaki is so called because cucumbers are the favorite food of a Japanese river troll or gnome called a *kappa*.) Two other popular options are *futomaki*, the "fat roll" of veggies and egg, and *inari-zushi*, which is sushi rice stuffed into thin tofu skins soaked in syrup. Like kappamaki, inari-zushi has a legend behind its name: Inari is the Japanese god of grains, and his messenger was a fox, whose favorite food, for some reason, was fried tofu.

Because of its vast popularity, and because of the Japanese drive to master the market, sushi is fairly easy to order. Many sushi chefs know the English words for fish even if that's all the English they do know; besides, on the table there is almost always a "cheat sheet" of pictures to go by. If you're sitting at the sushi bar, you can just point. The following is a list of the most common types of seafood you are likely to encounter.

Clams appear in at least a half-dozen varieties, ranging in size, color, and pungency as well as resilience; they include the almost rubbery abalone (*awabi*), large and small scallops (*kaibashira* and *kobashira*), the giant geoduck (*mirugai*), red clams, surf clams, and cockles (*torigai*), as well as cherrystones, littlenecks (*asari*), and other American regional varieties.

Crab may be either real, in which case it's called *kani*, or the imitation crab stick used in California rolls. Soft-shell crabs are increasingly popular in sushi, tempura-fried and served either in maki or hand-rolls. They're so popular, in fact, that they're available nearly year-round, which is a giveaway that many are frozen rather than fresh—but in truth, even the frozen ones are pretty good.

Eel also comes in two "flavors," freshwater (*unagi*), sometimes called conger, or saltwater (*anago*). They have very similar tastes, resembling smoked trout; though unagi is a trifle lighter in color and flavor and is frequently served as a main dish broiled and glazed with a sweet sauce over rice (*unagi donburi*). Unagi is so popular in Japan, where it is believed to restore energy and potency, that there are restaurants called *unagi-yas* that specialize in eel dishes. It's also the traditional dish to served on Doyo-no-hi, the hottest day of summer—to keep up your strength, don't you know. **Dojo**, which resemble baby eels but are actually small fish called loach, is a old blue-collar dish and also has its own restaurants; but they have not as yet become an export delicacy.

Flounder (*hirame*) is a term that in this country may be used to cover a number of flatfish or flukes and whitefish, including halibut, sole (*karei*), turbot, bream, and sea bass (*suzuki*), even though these are considered distinct in Japan. All are extremely mild-flavored fish, low in oils.

Fugu, or globefish or blowfish, though famous for its potentially lethal thrill (sushi chefs must be specially licensed to prepare it), is extremely rare in the United States, but precleaned frozen fugu is beginning to be available in the largest metropolitan cities. You're more likely to find *hire-zake,* which is a mug of hot sake infused by broiled fugu fin (which is not poisonous). Even if it were worth the risk, you may wonder if it's worth the price. In Japan, fugu is found both wild and farmed; it has a clean, stony flavor, like water from limestone, and is turned into a six-course banquet using all the nontoxic parts, including the milt. In the United States, only the flesh and some skin is common.

Mackerel sushi may be either Spanish mackerel (*saba*), king, or horse mackerel (*aji*); all are strong-flavored, oily fish with a grayish flesh; with their blue-striped skin, they resemble those leaping fish so often seen at the bottom of serving bowls, and indeed they were probably the models. If you are given a taste of mackerel cured in salt and vinegar, it's called *shimesaba.*

Octopus (*tako*) is almost always served cooked, even when served in salads, unless it is quite young and tender. (You can tell, because boiled octopus is red and white; raw octopus is actually gray.) It is somewhat chewy and surprisingly mild. Tiny whole octopus are boiled, glazed with a sweet sauce, and eaten whole.

Oysters (*kaki*) may be served raw on the half-shell dashed with a *ponzu* sauce of vinegar, grated radish, and chopped scallions (they beat Rockefeller every time); or served in the seaweed "cups" mentioned above. The most popular way to have oysters in Japan, however, is battered in *panko* (Japanese bread crumbs), fried, and dipped into Worcestershire sauce.

Red snapper (*tai*) is a particularly light and sweet-fleshed fish, good for beginners; the term is sometimes used to cover other similar fish, including red sea bream, perch, rockfish, or porgy.

Roe is very popular as a sushi ingredient. Among the most common varieties are the large orange salmon roe (*ikura*), usually served in one of those seaweed "collars" of nori and topped with a raw quail egg; the small, crunchy, poppy-red flying fish roe (*tobiko*), also used in California rolls; and smelt roe (*masago*) and herring roe (*kazunoko*), both of which are most often served still in the whole fish. Though salty, Japanese roes are not as briny as traditional caviar. Recently, many sushi bars have taken to adding chili or pepper sauce to tobiko paste to make what's called "spicy tuna roll," another example of indigenous American sushi.

You can also sometimes find wasabi tobiko, which is roe soaked in wasabi so that it is bright green instead of orange, served in a seaweed collar on rice—be warned, it can pack quite a punch.

Salmon is called *sake*, just like the drink, but without the honorific "o-" given the beverage; it can also be pronounced *sha-ke*, which is sort of blue-collar dialect but prevents confusion for those not yet confident around the sushi bar. At the sushi bar, sake usually refers to smoked salmon, but fresh (that is, raw) salmon is also available. As a main course, it might be salted, smoked, pan-broiled, or simmered in sake— the drinking kind. It is also popular in the dish called *shio-yaki*, in which fish is crusted in coarse salt and then broiled.

Sardines (*iwashi*) and **shad**, or *kohada*, may be served whole either as an appetizer or as sushi or, when full of roe, grilled.

Sea urchin (*uni*) is actually the gonads of the animal, a mustard gold or even orange custard whose originally delicate flavor quickly grows pungent and even bitter; in this case, quality is measured in days, if not hours. Even fresh, it has a distinctive and unique—one might almost say decadent—flavor; I usually describe it as tasting the way the sea smells.

Shrimp (*ebi*), is usually served boiled, even for sushi; but at more sophisticated sushi bars—or those with greater faith in their patrons— they may be served raw as a treat, in which case they are called *odori*, "dancing." (Really favored customers may get their shrimp only moments from live, anyway.) The most common treatment of shrimp, of course, is tempura, even when it is served in soups. It is also grilled. **Amaebi** are small "sweet shrimp" that indeed have a sweeter taste and slightly more gelatinous texture than regular shrimp. They will probably arrive with the heads still on but the body peeled down to the last tiny tail shell. Bite right behind the heads and eat the rest whole. The heads may be brought back later, fried and crunchy and served with a tempura dipping sauce. Don't worry; they'll be so crisp and brittle, particularly the long antenna, you'll think you're eating some sort of shrimp-flavored chip.

Squid (*ika*) is a translucent white (not unlike onion) and is served both raw and cooked. Depending on the size of the squid, it can be chewy and occasionally has a sort of soapy texture; but the flavor is mild and assumes whatever sauce it's served with. However, it wants gentle handling or it will turn tough; if it reminds you of rubber tires, as the saying goes, it's most likely the restaurant's fault, not the squid's.

Trout (*masu*) has quickly become popular for sashimi, sushi, and grilling. (Similarly, both orange roughy and tilapia, suddenly so chic among importers, are beginning to show up on the menu.)

Tuna (*maguro*) is probably the most famous sashimi and sushi fish in the world—although surprisingly, it wasn't particularly popular in Japan itself until about 200 years ago. A deep red, it tastes quite a bit like filet mignon and is surprisingly easy to swallow, even for the most dubious first-timers. You may see various species listed, but the ones usually used for sushi are bluefin (the best and the most common), yellowfin, and bigeye. *Tekkamaki*, or maguro roll, was probably the first maki roll made, since "tekka-ba" refers to a gambling house; the rolls were thrown together so the gamblers could eat without missing a hand.

Toro is an extra-rich (because it's extra-fatty) portion of the tuna belly; its seasonal availability, like that of soft-shell crabs, seems to have widened considerably, thanks to the commercial smarts of seafood wholesalers. Some will find its oiliness off-putting, but it grows on you, as they say. **Chutoro**, or near-toro, is a sort of half-and-half, richer than the lean maguro but not quite as buttery as toro. **Tataki**, skipjack tuna, is sometimes available as sashimi and is also half-rich. **Bonita** is a strong-flavored variety usually served seared to cut the flavor; bonita is even more important in Japanese cooking because the flakes of the dried fish, called *katsuobushi*, are, along with *kombu*, the ingredients for the *dashi* that is the basic broth of all soups and casseroles.

Yellowtail (*hamachi*) is, like the mackerel, a branch of the tuna family, with cream-colored flesh blending to a brownish-red and with a buttery, almost mushroomy flavor. Because of its richness, it is often combined with either scallions or the basil-like shiso; its jaw, with its meaty cheek, is a very popular grill dish. Incidentally, if you see *buri* on the menu, it's also hamachi, only full-grown, at least three years old.

The condiments traditionally served with sushi or sashimi are soy sauce, pickled ginger (*gari*), and wasabi, the hot green spread that is sometimes called Japanese horseradish but which is actually related to the hollyhock (the name may mean "mountain hollyhock"). Soy sauce is mixed with vinegar, citrus juice, and grated daikon radish to make either ponzu or tempura-dipping sauce; *nuta* sauce, usually served with spinach or octopus appetizers, is a thick miso paste. Sashimi is usually framed with edible decorations, either seaweed, radishes, or pickles. (See "How to Order and Eat Like a Native.")

Incidentally, if your sushi is served with scissored green plastic "doilies" underneath, you're seeing the last remnant of really traditional sushi service: In the old days, sushi was served on fresh banana leaves, cut into artistic shapes, because the leaves—like daikon and wasabi—contain a natural antibacterial agent. The shape seen most frequently nowadays, with two "feelers" at one end and jagged sawteeth on the sides, originally imitated a shrimp. Otherwise, if the garnishes look edible, they most likely are.

At the sushi bar, you will probably be served on wooden platters that the itamae will place before you; then, as you order, he will reach over the glass partition and place the sushi directly onto your plate. At the bar, you may receive your sushi a few pieces at a time, particularly if you order verbally and directly from the chef; or it may be prepared all at once, especially if you mark up a sushi ticket. A few trendier restaurants have set up conveyor belts to whisk sushi orders down the length of the bar; some even have tiny rivers and set the sushi on miniature boats to ride the stream to the customer. Somehow, though, these systems lack the personal touch.

Speaking of the personal touch, if you wish to tip your sushi chef, it is completely acceptable to offer him money directly over the counter; however, in this country, most people simply add it to the general bill.

THE MAIN DISHES

APPETIZERS The Japanese, with their love for artful restraint, long ago mastered what "nouvelle" chefs talk of now: grazing. (Kaiseki is, after all, the ultimate in presentation dining, and pretty near cuisine minceur, at that.) *Otsumani* are the nibbling things, to be eaten either as you drink away the evening or just as a warm-up to dinner—the tapas of Japan.

Virtually all Japanese meals begin with soup, either miso shiru, a cloudy soy paste broth with tofu and scallions in it (frequently served with a bean sprout salad), or suimono, a simple broth with sliced mushrooms. Sashimi is the most commonly ordered first course, but there are many intermediate choices, including gyoza, the Japanese version of fried dumplings; ika soba, squid julienned into soba noodles; and the particularly fine ankimo, a steamed mousse of monkfish liver so delicate that it's frequently referred to as "foie gras of the sea." Sunomono refers to vinegar-tossed salads or seafood appetizers; aemono are similar, but may have a more elaborate dressing. Boiled spinach (or other seasonal greens) with sesame seeds (goma-ae) and sliced octopus in miso dressing (tako nuta) are both very popular, for instance. Many restaurants offer a Western-style salad as well. Regular customers are often served a tidbit or two before ordering: a tiny whole octopus grilled and glazed, a morsel of boiled taro, or grilled mushrooms. Small orders of sushi and sashimi specials are sometimes offered as appetizers, too.

ONE-POT DISHES Japanese are fond of soups and casseroles, usually featuring either rice or noodles, although many noodle dishes, particularly those with broth, are served with rice on the side. Nabeyaki udon is a rich soup with shrimp tempura, chicken, vegetables, and thick udon noodles, often with an egg cracked over the top to poach. Yosenabe is a lighter seafood and vegetable version. Kamameshi is a rice stew; chazuke is rice with green tea poured over it. Oden is a sort of winter root stew, very hearty, full of potatoes, taro, fish cakes, greens, and tofu. Sukiyaki is a sort of fondue or stew of beef, vegetables, and tofu that are sautéed, then simmered in a sweet-and-soy broth; shabu-shabu, which uses a plainer broth (or just plain boiling water) and cooks for very short times (only a few seconds in some cases), is a derivative of the Mongolian hot pot—another Chinese inheritance.

Donburis are the original "rice bowl" dishes; the two best-known types are *unagi donburi*, which is topped with broiled glazed eel, and *oyaku donburi*, a combination of teriyaki chicken and egg (it's sort of a pun on "mother and child" donburi). Although it may surprise you, curry is one of Japan's most popular adopted foods. It's generally called *kairi raisu* (say it out loud), although it's more like the soupier American version of curry than the Indian or Thai originals. It comes topped or tossed with chicken, fried pork, scallops, grilled fish, and so forth. However, it's most frequently found at specialty carryouts and the few homestyle or street-fare restaurants located in Japanese neighborhoods.

Mushimono refers to steamed dishes; the best-known is *chawan mushi*, a nonsweet hot custard so named because it's prepared in a sort of teacup *(cha wan)*; it's studded with tidbits of chicken, shrimp, and gingko nuts baked in.

A dish that hasn't made much headway in the United States yet is *okonomiyaki*, or "pick-your-own" omelet. To a batter of flour and egg and a base of thin-sliced cabbage, the customers at an otonomiyaki restaurant add their choice of pork, beef, squid, shrimp, and so on; stir it up; and cook it on tabletop griddles. The customary seasonings are crumbled nori, katsuobushi, and mayonnaise.

MEATS AND POULTRY Sukiyaki, as mentioned, is a sweet-soy stew; customers fondue thin-sliced meat and vegetables in the pot, then eat it over rice. In restaurants where sukiyaki is offered in single portions instead of as a group dish, it may all be put together in the kitchen and served cooked, Tokyo-style. Shabu-shabu is its plainer cousin, in which the ingredients are dipped by the diners into simmering water; by the end of the meal the water evolves into a rich broth, noodles are added, and the customer drinks the soup, completing the meal. According to one explanation, sukiyaki got its name from a time when Buddhist emperors forbade people to eat meat. Defying this rule, poor farmers in the fields surreptitiously broiled food ("yaki" meaning "grilled") over campfires on the back of their iron farming tools (one translation of "suki" is "plow" or "shovel"). A slightly different version has it that even after meat was allowed, old habits were hard to break; rather than contaminate household pots, cooks fashioned cooking grills from old shovels. Shabu-shabu is said to have been named for the sibilant sound of beef being waved across boiling water—the Japanese equivalent of *shwooosh, shwooosh.*

Among other beef dishes still commonly served are negimayaki, beef rolled up around sliced scallions and broiled, then pinwheel-sliced; and teriyaki, a glazed and broiled chicken or beef. These days, in Japan as well as in America, one may see what is called "beef sashimi"—the Japanese version of carpaccio. Korean-style marinated beef, cooked on a table-top grill and dipped into sauce, is called *yakiniku* and is not uncommon in Japan but unusual here. However, if you want the teppanyaki beef, that knife-flourishing, speed-slicing, Popeil-gadget of a dinner, you'll probably have to seek out a so-called Japanese steakhouse: A true Japanese chef would consider all that sound and fury gauche and, well, barbarian.

Pork is most popularly served as tonkatsu, the breaded pork cutlet described above; it may also be marinated in sweet miso, rolled, coated in panko crumbs, and fried. *Kushi-katsu* is a variation of tonkatsu, a sort of kebab. A derivation of Chinese twice-cooked pork is steamed, then braised in a sweet-sour sauce made pungent with *ume*, the sour green plums. *Chusai* is pork belly or bacon slow-cooked in soy sauce.

Chicken is most commonly skewer-grilled, teriyaki-glazed, or used in casseroles; but when the breast is really fresh, the little filet may be cut away and served as sashimi. Fried chicken (*tori no kara-age*) goes back a lot further than Colonel Sanders (though his cheery presence is now familiar on the streets there); the Japanese version, marinated, dipped in potato starch, and deep-fried, is even better. Chicken is ground into dumplings as well, and although not commonly offered in American restaurants, such organ meats as livers and the small, yuzu- or lime-flavored wings are also popular skewered. Duck is particularly popular in Japan, where wild duck was common, but again, only the most upscale Japanese restaurants in this country are likely to offer it. The breasts are broiled and glazed with teriyaki sauce or seared and than battered and parboiled; legs and wings are grilled. There is even a sort of duck sukiyaki. Small game birds are popular in some regional cuisines, usually simply skewered.

FISH AND SEAFOOD   Sushi boom aside, the Japanese eat as much cooked seafood as raw. Fish, shrimp, scallops, octopus, squid, and shellfish are all broiled plain, but oily and fatty fish are generally braised or coated with coarse salt and then broiled very hot (the shioyaki mentioned above) so that the thin layer of fat just beneath the skin melts and seasons the meat. The lighter-fleshed fish are usually steamed or simmered; either may be deep-fried. The heads of certain whole fish, notably yellowtail, salmon, and grouper, are broiled or braised and served up separately (though most customers only get the jaw, the whole head, for those not too squeamish, is a real delicacy). The meat of the cheeks is extremely sweet. Small octopus, large prawns, and whole fish, usually red snapper or trout or mackerel, are apt to be charbroiled on the robotai grill. Swordfish (*kajiki-maguro*) is relatively new to the menu but is becoming popular as a grill option.

Seafood soups, called yosenabe, are whole meals—large pots of broth with shellfish, shrimp, and some chunks of fish, along with a gelatinous, candy-striped aspic misnamed "fishcake," and cabbage and onions. For one sort of oyster yosename, *kaki-nabe*, the kaki-nabe pot is coated with miso, which is scraped off with the chopsticks as the ingredients are eaten. *Anko*, the anglerfish or monkfish from which the liver mousse, ankimo, is made, is often cooked whole in a soup, but is rarely served grilled, as its meat toughens.

VEGETABLES In addition to pickling, braising, simmering, and tempura-frying vegetables, the Japanese grill almost any fresh produce, from asparagus to sweet peppers to eggplant and the large meaty mushrooms, especially matsutake and shiitake. Spinach and similar greens are often boiled, cooked, and then served as palate-cleansers.

SWEETS The Japanese are apt to end the meal as we think it should begin—with a bowl of plain rice—but they do enjoy some desserts, only not nearly so sweet as Western ones. (The amount of sugar in one American dessert would last a Japanese family for months.) They make exquisite, dainty cookies, particularly for the tea ceremony, that reflect seasonal images and flavors; the packaging of them is just as ornate, but again, they are much less sweet. Green tea–, red bean–, and ginger-flavored ice creams, fresh fruit (particularly melons, persimmons, oranges, and strawberries), and *yokan*, a red bean gelatin that tastes a lot like chestnut puree are common in restaurants here; less common, except on special occasions, are the fancier pastries, sweet doughy buns stuffed with nuts, sweet bean paste, and so on.

BEVERAGES By far the most famous Japanese drink is sake, and the availability of better and even "boutique" sakes in this country has increased Americans' interest in this ancient liquor. (See "The Sake Tsunami," below.) Sake bars are even opening in larger cities, where patrons may try out new labels and the more traditional light bites that go with them. A similar but more potent white liquor, something like a cross between sake and vodka, is called *shochu*; it used to be considered a blue-collar drink (it's originally Korean), but like many low-fashion items, it is gaining popularity, particularly with younger drinkers. There are also some so-called sakes made from other grains than rice, but although they're all clear, they have a tendency to taste like other grain alcohols: The "potato sake" tastes a lot like vodka, the "corn sake" like whiskey, and so on. In any case, these are usually offered only for novelty's sake.

As pointed out earlier, sake and tea are both addressed with great respect in Japan—o-sake and o-cha. Tea is both the homiest of beverages, drunk at all hours and with all foods, even with other beverages; and the most formal, the centerpiece of the elaborate social ritual of the tea ceremony. *Cha-do*, or "the way of tea," is a philosophy as well as an experience, designed to recall us out of the ordinary world into the natural Zen balance and to remind us of our essential equality with each other and the elements.

Green tea is produced in a range of qualities and textures (powdered or dried or whole leaf) and is not by any means the only type of tea drunk. Some are roasted, some have bits of roasted rice. American, Indian, and Chinese teas are called black teas as opposed to green tea (*kocha*, actually "red tea.") There are also teas made of seaweeds, flowers, rice hulls, chrysanthemum leaves, and herbs; cold barley tea is popular in summer. Americans tend to drink hot green tea after the meal, like coffee, but many Japanese drink it throughout the meal even if they are also drinking liquor.

Japanese beers are also good and increasingly available in this country, particularly the brands Kirin, Asahi, and Sapporo. Japanese winemaking in the French tradition dates back many decades, although it is not imported, and the Japanese public in general is just discovering fine wines. There are Japanese whiskies as well—the most famous is Suntory, and at least two single-malt Scotches are produced in Japan—and liqueurs, such as the honeydew-flavored Midori. In traditional sushi bars, a patron may buy a whole bottle of Suntory, put his name on it, and leave it from visit to visit, just as the old sushi bars used to keep regular customers' cups for them.

THE SAKE TSUNAMI

Sake has been brewed in Japan for more than 2,000 years and is as revered as it is loved. Usually described as rice wine, it's really closer to a rice beer, a fermented but not distilled grain alcohol; however, it has a stronger kick than traditional beer, generally ranging from 22 to 30 proof. It contains no preservatives and so should be drunk fresh (although it will keep for several weeks in the refrigerator). Sake is produced in a variety of flavors—sweet, dry, bitter, tannic, cedar-scented, flowery—you'll just have to find out what you like.

Traditionally, sake was made only of rice, water, and, since the eighth century, *koji*, a rice mold that encouraged fermentation; but during the worldwide depression and particularly in the aftermath of World War II, rice shortages nearly wiped out the industry. Manufacturers were forced to add small amounts of glucose and alcohol during the fermentation process to produce enough sake for domestic consumption (and most have continued to add some alcohol, though with more finesse).

These rougher sakes, called *futsu shu* or *sanzoshu*, were the sort shipped to the United States in the 1960s and '70s, and are responsible for the habit of drinking sake warm—to increase flavor and disguise the rough edges and decay from slow export and long shelf time. These bulk sakes, some with enough brewer's alcohol added to triple the output, still account for the great majority of sakes consumed, though obviously the quality is much higher now.

However, in the past 25 years, interest in better-quality sakes has inspired a revival in high-quality sakes as well as *jizakes*, which are the small custom brews also called country or local sakes, intended to be drunk cold or room temperature. These premium sakes are classified by the degree to which the hull is polished off the rice grain: The more polishing that is done, the purer the rice kernel—and the more expensive the sake, because it not only takes longer to polish but then requires more rice to produce the same amount of mash. *Honjozo* sake is made from rice polished to 70% of its original size. (Bulk sakes are made from rice polished by less than 30%.) *Ginjoshu* sakes must be made from rice polished to 60% of original size; *daiginjoshu* to 50% or less. *Junmaishu* is "pure" sake made the old-fashioned way—that is, without added alcohol, only rice and koji.

Namazake, which is unpasteurized, should be drunk as soon as possible or the flavor will go off. *Nigorizake* is only coarsely filtered, so that it remains "cloudy" with tiny fragments of the rice mash, which make it somewhat sweet.

Most restaurants serve sake in vase-like vessels or small bottles called *tokkuri;* better ones with a wider selection may also allow you to order by the glass or by the whole bottle—which, in the case of fine sakes, can be pricey. Sake is most often drunk from small cups (*choko* or, more politely, *o-choko*), but more formal sake cups are almost flat, like saucers. For special occasions, you may be offered the square balsa or cryptomeria boxes called *masu*, which grow more fragrant with continued use. The blue-collar tradition is to put a pinch of salt on one corner of the box and slug it down, à la tequila; in any case, turning the box so that a corner is centered on your mouth is a good idea.

If you are pouring sake for your companions—only if you are alone should you pour for yourself—you should hold the bottle lightly with both hands. It is also polite to lift your cup off the table when being served. A cup should be emptied before being refilled. The traditional toast is "*Kanpai!*" or "bottoms up!" and you should toss the whole thing down. (Remember, the cups are small.)

Again, most of these sakes are intended to be drunk chilled, with the exception of the *hirezake* (with char-grilled fugu fin in it). However, if you prefer it warm—and particularly in winter, this is perfectly acceptable—it should be heated only to what's called *hitohada* temperature— warm skin. If it's overheated, it loses both flavor and alcohol.

HOW TO ORDER
AND EAT LIKE A NATIVE

To begin with the utensils: The Japanese use chopsticks, which is why most foods are cut into small pieces or strips or cooked until soft, and a sort of flat-bottomed spoon primarily needed for the soupier one-pot meals or to cradle the bottom of a chopsticks-full of noodles. When you sit down, you will probably see a paper-wrapped package of chopsticks, a bottle of soy sauce, and, if you're at the sushi bar, a small rectangular or round saucer to pour the soy sauce into. In better restaurants, the chopsticks will only be attached at the very bottom, to facilitate splitting; in this case, rubbing the sticks together to remove possible splinters is a subtle insult, suggesting the restaurant might be supplying low-quality utensils. However, cheaper carryouts may use very stringy sticks that warrant a little polishing; you'll just have to judge the situation.

At most sushi bars, you will see a small dish for your shoyu; you may also see a tiny chopstick rest. You may lean your opened sticks against the soy sauce dish, or, if there is no chopstick rest, you could twist the paper wrapper (assuming you didn't rip it in half) around your fingers and tie a flat knot, then rest the small ends of the sticks on that.

If a washcloth or towel (*oshibori*) is offered, it will be carefully rolled and either presented in a little basket or placed via chopsticks directly into your hands. (It will likely be hot in winter, cold in summer.) Open it and wipe your hands, but don't refold it, just lay it neatly back in the cradle or beside your plate. If you wish to wipe your face, just press the cloth to your cheeks in a single movement; don't "scrub."

One of those flat-bottomed spoons will probably come with your preliminary soup, but the Japanese pick up the whole bowl with one hand, sip the soup directly from the lip, and use chopsticks to stir up the broth or eat the squares of tofu at the bottom. (If the top of the bowl sticks to the base, gently squeeze the sides of the bowl, and the lid will pop free.) On the other hand, although most Americans prefer to use chopsticks to eat sushi, many Japanese, particularly men, still pick it up with their fingers and pop it into their mouths.

Sushi is traditionally prepared with a dab of wasabi between the fish and rice with more on the side; with sashimi, you add your wasabi yourself by placing a small bit on the fish before dipping it in the shoyu. Americans frequently mash a chunk of wasabi into the soy sauce, but that's poor form; it's more polite to keep them separate, adding just a little wasabi—after all, your sushi chef has already put some on for you—and then dip it into the shoyu. In fact, in Japan, extra wasabi isn't even put out on the plate; you would simply ask the itamae to use a little more in preparing your sushi.

When dipping nigiri, the correct form is to dip not the rice side but the fish itself into the soy sauce; as a handy hint, try turning the sushi on its side and picking it up with your chopsticks the long way, sandwiching the rice in, rather than grabbing it across the middle; it is less likely to fall apart. Don't soak the whole piece in the soy sauce; not only will it collapse, you won't be able to taste anything else. Shoyu is a condiment, not a gravy.

Alternatively, you may eat sushi with your fingers; again, just make even more sure you don't overdouse the fish in soy sauce or get it on your fingers. Also, if you eat half a piece of sushi instead of eating it all in one bite, you should hold the remaining portion in your slightly lowered hand or chopsticks; don't put it back on the plate. If you are served an inside-out roll—that is, with the rice on the outside—finger a piece of the *gari* (ginger pickle) before picking it up: It will keep the rice from sticking to your fingers. You should not, however, wrap or layer your sushi in the gari.

If you're sitting at a table, particularly at one of the older-style shokuji dokoro establishments, food is considered something of a family affair. At a sushi bar, an obvious couple may be served from one wooden tray rather than two. When sharing food at a Japanese restaurant, whether you use your own chopsticks in a communal pot has to do with the closeness of your relationships. If you're related, or at least very close, you may do so; otherwise, use the longer serving sticks provided to place food on your rice bowl or plate. If you want to exchange tidbits, use your chopsticks to put food either on your companion's plate or directly into his or her mouth, but never— this is important—never pass food from one pair of

Noodles are eaten with chopsticks, but it's not hard; if they're in a bowl, you can pick the whole thing up with one hand and bring it close to your mouth and sort of shovel the noodles in with the other hand. If the noodles are either served dry on a plate or with a dipping sauce on the side, use your rice bowl as the saucer. Don't worry about catching up the strands neatly: Noodles are fast, sloppy, comfort food in Japan, and slurping is perfectly polite. In fact, it's essential, not only to keep the noodles from spilling all over the table but because sucking air in also cools the hot food. (This is also where those big spoons come in handy; you can pull up a strand of noodles in your chopsticks and sort of rest the ends of the strands in the spoon.)

To eat grilled chicken or fish from skewers, hold the tip of the skewer with one hand, slide the food off with your chopsticks and eat it, a piece at a time, over your rice. Pick up tempura with your chopsticks and bite off what you want; you may put the rest down.

Traditional Japanese dining tables are short platforms without chairs; diners are supposed to sit cross-legged on the floor, on straw mats called *tatami;* formal restaurants may still have tatami rooms for special parties. However, most Japanese restaurants in this country have Western-style seating; some that do have what look like traditional tables have pits or cutaways under the table for your legs to dangle.

If you are seated in a tatami room, you must remove your shoes and dine in your stocking feet; remove your shoes and leave them on the threshold just outside the sliding door. If the entire restaurant has traditional service, and you must remove your shoes at the front door, there will probably be slippers or sandals for you to slip on.

A Japanese meal begins with soup and some sort of pickle or salad (often served automatically), then moves through sushi and sashimi to grilled or fried seafood, then meat or poultry (or a one-pot stew). In a kaiseki meal (see below), each dish is presented and served separately, but in the home or in less formal restaurants all the food is served up together. (In this country, it usually falls somewhere in between.) There is one major exception—the bento box. The bento box, most popular for dinner or for such "carryout" occasions as the baseball game, holds four or five dishes, with rice as the mainstay—perhaps a couple of shrimp tempura, a little sushi, a little yakitori, and some pickles. Bento boxes are traditionally multilayered nesting boxes, but some look like the old TV-dinner trays, with odd-shaped dividers.

Kaiseki ryori, the most formal and elaborate cuisine, came from Zen tradition as part of the tea ceremony; like the tea ceremony, it demonstrates the extreme sophistication and sensitivity of both chef and diner by pretending to be very simple. (The word

Stick-y Situations
continued

chopsticks to another. This is a method used to transport funeral remains after cremation, so it is very bad karma.

It is also extremely rude to stab your chopsticks into the rice bowl and leave them sticking out, to point with them, to stab or spear food, or to lick them clean ("drumming" with chopsticks is beneath contempt but astonishingly common). Chopsticks are also used to say "when": Laying both sticks horizontally across your platter means you're full. Incidentally, it is perfectly acceptable to bring your own chopsticks if you have them; the Japanese have long since run low on wood and actually import tons of cheap disposable chopstick balsam from the United States.

"kaiseki" actually refers not to food at all but to the hot stones Buddhist priests used to pocket to keep warm and trick their empty stomachs into quiet.) It involves a number of courses, each relatively small, each prepared with great attention to the visual presentation. Courses include sashimi, a clear meat or seafood soup with seasonal vegetables, grilled fish, small tidbits intended to complement the drinking of sake, pickles, roasted rice, and so on, concluding with fine *matcha,* a high-grade green tea. At a meal like this, the diners should eat deliberately, after admiring the colors and displays of each dish as it is served.

If you only intend to eat sushi, it's more fun to sit at the sushi bar and watch the itamae (whose title means, literally, "before the board")

While the Japanese themselves generally eat lightly and, like other Asian cultures, value the rice over the protein, Japanese restaurateurs in the United States are accustomed to the greater appetites of American diners and have increased portions to match. Remember that most restaurants serve a bowl of soup and small salad with sushi or entrees.

work his magic. However, you don't have to sit at the bar to order sushi—and usually you don't have to give up tempura to sit at the bar, either. Just be courteous: If your party of four is only going to have a California roll before ordering beef teriyaki, don't take up the bar stools.

When ordering sushi, remember to keep track, as it's easy to run up quite a bill without really noticing. (This is one reason more and more restaurants are experimenting with all-you-can-eat nights; however, you should realize that establishments that offer all-you-can-eat all the time may be buying less expensive, i.e., lower-quality, fish.) Also, when ordering sushi à la carte, check to see whether that particular sushi bar counts one order of sushi to mean one piece or two; two is traditional, but many sushi bars in this country have shifted to one.

Although sushi meals range the most widely in price, depending on your appetite, many other Japanese dishes are fairly reasonable, particularly the one-pot meals, such as nabeyaki udon.

If you are feeling adventurous, you may ask for *omakase*—chef's choice. At some restaurants, however, an omakase meal, which depends on market ingredients, may have to be ordered 24 hours in advance. Omakase dinners will be more expensive, perhaps up to $50 depending on the establishment; omakase kaiseki meals can cost up to $100 a person.

COOKING AT HOME

Japanese dishes can be easily adapted to the American kitchen, often without adding new equipment. Sukiyaki and nabeyaki are prepared in cast-iron skillets or cauldrons; chicken or beef can easily be marinated in teriyaki sauce and broiled or grilled. Even chawan mushi can be prepared, with a little care, in any covered mug.

A flexible bamboo mat is needed for rolling maki sushi, but in a pinch, a stiffish grass-weave placemat would do. (These days, there are decent sushi carryouts everywhere; you might well find it worthwhile to spare the trouble of getting really fresh sushi-grade fish, slicing it—an art in itself—preparing sushi rice, and putting it together. In all honesty, it might be better to get the sushi from a pro and concentrate on the kitchen dishes, at least for a while.)

Automatic rice cookers, which originated in Japan, are now thoroughly Americanized and are worth owning whether you cook Japanese-style or not. Mongolian hot pots and fondue pots can be used for shabu-shabu, but small kettles or Dutch ovens or even woks can do; heavy skillets, especially cast iron, are perfect for sukiyaki. There are even miniature tappan-yaki grills for home Benihana practice.

As to finding ingredients, the number of Asian markets is booming, but in any case, more and more supermarkets are carrying such staples as tofu, Japanese rice, teriyaki and soy sauces, and prepared wasabi. The Asian markets will also have "convenience" foods, such as instant dashi broth in little packets like bouillon.

For entertaining at home, it is nice to indulge in a set of chopsticks and chopstick rests, soy sauce bowls, and covered soup bowls; at the least, a sake set and cups should be used to set the table. Don't overdress the table, though: A few fresh flowers, an interesting branch or bush cutting, even just handmade pottery would be more authentic in spirit. Remember *wabi* and *sabi*: Understatement is an essential element of elegance.

CUCUMBER SUNOMONO

4 tablespoons rice vinegar
3 tablespoons soy sauce
2 tablespoons sugar, mirin, or honey
1 teaspoon grated ginger with juice
1 large European cucumber
or 6 scrubbed, blemish-free pickling cucumbers

In a small bowl, combine rice vinegar and next 3 ingredients. If the cucumbers are waxed or thick-skinned, you may peel them; then slice thinly and spread on paper towels to drain for 30 minutes. Toss dressing with drained cucumber slices and divide into portions. If desired, top with crabmeat or baby shrimp.

TUNA NUTA WITH SCALLIONS

1 teaspoon hot mustard paste
(can substitute Coleman's or Chinese mustard)

3 tablespoons sweet white miso

1 tablespoon sugar

4 tablespoons rice vinegar, divided

1 tablespoon dashi (can substitute very diluted chicken broth)

1 tablespoon canola or light sesame oil

1 large bunch spring onions

or 2 naganegi (Japanese long onions) or leeks

8 ounces sushi-grade tuna

1 tablespoon soy sauce

To make dressing: Whisk mustard and miso in small saucepan until smooth; add sugar, 3 tablespoons of the vinegar, dashi, and oil, one ingredient at a time, whisking until smooth. Simmer for 3 minutes, stirring constantly, and let cool.

Trim onion tops at the point and any dried top edges where leaves completely separate, discard bottoms. Bring water in skillet to simmer; blanch greens for 3 minutes. (If using naganegi, cook 5 minutes, then flatten whites with the flat side of a large knife to release viscous juices.) Drain, cool, and slice onions into 1-inch pieces.

Cut tuna into 1-inch cubes. Combine soy sauce and remaining vinegar and marinate tuna for 20 minutes; drain and discard marinade. Gently toss tuna and onions in dressing; serve in bowls or on small plates.

CHICKEN YAKITORI

1/2 cup mirin

4 tablespoons sake

2 teaspoons grated ginger

1 tablespoon sugar

1/2 cup soy sauce

2 pounds boneless chicken breasts

4–5 green onions or scallions, cut into 1-inch pieces

2 tablespoons lemon juice

Prepare grill. Combine mirin, sake, and ginger in a small saucepan; bring to boil, lower heat, and add sugar and soy sauce. Simmer 20 minutes, stirring occasionally, until thick and glossy.

Slice chicken into 1-inch strips or cubes. If using bamboo skewers, soak them in water for 20 minutes.

Thread a piece of onion onto a skewer, followed by chicken (pierce in several places and slice down like ribbon); repeat. Grill (or broil) about 4 minutes per side, basting with sauce (or sprinkle with lemon juice and black pepper and serve sauce on side). Serve hot or at room temperature.

SUKIYAKI

3/4 pound fresh spinach, washed and stemmed
1 can whole bamboo shoots
8 large dried shiitake mushrooms, soaked in hot water
1 package firm tofu, cut into cubes
2–3 green onions, cut into 2-inch pieces
or 1/2 head bok choy, sliced 1 inch wide
1 large onion, cut into eighths (wedges)
1 1/2 pounds thinly sliced beef sirloin, all fat trimmed
2 ounces beef suet or 2 tablespoons oil
1/2 pound shirataki (gelatin) noodles
hot cooked rice
4–8 eggs (optional)

SUKIYAKI SAUCE

1 cup dashi or stock
2/3 cup soy sauce
2/3 cup mirin
1/2 cup sake
3–4 tablespoons sugar
1 tablespoon oil

Slice spinach leaves and bamboo shoots into bite-sized pieces and refresh in cold water. Drain. Trim hard stems from shiitakes; cut in halves or quarters.

Pat excess liquid from tofu. Arrange spinach, bamboo shoots, shiitakes, onions, and tofu cubes on platter with beef.

Stir together sauce ingredients (you may substitute the shiitake-soaking liquid for some of the stock) and pour into pitcher. If cooking at the table, have everyone seated before beginning.

Heat oil or suet in skillet to coat surface; add half the meat and cook partially; turn meat over, add half the onions and pour in enough sauce to cover. Add half of the other vegetables, including noodles and tofu (but keep them somewhat separate). Serve and repeat with the remaining ingredients. Serve with individual bowls of rice and top with a little extra sauce. (In Japan, the bowls of rice are topped with raw eggs, which cook under the stew; but current health concerns make that practice unfashionable; I still like it.)

KOREA

BASIC CUISINE

DINNER FOR TWO:
Mandoo dumplings, bulgoki, shrimp tempura

DINNER FOR FOUR:
Bindaeduk, bulgalbi, bibimbap, grilled fish

GROUP DISH:
Gulchupan

STYLE:
Earthy, robust, spicy

KEY FLAVORS:
Garlic, soy, sesame, chilies

EATING UTENSILS:
Chopsticks, fingers, spoons

DISTINCTIVE DISHES:
Kimchee, bulgoki, bibimbap

UNIFORMITY OF MENUS:
Good

NUTRITIONAL INDEX:
High sodium, high protein, medium cholesterol, low fat

COST:
Inexpensive to moderate

"THANK YOU":
"Kamsa ham ni da"

In many parts of the United States, Korean food is a sort of "stealth" cuisine. The Korean American community, made up largely of recent immigrants, is only beginning to move past the mom-and-pop grocery cooktop to the formal restaurant kitchen—or to put their own names on the scores of purportedly "Japanese" sushi bars opened by Korean entrepreneurs hoping to cash in on an already established market.

But Korean food, although it has old and strong ties to both Chinese and Japanese cuisines, has an earthiness, a robust kind of gustatory humor, that is very distinctive. Korean culture is at the same time Confucian and shamanistic, painstakingly ordered and richly symbolic. Early Koreans envisioned a universe of earth, fire, water, wood, and metal; that combination of assertiveness and delicacy characterizes Korean cuisine as well—simple but not exactly subtle.

Because Koreans make up one of the fastest-growing ethnic communities in the United States—there may be two million Koreans in this country, and the Los Angeles Koreatown, with perhaps a half million ethnic residents, is the largest Korean community outside Korea itself—restaurants advertising Korean-style barbecue and dumplings are sprouting up all over. The main difficulty now is getting them to "go public"—that is, to supplement their frequently Korean-only signs (and menus) with English ones.

THE COUNTRY

The Korean peninsula, a powerful thumb hitchhiking from southern China toward Japan, is primarily mountainous, crisscrossed by rivers (few of them navigable) and with a penumbra of nearly 3,500 small islands, most of them uninhabitable. It divides the Sea of Japan (or, as the Koreans call it, the East Sea) from the Yellow Sea; at its southern tip, the Straits of Japan are only 150 miles wide.

Korea's climate varies markedly, with cold, dry winters in the north and nearly tropical conditions in the south. About half the farmland in Korea has been turned over to rice cultivation, with paddies not only along the coast and in river valleys but also in painstakingly recovered flood plains. Livestock is raised somewhat sparingly, particularly in the north, where the uneven ground makes grazing difficult.

THE HISTORY

Except for a very small border with Russia, Korea has only one land neighbor—China, specifically, Manchuria; one of its most crucial roles in world history has been to serve as a cultural go-between for China and Japan. (The Koreans are ethnically closest to the Mongolians, but culturally closer to the more effete Manchurians.)

Around the beginning of the Common Era, Korea was divided into three kingdoms, but with the help of imperial China, the kingdom of Silla succeeded in unifying the country under a largely Buddhist rule. However, from the fifteenth century onwards, the impact of Buddhism in Korea began to weaken and was gradually replaced by secular Confucianism. Nevertheless, the Chinese influence continued. For centuries, Korean society adhered faithfully to the Chinese model—so faithfully, in fact, that in 1644, when the supposedly celestial Ming dynasty was overthrown by the Mongolian-bred Manchus, it seemed that heaven had literally fallen to the barbarians (the Korean upper classes having long since forgotten their genetic roots). Korea managed to escape the Western expansionism that spread throughout Asia until the late nineteenth century, when Japan forced it open and eventually annexed the entire country. Ironically, considering Korea's defiance of both the Mongol and Japanese invaders, both left indelible imprints on the cuisine. Mongols supplied the hot pot and the hot brazier used to grill meats (not to mention the chopped, raw steak tartare, called *yukhwe*), and the Japanese made sashimi and tempura staples.

THE CUISINE

Korean cooking brings together the five flavor types typical to Asian cuisine—salty, sweet, sour, hot, and bitter, that is, soy, honey, vinegar, chilies, and ginger—but unlike many neighboring cuisines, Korean cooking also spotlights five important colors: red, yellow, black, white, and green.

As in many cultures, Korean cuisine developed along two lines: the more complex court cuisine, in which a dinner might have as many as a dozen courses; and the home cooking of the common people, which even then consisted of three to seven courses. However, most Korean restaurants in the United States tread a sort of middle ground, mixing styles (and often putting courses together) to better fit the American lifestyle.

Because the marinated and grilled beef dishes, such as *bulgoki* (rump or round strips) and *bulgalbi* (short ribs), are so well known, Korean cuisine is sometimes thought of as heavier and more meat-dependent than most other Asian styles—and in the United States, perhaps this is the case. Like its neighboring countries, however, Korea depended historically most heavily on vegetables and seafood to accompany rice (*bap*). The real difference is in the forward, spotlight-grabbing seasoning.

Koreans enjoy powerfully flavored food, consuming more garlic per capita than any other ethnic group; they also use lavish amounts of soy sauce, red chilies, black pepper, and ginger. (For better or worse, the heat at most American restaurants tends to be turned down. If you want something a little spicy, ask for "*duhl mapge*"; if you want it really spicy, order "*mapge.*") Other common seasonings include *toen jang*, a fermented soybean paste; *gochu jang*, a sweet-hot red chili paste thickened with steamed rice; and *mirin* and rice vinegar. The most famous Korean condiment, really a staple in itself, is *kimchee*, a spicy, fermented pickle or relish most often made from radish or cabbage (though many other vegetables are substituted) with chilies, ginger, and lavish amounts of garlic. Kimchee can addict the most serious of chili-heads.

At the same time, Koreans know the value of contrast; the *payjun* or *p'ajon*, a large mung-flour pancake studded with oysters, shrimp, and scallions, could not be more delicate.

Incidentally, the names on Korean menus can look confusing, because Korean dishes are among the most variously spelled and transliterated. However, the majority have English subtitles, and even if not, you can generally puzzle out the phrase if you say it out loud.

THE MAIN INGREDIENTS

SEASONINGS   Kimchee provides one of the major flavor elements of the meal, but despite its power, it is usually "doubled" by heavy doses of garlic, ginger, ginseng, *perilla* (the basil-like herb called *shiso* in Japan), sesame seeds (which are usually crushed before being added to marinades, thus releasing a darker, richer flavor than the Middle Eastern sesame pastes), scallions and onions, soy sauce, red or black bean paste, the salty chili paste gochu jang, cinnamon, black pepper, dried red pepper, hot mustard, and citrus—particularly preserved or fermented lemons.

GRAINS AND STARCHES   Most of the Korean countryside is devoted to rice farming. However, farmers also grow several other types of grains (barley, wheat, corn, and sorghum) and starches (soy, azuki, mung beans, and white and sweet potatoes), any of which can be turned into flours or pastes and from that into noodles or thickeners.

VEGETABLES   Cabbage (usually either Chinese or celery cabbage), garlic, and radishes are particularly treasured for their role in kimchee, which occupies a nearly sacred position in Korean family life, as rice does in Japan. Other common vegetables include eggplant, mushrooms, leeks, lima beans, burdock, turnips, spinach, the giant daikon radish, some squash, carrots, tomatoes, potatoes, and yams; delicate sprouts, such as bamboo shoots, lotus roots, and sprouted beans, are also popular.

FRUITS   Although it is not generally obvious from restaurant menus, Koreans are fond of a variety of fruits, including apples, so-called Korean pears, persimmons, cherries, plums, oranges, lemons, winter melons, and grapes. These are commonly served at the end of a meal, as a digestive, or in the form of preserves and condiments.

MEATS AND POULTRY   Beef is the most popular entree, followed by chicken; rabbits are raised but rarely eaten here, and pork is only slightly more common. Goat is popular in some areas, but mutton is almost never served. (In the United States, however, it sometimes appears in a version of the Mongolian hot pot.)

SEAFOOD AND SHELLFISH Far and away the greatest natural food resource is the country's thousands of inlets and freshwater streams, which supply Koreans with an abundance of seafood proteins: anchovies, sardines, mackerel, tuna, cuttlefish, whitefish, pollack, flounder and fluke, cod, sandfish, herring, eel, octopus, clams, shrimp, squid, and abalone, along with various seaweeds and algae (used, as in Japan, both for wrapping sushi and for enriching stocks) and marine vegetables.

ANJU

Like most Asians, Koreans don't think of appetizers as a first course—although they can be—but more frequently as alternative meals, food to drink and talk by, in the way the Spanish consume tapas. (Soups, in fact, are more popular as snacks or on-the-run meals.)

The Korean word for such small tapas-like dishes is *anju*; this course commonly includes sashimi, oysters, bits of grilled pork, hard-boiled quail eggs, a sort of thin-sliced spicy corned brisket, and lettuce or even salted cabbage leaves to roll them in (and revive your thirst). In the United States, the anju frequently appear at the beginning of the menu, like hors d'oeuvres, but are apt to be much larger than expected.

Kejaeng is a highly distinctive and addictive anju: raw crab served in the shell but chopped into two-inch pieces, cured in salt

Stealth Health

Korean food is fairly healthful, although somewhat sodium-heavy. Cooking methods are simple—most foods that are not served raw are either pan-fried, grilled, broiled, steamed, or braised—and what little oil is used is vegetable or sesame. Very little animal fat is used even for frying. And although meat is popular, it is eaten, as in most Asian cuisines, in combination with starch and vegetables.

At the same time, because of its long Buddhist tradition, Korea has quite a few vegetarian dishes; but for whatever reason, they are not widely offered in American restaurants. There are a few chefs, however, who prepare what is called "temple cooking"—traditional monastery fare (again, simple but not dull), including dishes such as grilled bamboo shoots and wild sesame gruel. There are also restaurants that specialize in tofu dishes, with or without additional meats. Interestingly, some Buddhists believe that although they are forbidden to eat living things (i.e., seafood), they may consume food that is washed up—presumably "offered"— on the shore; however, no chef in the United States is going to serve two-day-old oysters, so don't worry.

and chili paste like a fiery ceviche, and served cold. Eating kejaeng requires either great skill or a certain amount of abandon; you can pick out a piece from the serving tray with chopsticks, but eventually you'll have to just grab hold with your fingers and eat it despite the chili sauce. Treat it something like an artichoke leaf, biting down on the shell to flatten it and gradually work the meat out—or just eat it anyway you can.

Gulchupan (or *guljeopan*) one of the most popular sit-around dishes, is more of a group order: Small pancakes are served in the center of a compartmentalized tray surrounded by a variety of ingredients ("gulchupan" literally means "nine varieties"), such as dried mushrooms, stir-fried matchstick carrots, and marinated shredded beef. Gulchupan is served at room temperature and thus can be eaten at leisure, so it frequently substitutes for a more elaborate meal.

THE MAIN DISHES

APPETIZERS As noted above, most of the items listed on American menus as "appetizers" are really light meals and can be quite filling. An order of sashimi, for instance, which might be six or eight pieces as a Japanese first course, may be literally dozens at a Korean restaurant—and that's not even the "large" size. Another dish frequently seen in the United States is *mandoo* (or *mandu*), Korean dumplings available steamed or fried or in soup; *cham maat* is a more general term covering dumplings and other dishes like the Chinese dim sum.

KOREAN BARBECUE In Korea, beef is prepared literally nose to (ox)tail, and there are said to be well over a hundred special soup recipes for virtually every portion, from shankbone to shoulder. However, the cuts most frequently offered in the United States are rump, round, short ribs, brisket, filet, tongue, liver, and tripe. Any of these are apt to be offered as "barbecue"—that is, marinated in a spicy and slightly sweet sauce and grilled over a hot brazier called a *hware*. (The increasing sophistication of these tabletop grills, which used to be propane-fueled but which now are frequently built in, gas-fired, and equipped with overhead smoke fans, is making these barbecue restaurants very popular with younger Americans, who grew up on the backyard grill.)

Bulgoki is usually sliced rump or round; bulgalbi (also known as simply *galbi* or sometimes *kalbi*) are short ribs sawed into two- or three-inch lengths. A suffix that indicates grilled food is *-gwhe* or *-kue*. *Yumtong-gwhe* is grilled heart, and *gobchang-gwhe* is tripe, so know what you're ordering. Yookwhe (or yuk whey) is raw beef; usually made of higher-quality cuts, it is served like steak tartare, topped with pine nuts, fresh apple, and egg, but is meant to be rolled up in lettuce leaves rather than spread on bread.

Fish Story

Korean sashimi is usually sliced more thickly than the Japanese version. Sometimes it looks almost chunky, because Koreans prefer to eat sashimi as they do meat, wrapping it in lettuce leaves with some radish or chilies for flavor and dipping it into sauces, either the traditional soy or even the hot bean paste. (This makes sashimi orders in Korean restaurants seem even larger.) Traditionally, the nori sheets used to wrap Japanese sushi are served as a side dish or condiment, brushed with sesame oil, lightly toasted, and cut up into squares to wrap around bites of rice. Korean sushi is also likely to seem more sturdy than the delicate Japanese version but is usually eaten in the traditional fashion, with chopsticks, soy sauce, and wasabi.

Though most restaurants in the United States use portable gas or propane grills instead of charcoal braziers, a few have the real thing in the back, so you might want to ask. If your whole party is having barbecue, let the staff know, because many tables have built-in grill tops that allow everyone to cook at the same time and taste everything. If only one person is having grilled meat (or if the staff thinks you seem new to the cuisine), it may be grilled for you in the kitchen and brought out on a platter, which is fine but not quite as much fun.

The barbecue method is also applied to pork, poultry, and even seafood. *Dwiji-gwhe* is sliced grilled pork; *jang-gwhe* (or *janguh-guyee*) is grilled eel (called *unagi* at sushi bars); and *ojingu-gwbe* is marinated grilled squid. *Takgoki* is barbecued chicken. *Soon dae* are sausages.

SEAFOOD Japan's long domination of Korea has made sushi a staple in that country as well, though subtly different in presentation (see Fish Story, page 353). Fish and shellfish preparations in general are also much like the Japanese: grilled or chargrilled, tempura-fried, and especially used to flavor soups and casseroles.

OMELETS AND CRÊPES *Bindaeduck* (or *pintaettuk*) are pancakes made of ground mung beans rather than flour, and mixed with eggs; they taste like a combination omelet and crêpe and are stuffed with pork, vegetables, and perhaps a touch of kimchee. Payjun, mentioned above, is a larger version—sometimes quite large, like a pizza—often made of seafood.

NOODLES Koreans are very fond of noodles and prepare them from a variety of flours and starches. Among the most popular dishes are *naengmein*, buckwheat noodles usually served cold with meat, vegetables, and chili paste; *jajaengmein*, wheat noodles in brown bean sauce with meat; and *chowmamein*, a seafood version. *Mein*, the Chinese word for noodles seen in variations all over southern Asia, may be spelled *myon* or *maen* as well. Interestingly, the nearest Korean version of pad thai or chow mein—stir-fried vegetables and noodles—is not called "mein" but *chap chae* (or *jap chae* or *chap chye*), and is most frequently made with glass or rice noodles. *Tangmein* is usually rice noodles, the see-through kind also called cellophane noodles or bean threads; but *tang* also refers to the clear stock prepared for soups.

BIG-BOWL DISHES AND ONE-POT MEALS Europeans and Americans tend to segregate different dishes on the plate and eat them separately, but many Korean dishes are toss-up meals; although the ingredients are served in bowls, along with the kimchee and condiments, the diner is expected to stir them all together in the largest bowl and season to taste. Among the favorites are *bibimbap*, a rice dish topped with chopped or strip-grilled beef, vegetables (usually spinach, bean sprouts, shiitake mushrooms, daikon, watercress or julienned zucchini, and carrots), egg, and hoisin or chili sauce, which is served layered like a composed salad and then stirred up by the diner; and *yookwhe bibimbap*, which has raw beef coated with sesame oil instead of the grilled version. Traditionally, yookwhe bibimbap is served with a raw egg, too, but like many Japanese restaurants, Korean establishments have often shifted to either serving cooked eggs or offering a choice. (In fact, bibimbap originated as a way of using up small amounts of leftovers; the generosity of the vegetables involved now reflects the reverse influence of American culinary culture on Korean tradition.) *Hwehdobap* (or *hwaidupbap*) is sort of a cross between bibimbap and Japanese chirashizushi, with thin strips of raw fish over noodles, seaweed, daikon radish, carrots, and so forth.

Jigae is a type of soup with hot bean paste mixed into the broth: *Ke-jigae* is a crab version, *dubu-jigee* is usually pork and bean curd, and *sook-jigae* is a jumbo gumbo of cuttlefish, pork, tofu, scallions, squash, and egg. *Jim* refers to a braise; *kalbi-jim* is short ribs braised in mirin and soy. *Jungol* means "casserole" and can feature shellfish, sea cucumber, seafood, and tripe or often, in a sort of deluxe version, all of the above; a particularly fancy variation, frequently translated as "caviar stew" (or, more bluntly, fish egg soup) features bean curd and cod or herring roe in a hot chili broth. *Haejaengook* or *baejangkook* is a hearty stew often prescribed as a hangover remedy, thickened with blood sausage and served with lots of scallions.

Koreans are also fond of a version of Mongolian hot pot called *sin sul lo* or *shin sun ro*, which uses a steamboat or firepot dish with a chimney for charcoal. (See "How to Order and Eat Like a Native".) A similar dish involving seafood, called *maeun-tang*, can be either a light stew or a thicker gumbo.

BEVERAGES With meals, Koreans generally drink beer or rice wines. *Shochu* (or *shoju*), a sort of vodka-sake cross; and *makkolli*, a cloudy, fermented-rice liquor particularly suited to anju, are the most common beverages. A slightly more refined makkolli, closer to Japanese sake, is called *tongdongju* or, more slangily, *popju*; ginseng wine is called *insamchu*. Western-style liquor and beer are also popular.

Koreans take tea very seriously; in the teahouses, dedicated to traditional enjoyment and contemplation of the beverage, there may be imaginative brews flavored with roasted corn or barley, wild sesame, ginseng, ginger, cinnamon, arrowroot, citron, or quince.

SWEETS Koreans do not generally eat desserts, although they will occasionally offer children crackers or American candy; fresh fruits are more common at the end of a meal. Sweets are usually limited to holidays or special occasions.

HOW TO ORDER
AND EAT LIKE A NATIVE

Many Korean restaurants in Korea, and a growing number in the United States as well, are specialty shops, preparing only particular kinds of dishes. A *bulgoki-jip* is a barbecue joint (literally, a "beef house"), a *saengsan-hweh-jip* the local sushi bar, a *mandoo-jip* a dumpling kitchen, and a *poonsik-jip* a noodle counter, where you can watch the cooks hand-pull, stretch, thin, and finally cut the chewy noodles that are the third major food group. There are also what are called *suljip*— the tapas bars of Korea, serving mostly anju and cocktails and catering primarily to students and happy-hour types.

However, the vast majority of Korean restaurants in the United States are full-service establishments, where you can sample some of everything, including sushi. But start slowly, because every meal comes with rice (even breakfast, when it may be a kind of gruel) or rice mixed with other grains and a number of small side orders, called *panchan*—bowls of mung bean spouts, squash or spinach in sesame oil, garlic stems, raw or dried squid, dried shrimp, watercress or cilantro, grated turnip or radish, and of course kimchee. (The assortment should provide the mouth with contrasts of textures, spices, and flavors.) All dishes after the panchan are served at once, including soup and sushi (although some restaurants here have shifted to a dual-course service). It's customary to share at least a couple of dishes, such as a noodle dish, payjun, or bulgoki. Individual bowls of steamed rice come with dinner; unlike the manners in other Asian countries, where the bowl is held up to the mouth, it is considered more polite in Korea to eat without lifting the rice bowl off the table. Remember that "appetizers" may be more like light entrees.

Most foods are eaten with either chopsticks and spoons, in the case of one-pot meals, or chopsticks and fingers for barbecue, sushi or sashimi, and anju. (As elsewhere, it is considered rude to leave your chopsticks jammed into your rice.) Barbecued meats are taken off the brazier with chopsticks, placed into a lettuce leaf with a bite of rice, green onion, and chili or bean paste, rolled up, and then eaten with the fingers. (In the United States, especially for American customers, the waitresses may come along and take the grilled meat or chicken off the brazier for you and place it on a plate, which will allow you to eat it with chopsticks, if you prefer.) Yookwhe, the sesame-flavored beef tartare, is eaten the same way. Short ribs are eaten with the fingers.

The "flat dishes," such as bindaeduck, can be eaten either with your fingers or with chopsticks; the larger payjun can be torn into smaller pieces with the chopsticks and then attacked either way. To eat gulchupan, use your chopsticks—the thicker ends, not the eating ends—to place the fillings into your pancake, then use your fingers to roll it up, dip it into the sauce, and eat it; ditto for most anju. The large-bowl dishes—the rice-based bibimbaps and noodle dishes—are eaten with both the chopsticks and with long-handled teaspoon-like spoons, used primarily for stirring ingredients and seasonings together. You may slurp your noodles, within reason. For soups, use the chopsticks for picking out the meats or seafood and the spoon for the broth.

Sin sul lo, the hot pot meal, is eaten communally and requires chopsticks. The traditional firepot looks something like a stovepipe hat with the brim turned up and the crown sliced off; thin slices of beef, onions, carrots, scallions, chrysanthemum leaves, shrimp, pork meatballs, and perhaps walnuts or pine nuts are arranged around the bowl. When it is brought to the table, hot coals are transferred to the chimney, the lid is replaced, and boiling stock is poured into the "moat"; and as the food cooks, diners remove bits from the broth, dip them into a sesame-flavored sauce, and eat them over the rice bowl.

A meal for two might consist of an order of steamed or fried dumplings, one order of bulgoki, and perhaps a charbroiled fish. A party of four should order bindaeduk or some sashimi or, if you don't like raw fish, perhaps soon dae sausages; two barbecues (bulgalbi and either chicken or, if available, eel) or one beef dish and a rice or noodle dish such as bibimbap or jajaengmyon; it will be a lot of food.

If you have several people in your party, or perhaps a family group, find out whether the restaurant offers *chongsik* dinners, banquet-style meals that usually require 24 hours' advance notice; a chongsik menu is apt to run to as many as 20 dishes, including baked shellfish, meat-stuffed peppers, fried oysters, and elaborate stews as well as grilled meats. (*Hanjungsik* banquets, formal court affairs, run to 100 dishes or more.)

Dining in Korean restaurants is typically inexpensive to moderately expensive; most dishes cost under $10. After discovering how much food it can be, you may order less and save more. The chongsik dinners may be somewhat more costly, perhaps $25 a person.

COOKING AT HOME

Re-creating Korean food at home is fairly easy, even if you don't have a hot pot for sin sul ro; it can be made in a large wok or electric frypan, and barbecues can be made either outdoors on a grill or inside in a skillet (galbi can be broiled or oven-roasted as well). If you have a small hibachi, you can even grill tableside. Because the panchan (side dishes) can be made in advance, the meat marinated overnight, and the rice timed, you can eat whenever you decide to fire up the grill.

Traditionally, Korean men and women dined separately (aristocrats and scholars often ate in their studies), dining off low, wide tables more like footed trays, so you could sit around the hibachi on the floor or set on the coffee table. Use bowls only—small for the panchan (you can refill them as needed), medium for rice, and larger for the main dishes and noodles. Offer plenty of spices: red chili paste, dried red chilies, soy sauce, and lots of kimchee. This essential relish can be obtained in any Asian market, but there are relatively quick versions, like the one offered here, that allow you to control the heat and garlic level.

Incidentally, a great many of the dishes used in Korean restaurants, particularly to serve rice, are stainless steel or perhaps brass; this is a remnant of the tradition that required all bowls, spoons, and chopsticks to be silver, because silver was believed to discolor in the presence of poison, thus conflating hospitality and precaution. Even today, bridal dowries contain at least some silver pieces. However, more and more restaurant settings are simply porcelain; some larger one-pot dishes or casseroles are served in preheated stoneware bowls or crocks or even cast-iron skillets.

BARBECUE MARINADE
(for bulgoki, bulgalbi, chicken, etc.)

6 tablespoons soy sauce
1/2 cup mirin or dry sherry
2 tablespoons water or beef stock
2 tablespoons toasted, crushed sesame seeds
or 2 tablespoons sesame oil
2 heaping tablespoons sugar
4 scallions, white and pale green parts, finely chopped
2 tablespoons finely minced garlic
2 tablespoons grated ginger
ground black pepper to taste

Combine all ingredients. Marinate meats 3 to 4 hours, covered, or overnight in the refrigerator. Grill or broil meat as desired; serve with steamed rice, dipping sauce, and spinach (cooked, squeezed dry, and dressed with sesame oil and a touch of vinegar) and kimchee. This amount of marinade will cover about 2 pounds of sirloin, flank, or rump roast and 3 pounds or more of short ribs.

BULGOKI DIPPING SAUCE

1/4 cup soy sauce
2 teaspoons sesame oil
1 teaspoon Chinese bean paste or red miso (optional)
1/4 cup mirin, sake, or dry sherry
1 teaspoon roasted ground sesame seeds
1 tablespoon finely chopped spring onion
1 heaping tablespoon honey or sugar
1 teaspoon grated fresh ginger
1 teaspoon crushed dried red chili, chili paste,
or pepper sauce (more to taste)
1 clove garlic, minced (more to taste)
salt to taste

Combine first nine ingredients (up to the chilies, if using honey). "Cream" garlic with salt and (if you are using it) sugar into a smooth paste and mix into sauce. Serve in individual bowls.

"QUICK" KIMCHEE

1 large head Chinese or celery cabbage
3 cloves garlic
1 dried red chili, crushed (more for second variation),
or 2 teaspoons hot pepper sauce
1 tablespoon soy sauce
2 teaspoons grated fresh ginger
2 tablespoons sea salt or coarse kosher salt
(more for second variation)
2 teaspoons seasoned rice vinegar
1 tablespoon sugar

For "instant" kimchee, simply chop the cabbage into small pieces, crush the garlic, blend with remaining ingredients, and let stand at room temperature until ready to serve (refrigerate if you will be waiting more than 3 or 4 hours).

For a slightly more powerful and somewhat more traditional version, begin a week or 10 days before the day of entertaining. Cut the bottom off the cabbage, slice lengthwise into five or six sections, and let dry (in the sun, to be really authentic) for 3 or 4 hours. Then coarsely chop and layer in a crock, interspersed with generous coverings of salt and red pepper. Top with a wooden tray or plate small enough to fit inside the dish, weight it down with a large stone or iron, and let it sit for up to a week (allowing another 4 days before serving). Then rinse thoroughly under cold water (and wash the crock as well); squeeze out as much moisture as possible; and return to the crock, this time layering with the combined remaining ingredients. Add water or light stock to cover cabbage. Cover with wax paper or slightly loose plastic wrap, replace top, and refrigerate until serving.

PART VI

THE AMERICAS

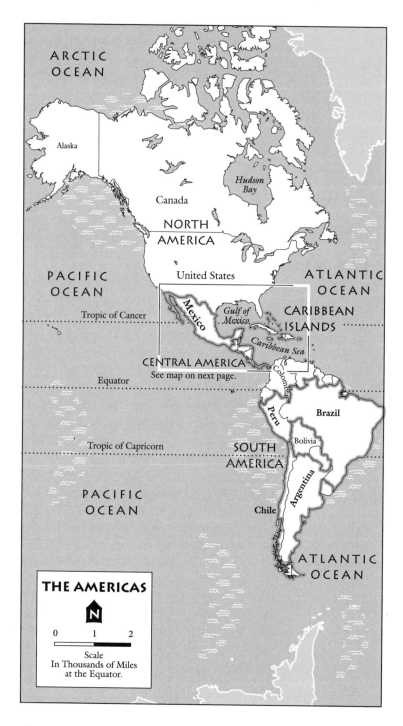

THE AMERICAS

N

0   1   2

Scale
In Thousands of Miles
at the Equator.

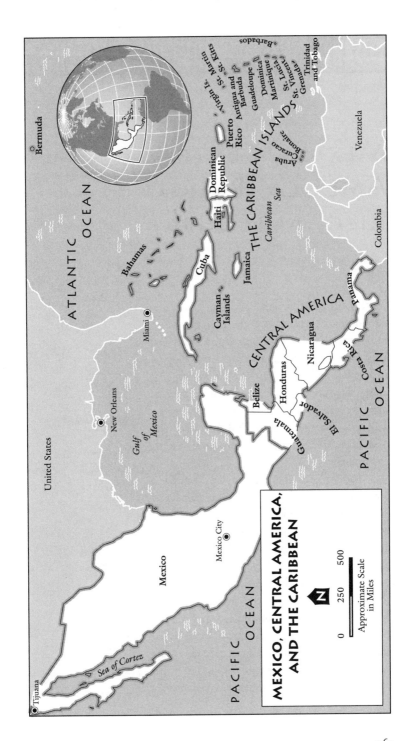

MEXICO, CENTRAL AMERICA, AND THE CARIBBEAN

Approximate Scale in Miles

0   250   500

N

THE CARIBBEAN ISLANDS

Barbados

Virgin Is. St. Martin St. Kitts
Puerto Rico Antigua and Barbuda
Guadeloupe
Dominica
Martinique
St. Lucia
St. Vincent
Grenada
Trinidad and Tobago

Bermuda

ATLANTIC OCEAN

Dominican Republic

Haiti

Bahamas

Cuba

Jamaica

Cayman Islands

Aruba Curaçao Bonaire

Caribbean Sea

Venezuela

Colombia

Panama

Costa Rica

Nicaragua

Honduras

El Salvador

Belize

Guatemala

CENTRAL AMERICA

PACIFIC OCEAN

Miami

New Orleans

Gulf of Mexico

United States

Mexico City

Mexico

Sea of Cortez

Tijuana

PACIFIC OCEAN

363

MEXICO, CENTRAL AMERICA, PUERTO RICO, AND CUBA

Perhaps the most astonishing thing about Central America, Mexico, and the islands of Cuba and Puerto Rico is how thoroughly we have confused language with culture. The terms *Hispanic* and *Latino* both refer to the Spanish language, paying lip service to the conquistadors rather than the natives, even though the Indians still dominate the population. "Indians" itself is a misnomer, as Columbus was nowhere near the East Indies.

"Latino" or not, more than a million Mexicans speak only Indian languages. El Salvador is 80% *mestizos*—people of mixed native, European, and African blood. Guatemala is evenly divided between mestizos and Indians; Honduras and Nicaragua have only small white minorities. Despite the importance of pork, beef, chicken, and rice, which were introduced by the Spanish, the cuisines of Mexico and Central America are still heavily dependent on the Indian staples: chilies, tomatoes, beans, avocados, nuts, sweet potatoes, and, most important, corn, which they have been cultivating for 7,000 years.

Moreover, although it may be a poor substitute for revenge, the foods of the New World revolutionized the cuisines of the Old World: Mexico was the source for what became "French" vanilla, "Italian" tomatoes (spaghetti sauce! pizza!), "Hungarian" paprika, and, from the cocoa that the Aztecs reserved for their priestly class, "Swiss" chocolate. The *gran turco* of sixteenth-century Venice, which they called the "Turkish grain," was actually Mexican cornmeal that came to the Mediterranean via Middle Eastern trade routes. Native Americans were making whiskey long before Columbus arrived; though the Europeans swept agricultural concern aside in their quest for American gold, the chilies, peanuts, and particularly the chocolate, tomatoes, and tobacco they sent back eventually provided greater wealth than Ferdinand and Isabella could ever have imagined.

(Although Cuba and Puerto Rico are included in this chapter because of the heavy Spanish influence on their cuisines, it may be helpful to skim the following chapter on "The Caribbean Islands" for additional information.)

THE HISTORY

Central and southern Mexico and Central America were the site of a series of great native civilizations going back four millennia to the Olmec, whose gigantic stone sculptures survive today. The Mayans' writing system, calendars, astronomical calculations, and conceptually dazzling mathematical system were fully developed by about 1500 B.C.E. At its peak, about the eighth century B.C.E., the Mayan empire ruled an estimated 14 million people; about 2 million ethnic Mayans still live in the Yucatán and in Guatemala and Honduras. They were gradually dominated by a series of increasingly aggressive tribes, leading up to the Toltec (the "master builders" of pyramids) and finally the Aztecs—or Mexicos, as they called themselves—who under their last king, Moctezuma (Montezuma), made the fatal error of welcoming the Spanish conquistadors as celestial visitors.

Once the Spanish had taken control in the early sixteenth century, however, such glories were forgotten. The conquistadors established a three-layer caste system, with the Spanish at the top, the natives at the bottom, and the mestizos caught in the middle. Within a few decades, the system had become even more ornate, with the Spanish-born governors and military lording it over even the "pureblood" Spanish born in the New World, or Creoles. This societal divide would gradually cripple the native underclass and define the nation's subsequent history of civil wars, coups, presidencies, dictatorships, and so on. (Just look at how many reformist names are familiar, despite their failures: Father Hidalgo, Benito Juarez, Pancho Villa, Emiliano Zapata.) Since World War II, increased U.S. economic aid has helped somewhat, but the legacy of the Spanish caste system remains Mexico's most visible social and economic failure.

Culinarily speaking, the Spanish have kept their grip as well. The only other major influence has come from the brief residencies of French governments in Mexico City, one during the reign of Napoleon I, who conquered Spain in 1808; and the other under Napoleon III, who dispatched the unfortunate Hapsburg Maximilian to rule Mexico as emperor (he lasted three years). Not even the loss of California, Texas, and the Southwest to the United States during the war of 1846–48 has altered the cuisine too drastically; in fact, the revival of interest in Native American cuisine has found some of its strongest proponents in the United States.

Cuba, which was visited by Columbus on his first voyage in 1492, was strategically positioned to become the base of Spanish operations in the New World, because it stretches out across the mouth of the Gulf of Mexico and offers access to both the Caribbean and the Atlantic. Not surprisingly, it was equally attractive to French, British, Dutch, and Carib marauders. It was also an early mainstay of the slave trade: The gentle Arawaks, beset by disease, enforced labor, and punitive living conditions, were all but wiped out within decades of the Spanish landings and were replaced by African and other Indian captives. Nevertheless, thanks to a constant influx of Europeans, the island prospered; today the population is an ethnic mix of black, European, and transplants from other Latin countries, along with a trace of Indian.

One of Spain's earliest cash cows, Cuba was thickly planted with the sugarcane that was used for making molasses (and, more profitably, rum); even today, two-thirds of its arable land is given over to cane and another large chunk to tobacco. On what remains, subsistence farmers raise rice, corn, beans, citrus fruits, squash, sweet potatoes, and yucca, but they depend heavily on livestock, particularly chicken and pigs, and on fish and seafood. (The love-hate relationship between Cuba and the United States, which first liberated the island from Spain in 1898 and then "protected" the fledgling republic, is intertwined with the sugar economy.) However, in culinary terms, the most important connection is the bustling community of Little Havana in Miami, which is reviving classic Cuban cuisine and also helping develop a new "Miami spice" style. (For more on *norteño* or Tex-Mex cooking and new Miami cuisine, see the Appendix on regional cuisines of the United States.)

Puerto Rico—the "rich port" of the Spanish colonists—sits at the eastern gate of the Caribbean and so was also an early fortress and trading center for the Spanish; despite the repeated attempts of the French, British, and Dutch to acquire it, it remained staunchly Spanish, at least in the north. In the south, facing South America and the other islands, it was a busy contraband market. Like Cuba, it is a virtual sugarcane factory and also produces coffee and tobacco. It is the most populous of the Caribbean islands, having been the most prosperous; it still has one of the densest populations in the world. As a U.S. protectorate (also since the Spanish-American War) and increasingly popular tourist destination, it has served to introduce many travelers to traditional Spanish-Caribbean fare.

THE CUISINES

Real Mexican food used to be an oxymoron in the United States, and there are still many important ingredients, fruits, vegetables, herbs, and even flowers, that have never made it to U.S. markets. Nevertheless, the culinary scene has improved tremendously, partly because of the improved economic position of Mexican-Americans and partly thanks to the interest of modern Mexican, Southwestern, and Tex-Mex chefs. (Mexico itself has some 500 registered culinary schools.) Mexican cuisine is just barely recognizable in the refried beans and other internally confounding dishes found in the frozen-dinner and fast-food lanes: "Refried" beans aren't actually fried twice at all, only very well fried; burritos, in fact, are a norteño invention. Mexican rice is not a ketchup-coated porridge, as it is in U.S. cafeterias, but a kind of pilaf, with the grains blanched, simmered in oil, and then cooked in broth and fresh tomatoes.

In fact, authentic Mexican cuisine would seem very modern today. The Native Americans were cooking with sun-dried tomatoes centuries ago. (Intriguingly, the Mayan language differentiated between foods not so much by type as by texture—firm versus soft, for example—or methods of consumption.) The Aztec priests and aristocrats drank chocolate, though probably in a bitter form; and created *mole* (pronounced MO-lay, from the Nahuatl word for "mixture"), the distinctive chili sauce, often spiked with bitter chocolate, that is one of the signatures of Mexican cooking. Moctezuma's imperial kitchen prepared hundreds of dishes, including shrimp casserole with tomato sauce and *pepitas* (pumpkin seeds). They grew corns, beans, Jerusalem artichokes, and chilies; hunted wild boar, tapir, and such neo-Southwest delicacies as armadillo and rattlesnake; snared turkeys and other game birds, as well as waterfowl; and fished for fresh- and saltwater delicacies. (Less "modern," perhaps, but indicative of the often underestimated variety of their diet, are other protein sources: guinea pigs, dogs, manatees, monkeys, and even large grasshoppers. But such ingenuity was essential in a country where only 15% of the land mass is arable.)

Chilies were both spice and preservative, preferred to salt; of the 20 or so wild varieties of the *capsicum* species, four or five had already been domesticated by Native Americans before the European incursions, including the Tabasco, the habañero, jalapeño, the cayenne, and its mild offspring, the bell pepper. Chilies were believed to be medicinal and healthful as well, and modern nutritionists agree. The Native Americans also had honey for sweetening, and a great many spices and herbs not familiar today. They used peanut oil for cooking.

It was a healthful diet, high in carbohydrates and protein and extremely low in fat, at least until the Spanish arrived. They introduced sugar, pork, beef, cheese, and butter, and one of the region's least nutritious habits, frying in lard. To an overwhelming extent, Mexican cuisine is still a combination of Indian/mestizo and Spanish elements. Over the centuries, black and Creole slaves; French, British, and Portuguese traders; and Chinese and Indian laborers provided a few flourishes, but only a few: One of the scant traces of the brief French "empire" of the mid-nineteenth century is a fondness for crêpes and crisp bread.

One of the greatest distinctions between Mexican cooking and the cuisine of its Caribbean neighbors is in the preliminary handling of seasonings: The roasting or toasting of chilies, onions, garlic, and tomatoes before cooking is a hallmark of authentic Mexican food. In fact, the three-legged stone *molcajetes*, the bowl-like pestles in which mole is traditionally mixed, is enjoying a sort of revival among culinary trendies.

Most dishes are either grilled or stewed or braised in clay pots. Soft dishes, such as rice and beans or meat stews, are eaten with a fork, but thick bean or sausage dishes are often wrapped in tortillas and eaten by hand. (Again, this may have something to do with the geography of the region: The poorest Indians, many of whom were field laborers or live-stock herders, packed along foods that required the fewest utensils or containers; the coastal dwellers, whose more tropical foods were picked fresh and spoiled quickly, preferred pots for combining ingredients.)

Considering the geographical and climatic variety of the region—mountainous coasts, especially along the Pacific, prairies, plateaus, and thick jungles, all susceptible to hurricanes, earthquakes, and volcanic eruptions—it is surprising how similar the cuisines are. However, there are some local distinctions: The northern sections and the large ports, such as Veracruz, tend to show the strongest Spanish influence; the north is also the wheat-growing and cattle-grazing area, so flour tortillas and steaks are most popular there. Corn meal—that is, *masa harina*, or tortilla dough—is a little more textured in the north, and the tamales are smaller.

The Yucatán region produces particularly spicy fare, and Chihuahuan dishes tend to use a little more vinegar than most others. Oaxaca, home of tequila and mescal, also produces moles that are considered some of the finest. The central plateau, particularly Mexico City, has the most cosmopolitan fare and the most visible French influence. Masa from the region is very fine, and the *tamales* famously light and spongy (and large). The higher plateau-dwellers, particularly Indians, still lean on the precolonial staples of their ancestors—tortillas, beans, tomatoes, and hot chilies, plus cheese and other dairy products. The tropical lowlands and coastal areas are more reliant on fruits, nuts, vegetables, seafood, and poultry.

Thanks to its Spanish imprint, Puerto Rican cuisine is noticeably more meat-heavy than most of its Caribbean neighbors—livestock cultivation runs a close second to sugarcane production—and its otherwise fairly straightforward dishes are primarily distinguished by their Spanish, rather than curry- or jerk-style, mixtures of spices. *Adobo*, a chili spice–vinegar barbecue that the Spanish developed in Puerto Rico, turned out to be so addictive that they carried it through Mexico and westward to the Philippines, where it is now the national dish. In return the Puerto Ricans adopted paella, and they still serve an elaborate version. In Puerto Rico's more upscale restaurants there are also strong reminders of the Italians, Germans, and French, who began vacationing and trading there in the nineteenth century, but little of that has moved to the United States.

Cuban food is much like Puerto Rican, though both have one foot in Mexico and one foot in the West Indies, so to speak. Unlike its more tropical neighbors, however, Cuban food is not so highly spiced and rarely incorporates fresh fruit or fruit salsas into meals; instead, they tend to consume fresh fruit separately or to drink juice.

THE MAIN INGREDIENTS

To grasp just how "American" these cuisines are, consider the list of foods unknown to Europeans until the sixteenth century: tomatoes, coriander, chilies, cocoa, avocados, bananas, beans, corn, potatoes, yams, vanilla, turkey and various other game birds, pine nuts, pecans, peanuts, squash, and tobacco. What the Europeans did bring was significant— rice and wheat, olives, beef, mutton, goat, pork, almonds, cinnamon and nutmeg, raisin and wine grapes, and Seville oranges and limes. (Oddly, they would later attempt to stamp out the production of both olives and wine grapes, fearing the loss of valuable monopolies in Europe.) With these foods, they also introduced the techniques of making bread, oil, wine, and vinegar; for distilling hard liquor; and for transforming milk into cheese—but their contributions, though absorbed into the New World cuisine, did not eradicate it.

SEASONINGS Among the most popular flavorings in the region are cilantro, the lemony parsley also known as coriander, and its seeds; cinnamon; *annatto* (achiote) seeds, which provide a pungent flavor and distinctive red coloring; cloves; bay leaves; oregano; sesame seeds; ground nuts and seeds, particularly pumpkin (*pepita*); dried shrimp; citrus and vinegars; and *epazote*, a pungent, sawtoothed herb sometimes called "Mexican tea." The leaves of the avocado are also very popular, slipped fresh into stews, roasted, dried, or ground.

Seasoning blends include mole, a combination of chocolate, chilies, ground nuts and spices, and herbs; *adobado*, a garlic-based chili marinade or rub that underlies the Spanish adobo, or stew; and *recado*, a garlicky chili paste particularly popular in the Yucatán and Tabasco. *Chile colorado* is a red sauce, the salsa most Americans are familiar with, and *chile verde* is a green sauce that is usually not as hot. "Salsa" simply means sauce; true salsas can be of all raw ingredients (most often used for kid or lamb), simmered (for tortilla dishes), or green with parsley (for chicken and pork). The most basic version is raw chopped tomatoes, chilies, fresh cilantro, and onions; *salsa ranchero* is very similar version but cooked. However, more ornate salsas are made with dried shrimp, *huitlacoche* (corn fungus), or extra-hot chilies, like the habañero salsas of Yucatán. An old Oaxaca recipe calls for roasting pumpkin seeds, dried shrimp, avocado leaves, and chilies and grinding them all together for gamier meats, such as rabbit or armadillo.

Puerto Ricans have adopted the Italian seasoning blend called, just as it is in Italy, *sofrito*, a sauté of diced onions, tomatoes, garlic, and parsley, but they usually give it a characteristic spicy and meaty punch with the addition of chilies and salt pork or ham.

Chilies are an entire chapter in themselves—more than half the 200 recognized varieties of chilies are grown in Mexico—but among the most important (and those commonly found in the United States) are the notoriously fiery habañero; the familiar dark green jalapeño, used both fresh and pickled; the chipotle, a dried and then smoked jalapeño; the blistering serrano, which is smaller than a jalapeño but similar and which turns from green to scarlet and finally yellow; the large, green, triangular poblano, which is relatively mild and almost always roasted before being used; and the ancho, which is a dried poblano with an especially rich, almost sweet flavor.

The southerly cuisines lean less to chilies and bitterer spices, such as cinnamon, cloves, and nuts, and more to vinegary, citrusy flavors. *Aji* means both the hot aji pepper itself and a South and Central American condiment or dipping sauce.

FRUITS The Mexican coastal regions and the Central American countries are rich in citrus, bananas and plantains, and *maguay*, the plant from which the tequila-like mescal is derived. The farther south one goes, the more "Caribbean" the landscape: Coconuts and coconut milk, avocados, dates, figs, watermelon, mangoes (not introduced until the nineteenth century, but a perfect fit), pineapple, and other tropical fruits begin to make appearances.

VEGETABLES Many people think the region's vegetable dishes begin and end with beans, and in fact a rainbow of black, brown, purple, pink, white, and green-and-white striped beans are available, along with broad beans and green and long beans. (Beans are traditionally the fourth course of the major midday meal, served after the meat or fish.) In addition, however, these countries produce many squashes and pumpkins, along with the now-trendy squash blossoms, peas, chayote (vegetable pear), jicama, various edible cacti (particularly *nopales* paddles with their okra-like viscosity), sweet peppers, a wide variety of mushrooms, the tangy-sour tomatillos (often incorrectly referred to as green tomatoes), true red and green tomatoes, avocados, white and sweet potatoes, cassava, and the versatile yucca. In addition to corn itself, the Mexicans in particular value the mushroomy corn fungus called huitlacoche, which is beginning to be popular in new Mexican and Southwestern restaurants in the United States.

GRAINS AND STARCHES   Corn is far and away the most vital grain crop, of course, but both rice and wheat are widely cultivated (the latter primarily for tortilla flour). Amaranth, a tiny and nutritionally rich grain that is as old as corn, has recently become popular in the United States as a health food, although few restaurants offer it. Mexican chefs interested in older Indian dishes have also revived other alternative grains, such as quinoa (pronounced KEEN-wah) and wheat berries. In poorer areas, plantains, cassava (taro root), and yucca may be used to produce dough.

MEAT   Ever since the Spanish introduced pork, it has been a mainstay of the diet, although in the north in particular, beef is preferred. Goat and lamb are almost equally popular. *Chorizo* is a spicy, unsmoked pork sausage. Some of the more ambitious establishments in the wealthier tourist areas, such as Acapulco, and in the United States offer European-style dishes of venison or boar. Organ meats and offal are extremely popular, particularly brains, kidneys, and tripe; grilled chicken hearts and livers are a Central American favorite.

POULTRY AND EGGS   Chicken have been cultivated since the Spanish arrived, but stronger-flavored birds, such as turkey (the primary bird in ancient times), pheasant, quail, and squab, are still preferred.

DAIRY PRODUCTS   Cheese is widely consumed throughout the region, but despite the ubiquity of sour cream on U.S. fast-food menus (along with "nacho-flavored" tortilla chips and sugary salsa), other dairy products are not major ingredients. Among the most popular cheeses are *cotija*, which is something like a Parmigiano; *queso ranchero*, which is a mild but fresh-tasting white cheese; *queso fresco*, used for stuffings and toppings (the closest thing to the orangy plastic used in the United States); the feta-like *oñejo;* the stringy, mozzarella-ish *asadero;* the dry, strong, Romano-style *ranchero seco;* and *manchego*, a ripe, full-bodied cheese used for smooth melting.

FISH AND SHELLFISH   Few countries enjoy the variety of seafood that Mexico and its neighbors do: marlin, black bass, tuna, trout, sailfish, swordfish, dogfish shark, amberjack, grouper, pompano, dorado, gar, sole, bream, skate, shrimp, mussels, squid, freshwater snails, scallops, oysters, lobsters, crabs, and even sea turtles. So-called chocolate clams (*almejas chocolates*), far from being dark brown, are rimmed with a coral red as if they were wearing lipstick; pismo clams are pink, and pinna clams look like scallops.

STREET FOOD

Mexicans and Central Americans love what they call *antojitos*, or "little whims," which they pick up from street vendors and grilling stalls and consume at long wooden communal tables. These antojitos—the originals of the tacos, burritos, and such that are now mass-produced in inferior form by Tex-Mex chain restaurants—are a perfect example of what we described in the preface as "first-generation food"—quick and cheap market dishes. Many of these street fare items are also popular home cooking, not white-linen table fare but somewhere in between: The central course of the main meal, the meat or fish dish, is nearly always accompanied by some kind of tortilla dish; and a sort of giant tamale stuffed with pork and chicken is a traditional dish on All Saint's Day (a slice is usually left for the spirits).

TORTILLA DISHES In Mexican markets, the street cooks have a variety of grilled meats, barbecue, vegetables, fish, shrimp, and even organ meats, which they chop with a cleaver, toss into a tortilla, and top with salsa or onions to suit your taste. This is pretty much the sort of food found in cheap-eats diners called *cochinas economicas* or in restaurants with the sign *comida casera*—"home cooking." (Mom-and-pop Central American restaurants that dish out blue plate specials, working-class meals of beans, rice, and a bit of meat are called *comefores*.)

Handy Food

Virtually every meal in Mexico, even the more formal dinners of several courses, will include some finger food. The French say "A meal without wine is like a day without sunshine," but Mexicans would substitute the word "tortilla" for "wine." Most mercado or vendor food can be eaten by hand, wrapped in tortillas. Similarly, any restaurant dish that is thick enough can be turned into tortilla stuffing—the meats from the thicker stews, organ meats, and even some seafood: Oyster tamales are popular in Veracruz.

Stuffed chilies, grilled meats on the bone, and tortas sandwiches are all, likewise, finger food. (Incidentally, most tortas include beans, which may surprise first-timers.) Meats that involve bones—such as goat *birria*, which in some places you can order by cut (shoulder, rib, leg)—can be eaten by hand as well. Tamales are wrapped in corn husks or banana leaves before steaming; these wrappings are not edible but should pull away cleanly from the tamale if it has been cooked long enough.

Central American *mercados*, or markets, are also dotted with stalls and vendors serving *comidas corrientes*—roughly, "the local stuff." Frequently, street vendors just place a sheet of metal across a simple fire and fry tortillas on them. Guatemalans particularly enjoy *chiles rellenos*: Whole peppers are used as the "wrapping" for chicken and vegetables or cheese and are then fried.

To clarify the confusion about the names of such dishes: Tortillas are the disks, either large or small, that are used to hold other ingredients. They may be made of masa harina or wheat flour. Tortillas are usually soft and pancake-like, not the hard, crumbly version common in the States, though you do sometimes find harder-fried tortillas in Jaliso and Yucatán. When they are fried, either to use for dipping or being recycled into stews, they are called *tostadas*, but even tostadas are rarely as hard as mass-market chips.

Tacos are the stuffed tortillas you can eat with your hands; enchiladas are rolled, filled, and sauced. Other tortilla-based foods include *sopas*, which are somewhat thicker, fried tortillas used to hold chilies or beans, a bit more like tacos in the United States; chalupas, or "small canoes," oval-shaped tacos; and quesadillas, filled and then grilled tamales stuffed with chicken, cheese, potatoes, and even scrambled eggs. *Chimichangas* are tortillas stuffed with chicken, cheese, or beef, and then fried. *Panvidos* are fried tortillas stuffed with turkey, black beans, and cheese.

TAMALES Tamales are made from the same corn meal dough as tortillas, but instead of being griddled or roasted, the meal is wrapped (traditionally in banana leaves or corn husks) and steamed. The whole process—grinding, forming, stuffing, wrapping, and steaming—takes a while, so tamale meals are often served at informal parties or family get-togethers. Tamales can be stuffed with pork, shrimp, plantains, potatoes, fresh corn, peanuts, chicken in tomato sauce, or chicken and cheese—but almost always with chilies. Sometimes tamale dough is sweetened with cinnamon, sugar, and raisins and served for breakfast or a late snack with coffee. The Nicaraguan *nacatamal* is served with a generous stuffing of braised pork, raisins, sweet and sometimes hot peppers, yucca or potatoes, and rice.

PUPUSAS Salvadoran *pupusas* are extremely popular; the "pat, pat, pat" sound of a pupusa maker is as familiar and telling to Central Americans as the "clap-slap" of sushi makers is to the Japanese. Pupusas are made from the inside out: A ground corn dough is patted around the meat, bean, or cheese filling and then grilled. They are traditionally served with pickled cabbage, called *curtido* or *repollo*, which is ladled onto the split-open pupusa to taste. *Pastelitos* are also ground corn dumplings filled with seasoned, minced meat. (The word *pastes* is derived from the "pasties" or meat pies that British silver miners used to make.)

In addition to the foods above, market fare is almost certain to include candied sweet potatoes, whole roasted ears of corn seasoned with chilies and lime, boiled peanuts or green garbanzos, pork cracklings, and fresh fruits and juices of many kinds.

Watch Your Mouth

It is important to note that the nomenclature of Mexican, Central American, and Cuban dishes is not uniform, and in this case it is not merely a matter of spelling. A Cuban tortilla is an omelet, not a flat corn pancake; a Mexican *torta* is a sandwich, not a sweet. A Central American *empanada* may be made of a mashed plantain dough and may have a sweet filling instead of pork or cheese; a Mexican or South American empanada is a fried wheat turn-over stuffed with meat. A Central American *quesadilla* is a dessert, not a cheese-stuffed soft tortilla, and a real Mexican quesadilla is a stuffed cornmeal turnover related to the papusa. (Again, see the appendix on American regional cuisines.) Cuts of meat are also rather loosely translated, and Cuban "ham" is frequently unsmoked. If you can't tell from the menu, you may want to ask.

MEXICAN SPECIALTIES

Although many of the dishes listed here originated in Mexico, many have spread throughout the region and are apt to appear on any Central or even South American menu. More Cuban and Central American dishes are described below.

APPETIZERS Any of the antonijos listed above might be offered as first courses, particularly at home. Among more formal appetizers, the most famous include *ceviche* (also spelled *cebiche* or *seviche*), raw seafood and fish "cooked" in the acid of fresh lime juice and chilies; *camarones*, shrimp, most often grilled or sautéed in butter and garlic; and *queso fundito*, a melted cheese with chilies and sometimes chorizo that is much more flavorful than the Americanized "nacho" cheese

SOUPS Black bean soup is probably the most famous Cuban and Puerto Rican starter, and is also popular along the Gulf Coast of Mexico, particularly in Veracruz; but the most common soups in Mexico are chicken-based, particularly chicken-and-rice soups and the tortilla soups that combine chicken broth (and perhaps a little leftover chicken) with leftover tortillas, tomatoes, cheese, and chilies. Regional soups also include *albondigas* (meatballs in broth); corn and/or crab chowders; avocado purees; the cold coconut soup that is a specialty of Jalisco, the beach resort region; the tangy tomato-and-crab soup of Veracruz; Yucatán's chicken and chicken liver soups spiked with bitter lime; citrus- and chili-spiked broths with strips of tortilla or rice; creamy shrimp soups (Mexican *crema* is more like crème fraîche than heavy cream); and squash and potato soups with cheese. *Sopa de pan*, or bread soup, is more like a layered appetizer casserole of bread, onions, tomatoes, plantains, beans, and hard-boiled eggs, soaked in broth and baked.

STEWS *Cocido* (also called *puchero* in some areas, although that term can just refer to stews in general) is a hearty soup, closer to a beef stew, that sometimes serves as a main course; in the chunkiest versions, the meat is spooned into tortillas, dashed with salsa, and eaten by hand. *Caldillo* or *cazuela* is close to what Americans generally mean by "chili"—ground beef cooked with tomatoes, chilies, onions, and beef broth. *Caldo* is a rich seafood soup; it is sometimes called *caldo siete mares*, which means "seven seas soup." *Sopa de mariscos* is a lighter, broth-based seafood soup. The tripe stew or soup called *menudo* is the Mexican hair of the dog, legendarily consumed as a hangover cure and always prepared on New Year's Day. (The Central American name for it is *mondongo*.) *Chocolomo* is a Saturday night special, because Saturday is usually market day, and this stew is made of freshly butchered beef and offal and seasoned with bitter lime. *Posole* is sometimes used to mean cornmeal mush made from the large whole hominy corn, but the term is also applied to a pork and hominy stew.

SEAFOOD Fish may be grilled, rubbed with achiote and lime, roasted, deep-fried, stuffed with crab or shrimp (*pescado relleño*), rubbed with a garlic paste or caper sauce, or pan-stewed with tomatoes and onions (known as *veracruzana*, or Veracruz-style). *Pescado envuelto* is usually a whole fish, such as black bass, dashed with olive oil, cilantro, and lemon, then wrapped in corn husks and steamed or poached. Newer-style Mexican restaurants also offer grilled and/or marinated squid, octopus, swordfish, or salmon steaks; some bake fish and seafood *al espanole*—in the Spanish or Mediterranean style—with olives and capers.

One traditional lobster treatment is to simmer it with its head and generous amounts of oregano and garlic, then thicken the broth at the end with masa harina. Shrimp is frequently baked in Veracruz sauce, grilled, as part of a mixed seafood platter, or simmered in a hot chili *escabeche* sauce; they also sometimes pop up inside quesadillas or "shredded" (really chopped) in empanadas. Turtle is not offered much in the United States, although you may see turtle stew or soup on the menu.

RICE DISHES Rice is often treated as a sort of dry soup, served as an intermediary course between the "wet" soup and the meat dish. It is always made with a long-grain variety. The basic choices are white (plain boiled rice), red (the Mexican rice described above), or green (cooked with fresh parsley, cilantro, and green chilies). However, various versions of *paella* and *arroz con pollo*—the Spanish all-in-one dish and the baked chicken casserole—are made everywhere across the region.

MEATS Pork being the mainstay, it receives the widest range of treatments. Pork may be roasted, marinated, rotisserie-grilled, stewed with prunes, dressed with green chili sauce or vinegar (*pibil*), or wrapped in banana leaves and steamed or braised. Sometimes pork is first braised in a seasoned broth and then pan-fried to crispness. The word *carne* simply means meat, but *carnitas* are usually chunks of fried pork. A raisin-and almond-stuffed boneless pork loin basted in a sweet-hot sauce is a popular holiday or banquet dish. Pork may also be done in an almost North African manner: stewed with green olives, raisins, almonds, cumin, and garlic and turned into mini–pot pies with masa dough crusts. *Albondigas*, or meatballs, are usually made of pork and beef together, mixed with rice and frequently diced zucchini, and generally served either in soup or as an entree with tomato sauce.

Among beef dishes, one of the most common is *carne machacada*, literally "pounded beef" (often shortened to *machaca*): Beef is thinly sliced and dried (or in some areas salted and dried) and then broiled before being pounded to a finely shredded, almost feathery consistency and mixed with onions and chilies and layered with tomato sauce. *Carne asada* is fairly well known in the United States, but this recipe was actually invented in the 1940s: beef marinated in Seville orange juice and served with green enchiladas. *Tinga* is a braised seasoned beef stewed with hot chilies. *Parilladas* are mixed grills, sometimes cooked on tabletop braziers, and may include spare ribs, flank steak, chicken, chorizo, blood sausage (*morcilla*), sweetbreads (*mollejas*), tongue (*lengua*), pork chops, seafood, fish, and even vegetables or plantains. *Bisteca ranchero* is a steak (often rib-eye or blade) layered with potatoes, tomato sauce, and chilies. In some areas very prime beef is turned into a sort of cross between steak tartare and ceviche, raw beef "cured" in escabeche spices. Fried beef, that is, the "chicken-fried steaks" of Texas, are more often found in the north.

Goat, particularly kid (*cabrito*), is almost always either roasted or braised for the vinegar- and clove-flavored birria; lamb is roasted, stewed, or braised for birria. (Birria and other stews are eaten with either tortillas or the French-style rolls called *bolillos*; see "How to Order and Eat Like a Native," page 382.) The braised heads of both kids and lambs are considered delicacies. Venison is roasted or stewed.

Organ meats from any or all of these animals are prized: kidneys, livers, tongues (particularly cabrito), and tripe. One dish is something like the Scottish haggis: sheep stomach stuffed with other organ meats. And in some big-city restaurants, particularly in Mexico City, where the French imperial influence was the strongest, plates of chilled assorted meats are served with vinaigrette.

POULTRY Chicken is frequently grilled—the charcoal-grilled chicken of Sinaloa is particularly famous—and then sauced with ground nuts and spices or tomatoes and onions. Chicken is especially well suited to the sweet-hot mole sauces and may be either stewed with the mole or grilled and then sauced. Chicken is also frequently stewed with earthy vegetables such as pumpkin and turnips, carrots, or sweet potatoes; or, especially in the southern Gulf regions, it may be flavored with citrus, cilantro, and coconut milk. Turkey, squab, and quail are very popular, often marinated in olive oil and wine vinegar before grilling; however, in the United States, restaurants generally offer only chicken or quail.

DAIRY PRODUCTS Eggs are an important source of nutrition, most often scrambled and served over or in tortillas; in the United States they are most frequently served in the hearty *huevos rancheros*—eggs fried sunnyside up, served over tortillas, and topped with tomatoes and salsa, chorizo, or the shredded meat called machaca. Eggs also pop up hard-boiled and chopped inside tortillas.

Cheese is more commonly an ingredient, but there is one dish worth mentioning because it sounds like an inside-out cheeseburger: *queso relleño*, a large, soft, Dutch-style cheese stuffed with spiced meat that is steamed until soft and runny and then topped with tomato sauce.

BEVERAGES The most popular nonalcoholic drinks in the region are milk and fruit shakes, sometimes with a raw egg added, called *batidos* in Cuba and *licuados* in Mexico. *Agua frescas* are slightly sweet fruit drinks. *Orchata* or *horchata* is a rice and milk version, something like rice pudding in a glass, flavored with vanilla, almond, or cinnamon (this in particular reminds us that Columbus first sailed to the New World in the same year that the Moors were expelled from Spain after centuries of culinary influence.) *Atole* is more corn, a sort of masa milkshake that comes with chocolate or other flavorings.

Among alcoholic beverages are beer—an industry vastly improved in the nineteenth century by the influx of German and Swiss immigrants, to the point that several brands are popular in the U.S. market as well—the trendy tequila, and its even trendier relative, mescal. (An over-enthusiastic first-time indulger in tequila might well have a new definition for "Moctezuma's revenge.) *Pulque* is a milder, self-fermented liquor made from the same plant as tequila, the agave, but it's a more rural or blue-collar drink and not available in the United States. Some upscale restaurants may serve coconut brandy or a surprising tequila "chaser" called *sangrita*, which is not to be confused with the more familiar wine-and-fruit punch called *sangria;* sangrita is a spanking mix of orange juice, grenadine, salt, and ground pequin chili.

One should also note that the Mexican wine industry, though very old—it dates to the Conquest of 1523, and the first grapevine planted in what is now the United States was a cutting from Baja California, transplanted in 1701—has just begun to draw international attention. Most promising are the Cabernet Sauvignons and Chenin Blancs of Baja.

CUBAN AND PUERTO RICAN SPECIALTIES

Cuba's unofficial national dish is black beans and rice, known as *moros y cristianos*, or "Moors and Christians," a name that dates back to the early days of the Spanish conquest, when the liberation of Spain from the Muslims was still a fresh memory. But in general, like the Puerto Ricans, Cubans have acquired the Spanish habit of preferring meat and seafood proteins to beans. Puerto Ricans, too, like the combination: They're particularly fond of what they call *asopaos*, rice-based stews featuring either chicken or seafood.

MEATS AND POULTRY Called *puerco asado* or sometimes *lechon asado*, roast pork marinated in citrus and garlic is a Cuban favorite (and no cooks seem to have more patience in slow-cooking onions to a caramel perfection than they). It is so commonly a Sunday-dinner sort of dish that in many restaurants it may be available even if it is not listed on the menu. Pork is also frequently cut into chunks and fried, or smoked into hams to be cooked with the black beans or with rice. Chorizo, the spicy sausage, is another pork specialty, and one habit-forming (though not exactly low-cal) Cuban appetizer is a quesadilla topped with sliced chorizo, then covered with melted cheese.

Adobo, the vinegar-chili marinade that the Spanish took with them to the Philippines, where it became a staple, originated in Puerto Rico, and adobo-flavored pork roasts are very traditional. Another Puerto Rican favorite is *mogongo*, a sort of skillet torte with a mashed plantain "dough" and grilled or fried meat on top.

Ropa viejo (literally, "old clothes") is a seasoned beef stew cooked till it falls into shreds; *tasajo* is a dry-cured seasoned beef that originated in Brazil and the Caribbean but is also popular in Cuba and Puerto Rico. *Picadillo* is a dish of ground beef and/or pork sautéed in lard or drippings with onions, chorizo, and salt. *Bolicha* is a pot roast or braised brisket. Cubans are expert at preparing lamb and goat as well, although these meats are not quite so common in the United States; in the most authentic spots in established Cuban or Puerto Rican neighborhoods (Miami or Los Angeles, for example), you may find organ stews, such as tripe and brains.

Chicken may be quick-fried (called *chicharron*) or stewed in tomatoes and wine as well as roasted; rabbit (which, just as promised, tastes very much like chicken) is not infrequently offered in similar dishes.

SEAFOOD Cuban shellfish, although perhaps not as famous as the country's meat dishes, is delicious; *mariscos* means "seafood" and is often written on the outside of Mexican or Cuban (or Puerto Rican advertising as Cuban) restaurants to demonstrate that fresh seafood is prepared inside. Spanish-style paella, the shellfish- and ham-studded rice casserole, is very popular, along with garlicky sautéed shrimp, Caribbean-style salt cod stews, and pan-fried whole fish, such as red snapper. *Choros* are steamed mussels, usually with lots of broth to sop up. *Calamares*, or squid, is usually braised in tomatoes or wine and served over rice; as an appetizer, squid is usually fried, but grilled is better.

BEVERAGES Rum, of course, is one of the original Caribbean exports; Puerto Rico in particular is the source of many of the most popular rum brands sold in the United States. Rum is also classically Cuban, and despite the embargo that prevents authentic Cuban liquor from being imported, its cocktail recipes, notably the daiquiri—actually invented by an American engineer during the Spanish-American War—and the mojita, are everywhere.

CENTRAL AMERICAN SPECIALTIES

Central Americans have traditionally migrated among nations, and although there are regional specialties—tripe in Honduras, stuffed pupusas in El Salvador—the food, particularly as prepared in the United States, is fairly uniform.

MEATS Among beef dishes are *pipian* (or *pepian*), a spiced stew thickened with ground nuts or sometimes rice or tortilla strips; *picadillo*, here not as heavy as in Cuba, but a meat stew flavored with tomatoes and raisins; and the shredded meat–corn flour mix called *indio viejo*, which means "the old Indian," and may refer to the age of the recipe or to the fact that it was a way of using up older ground corn. It may even be a sort of joke on ropa viejo. *Carne deshilachada* is a skillet hash of minced or chopped beef, eggs, tomatoes, onions, and peppers all fried together. *Hilachas* is stew made with braised then shredded beef. (Interestingly, a number of Central American restaurants in the United States have begun offering what used to be considered South American–style grilled meats like those in Argentine or Brazilian *churrascarias*. See the chapter on "South America: Brazil, Peru, and Argentina," page 400.)

Vigaron is a Nicaraguan specialty of fried and chopped pork, shredded cabbage, and yucca, with a tangy dressing. *Revolcado* is a Guatemalan pork-organ stew, usually featuring brains, tripe, and all. *Caballo bayo* is marinated grilled beef, the Nicaraguan fajita.

VEGETABLES Unlike Mexicans, Central Americans frequently start and end the veggie list with beans, with corn, tomatoes, and chilies in between. The Central American version of beans and rice usually uses red beans (as in the Nicaraguan *gallo pinto*), but white beans are popular in vinegar-flavored salads and in other, softer dishes, such as *frijol blanco*, a Guatemalan dish flavored with pork. Cabbage and the heavier squashes make rarer appearances.

SWEETS The whole region is fond of sweetened breads, both for breakfast (the Guatemalan *campechadas*, the Mexican *pan dulce*) and dessert (the Caribbean-influenced ginger bun and the tropical coconut coco roll). A particular version, flavored with orange and orange-blossom extract, is called *pan de muerto*—"bread of the dead"—and is traditionally served on the first two days of November, All Saints' and All Souls' Days.

Other sweets include *marquesote*, either a sponge cake or a custard cake, and *rodojas*, the orange-flavored version; *arroz con leche*, rice pudding; and *capirotada*, bread pudding. *Flan de horchata*, a Spanish import, is a custard made from a tuber related to the water chestnut called the earth almond, tiger nut, or *chufa*. In El Salvador particularly, a pineapple torte called *La Semita* is popular. Cheesecakes and ricotta-like flavored cheese custards are popular in Mexico particularly. Fresh or crystallized fruits—pineapple, coconut, or mango—are frequently served as dessert as well.

HOW TO ORDER AND EAT LIKE A NATIVE

Most of the more formal restaurants in the United States are Mexican or Cuban; the Central American (or combined Mexican–Central American) tend to be more family-style cantinas. Main courses are generally eaten with the common utensils, but almost any entree may be placed into a roll or tortilla and eaten by hand.

The main meal in Mexico is a midday dinner that may last from 2 until 5:30 p.m., and that is where the more substantial dishes will be served. Between the big dinner and the last supper, about 9 or 10 p.m., comes a sort of high tea, featuring coffee or hot chocolate and as likely to mean tamales as pastry. In the United States, however, restaurants have adapted to the American meal schedule.

The general order of dinner is appetizers, soup, rice, the *platido fuerte* (the "heavy plate" or main course, usually fish or meat), beans, and dessert. A fancier meal might be Europeanized a little, so to speak, with two entrees, one probably seafood or possibly chicken or vegetable and the other a meat or chicken, followed by a salad and, finally, the dessert. Two people will probably find soup, a quesadilla, one fish dish and one meat (preferably pork adobado)—plenty to eat. A party of four might order ceviche and two soups (avocado and crab), a shrimp dish, roast kid, chicken mole, and paella. If Cuban black bean soup is offered, be sure to get that, too.

Some more formal restaurants that specialize in Spanish-influenced dishes may offer tapas, the small appetizers ranging from $4 to $5 to perhaps $15 for mini-paellas: These can be more expensive, but allow you to taste more dishes. In such an establishment, you should try some of the fine Spanish sherry varieties, especially the nuttier and drier styles, such as palo cortada and amantillado.

A few restaurants with a special interest in traditional Indian cuisine may serve atole, the clove- or almond-flavored corn drink that comes with a platter of finger foods, such as fried tortillas or yucca; the idea is to alternate bites of the sweetish appetizers with sips of the spicy atole.

In Central American restaurants, particularly the informal ones, so many side dishes come with the entree—for instance, an order of enchiladas is usually served with rice, beans, lettuce and tomato, guacamole, and picante sauce—that moderation is advisable in the beginning: Just order an entree apiece. These establishments are generally extremely inexpensive; only rarely, and usually just for fancier seafood dishes or perhaps steaks, do they reach $12 per person.

COOKING AT HOME

Central American and Mexican cooking is sometimes labor-intensive, but it is not terribly complex; now that there are so many markets from which to buy fresh tamales and tortillas, entertaining at home is relatively simple. Most foods are either grilled or stewed; the only important thing to remember is that acidic foods, such as salsas and chilies, should be prepared in nonreactive ceramic, glass, clay, or enamel-coated cookware.

(You'd be smart to wear rubber cloves when handling chilies, and wash your hands and the knife immediately after slicing.) Similarly, wooden utensils are best.

QUINOA WITH SUN-DRIED TOMATOES

1 cup quinoa
1 scant tablespoon olive oil
2 green or spring onions, white and tender greens chopped
6–8 dry-packed sun-dried tomatoes
1 small jalapeño or serraño chili, chopped (optional)
1 clove garlic, minced (optional)
2 cups stock, water, or a mixture of both
3 tablespoons chopped cilantro

Rinse quinoa under warm running water and drain. Meanwhile, heat oil in heavy saucepan over medium and sauté onions, tomatoes, chili, and garlic until soft but not brown. Add stock and bring to a boil. Stir in quinoa, return the mixture to a boil, then reduce heat and simmer, covered, until liquid is absorbed (about 30 minutes). Let sit 5 minutes, fluff with fork, and top with cilantro. Makes 4–6 side servings.

STEWED BLACK BEANS CUBANO

1/2 pound dried black beans
1/3 cup olive oil
1/2 cup chopped onion
1 bell pepper, seeded and cut into large chunks
1 clove garlic, pressed or minced
2 large mild chilies (such as poblanos), seeded and chopped
1 bay leaf
pinch of sugar
oregano, cumin, and salt to taste
1 teaspoon vinegar or wine or sherry
hot, cooked white rice

Soak beans overnight, or bring to boil and allow to sit in boiling liquid for 1 hour. Drain, cover with fresh water, and cook until tender. (Depending on the beans, this may take anywhere from one hour to two.) Pour off some of the water, leaving about an inch covering the beans. *Note:* It's tempting to use canned beans, but the texture will be too mushy; if you must use them, be sure to rinse well.

Heat oil in a small skillet over low heat, sauté onion, pepper, garlic, chilies, and all seasonings except vinegar until softened but not browned. Add to cooked black beans. Bring to boil and add vinegar. Reduce heat, cover partially, and simmer 15–20 minutes, or until somewhat thickened. If it remains runny, remove about 1/2 cup of the beans, mash or puree them, and stir them back into the pot. Serve with white rice. Serves 6.

CHICKEN FRICASSEE

3-pound chicken, cut into frying pieces
1 tablespoon coarse salt
4 cloves garlic, minced
1/4 teaspoon ground black pepper
1/4 teaspoon ground oregano
1 tablespoon olive oil
1 teaspoon vinegar or cooking wine
oil for frying
1/2 cup diced ham
1 small onion, chopped
1 tomato, skinned, seeded, and chopped
1 small bell pepper, chopped
2 mild chilies, seeded and diced
1/2 cup tomato sauce
6–8 pitted green olives
1 teaspoon capers (optional)
1/4 cup stock or water
3 medium potatoes, peeled and cut into chunks
1/2 cup canned or thawed frozen peas

Rinse chicken pieces and pat dry; rub with salt, garlic, ground pepper, oregano, and oil. Place in a nonreactive dish, sprinkle with vinegar, and marinate at least 30 minutes. Heat 1/2 inch of oil in heavy skillet over medium-high heat, brown chicken, and set aside. Reserve 2 tablespoons oil used to brown chicken and heat in a heavy enamel-coated casserole or Dutch oven. Sauté ham, onion, garlic, pepper, tomato, and chilies for 5 minutes; add tomato sauce, olives, and capers and sauté 5 minutes more. Add chicken pieces and 1/4 cup stock and bring to simmer; add the rest of the stock and the potatoes and peas and raise heat slightly to maintain simmer; cook until chicken is tender. Serve with rice. Serves 4–6

RED SNAPPER VERACRUZANO

4 large white or red onions
2 bulbs garlic, peeled
6 large ripe tomatoes
1 1/2 cups olive oil, divided
1 cup pimiento-stuffed green olives, chopped
10 bay leaves
12 tablespoons dried oregano, divided
4 teaspoons thyme, divided
salt and pepper to taste
10 dry-packed sun-dried tomatoes or roasted tomatoes
3 cups fish stock or mixed clam juice and water
3–4 hot chili peppers, seeded and coarsely chopped
1/4 cup sherry or balsamic vinegar or red wine
1/2 cup lime juice
1 4- to 5-pound fresh whole red snapper
1/2 tablespoon chopped fresh cilantro
hot, cooked rice

For the basic tomato sauce, chop 2 onions and mince 4 cloves of garlic; peel, seed, and chop tomatoes. Heat 1/2 cup olive oil over medium-high heat in skillet and add 4 whole cloves garlic; fry until browned, then discard the garlic. Reduce heat to medium-low; add the minced garlic and onion and brown lightly; add tomatoes, olives, 4 bay leaves, 1/2 tablespoon oregano, 2 teaspoons thyme, and salt and pepper to taste. Reduce heat further and simmer until very thick, stirring occasionally (it may take 2 hours). Set aside.

Meanwhile, coarsely chop sun-dried tomatoes (see note below). Cut remaining 2 onions into quarters. In a food processor, combine sun-dried tomatoes, onion quarters, 3 cloves garlic, and fish stock. Heat 1/2 cup olive oil in skillet and add blended mixture. Add 1 teaspoon oregano, remaining thyme, and half the chilies. Simmer 1 hour. Add reserved fresh tomato mixture and vinegar or wine and simmer another 30 minutes.

Rinse out processor bowl and add lime juice, remaining garlic, bay leaves, oregano, remaining 1/2 cup olive oil, and a dash of salt, blend. Place fish in baking dish, cover with lime mixture, and marinate 1–2 hours in refrigerator. Remove fish from marinade, pat dry, and place into larger oven-proof dish.

Preheat oven to 350°F. Cover fish with a small amount of tomato sauce and bake for 90 minutes, basting with pan juices a couple of times early on. When done, rewarm remaining tomato sauce and spoon more over the fish; put remaining sauce in dish to pass around. Garnish with chilies and cilantro. Serve with rice. Serves 6.

Note: To roast tomatoes, broil on baking sheet or on griddle over flame, turning occasionally until they turn brown but not black on each side. You can also substitute tomatoes baked until dried or sun-dried tomatoes soaked in warm water and squeezed partly dry.

THE CARIBBEAN ISLANDS

The Caribbean Sea has been called the "American Mediterranean," partly because of its clear and fertile water but also because it was first colonized by the Mediterranean rivals—Spain, Portugal, and France—before the Netherlands and England followed them in. It might also have to do with the great pirate fleets: Henry Morgan, Blackbeard, Jean Lafitte, and Sir Francis Drake all made and lost fortunes trading spices and rum in the American waters.

But as strong a place as it has in our romantic topography, the Caribbean has barely begun to take shape on our culinary map—outside, perhaps, of Miami. Their contributions to the North American diet are generally forgotten or underestimated. In 1621, the governor of Bermuda sent a shipment to his colleague, the governor of Virginia, containing all "kindes and sortes of the country plants and fruits, as Virginia . . . until then had not," including figs, oranges, lemons, pomegranates, plantains, potatoes, papayas, cassava root, chilies, and sugarcane. One of its most popular inventions, barbecue, isn't generally recognized as Caribbean at all.

The great majority of "Caribbean" restaurants in the United States are Jamaican, which has produced interesting cultural sidelights: Many Jamaican immigrants who had previously sought assimilation have found new ethnic pride in the youth market's embrace of reggae music and Rasta slang and fashions. The Rastafarian prohibition on eating meat dovetails with the increasing interest in vegetarian establishments, and the traditional spicy-style "jerk" dishes fit the boom in peppery cuisines.

And, like the West African restaurants, Caribbean restaurants—particularly those that feature Creole specialties—recall the islands' ethnic ties to American black culture, a fact that has made them "politically correct" in many urban areas and has contributed to their growing numbers. (Although Cuba and Puerto Rico are geographically Caribbean islands, their cuisine is far more traditionally Indian and Spanish; see the chapter on "Mexico, Central America, Puerto Rico, and Cuba.")

THE COUNTRIES

There are hundreds of islands included in the sweeping term "Caribbean," the vast majority of them small and virtually unknown except to fishermen and scuba divers. The largest land masses—Cuba, Jamaica, Hispaniola (Haiti and the Dominican Republic), and Puerto Rico—form a short, thick line called the Greater Antilles, which juts out from the mouth of the Gulf of Mexico like a rude tongue. The Bahamas mark a long, slightly flattened curve from offshore southeast Florida to near Haiti; the Lesser Antilles, including Trinidad and Tobago, Curaçao, Barbados, Aruba, St. Martin, Guadaloupe, St. Lucia, Grenada, St. John, St. Thomas, and so forth, bulge out again and touch down near Venezuela. "Aruba" is Arawak for "well-placed" because it was so near the mainland. In fact, the cuisines and cultures of much of northern South America, particularly, Guyana, Suriname, and French Guiana, are more closely related to the Caribbean islands than to the greater continent.

Within this great crescent, framed by the curve of Mexico and the Yucatan peninsula, the Caribbean Sea flows in a warming, counterclockwise direction, brushing the Gulf of Mexico and opening via straits and canals to both the Atlantic and the Pacific. Despite frequent volcanic eruptions and violent storms and hurricanes, the region has a benevolent climate; temperatures rarely stray outside the 70° to 85°F range. The water is always warm and is less salty than the Atlantic as well, almost pollution-free and famously filled with exotic plant and animal life.

Traditionally, the great plantation crop has been sugarcane, used for making molasses and, even more profitably in the beginning, rum. Another cash crop, intriguingly, was horses, which flourished on the islands so readily that they became a sort of trans-oceanic stables. The other cash crops are coffee (particularly in Jamaica, where the Blue Mountain beans are a premium export), tobacco (which gave the island of Tobago its name), bananas, cocoa, and spiny lobsters. Subsistence farmers, meanwhile, depend heavily on plantains and yams, breadfruit, cassava, sorghum, rice, and corn, along with a wide variety of citrus and tropical fruits and beans. Spice is legion here, seafood is plentiful, and goat is the most popular meat—particularly since the mountainous terrain makes grazing sheep and cattle problematic. (In fact, "Haiti" means "land of mountains" in Arawak.)

THE HISTORY

The islands are naturally fertile and hospitable. The original inhabitants, the Arawaks, were a pacific people who scarcely even needed to cultivate land; they lived comfortably on the available fruits and vegetables, primarily cassava, yams, papayas, and pineapples—and caught fish and the odd iguana or boar for meat. However, a closely related tribe, the Carib, were extremely aggressive and ritually sacrificial—their name, corrupted by the Spanish to "Galibi," is the source of the word "cannibal"—and they easily overran the Arawak, scavenging freely among the islands. So many Carib warriors took Arawak women as wives (or slaves) that it became customary for all women to speak Arawak, the subservient tongue, and men to speak Carib.

It was in the islands that a physician among Columbus's second expeditionary force first recognized that the chilies the natives used as preservatives not only aided in digestion but also packed a powerful gustatory punch. And since this was only a few years after Vasco de Gama's tour around the toe of Africa had launched an inflationary market for Eastern spices, the pepperlike chilies the Spanish fleet carried back eventually proved to be of immense value.

Not so, apparently, the natives, who suffered violently from the combined onslaught of European pestilence, slavery, enforced conversion, and in some cases unilateral removal: The entire Arawak population of Aruba was transported by the Spanish in 1515 to work the copper mines in Hispaniola. The indigenous populations were virtually wiped out by the end of the sixteenth century, only 100 years after the Europeans arrived; and to replace their labor, the colonists soon began importing slaves—not just West Africans but also Southwest and Mexican Indians taken by the Spanish and French, as well as a few indentured Europeans hoping to escape poverty at home. The Caribbean became one vital point of a merchant triangle that exchanged African slaves for Jamaican rum and the rum for tea and European textiles.

After the banning of slavery by Great Britain in 1838, Indian and Chinese laborers were imported to work the plantations. Even the fledgling United States had a part in the Caribbean melting pot, particularly after the discovery of gold in California made the Panama passage so important.

Today, the descendants of Africans are the dominant ethnic group in all but the Spanish-colonized islands (Cuba, Puerto Rico, and the Dominican Republic). The intermixing of African, European, and Indian blood ironically produced the very thing the Eurocentric caste system was designed to prevent—the Creole, a new and inescapably New World creature. Even the languages have melded: Most of the islands have a pan-dialectic patois, and the *lingua franca* of Aruba and Curaçao, called "Papiamento," is a mix of Spanish, Dutch, Portuguese, English, French, Indian, and African languages.

THE CUISINE

Like the people themselves, the cuisine of the Caribbean is a little this, a little that, part native, part imported, and part synthesized and new. Although the obvious culinary influences are African, French, and Spanish, there are strong Middle Eastern and Indonesian elements that recall the Dutch, Portuguese, and British trade empires (notably tamarind,

---

BBQ Bonanza

Barbecue, that great American favorite, is not Texan or Southern, though both areas claim it; instead, it is Indian. The Arawaks preserved their meat by smoking it over green wood, a method that the Spanish later disseminated into Mexico (i.e., Texas) and Florida. The Arawak word for the smoking pit was *brabacot*, which the Spanish corrupted to *barbacao*. Its similarity to *barbe a queue*, meaning "whiskers to tail," is strictly coincidental, but it makes a great pun.

ginger, coconut milk, eggplant, olives, as well as nutmeg and its side-product, mace). The overwhelming popularity of curry spices, along with rice and *roti* (wheat-flour crepes), recalls the Indian immigration; while St. Thomas, which was permanently occupied by the Danish in the 1670s, has not only Danish and African but Sephardic, Spanish, and English ethnic strains, thanks to its long-standing free-port policies.

The British installed the custom of afternoon tea, along with York-shire pudding and other doughy reminders of the empire—Irish stew, hot cross buns, and fish and chips; the working-class staple called a "Cornish pastie," dough stuffed with ground meat, is now an island favorite called a *pasty*. Residents of Curaçao and Aruba, longtime Dutch strong-holds (and home of the citrus-spiked liqueur that bears the former's name), are addicted to a dish called *keshy* (or *keshi*) *yena*—Edam or Gouda cheese stuffed with meat. Indonesian satays, both chicken and pork, are popular throughout the islands, as are French fries called *batata* or *friet*, served in paper cones with a multi-culti choice of toppings: curry sauce, ketchup, mayonnaise, chili sauce, or peanut sauce. And one of the most famous elements of Jamaican cuisine, "jerk" spices, is proba-bly a memento of the fiercely resistant Maroons—black slaves who fled into the mountains in the mid-seventeenth century, when Britain wrested the island away from the Spanish, and remained there for nearly a century until being guaranteed independence.

The most visible influence is the West African, and many ingredi-ents and recipes of the islands directly replicate those of Gambia and the Ivory Coast area: The Africans introduced yams and the fermented cassava dough called *gari*. They also "returned" the peanuts, black-eyed peas, okra, and plantains that early Portuguese traders had discovered in South America and taken to Africa.

Although the Spanish imports such as olives, capers, pork, garlic, vinegar, oranges, raisins, and cilantro are primarily essential to Cuban, Dominican, and Puerto Rican dishes, they have inevitably been dispersed around the region; the Spanish also established the practice of raising chickens, for meat as well as eggs (the Indians had relied on waterfowl and the occasional nest raid), and deep-frying. French colonies, such as Guadaloupe and Martinique, had a very strong relationship with the mother country, particularly in the lavish mid-eighteenth century—Napoleon's Josephine was born in Martinique, and her rather loose morals were often blamed on the tropical climate—and their cuisine still features cream sauces and green herbs. In the mid-nineteenth century, the Chinese and Indian laborers radically expanded the regional diet by introducing tofu, rice, wheat flour, mangoes, and curry spices; a technique for boiling coconut milk down into a cream base; and the wok, used to stir-fry vegetables.

However, the Caribbean is so internationally renowned as a tourist attraction, and the islands' economies so heavily entertainment-dependent, that nowadays most islands boast "Continental" restaurants—French, Italian, American regional, German, Argentine, Chinese, Japanese, Indian, and Asian fusion. In some places, "authentic" local cuisine is hard to find.

THE MAIN INGREDIENTS

SEASONINGS The most popular flavorings are chilies, ginger, cane vinegar (slightly sweetened with molasses), curry mixes, grated coconut (coconut oil is the cooking medium of choice), nutmeg, peppers, and the evocatively named *piment negresse*—whole allspice (both berries and leaves), which is not only indigenous to this region but even today cultivated solely in the Americas. One of the oldest condiments in the islands, piment negresse is essential for traditional pepperpot stew. *Cassareep* is a thick blend of boiled-down cassava juice, cinnamon, cloves, brown sugar, and other flavorings. Of these, the chilies are the most obvious; some of the world's hottest chilies originate in the Caribbean, including the notorious Scotch bonnet (actually *habañero*) and fierce bird peppers. Rum, of course, is also a flavoring, along with molasses. And since curries are so popular, Indian-style chutneys—particularly light, fresh versions that mix peppers and fruits or herbs—are common condiments for both fish and meat.

The distinctive *ackee* is served almost exclusively in Jamaica. The red pod of an ornamental tree, ackee can be deadly if picked before it ripens. (When the pod splits to reveal the edible yellow flesh within, natives say the fruit is "smiling.") It looks like scrambled eggs but has a lemony flavor.

FRUITS Thanks to the generous climate, the region offers both sweet and citrus fruits: mangoes, pineapple, passionfruit, coconuts, guava, bananas and plantains, plus oranges, lemons, limes, and grapefruit. So-called jelly coconuts are unripe coconuts whose meat has a jelly-like consistency. Tamarinds are sold in markets as pulp as well as a seasoning juice. *Carambola*, known in the United States as star fruit or star apple, is a starfish-shaped citrusy fruit. Another exotic fruit is *cherimoya*, sometimes called the custard apple; the fruit is halved and its soft, creamy flesh is eaten with a spoon.

Papayas, called "paw-paws" in the southern United States, are rosy-colored and quite large; they contain a natural tenderizer (which is now being synthesized), and meats are traditionally wrapped in papaya leaves overnight. The sorrel is a bright red fruit with a green pit and sweet-tart flavor. The soursop, also known as the corossol or guana-bana, is a shiny, dark-green fruit that vaguely resembles an artichoke on the outside but has a cottony or creamy white flesh inside. Avocados are also indigenous to the region.

STARCHES The staples are corn, breadfruit, cassava, rice, and sweet potatoes and yams (which are actually different species, though in the United States what's called a "yam" is a sweet potato). Breadfruit, the notorious diet of the *H.M.S. Bounty,* was imported from Tahiti and is used much as potatoes are—fried, roasted, or sliced into chips. (It doesn't look like bread, incidentally, but like a dimpled beachball or overripe melon.) Cornmeal is usually called fufu, as in West Africa, but is also referred to by its Mexican name, *masa harina,* if it is ground particularly fine. Cassava root is variously known as yucca and manioc and is the source of tapioca flour as well; sometimes it's ground and fried into a mealcake called *bammy. Gari* is roasted, rough-ground, and fermented cassava flour. Wheat flour, introduced by the Indian laborers, is used for a variety of (primarily flat) breads.

VEGETABLES Beans and peas—red, black, pink, kidney, and turtle beans, garbanzos, and pigeon and black-eyed peas—are a reliable source of protein. The most common squashes include pumpkin (or *calabaza,* a corruption of "calabash"), butternut, and hubbard, along with the chayote or christophene, which has become a supermarket staple. *Callaloo* refers to greens, but broadly—it can be either of two plants, one called taro or *choux Caribe,* among other names, and the other known as Indian kale or Chinese spinach. (In some islands callaloo is a stew; see "Soups," page 395.) *Dasheen* is a root vegetable with purple flesh.

FISH AND SHELLFISH Obviously, seafood is abundant in the islands, including conch, shrimp, crayfish, grouper, mullet, sunfish, spiny lobsters (actually a variety of crawfish, with two large meat-filled "antennae" instead of enlarged front claws), crabs, flying fish (so abundant that Barbados is nicknamed "Land of the Flying Fish"), codfish, snapper, and jackfish. Spiny mollusk roe is eaten much as sea urchin roe is. The Iberian occupation ensured the adoption of salt cod into the diet; West African–style smoked fish is also quite common.

MEATS AND POULTRY   Goat and kid are prized meats, but pork and mutton and the occasional game, venison, or boar are also popular. Beef as steak is primarily tourist resort fare, but the lesser cuts, particularly ground beef, are fairly common.

POULTRY AND DAIRY   Both chicken and ducks are widely raised, and some islands have some game birds available; turkey is becoming more standard. Eggs were not a traditional element in Caribbean Indian cooking, and since cattle were unknown until the Spanish conquest, milk, cream, cheese, and butter have limited roles as well.

THE MAIN DISHES

APPETIZERS   Jerked chicken wings or "drumettes," miniature beef pasties, and codfish balls are common first courses. *Bitterballen* are bite-sized meatballs; their cigar-shaped twins are called *kroker* and are usually served with mustard. *Nasibal* are Indonesian-style lumps of deep-fried seasoned rice. Bakes are peppery biscuits or beignets that can be plain or stuffed with shark or swordfish or some other fish; they may be called "floats" if fried. Crab may be fried into cornmeal fritters. Conch needs to be tenderized through pounding or scoring and is most commonly turned into fritters or chowders. *Pates* (pronounced "PA-tays") are little deep-fried pies filled with garlicky ground beef. Similar turnovers are called *empanadas*, in the Spanish style, or may be referred to as *pastechis* if they are a little larger. These may be seafood- or cheese-stuffed as well. Many restaurants also offer smoked fish or fish-and-cornmeal crackers. Chinese-style barbecued or sweet-and-sour ribs and egg rolls are common in some areas. Any of these fast or finger foods are apt to be sold by vendors on the street or near the beach bars. One of the most popular snacks in Jamaica is a shark float topped with cole slaw and chutney or tomatoes and onions.

SOUPS   Whether as a first course or as a whole meal, Caribbean soups tend to be hearty and filling. Fish and/or meat is often added to a broth that is thickened with starch, either cornmeal or ground rice. Peanut soups with either chicken or dried shrimp are popular, and pumpkin soups are quite common. Callaloo is both a vegetable and a Creole soup, sometimes identified as pepperpot soup; although there is no standard recipe, it generally includes the spinach-like callaloo leaf, crabmeat, okra, chilies, and sometimes coconut milk; it's not unusual to find callaloos that mix fish and pork together.

ONE-POT DISHES Almost every Caribbean restaurant has some version of "hoppin' John," that African-American staple of rice and beans (black-eyed peas, red or pigeon beans, etc.), sometimes cooked with coconut milk. *Souse* is not a sausage-meal mix, as in the United States, but a pork stew. *Cou-cou* is not cous-cous, though it looks similar; it actually derives from the Gambian way of mixing fufu with okra, and in some places is known, even more confusingly, as *fungi. Pelaus* are flavored rice dishes derived from Indian pilaus and, before that, from Persian pilafs; in creole fashion, they've been hybridized with typical seasonings ranging from pork and bacon to Worcestershire sauce or brown sugar and olives or peanuts.

Metagee is a sort of layered casserole, with root vegetables on the bottom, followed by okra or greens, potatoes, and pumpkin and then fish or shellfish on top. It is most popular in the southern islands and South American coast and is sometimes called *sancoch*.

MEATS AND POULTRY Caribbean recipes are defined more by style than by main ingredient. Jerk can be applied to almost any meat, though chicken and goat are the most common. Curry is probably the second most common type of recipe. Goat is the most popular curry meat, but the dish is also made with shrimp, mutton, lamb, or whole fish, and frequently with vegetables or tofu. Roti, a split wheat or pea-flour pancake, is often rolled around chicken or conch or vegetable curry.

Chicken is also stewed with peanut butter, as in West Africa; mixed with coconut and orange juice, as in Malaysia; and smothered in tomatoes and olives, as in Spain.

SEAFOOD A characteristic treatment for seafood is a vinegary chutney called *escabeche* (or *eschovishe, escoveitche,* or *caveach*), which can refer either to the cooking sauce itself or to a sauce-"cured" raw seafood, like a Caribbean ceviche. Whole fresh fish, particularly snapper, may be stewed in a tomato and onion sauce, curried, or even jerk-rubbed. Catfish appears stuffed with crab and shrimp and sauced with béarnaise in a classic French Creole dish you'd expect to see in New Orleans. On the other hand, the Chinese influence shows up when fish are steamed with ginger and garlic; and tamarind, an Indonesian flavor, is popular in Trinidad. Fish is sometimes smoked as well, particularly for use in West African–style stews featuring peanut butter. The more modern or international kitchens, particularly in the resort areas, have taken to jerk-rubbing tuna and just searing it into a cross between sashimi and Cajun blackened fish.

Salt cod is often chopped into patties and fried into the island quick-snack called "stamp and go." Whether that phrase refers to stamping out the cakes and passing them out or stamping your foot in impatience isn't clear. Salt fish is also essential for "rundown," which is a sort of curry or stew using simmered-down coconut milk.

BEVERAGES The Caribbean islands may be as well known for their drinks as for their cuisine. Rum comes in hundreds of varieties and flavors and is mixed with any and all fruit juices. (Juices themselves are available in dizzying supply: passionfruit, guava, guana, mango, papaya, pineapple, coconut milk, etc.) "Irish moss" is a sort of seaweed brewed into a very soothing creamy shake. Ginger is the source of several popular drinks, not only the original ginger ale but also ginger wine (a currant wine steeped in ginger) and ginger beer, which is not alcoholic. Other "real" beers are also brewed locally—the most famous example is Red Stripe—and a Guinness factory in Jamaica keeps the islands supplied with stout.

DESSERTS Among the most popular desserts are banana puddings, bread and rum puddings (along with some rather bland and doughy puddings that recall the dimmer facets of the British Empire), mixed fruit salads, fried plantains, coconut custard, ginger cakes and cookies, and plain preserved ginger. "Tie-me-up" is a cornmeal mush "tied up" or wrapped in a banana leaf for steaming; it can be either sweet or savory. Sweet punches are often served in lieu of desserts.

HOW TO ORDER
AND EAT LIKE A NATIVE

Ordering in a Caribbean restaurant is fairly easy, since most menus are divided American-style into appetizers and entrees, and their names are quite uniform (except for that pesky escabeche). The best way to become familiar with the food may be to order as many appetizers as are appealing, two at a time, and then perhaps try a goat curry or escabeche. (It is also wise to go slow, because "appetizers," like most street foods, sometimes show up in large portions.) Many of these are finger foods, ideal for conversation: crab fritters, "shark bites," cod fritters, jerk chicken wings, etc. Two people should try one fried-seafood dumpling or bakes and some jerk chicken wings, then share a curry, preferably goat or vegetable, and a whole fish either baked or escabeche-style. For four add a soup—callaloo if available—and a peanut butter and chicken stew or okra gumbo.

When it comes to curries and stews (or any dish that comes sided with red beans and rice, revealing its Spanish origins), you may use a fork, although many Caribbean residents continue to eat African-based and Indian dishes with their fingers.

COOKING AT HOME

Most Caribbean cooking is done outside, either on grills or in large pots. However, unless you feel up to digging a real smoke pit, most island foods can be reproduced using pots or an outdoor grill; even the broiler will do. Like curry powders, jerk rubs are individualized and can be customized to taste. There are a fair number of hot sauces and jerk rubs available in specialty groceries in the United States, but it's fun to develop your own version. Here's a starter—and, incidentally, a little goes a long way.

JERK RUB

1 onion, finely chopped
2/3 cup scallions, finely chopped
2 teaspoons fresh thyme
1 1/2 teaspoons salt
1 teaspoon ground allspice
1/4 teaspoon ground nutmeg
2 teaspoons ground cinnamon
2–4 hot chilies, such as habañero, jalapeño, or serraño, chopped
1 1/2 teaspoons ground black pepper
1 tablespoon dark rum or molasses (optional)

Mix ingredients in food processor or blender to make a paste; rub well into uncooked meat or poultry. Store rub in a jar or tightly covered container for up to a month. Makes approximately 1 cup.

JAMAICAN JERK CHICKEN BREASTS

1 tablespoon Jerk Rub (see recipe above)
4 large chicken breast halves, skinned, bone in

Smear chicken breasts with thin coating of jerk rub (or to taste) and place in lightly oiled glass baking dish; cover and marinate in refrigerator 2 to 3 hours. Preheat oven to 275°F; bake, covered, about 25 minutes or until nearly done, then brown under broiler. (Note: If crispier finish is desired, leave skin on.)

CODFISH FRITTERS

1/2 pound codfish fillet, skinned
1/4 cup grated coconut
1/4 cup spring onion, finely chopped
1 egg, lightly beaten
2 tablespoons bread crumbs
1 clove garlic, minced
1 teaspoon Worcestershire sauce
2 tablespoons fresh cilantro or parsley, chopped
2 teaspoons Jerk Rub (see recipe above) or curry mix
Oil for frying

Puree fish in food processor, combine with other ingredients except oil, and shape into patties; fry until deep golden, about 1 minute on each side; drain on paper towels. Serve with chutney, salsa, or any fresh fruit chopped with mint and lime juice.

SOUTH AMERICA: BRAZIL, PERU, AND ARGENTINA

South American cuisine is as yet little known in most parts of the United States, although that is likely to change quickly. Many supposedly Central American establishments are actually Peruvian or Ecuadoran, which, while displaying many similarities, downplays the authentic dishes. The prime per-pound beef of Argentina and the all-you-can-eat Brazilian churrascarias, or grill houses, have moved in with the revival of the big American steakhouse craze. (Such steak palaces make one wonder what the meat-loving Spanish would have done if they had not stumbled into the Americas and discovered the potato or the "beefsteak" tomato.) In addition, a growing number of east Brazilian (i.e., Bahia-style) restaurants are moving in behind the craze for Caribbean island foods and rum punches (and such suspect "native" Rio dances as the lambada and commercialized samba).

THE COUNTRIES

The ice cream cone–shaped continent is the fourth largest, though not one of the more popu-

BASIC CUISINE

DINNER FOR TWO:
Black bean soup, ceviche, smothered whole fish, cabrito

DINNER FOR FOUR:
Antichucos, crab chupes, potatoes huancaína, escabeche fish, roast pork, grilled chicken

GROUP DISH:
Feijoada

STYLE:
Spicy, tropical, nutty

KEY FLAVORS:
Chilies, coconut and palm oil, corn, tomatoes, beef

EATING UTENSILS:
Forks and knives, fingers

DISTINCTIVE FOODS:
Feijoada, empanadas, churrasco

UNIFORMITY OF MENUS:
Good

NUTRITIONAL INDEX:
Starchy, high fiber (north); high fat, creamy (Brazil); high cholesterol (south)

COST:
Inexpensive to moderate

"THANK YOU":
"Gracias" (Spanish), "Obrigado" or "Obrigada" (Portuguese, masculine or feminine)

lous. Although South America is so large—4,750 miles top to bottom and 3,300 miles at the widest—it is sharply marked by the high spine of the Andes Mountains, which run north to south and separate the deserts from the well-watered territory; the highlands of the northeast and upper Brazil, wedged apart by the equatorial Amazon River basin; and the long continental slope into the flat pampas of the south. The continent has limited natural ports or arable land; it is part tropical, part alpine, part desert, and only rarely temperate.

The northeast curve of the continent snuggles up into the shoulder of the Caribbean Sea and enjoys its warm climate and abundant seafood. Below that is the broad bulge of Brazil, with the vast Amazon basin and rainforests covering the upper third; the fertile southeast "belly" of the Bahia region and Rio de Janeiro; and the plains tapering toward the pampas in the south. On the Pacific coast, the Andes slice right down the

America, America

In many ways, the regional cuisines mirror those of North America; if you folded the two continents at about the middle of Central America, the Guianas and Brazilian coast would meet the Caribbean and Florida Keys, Peru would overlie Mexico, and the cattle ranges and sheep ranches of Argentina would come close to matching the old Texas-Montana cattle trails. Even the long stretch of Chile, with its pockets of temperate-to-wet mountainside and the lightly acidic soil now increasingly turned to viniculture, would follow the wine-growing west coast from California to Washington.

continent, from just west of the Central American isthmus to the tip of Chile. A large percentage of the coastal region is desert, and although the Peruvian portion of the Andean ranges are wide and relatively fertile, in Chile they are steep and arid. To the east the mountains stretch away into great pasturelands and plains.

The population of the northwestern Andes, Peru, Ecuador, Colombia, and Bolivia, is overwhelmingly Indian and mestizo; Chile is also primarily mestizo, with small but distinct German, French, British, Italian, and even Yugoslavian communities.

Argentina, on the other hand, is predominantly European—Italian and Spanish, but also French, German, Swiss, and Eastern European—except for some mestizo villages in the northwest, near Peru. Southeastern Brazil, the most populous region, is truly Creole—a mixture of Indian, African, and European that its citizens boast of as "a new race." The Amazon rainforest is inhabited almost entirely by natives.

THE HISTORY

Like North and Central America, South America has seen much of its native civilization obscured, if not erased, by the European colonial empires. However, the great Quechua empire of Peru (ruled by the Inca, whose title is often applied to the entire nation) had developed highly sophisticated techniques of irrigation and selective breeding thousands of years before the Spanish and Portuguese arrived at the turn of the sixteenth century. By about 3,000 B.C.E. they had domesticated the remarkably intelligent and willing llama—an animal whose virtues are gradually becoming known in the United States—which supplied not only transportation but also food, clothing, and fuel. They had several ways of preserving food and built silos or warehouses throughout the empire to guard against times of drought or extended winter cold.

As was true in Mexico, the predations of the Spanish conquistadors and the Anglophilia of historians have combined to obscure the accomplishments of the American natives the Europeans subjugated. The Quechua empire, though centered in Peru, included modern-day Colombia, Ecuador, and Bolivia and reached into Brazil and down into Chile and Argentina. They constructed highways the Romans would have envied: Two extended the 2,500-mile length of the empire, one down the coast and another actually through the Andes. They also established a remarkably sophisticated system of aqueducts that carried water up the mountains to the terraced farms, where quinoa, maize, amaranth, barley, potatoes, sweet potatoes, and beans were cultivated. It was an orderly empire, with prohibitions against murder and theft that made the Quechuas all too susceptible to the warlike Spanish. Because they refused to serve as slaves, even after Pizarro's conquest of Cuzco and the assassination of the Inca, more Quechuas actually died by mass execution than by the epidemic diseases brought by the Europeans.

Thanks to the 1494 Treaty of Tordesillas, which may have preceded the actual discovery of Brazil, the Portuguese were "given" Brazil and the Spanish received the rest of South America; hence the Brazilians speak Portuguese, while in most of the other countries, the official language is Spanish (see the chapter on "The Iberian Peninsula: Spain, Portugal, Catalonia, and the Basque"). In the northeastern nations (the Guianas), Dutch, English, and French are spoken.

THE CUISINES

Although there are more than a dozen countries on the continent, three regional cuisines dominate both the other South American countries and South American restaurants in the United States: Brazilian, with its mixed Portuguese, African, and East Indian influences; Peruvian, based (like Mexican and Central American cuisine) on the foods of its pre-Columbian natives; and the European-influenced food of the southern "cone," particularly Argentina and, to a lesser degree, Chile. (The northeastern countries, which are near neighbors and climactic cousins of the Caribbean islands, have Caribbean-style cuisines; see the chapter on "The Caribbean Islands.")

Brazilian food is the most truly Creole, partly because it was a Portuguese rather than Spanish colony, and the Portuguese were heavily involved in Indonesian trading; partly because a large number of West African slaves were imported to work the sugar plantations; and partly because its tropical climate not only provides it with abundant seafood but is hospitable to more fresh fruits and flavorings. The eastern and southeastern part of the country, particularly along the coast between Salvador and Rio de Janeiro, is the most populous region, with many excellent harbors that historically attracted the attention of other European fleets as well: The Dutch actually held Bahia for about 30 years in the middle of the seventeenth century, contributing more Indonesian spices and a taste for cheese; and the Italian sailors found the climate so homelike that thousands never went home—hence the surprising number of Italian restaurants in both Brazil and Argentina.

Before the arrival of the Europeans, the few indigenous Indians of Brazil—mostly Quechuas, in the west—depended primarily on manioc, from which they made a flour called *farinha* (and from that the toasted, nutty thickener/flavoring called *farofa*); Mexican maize, from which they made both tamale meal and mush; greens such as collards and kale; beans; citrus fruits; and fish. Like most of the middle Americas, the region had indigenous chilies, and the most potent of all, the habañero, comes from Amazonia. The restless Portuguese immediately established in Brazil, as they did everywhere, their beloved salt cod *(bacalao)* and fried shrimp (the same "tempura" they later introduced to the Japanese), olives, almonds, onions, garlic, wine, the sugar that became the first great plantation crop, and the use of egg yolks to emulsify and bind sauces. They also taught the natives, who traditionally slow-cooked meats whole in pits lined with heated stones, to stew meats and vegetables together.

The Africans introduced yams, okra, dried shrimp, bananas, palm nuts and palm oil, and coconut and coconut oil; although the peanut was native to North America, the Africans had quickly mastered its potential and carried it back and forth to the Caribbean and Brazil. The slaves were also the first to create what might be considered a "culture" of cuisine in Brazil, by infusing the practice of cooking with mystical and religious elements that made recipes (and cooks) far more respected institutions.

Brazilian Creole cooking is best known for a flavoring combination of coconut milk (squeezed from freshly grated coconut meat), dried shrimp, malagueta peppers (the gingerish grains of paradise), and chilies, along with rich avocado and ground nuts. Its other most obvious element is *dende* oil, the West African palm oil that lends not only a unique flavor but also a characteristic yellow-orange color to dishes and is thus sometimes confused with saffron or achiote. This visibly hybrid cuisine, which is increasingly popular in the United States, is also referred to as "Bahia" cuisine, after the port of Bahia on the east coast of Brazil, just below the lip.

Brazil is also home to a number of East Indian and Chinese immigrants; and curry spices, lamb dishes, stir-fries, lentil and vegetable stews, tamarind sauces, and chutney and rice dishes show these influences.

Peruvian cuisine is, like that of Mexico and Central America, still heavily influenced by the indigenous foods, though central elements have been borrowed from the Spanish. (One could consider the foods of the Andean villages, where the Quechuas retreated as the Europeans advanced, the only "authentic" South American cooking.) The Quechua raised some 80 varieties of potatoes—there have been remnants of sweet potatoes at least 12,000 years old found in Peru—of which more than 30 are still eaten, including the newly trendy purple, golden, and "transparent" varieties; potatoes in a variety of chili-spiced, chicken-flavored, and cheesy (*papas a la Huancaina*) dishes are still prominent on Peruvian menus. Although the Quechuas were first given corn by their neighbors to the north in Mexico and Central America, they themselves eventually isolated hundreds of varieties; one, called *callemote*, has kernels the size of popped corn that are peeled and eaten as a snack. They also turned corn into a beer, called *chicha*.

Two of the other grains cultivated by the Quechua, amaranth and quinoa, are modern-day nutritionists' darlings: With only slightly more calories per half-cup than barley or buckwheat, amaranth has twice the percentage of protein, and though twice as caloric as corn, it provides five times the protein. Quinoa, which the Quechua called "mother of all grains," has more calories, but even more protein.

The Quechua employed a variety of preservation techniques: air-drying, freeze-drying, salting, and sun-drying. They were the ones who first air-dried potatoes and powdered them into the cornstarch we still use in cooking and cosmetics today. The local chilies were likely a domesticated form of the aji in the lowlands and the rocoto or manzana in the highest reaches of the Andes, but the other chilies of the Americas were known here long before the Europeans arrived.

The primary meat, although it was wisely limited, came from the llamas and vicuñas that were domesticated millennia earlier; air-dried llama meat is called *charqui*—the original "jerky." Chickens were, by some accounts, already present, though they were not raised as livestock until the arrival of Europeans.

The Spanish introduced beef, sheep, goats, and hogs to the Indians, thereby not only increasing the proportion of meat in the diet but also vastly upping the fat quotient; instead of baking or boiling, the Indians were now frying, and dairy products such as cream and cheese also became common. They brought wine, and introduced the planting of vines, along with the eggplants, rice, coffee, almonds, and spices they had adopted from the Moors. They also brought olives, though here,

Ethnic Imports

Despite its great land mass, South America is populated primarily at the edges; nearly everyone, with the exception of some deep-Amazon tribes, lives within 200 miles of the coast. Most of the major cities are along the coast, too; and the many European immigrants have established tight communities and restaurants to feed them. Italian immigrants have outnumbered all others in the last century; hence, a surprising number of the restaurants in Rio de Janeiro are Italian, and most Argentine kitchens, even the steakhouses, offer pastas as the alternative. It's not uncommon to find German dumplings and strudels in Chile and Venezuela, Dutch/Indonesian rijsttafel in Guyana (which is so near the former Dutch islands of Aruba and Curaçao), even Scotch haggis in Brazil. Chinese, Japanese, and Greek restaurants, with their flair for seafood, are increasingly common along the eastern coast as in Mexico, they prevented the Indians from raising their own and challenging their market monopoly.

Argentina was only lightly populated before the Europeans arrived, and consequently has almost no indigenous cuisine. Its greatest influences are topographical rather than historical—the interior plains and the rich northeast seacoast.

The pampas, the 400-mile-wide grasslands, are the breadbasket of the region, supplying wheat, alfalfa, and corn and also pastureland for the cattle, sheep, and dairy cows and the horses used to herd them. Cattle-ranching has much the same mystique in Argentina as it has in the American West, and the gaucho, the cowboy of the Argentina plains, is similarly a figure of legend. (Many of them were actually black or mestizo Brazilian slaves who fled the sugar plantations and signed on to cattle drives.) Beef was introduced into the area in the mid-sixteenth century, and by the eighteenth century cattle were running wild. Today Argentine beef is among the world's most prized, and Argentinians consume more beef per capita than any other country in the world. Along the eastern coast and in the oases of the western desert, farmers cultivate fruit, including wine grapes, corn, and some sugarcane.

Chile offers a rather daunting vista on a map—265 miles at the widest and squeezed between the Andes on the east and the desert seacoast on the west—but it has a hospitable, Mediterranean region in the center that allows for the cultivation of oats, potatoes, wheat, corn, vegetables, and fruits, including wine grapes. Cattle and pigs are raised in the north, sheep and cattle in the south. And the thin, cold-current ocean supplies unexpected luxuries: the conger eels called *congrios*, giant sea urchins (*erizos*), crabs, shrimp, abalone, mussels, oysters, and many oily-fleshed fish.

THE MAIN INGREDIENTS

SEASONINGS The strongest indigenous spices are, of course, the chili peppers, followed by the achiote or annatto, a reddish spice something like nutmeg with an orange-colored punch, and chocolate—used, in the Aztec manner, to flavor some stews. The other major flavors are coconut, rums and fortified wines, the Indonesian spices (turmeric, ginger, mace, cinnamon, cumin, allspice, coriander), malagueta peppers, garlic, vanilla, flavored vinegar, olives and olive oil, palm oil (dende), cilantro, lime, lemon, thyme, dill, mint, sage, and rosemary. Marinated anchovies and dried shrimp are often used as a flavoring, too, and the toasted farofa called farina is indispensable in Brazilian cooking; it is almost always served in a bowl on the table, as Americans would have sugar.

Molho de Nago is an African-style sauce made of dried shrimp, lemon juice, okra, and malagueta peppers. *Chimichurri* is an Argentine meat sauce made of parsley, garlic, oil, and lemon juice or vinegar.

VEGETABLES As mentioned above, the Quechuas cultivated some 80 varieties of potatoes, and perhaps three dozen types are still fairly common. Beans (kidney, black, red, yellow, white, garbanzo, string, and lima), peas, and lentils provide crucial proteins; greens (lettuce, watercress, mache, kale, cabbage, chard, spinach), root vegetables (turnips, carrots, fennel, celeriac), squashes and pumpkins, jicama, avocado, broccoli, tomatoes, onions, and olives are also common. Brazilians are extremely fond of okra and also have access to a variety of ferns and fungi.

> ### Imported Fat
>
> South American cuisine employs an unusual variety of cooking fats, most of them imported: rendered duck and goose fat, lard, butter, clarified butter, sesame oil, palm oil, coconut oil, rendered bacon and ham fat, olive oil, and corn oil. In some areas, particularly in the cities, American vegetable shortening has become popular, apparently because many people believe it (from its appearance) to be lard.

GRAINS AND DOUGHS Corn is, of course, the most important, and is used as hominy, as whole-grain meals, as finer meals (masa harina), fermented, and as mush; when dried, it produces a very fine starch. Rice is the second most important grain. Quinoa and amaranth are highly nutritious, nutty-flavored grains; barley and some wheat are also grown, particularly in the south-central plains. Yucca and cassava flour are very common toward the north; manioc meal or farofa is characteristically Brazilian. Doughs for empanadas may include extra butter (some are virtually puff pastries), lard, or potato, yucca, or plantain mashes as well.

FRUITS AND NUTS The South American *limon* tastes more like a lime (they call the North American type "sweet lemons"). Pineapples, quinces, mangoes, plantains, figs, dates, prunes, oranges, custard apples, papayas, breadfruit, grapes and raisins, pears, apples, and coconuts are the most common fruits, but a few areas, particularly in the north, also grow peaches and berries.

Some nuts grew wild in South America, such as pecans, Brazil nuts, and walnuts, but the Spanish brought along a lot of the Middle Eastern nuts and spices the Moors had brought to them, particularly almonds, cashews, hazelnuts, and walnuts, and pignolis from their North American territories; the Africans passed along the peanuts they acquired farther north.

FISH AND SEAFOOD   Chile, Argentina, and Brazil, with their long coastlines, and the northern states adjoining the Caribbean islands enjoy a huge variety of fresh fish, including anchovies, abalone, bonito, tuna, swordfish, flounder, sole, trout, bass, sardines, a rainbow of snapper, shrimp in all sizes, shellfish (mussels, clams, scallops, crabs), squid, octopus, lobsters, and crabs. Peru and Ecuador specialize in scallops, abalone, prawns, and crayfish. In Bolivia, which is landlocked but opens onto Lake Titicaca, freshwater species such as trout and smelt, giant frogs, and river shrimp or crayfish are specialties. And in Chile, conger eels are highly prized.

POULTRY AND WILDFOWL   The chicken may have reached South America before Columbus arrived (it is one of the possible bits of evidence of a very early Chinese trade), but it was considered a poor alternative to wild turkey, squab, duck, quail, grouse, pheasant, and partridge. Argentina even has a kind of ostrich, the emu, the huge legs of which are considered delicacies (and whose lean red meat is increasingly popular as a beef alternative in restaurants in the United States).

EGG AND DAIRY PRODUCTS   Since the arrival of the Europeans, eggs have become a fairly important ingredient in soups, emulsions, and sauces; but they are often now used as meals in themselves: scrambled, fried, as omelets, etc. The Portuguese-influenced Brazilians, in particular, use a lot of egg yolks. Cheeses, both goat's and cow's milk, are extremely popular.

MEATS   Although pork wasn't known until the beginning of the sixteenth century, it has become one of the most popular meats in South America, along with beef, and mutton and goat are widely eaten. However, the traditional favorites include rabbit (which is usually treated as poultry) and the huge Argentine hare called a *viscacha*; venison; boar and peccary; and the *cuy*, a guinea pig the size of a small dog. Llama meat is still popular, particularly in Peru, where it is often air-dried (the charqui mentioned above). Organ meats are extremely popular, particularly kidneys, liver, sweetbreads, heart, and tripe (*modongo*). Even offal, such as snouts, pig's ears, tails, and hocks, are used in stews and sausages, especially the Brazilian national dish, *feijoada*. Calves feet are also much admired.

Sausages reflect a variety of influences, including German, Spanish, and Italian. *Morcilla* (blood sausage), the spicy chorizo, and the lightly smoked *paio* are among the most common.

THE MAIN DISHES

APPETIZERS   As in Central America, many of the finger foods—empanadas, tamales, fritters, etc.—that are listed as hors d'oeuvre on menus in South American restaurants in the United States are really light meals or snacks. In Brazilian restaurants they are sometimes referred to as *salgadinhos*—literally, "salty things" designed to go with drinks—and these are often taken right out of the Portuguese cookbook: salami-like sausages, batter-fried shrimp, pickles, raw cured hams, tuna, or sardines. However, some are genuinely native first courses: fried smelts, potato tortillas, black-eyed pea fritters, shrimp or crab cakes, fried fish cubes, and *acarajé*, ground dried beans mixed with dried shrimp and fried.

In the Italian and grill-happy Argentine restaurants, chargrilled sweetbreads or kidneys, "mixed fries" of organ meats or seafood, fried marinated fish cubes or grilled sweet peppers or eggplant are common. In some Peruvian kitchens, the cheesy potato dish called huancaina is served as an appetizer as well as entree. *Fiambre* means the dish is cold, but that may include meat and seafood dishes as well as vegetables or salad. *Carne seca*, a pickled and then dried meat (also called *xarque*), is a popular Brazilian snack.

SOUPS AND STEWS   South American cuisine is particularly rich in seafood soups and vegetable purees, often called "cream" soups, but with no dairy product in sight. Among the most popular are black bean soup; a Chinese-inspired hot broth with beaten raw eggs stirred in; calves' foot consommé; chicken with rice; dumpling soups; chowders of clam, crabmeat, or shrimp with corn (called *chupes*); beef and dried-potato soups; and soups with greens, squash, or pumpkin. Fruit soups are particularly characteristic of Brazilian menus, as are soups flavored with coconut milk or ground nuts.

Migas here are not bread salads but stews or thick soups with bread crumbs, often shellfish-flavored. *Mariscadas* are South American bouillabaisses that mix fish and shellfish. *Seco* denotes a (relatively) dry stew, generally a meat or red-meat fowl dish.

ONE-POT MEALS   Feijoada, or more formally *feijoada completa*, the national dish of Brazil, is a casserole of variety meats (usually pork), greens, black beans, and some powdered cassava and usually flavored

Wrap Session

Known variously as empanadas, empadas, empanaditas, pasteles, or *salteñas*, stuffed pastries are as ubiquitous in South America as they are in Central America. They may be made of pastry dough, bread dough, or corn, yucca, or plantain dough; fried or baked, sweet or savory; shaped as triangles, half-moons, rounds, or squares. Fillings can be meat, seafood, vegetable, poultry, cheese, or even fruit. Peruvian and Ecuadorian tamales are slightly sweeter than Central American versions. In Chile, where the stuffing is often slowly simmered in a rich stock and spiced with raisins, they are called *caldudas*, from the stockpot, *caldo*.

Tamales, too, have a variety of Indian names—*hallaca*, *bollo*, *juanes*, *pamonhas*—to go with the Spanish one we know. They can be made from corn, wheat, yucca, rice, potato, plantain, or quinoa doughs; and filled with chicken, duck, pork, seafood, veal, vegetables, or even curry. In Venezuela, there is a Mexican-influenced version that combines chicken and potatoes with a tomato sauce.

There are two debates among tamale cooks: Should they be wrapped in banana leaves or corn husks? and should they be steamed or simmered?

with palm oil. *Cuzcuz paulista* is Moorish couscous, only made with cornmeal. Argentines like *carbonada*, another Moorish-sounding beef stew that mixes pumpkin meat and dried or fresh fruits and is served in the pumpkin shell.

Cochido is a general word for stew, but it's not to be confused with Brazilian *cozido*, a combination of sun-dried beef, pork, and plantains (which distinguishes it from its Portuguese ancestors). A stew called, variously, *sancochado*, *sancocho*, *hervido*, or *cazuela puchero* is something like the New England boiled dinner—a mixture of meats and vegetables cooked in water or stock. The most vivid version of this is called, affectionately, *olla podrida*, or "rancid casserole," and combines various cuts of beef (usually starting with a brisket, though a calf's head is the traditional centerpiece), chicken, pork (hams, hocks, and bacon), and veal with a couple of types of sausages as well as garbanzos, limas, and perhaps potatoes or yams. The nickname may refer either to the well-hung (i.e., green) bacons of South America or to the fact that traditionally such stews were never entirely finished, just refueled.

RICE AND GRAIN DISHES There are a number of rice, quinoa, and even barley dishes that feature meats and poultry simmered into the cooking grains. Among the most popular are *arroz con pollo* (rice with chicken), *arroz de cuxa* (rice with dried shrimp and vinegar), barley with quail, orzo with rabbit or duck, and quinoa with chopped clams. Brazilians often flavor rice with tomatoes (the original version of what cafeterias used to call "Spanish rice"), and East Indian–style pilaus, flavored with spices and nuts, are also common.

Brazilian farofa is often sautéed in butter and mixed with scrambled eggs. *Locro*, a whole grain wheat stew flavored with meat and vegetables, is also derived from the couscous that Spanish-Arab settlers remembered.

SEAFOOD   One of the greatest contributions of New World cuisine is *ceviche*, the combination of fresh fish and seafood "cooked" in hot chilies, lime or lemon, and onion. The most popular ingredients of ceviche (also spelled *seviche* or *cebiche*) are flounder, sole, trout, snapper, shrimp, crab, lobster, prawns, mussels, clams, octopus, and squid. Ceviche is served any time of day, as appetizer, snack, or light meal; a whole dinner of ceviche is called a *cebichada*. It is also considered a hangover remedy, and the booths that dispense fresh-out-of-the-water ceviche at dawn are called *cebicherias*. *Escabeche*, that vinegar-based Caribbean marinade, is also popular in South America.

In general, fish is steamed, fried, braised in banana leaves, baked, smothered in hot chilies and onions, stewed with sausage or chicken, topped with coconut, mustard, or peanut butter sauce, or stuffed with crab meat or flavored bread crumbs. Squid is often stuffed with ground pork (an Indonesian import) or stewed in its own ink (Portuguese). Crabcakes, sea turtle soup, and okra gumbos with shrimp, mollusks, and cashew nuts (called *caruru* in Brazil) are popular. Stuffed crabs with coriander, tomatoes, and even coconut are a favorite, particularly in Brazil. Among the seafoods Peruvians love most are anchovies, which are grilled fresh, salt-cured, or marinated as a seasoning; shrimp heads are also popular as a seasoning ingredient. The Portuguese salt cod and marinated or salted anchovies are used in hashes, fritters, stews, and stuffings.

POULTRY AND RABBIT   South American cooks staunchly maintain that the only way to eat wild pigeon, pheasant, and grouse is grilled rare, to keep the red meat from drying out; wild duck and most wildfowl should also be treated lightly. Turkey is the favorite, and richly fed toms are stuffed with walnuts and corn both before and after stewing, so to speak. The Moorish tradition lives on in such recipes as duck with olives or figs, the Portuguese in quail braised in sweetened fortified wines such as sherry, madeira, or brandy. One popular Bahia version is chicken with shrimp and almonds. Whether or not the chicken was known to the Quechuas before the Spanish arrived, the Peruvians have perfected

In Argentina and Brazil, where the muscular skirt steak called *churrasco* is so popular, all-grill restaurants are called *churrascarias;* they skewer such organ meats as kidneys, livers, hearts, and sweetbreads; pork and lamb chops; beef short ribs; tenderloins; chorizo and blood sausages; and sometimes chicken or veal loin, and serve them as mixed grills. Other churrascarias spit-roast whole quarters of mutton, kid, beef, and pork and then carry them from table to table, slicing off meats to order—a point-and-eat style that is becoming trendy in the United States.

the lemon-marinated and charcoal-grilled chicken so popular in the United States today; Brazilians often cut up chicken or smaller birds such as quail and quick-fry them with the bones still in. Poultry is also stir-fried in a number of Chinese-influenced sauces. *Aji* and *picante* mean that the dishes are chili-hot; *aji de gallina* is a very popular chicken dish flavored with ground nuts, coconut milk and chilies.

Rabbit is fried, coated with mustard or coconut (French and Indonesian), stewed with honey and fruit (Moorish), or flavored mole-style, with bitter chocolate (Mexican).

MEATS Grilling and braising are the two most common methods of cooking meat; the leftovers, served cold, are called fiambres. Venison and guinea pig are usually grilled or roasted; pork is stewed or roasted (particularly with garlic, as the Portuguese preferred, or spiced with a chili mixture—another variant of adobo), or its chops are used in mixed grills with sausages, sweetbreads, and beef. Veal is usually roasted or shank-braised, except in the Italian restaurants of Buenos Aires, where scallopini turn up piccata, parmagiana, and any other classic way.

Goat is grilled, particularly kid (*cabrito*), or curried; lamb is roasted, rubbed with garlic and anchovies, and butterflied or used on mixed grills. (The Brazilians, who pronounce the letter X as "*sh,*" have a wonderful Gaelic casserole they call *airixtu*—phonetically, "Irish stew.") Among the Argentine steakhouses, the most popular cuts of beef are the flank steak, which is the cut usually meant by *bistek*, and the skirt steak, or *churrasco*. A dish from Chile often found in Argentina features a beef-steak topped with fresh corn and sugar. Almost any meat, pork, beef, lamb, or goat can be ground into meatballs (*abondigas*). *Ropa viejo*, meaning "old clothes," is a mixture of shredded marinated beef and cabbage. *Antichucos*, marinated and grilled beef heart, is a Peruvian specialty. *Lomos saltados* is marinated beef strips cooked with onions and peppers—the Peruvian Philly steak. Argentines also frequently stuff and braise rolled steaks in the Italian manner.

BEVERAGES In Brazil, the most popular alcoholic spirit is *cacha-ca*, which is 100 proof and related to rum; it is most commonly served in a lime and sugar cocktail called *caipirinha*, which is (not surprisingly) popular in restaurants in the United States. The Peruvian *pisco* sour, often compared to a margarita, is actually closer to a brandy punch and includes sugar and egg whites. *Yerba mate* is a sort of bitter herb tea of the grasslands; in most urban areas, coffee is a staple. Beer is also popular, and many good brands, such as the Brazilian "black beer" Xinhua, are now being imported more broadly.

DESSERTS In general, fresh fruit is eaten after meals, and sweets, such as coconut cakes, cookies, and meringues, are considered either late-morning, coffee-break snacks or afternoon delights. The primary exception, particularly in the strongly Spanish Chile and Argentina, are flan-like custards or cream puddings.

ARGENTINE AND CHILEAN WINES

Although many people assume that South America comes in at the short end of "New World" wines, Argentina is actually the fifth-largest wine-producing country in the world. (The Argentineans themselves are the fourth-greatest per-capita consumers—a fact that may explain why 90% of those wines never leave Argentina.)

Nevertheless, many critics think Argentina is poised to become the success story of the new decade: Its winemakers, and several in neighboring Chile and in California, are increasingly impressed by its dependable climate (300-plus days of sunshine) and ability to turn out softly tannic, dark, and spicy wines, many retailing in the United States for under $10 a bottle.

For the most part, Argentina is a 3-M country: Mendoza, Malbec, and Merlot. Mendoza is the most important grape-growing region. The focused, leathery/woody Malbec that is primarily a "blending" varietal in France turns supple, muscular, and earthy in the Southern Hemisphere, producing medium-bodied wines with dark black-red color and lots of black-fruit flavors. The Merlots are equally accessible, with plenty of raspberry and a bit of smokiness; not surprisingly, some companies are experimenting with Syrah. (Although less widely publicized, Argentina's white wines, particularly its tropical and buttery Chardonnays, are also making inroads into the U.S. market.)

Although the wine industry in Chile dates to the 1550s, it has come into its own only in the last 20 years or so, since the lifting of a 40-year government ban on new vineyard plantings and, more recently, the increasing influx of investors from the French and American wine industries. In 1995 there were only 12 wineries in Chile; today there are about 75, which have swept into the market for inexpensive (generally under $15, and many under $8 a bottle) and user-friendly wines. Chile's fat, plummy Merlots—most of them actually now recognized as Carmenère, an almost forgotten Bordeaux varietal—and brilliantly colored, fruit- and mineral-tinged Cabernet Sauvignons are its best-known wine styles; in general, they should be drunk fairly young.

In the last four or five years, wines in the $15–20-a-bottle range have made inroads into the once immovably loyal California audience, thanks primarily to wineries either owned or in partnership with major international labels. For example, Casa Lapostolle belongs to the (Grand) Marigny-Lapostolle family; Lafite Rothschild has a stake in Los Vascos; Australia's giant Hardy's owns Mapocho. Miguel Torres, one of Spain's most respected winemakers, has another eponymous company in Chile; Pernod-Ricard is increasing its holdings.

Even more recently, the Chilean wine industry has made another remarkable leap: into the over-$50-a-bottle market. The joint Mondavi–Vina Errazuriz venture called Seña and the Concha y Torres–Mouton Rothschild collaboration Almaviva are pushing prices even over that mark. These super-Chileans have been well received by critics, but as yet have been only cautiously explored by consumers.

HOW TO ORDER AND EAT LIKE A NATIVE

The European influence ensures that almost every meal is served in courses, although some Peruvian restaurants may serve everything at once. In general, Peruvian restaurants are quite inexpensive, and Brazilian establishments are moderate; Argentine restaurants, because of the meat, may be somewhat more expensive but are still relatively reasonable.

Where feijoada is served in the traditional manner, the various meats—tongue, bacon, sausage, spareribs, beef chunks, etc.—and greens are served on one platter with the tongue in the center; the beans, white rice, and toasted farofa arrive in their own tureens. Take some rice on your plate, arrange a pile of meats alongside, then top the whole thing with beans and the bean liquor and sprinkle farinha over the top.

In a Brazilian restaurant, two people should start with a soup—either chicken and rice or black bean—and then have smothered or grilled whole fish and cabrito; for four, add ceviche and feijoada. However, feijoada is often prepared only on certain days, or with prior notice; it may also be a group dish, in which case you should look for a seafood/sausage stew or *carne del sol*, air-dried roast beef. For two, a Peruvian menu may offer antichucos on skewers, seviche, escabeche-flavored fish, and roast pork; four people can add a shrimp or crab chowder, potatoes huancaina, and a seafood or goat stew. Argentine restaurants often serve empanadas or delicate organ meats, such as sweetbreads, as appetizers; share a grilled sausage plate or mixed grill and a stuffed flank steak with green chimichurri sauce. Four people should try a squash or pumpkin stew, if possible, and grilled shrimp.

COOKING AT HOME

There is, of course, no "official" recipe for feijoada; one authority says it should be pork, another says beef and pork, a third adds greens. You may want to add or subtract cuts of meat or even substitute lamb or goat; but jerked meat, available at Hispanic groceries and frequently in convenience stores, adds a characteristic tang to the stew. In a pinch, plain dried beef can be substituted, but not the super-thin variety. Serve cold beer or, if you can find cachaca, caipirinhas. (The closest substitute would be a good homemade daiquiri.)

FEIJOADA COMPLETA

1 pound dried black beans
1/2 pound jerked beef, cubed or sliced
3 1/2 cups water
2 ham hocks, cubed
1/4 pound smoked tongue
1 bay leaf
4 slices bacon, cut into eighths
2 cloves garlic, finely chopped
2 hot chili peppers, finely chopped
2 green onions, chopped
1/4 cup dry or medium-dry sherry, port, or madeira

1/2 pound pork sausage
1/2 pound blood sausage
1 1/2 cups orange juice (optional)
8 ounces fresh kale, mustard greens, collards, or spinach, coarsely chopped
2 tablespoons palm oil (optional)
hot, cooked white rice
toasted farinha
hot, cooked pumpkin or squash
orange slices for garnish

Pick over dried beans for gravel and soak overnight; also soak jerked beef. The next day, drain beans, cover with 3 1/2 cups fresh water and simmer until done (about 1 1/2 to 2 hours); drain, and reserve liquid. Meanwhile, in a stockpot, cover jerked beef, ham hocks, and tongue with water and add bay leaf; bring to boil and simmer 1 1/2 hours, skimming foam as it rises. Remove beef, hocks, and tongue and cut meat off bones into chunks; set meat aside, return scraps to stock, and continue simmering 30 minutes. Strain and set stock aside.

In a Dutch oven or casserole, cook bacon until rendered and sauté garlic, chili peppers, and onions until golden; add sherry and bring to a simmer, then add reserved stock, beef, tongue, hocks, sausages, black bean liquid, and orange juice, if desired. Cook for about 10 minutes, stir in greens, and simmer until wilted. Add black beans and simmer another 20 to 30 minutes, adding palm oil if desired, or a little more water if the stew seems dry.

Transfer feijoada to serving dish, garnish with orange slices, and serve with white rice, toasted farinha (available at specialty groceries), and pumpkin or squash. Serves 6.

SMOTHERED TUNA

4–6 tuna (or swordfish) steaks, about 1/2 pound each
2 cloves garlic, peeled
2 teaspoons salt
1 tablespoon fresh ginger root, peeled
1 teaspoon lime zest
1 teaspoon orange zest
1 tablespoon dry sherry

2 teaspoons lime juice

2 tablespoons palm, coconut, or olive oil, divided

2 ounces pancetta, bacon, or ham, cubed

1 large onion, sliced

1 large bell pepper, sliced

2 hot chilies, thinly sliced

3 large tomatoes, chopped and drained

3 tablespoons parsley, chopped

Skin and pat dry fish steaks; set aside. Combine next seven ingredients in mini-processor or pestle and make into a paste; add 1 tablespoon oil and combine again. Rub fish with paste and let it marinate while grill or broiler heats.

Meanwhile, sauté pancetta or bacon in remaining oil; add onion and pepper and sauté until they have given up liquid and nearly dried out; add chilies and tomatoes and cook until liquid is again nearly drawn out.

If you are broiling the steaks, cook them a few minutes on either side until browned but still raw in the center; stir in pancetta sauce, moving sauce under and alongside the steaks, and place the pan back under the broiler until steaks are hot through but still pink. If you are grilling the steaks, grill them until done and top with sauce before serving. Garnish with parsley.

APPENDIX: AMERICAN REGIONAL CUISINE

The United States is a huge country, encompassing more than 3,750,000 square miles—larger even than China. Italy, with its many regional cuisines, is only two-thirds the size of the state of California, France three-quarters the size of Texas. In the continental mass alone, the topography includes prairie, mountain, forest, pastureland, marsh, river valley, coastal lowland, and desert. Yet the United States may well be the most homogenized country in the world when it comes to food. The culture of the supermarket, the chain restaurant, and the national fast-food commercial encourages an expectation of conformity, from "home cooking" to the steakhouse to the canned escargot at the continental joint—Chez What? The fact that the latest trendy menu description is "New American" or "Modern American" only adds to the confusion, since it pops up in New York, Washington, Charleston, Houston, Santa Fe, Boston, Los Angeles, Miami—everywhere and anywhere, and on menus that otherwise bear little resemblance to one another.

There is that one word that links them all—"American"—and it holds out the first hope of a revolution in restaurant cuisine. After decades of imitating the Old World masters, New World chefs are finally taking their places as stars in their own right. Not merely "cooks" in the traditional sense, often not even formally trained, they are adventurers, culinary explorers in search of their roots—even, as in the case of New Southwest proponent Mark Miller, anthropologists.

And many are New World converts—culinary immigrants. Jacques Pepin has tried to recreate the real spirit of French country cooking in California by stripping off those pompous layers of sauce. The late Pierre Franey, longtime New York restaurant chef and author, spent the last several years of his life leading TV audiences around such uniquely American scenes as the kitchens of Disney World, a bayou cookout, and a cattle ranch. Austrian Wolfgang Puck was one of the first and most visible crafters of L.A. haute cuisine. Nor are chefs any longer content to remain behind the scenes, either physically or culinarily. An ever-increasing number are proponents of various ethnic or social agendas, helping to turn the spotlight on soul food or on vegetarian or organic or feminist or boycott-correct menus. Puck, in an effort to persuade Congress to tighten labeling of fresh poultry, "bowled" a frozen chicken down a hallway. And the tidal wave of TV and cable cooking shows, which have turned chefs into celebrities able to market themselves as mini-franchises, opening restaurants on both coasts and Las Vegas and even Disney World simultaneously, only adds to their potential influence on the American dining public.

If there is any common philosophy among all these self-described New American cooks, the serious and the showboating, it would be their interest in integrating native ingredients into their work. Many chefs prefer the term "modern," as in modern American or modern Southwestern cooking, to suggest an evolution or progression of traditional cuisine, rather than "new," which implies invention. There is renewed affection for the old favorites—variously called soul food, family-style, mom's cooking, and comfort food—only made up fresh, with local flavors and fewer brand-name recipes. Domestic chevre, caviar, chicory, pâté, wild mushrooms, wines, and even wasabi now command the respect that used to be reserved for imports.

And with that increasing confidence, our melting pot has come to an appetizing simmer. American recipes are being reconsidered in the light of Asian cooking techniques, European sauces are being tailored to native ingredients, and so forth. The emphasis has shifted from commercial groceries to local produce, regional game and fish, free-range and additive-free livestock, native vegetables, and even wild greens and herbs. American chefs have a broader array of methods to choose from than ever, thanks not only to the many other cuisines and ingredients but also to a plethora of time-saving utensils and appliances. And with more time to reflect, they are rediscovering the various ethnic and historical influences that make regional cuisine vital.

Not all "new" cuisine is particularly authentic. California cuisine is really more a philosophy than a specific style. European and Asian ingredients are used in traditional recipes, and American ingredients are given classic treatments. Because California was in the forefront of the body-conscious culture, restaurateurs on the West Coast were also early proponents of cuisine minceur (now renamed, less punitively, "spa cuisine").

What is beginning to be called "Pacific Rim food," a style increasingly associated with Hawaii, Vancouver, and Southern California cuisine, as well as that of Sydney, Australia, mixes ingredients and techniques from Indonesia, Southeast Asia, Japan, and other Asian nations with local specialties. "Atlantic Rim," a newer phrase, is being used to encompass updated Caribbean and South Florida cooking—a style previously known jocularly as "Miami Spice" or Gulf Coast fusion or, more seriously, nuevo Latino. New Southern cuisine isn't so much new as remodeled by a little more seasoning, a little less fat, and a shorter cooking time. (For a little background on soul food, see the chapters on West African and Caribbean cooking.)

Many cities—especially those on the coasts, which naturally absorb the most immigrant traffic—have successfully exploited their culinary inheritances, and with fascinating results: Boston, with its blend of New England seafood and Mediterranean flavors, suggests some street-theater version of *Captain Courageous* featuring the spoiled American rich kid, the African cook, and the Portuguese hero. And Seattle, with its large Japanese and transplanted Californian communities, is developing a reputation for innovative seafood dishes.

But only a few regions have established such distinct culinary styles that you might find their cooking in other parts of the country. Those "exportable" styles include nuevo Latino; modern Southwestern, which includes Santa Fe and Tex-Mex; and the New Orleans siblings, Cajun and Creole. (Although it seems likely that, with the first Hawaiian imports appearing among restaurants in Los Angeles and New York, Pacific Rim may soon join the list, it's still in the early stages.) That these are all somewhat related is not so surprising when you remember that the two great colonial powers, Spain and France, and the Africans they imported worked their way into the North American continent primarily via the Gulf of Mexico and the Caribbean.

Although they may not be "ethnic" in exactly the way the foreign cuisines covered in this book are, these three regional styles are more and more popular and deserve at least a quick description.

NUEVO LATINO

Despite its rich and varied influences—Spanish, Mexican, Afro-Caribbean, French, Greek, Indian, and Chinese—the food in chic new South Florida restaurants and many Caribbean resorts is light, bright, and bracing. The most characteristic elements are seafood, citrus fruits, and chilies, with avocado, tomatoes, and rum or brown sugar close behind. Color is more of a consideration in this cuisine than in any other; in fact, this is the only region where "hot pastel" is both a visual description and a recipe. Pink grapefruit, grass-green key limes, golden mangoes, black beans, scarlet tomatoes, honeydew melons, orange yams, deep-green cilantro, and purple onions are matched to fish of every hue, from red snapper to silvery mackerel.

Florida cooking has many Caribbean echos, from *bacalao*, the Spanish salt cod, to *barbacao*, the Indians' smoked meat. *Escabeches*, *ceviches*, okra gumbos, black-eyed peas, coconut, yucca chips, fried plantains, cornmeal, and hominy are common; so are French cream sauces, seafood mousses and bouillabaisses, Greek fried calamari and oregano- and feta-flavored fish, and Jamaican jerk spices.

The wealth of fish includes pompano, grouper, red and yellowtail snapper, redfish, tilefish, trout, mullet, flounder, yellowfin and bluefin tuna, swordfish, mackerel, amberjack, wahoo, and dolphin fish (also known as mahi-mahi or dorado to distinguish it from the mammal dolphin). Other seafood includes blue and stone crabs, shrimp of all sizes, spiny lobsters, oysters, squid, alligator, sea turtle (now politically incorrect), conch, and scallops. Small birds, lightly grilled or smoked, are a regional tradition; they include squab, quail, rail, duck, doves, and so on. (Seafood is fried, but poultry rarely is.) Pork is the most common meat.

Sometimes a restaurant refers to "Gulf Coast cuisine," which can be South Floridian but can also be Texas Gulf Coast–style. This cuisine tends to be meatier, with particular emphasis on roasts, pan-fries, and barbecues; favors more fried dishes; and features more thick, flour-based west Louisiana sauces. "Gulf Coast" can even refer to dishes from Veracruz or Tabasco.

NEW OR MODERN SOUTHWESTERN

This category lumps together several cuisines frequently served up in combination: what's usually called Santa Fe style in recognition of Coyote Cafe founder (and chili poster designer) Mark Miller as well as the Inn of the Anasazi and other popular Santa Fe restaurants; Tex-Mex or *norteño* cuisine, which generally includes dishes from the Sonora and Chihuahua regions of Mexico and Arizona as well as Texas; and even some premissionary Native American dishes that show up on New Southwest menus.

The hottest, and hautest, variety is Sante Fe. Over the last decade, the boom in New Mexican cuisine has influenced nearly all other regional styles with its emphasis on smoking, low-fat cooking techniques, and, above all, chilies, which are suddenly one of the most popular foods in the United States. Anywhere in the Southwest you can find a restaurant that serves either shredded meat chili, ground meat chili, red tomato chili, green chili, chicken chili, venison chili, boar chili, or black bean chili, and probably several at a time; but only in New Mexico could you order a chili dish of pure chilies, roasted, peeled, pureed, simmered, even "seasoned." Whole magazines, gourmet catalogs, and accessory stores are devoted to salsas, chili sauces, and seeds, and scores of species—yellow, green, orange, red, purple, and even black—are jealously cultivated. A few years ago, sales of prepared salsas in this country passed sales of catsup.

In Santa Fe itself, a city that is nearing the end of its fourth century, the cuisine combines Native American, Spanish, and Mexican dishes with some bits of Louisiana and railroad Anglo flavoring. Santa Fe cooks were among the first to use mesquite wood for smoking meats and poultry, and they "rediscovered" such indigenous ingredients as sun-dried tomatoes, piñon nuts, blue cornmeal, cilantro, pumpkin seeds, wild oregano, cumin, and Mexican-style chocolate moles flavored with nuts and vanilla. Prickly pears and their fruit, also called cactus pears, are another characteristic ingredient. Turkey, which ran wild here, was a staple of the Pueblo Indian diet, along with game venison, bison, rabbit, prairie dogs, beaver, and other large rodents; traditionally, the Indians spitted and roasted meat, but after the introduction of the iron pot by the Spanish, they began stewing beans and meat with green chilies, nuts, and seeds. The Spanish also brought sheep and cattle (and dairy products), pork (and the lard that is still many cooks' favorite fat), and they planted olive trees, orchard fruits, and vineyards. Since the Moors had just been evicted from Spain as Columbus was landing in the New World, their culinary influence was still strong when Santa Fe was founded. Hence the presence of raisins and almonds along with the sherry, garlic, and olive oil. ("Texas toast," after all, is transplanted bruschetta—grilled bread spread with olive oil and lots of garlic.) Spanish-style sausages and hams are also fairly common.

The territories of Sonora and Chihuahua, which border Arizona and Texas, were transformed by Spanish wheat and cattle into huge ranges, so Tex-Mex or norteño cuisine started out as, in effect, cowboy food. Much of it was originally limited to what simple outdoor fires and minimal utensils could create (hence quesadillas, which started out as fried turnovers, wound up as the flat cheese and tortilla "sandwiches" we know in the United States). It also meant that although maize and corn-meal were available, wheat-flour tortillas became the standard. El Paso, the quintessential border town, has long claimed credit for inventing the nacho, which is, after all, a way of eating a whole dinner without a fork—or without getting out of the saddle. It may also be responsible for the burrito, or stuffed flour tortilla. It is believed that charcoal grilling began here, where it is called simply *al carbon*, and the flavor of char smoke is characteristic of Chihuahuan food. Chihuahua was also the site of a large Mennonite settlement and traditionally produces a lot of mild and easily melted cheese and *crema*, a cultured thick cream like crème fraîche. *Queso fundito*, the melted cheese eaten with fried tortillas that has evolved into a bar staple in the United States, is a Sonoran tradition; refried beans with cheese is Chihuahuan.

In the larger ranches, hacienda cooks began to mix traditional Mexican tortillas and enchiladas, beans, chilies (red and green), and salsas with prime meat and game, cheese and sour cream, and wine and olives to recreate Spanish dishes for their homesick employers. *Menudo*, the tripe stew recommended as a hangover remedy, and *adobo*, the chili paste that so captivated the Spanish that they carried it around the world, are specialities of this region.

Barbecue, the Indians' spicy pit-smoked meat (which may or may not have been served with tomatoes), gradually worked its way from the Yucatan and coastal Mexico into Texas, picking up Spanish vinegar, Jamaican molasses, and various other refinements along the way. Both beef and pork are given serious attention in Tex-Mex cuisine; more recently, goat, venison, bison (or farmed buffalo), and game birds, particularly quail, rabbit, doves, and squab, are returning to menus.

NEW ORLEANS

It's not surprising that so many people are confused about the distinction between Cajun and Creole cooking. For one thing, they share similar influences and similar ingredients; they're both associated with Mardi Gras and crawfish and oysters and New Orleans music (Dixieland, Cajun, and zydeco bands have all become increasingly popular outside their home state); and in fact the styles are beginning to merge—so much so that many people are starting to refer to them jointly as New Orleans cuisine. (Although in the case of many tourist-trap establishments, the term "Cre-jun" is more appropriate.) Etouffées, jambalayas, and gumbos seem to be popular on both sides.

However, there are a few differences, and history helps explain them. Cajun is a mixture of French, Spanish, African, coastal Mexican, and Choctaw and other southern Indian cooking; it's also a working-class cuisine, largely dependent on subsistence crops and hunting and with relatively few intricate techniques. (Because food was often tough and utensils few, long-cooked one-pot meals are the most common). Creole food is upper-class European at heart, and while it also has African and Indian strains, it's a more elaborate style, developed by the cooks—some of them professionally trained and imported—who worked for the wealthier residents and colonial rulers. It involves more sauces (it's hard to imagine a New Orleans brunch without eggs Benedict and hollandaise), has shorter cooking times, and in traditional French style is served in courses.

"Cajun" is a corruption of the word "Acadian," and the Cajuns are descended from southern French farmers who moved to Nova Scotia in the early seventeenth century. When Canada fell to the British a century later, they were exiled and began the long trek south (an exodus memorialized in Longfellow's "Evangeline") to what was left of French territory—namely, Louisiana. They settled in and around the bayous, where they found abundant fish and shellfish and game. The local Indians showed them how to powder sassafras leaf into a thickening and flavoring agent (filé) and how to barbecue meat and make cornmeal; they may also have been the first to "cook" flour into a roux ("red"), the basis for gumbos, fricassees, and so forth. The West African slaves brought with them okra, which in one dialect was called "gombo," leading to the name "gumbo" for an okra-thickened stew. (The word "jambalaya" is variously said to derive from an African dish of stacked, simmered fish, called *jomba*, or to a combination of *jambon*, the French word for ham, and *ya*, an African name for rice.)

Though the word has come to mean ethnically mixed, the original Creoles were French and later Spanish nationals born in Louisiana. They maintained a "first families" roster within the city well into this century and spoke French as a first language. (The Cajuns do too, though their dialect is somewhat different and they have had a more difficult time defending their ethnic heritage.)

Cajun cooking depends heavily on spices: filé, onions, celery, hot and bell peppers, green onions, garlic, and, especially, hot peppers. Cajun chefs often speak of "the three peppers," meaning black, white, and Tabasco; and spicy "blackened" seafood is a typical Cajun dish, though one poorly represented by most mass-market renditions The more classic Creole cuisine emphasizes marjoram, sage, fennel, leeks, mustard, and so on. Cajun spices are more commonly cooked into the dish, either in the stew or in the roux, while Creole seasonings are often included in the sauce.

Cajuns lived upriver and used more freshwater fish (particularly crawfish), turtles, water birds, and squirrel; Creole dishes emphasized saltwater fish, venison, beef, geese, shrimp, and so forth. Cajun cooks are more prone to fry fish or even meats and vegetables; Creole chefs prefer to sauce them, stuff them, or sauté them in butter. The Cajuns traditionally cook with lard and eat more fatty meats, particularly sausages; but during the cooking process, they frequently pour off excess oil or fat or deglaze the pan. Creole cooks, who use much more butter and cream and olive oil, do not remove fat and in fact often "finish" sauces with more butter or cream.

Both eat a great deal of rice, the southern staple, but the Cajun diet also features cornmeal and hominy (cheap, indigenous corn), while the Creole diet includes more breads and rolls (requiring wheat flour, originally a rich family's indulgence). And finally, because they were wealthier, the Creoles were more likely to expect sweets and desserts and to get them.

THE LAST WORD

Now, if this armchair voyage has piqued your curiosity or your appetite, we urge you to go out and explore these cuisines yourself. Show both your interest and your appreciation to the chefs and staff who serve you. Maybe you won't always like everything, but you will find many dishes, and people, to enjoy. We wish you many fine meals and many new friends. As the great and hilarious Julia Child would say, "Bon appetit!"

INDEX

428